HEALTHCARE DECISION-MAKING AND THE LAW

Autonomy, Capacity and the Limits of Liberalism

MARY DONNELLY

CAMBRIDGE
UNIVERSITY PRESS

CAMBRIDGE
UNIVERSITY PRESS

University Printing House, Cambridge CB2 8BS, United Kingdom

Cambridge University Press is part of the University of Cambridge.

It furthers the University's mission by disseminating knowledge in the pursuit of education, learning and research at the highest international levels of excellence.

www.cambridge.org
Information on this title: www.cambridge.org/9781107470927

© Mary Donnelly 2010

First published 2010
First paperback edition 2014

A catalogue record for this publication is available from the British Library

Library of Congress Cataloguing in Publication data
Donnelly, Mary, M.A.
Healthcare decision-making and the law : autonomy, capacity and
the limits of liberalism / Mary Donnelly.
p.   cm. – (Cambridge law, medicine and ethics)
Includes bibliographical references and index.
ISBN 978-0-521-11831-6 (hardback)
1. Medical care–Law and legislation–England.   2. Medical care–
Law and legislation.   3. Medical care–England–Decision making.
4. Medical care–Decision making.   I. Title.
KD3395.D66 2010
344.4203′21–dc22
2010033023

ISBN 978-0-521-11831-6 Hardback
ISBN 978-1-107-47092-7 Paperback

For John, Cormac, Kevin and Brendan

CONTENTS

ACKNOWLEDGEMENTS

I have incurred many debts of gratitude in writing this book. I have learned a great deal from Professor Phil Fennell, University of Wales, Cardiff, and have benefitted from his expertise and from exposure to his thoughtful approach to this area of the law. The book has also benefitted from conversations and collaborations, in many different contexts, which have helped to shape my thinking (although, of course, responsibility for the conclusions reached and the arguments presented is mine alone). In this respect, I am grateful to Professor Peter Bartlett; John Billings; John Danahar; Dr Dolores Dooley; Professor Caroline Fennell; Mr Justice Finnegan of the Supreme Court of Ireland; Professor Ian Freckelton; Professor Søren Holm; Dr Mary Keys; Dr Ursula Kilkelly; Dr Deirdre Madden; Professor Maeve M'Donagh; Professor Bernadette McSherry; Dr Joan McCarthy; Dr Siobhan Mullally; Dr Claire Murray; Dr Tanya Mhuirthile; Donal Nolan; Shaun O'Keefe; Professor Sidney Watson; and Dr Darius Whelan. I have also benefitted from interacting with my undergraduate and postgraduate students in medical law at University College Cork. In addition, the work was enhanced by my attendance at a workshop at the Monash University campus in Prato, Italy, in 2009 entitled 'Rethinking Rights-Based Mental Health Law' and I would like to thank the organiser, Bernadette McSherry, and the other participants.

Some of the work on this book was undertaken during a period as visiting Research Fellow at the London School of Economics in 2009 and I am grateful for this opportunity. I would like to thank Helen Mulcahy and the other staff of the law library at University College Cork. I have also benefitted from the library facilities at the Institute for Advanced Legal Studies, London and from the online resources available to Irish universities as part of the Higher Education Authority's IReL project. I am grateful also to Finola O'Sullivan at Cambridge University Press and to the series editors, Professor Margaret Brazier and Professor Graeme Laurie, for giving me the opportunity to publish this book in the present series.

For personal support over the period of writing this book, I am grateful to my parents, Bertha and Paddy Donnelly, and to Claire Mee, Anne Marie Mullally, Áine Ryall and, most especially to my wonderful sons, Cormac, Kevin and Brendan Mee. Finally, my husband and colleague, John Mee, read many drafts and successfully negotiated the sometimes dangerous territory between encouragement and critique. I am deeply grateful to him for both.

CASES

A v. *United Kingdom* (1998) 27 EHRR 611

A Hospital NHS Trust v. *S* [2003] EWHC 365 (Fam)

A National Health Trust v. *C* unreported High Court (Family Division) 8 February 2000

Ahsan v. *University Hospitals Leicester NHS Trust* [2006] EWHC 2624 (QB)

Airedale NHS Trust v. *Bland* [1993] AC 789

Al Hamwi v. *Johnston and Another* [2005] EWHC 206

An NHS Trust v. *A and Another* [2005] EWCA Civ 1145

Arato v. *Avedon* (1993) 858 P 2d 598

Auckland Area Health Board v. *Attorney General* [1993] 1 NZLR 235

Austen v. *Graham* (1854) 8 Moo PCC 282

B v. *Croydon Health Authority* [1995] 2 WLR 294

B v. *Dr SS, Dr G and the Secretary of State for the Department of Health* [2005] EWHC 1936 (Admin); [2006] EWCA Civ 28 (CA)

Baby Boy Doe (1994) 632 NE 2d 326

Bailey v. *Warren* [2006] EWCA Civ 51

Banks v. *Goodfellow* (1870) LR 5 QB 549

BD v. *Stone and Eastern Regional Health Integrated Authority* (2006) NLTD 161

Bee v. *Greaves* (1984) 744 F 2d 1387

Bensaid v. *United Kingdom* (2001) 33 EHRR 205

Birch v. *University College London Hospital NHS Trust* [2008] EWHC 2237 (QB)

Bolam v. *Friern Hospital Management Committee* [1957] 1 WLR 582

Bolitho v. *City and Hackney Health Authority* [1998] AC 232

Bolton Hospitals NHS Trust v. *O* [2003] 1 FLR 824

Bolton v. *Blackrock Clinic* unreported Supreme Court, 23 January 1997

Boughton v. *Knight* (1873) LR 3 P & D 64

Bouvia v. *Superior Court* (1986) 179 Cal App 3d 1127; (1986) 225 Cal Rptr 297

Brightwater Care Group Inc v. *Rossiter* [2009] WASC 229

Bush v. *Schiavo* (2004) 871 So 2d 1012

Bush v. *Schiavo* (2004) 885 So 2d 321

Canterbury v. *Spence* (1972) 464 F 2d 772

Cartwright v. *Cartwright* (1793) 1 Phillim 100

Centre for Reproductive Medicine v. *U* [2002] EWHC 36 (Fam)

LEGISLATION

Constitutions and conventions

Bunreacht na hÉireann 1937, the Constitution of Ireland 1937
Canadian Charter of Rights and Freedoms 1982
Constitution of the United States 1776
Convention for the Protection of Human Rights and Fundamental Freedoms
(the European Convention on Human Rights) (Rome 4 Nov. 1950; TS 71 (1953);
Cmd 8969)

Statutes, statutory instruments and bills

England and Wales

Access to Justice Act 1999
Court of Protections Rules 2007, SI 1744/2007
de Prærogativâ Regis 17 Edward II
Draft Mental Health Bill 2002 Cm 5538-I (London: HMSO, 2002)
Draft Mental Health Bill 2004 Cm 6305-I (London: HMSO, 2004)
Health and Social Care Act 2008
Human Fertilisation and Embryology Act 1990
Human Rights Act 1998
Lasting Powers of Attorney, Enduring Powers of Attorney and Public Guardian
Regulations 2007, SI 1253/2007
Lasting Powers of Attorney, Enduring Powers of Attorney and Public Guardian
(Amendment) Regulations 2009, SI 1884/2009
Mental Capacity Act 2005
Mental Capacity Act (Independent Mental Capacity Advocates) (General)
Regulations 2007, SI 1832/2007
Mental Capacity (Deprivation of Liberty: Standard Authorisations, Assessments and
Ordinary Residence) Regulations 2008, SI 1858/2008
Mental Capacity Act 2005 (Deprivation of Liberty: Monitoring and Reporting)
Regulations 2009, SI 827/2009
Mental Health Act 1959

Mental Health Act 1983
Mental Health Act 2007
Mental Health (Hospital, Guardianship and Consent to Treatment) Regulations 1983,
SI 893/1983
Public Health (Control of Disease) Act 1984
Public Health (Infectious Diseases) Regulations 1988, SI 1546/1988

Other jurisdictions

Adults with Incapacity (Scotland) Act 2000 (Scotland)
Bill of Rights Act 1990 (New Zealand)
Californian Welfare and Institutions Code (Cal Welf & Inst Code 5000)
(the Lanterman-Petris-Short Act) (California, United States of America)
Charter of Human Rights and Responsibilities Act 2006 (Victoria, Australia)
European Convention on Human Rights Act 2003 (Ireland)
Health Act 1947 (Ireland)
Health Care Consent Act 1996 (Ontario, Canada)
Human Rights Act 2004 (Australian Capital Territory, Australia)
Mental Health Act 1986 (Victoria, Australia)
Mental Health Act 1990 (Ontario, Canada)
Mental Health Act 2001 (Ireland)
Mental Health Act 2007 (New South Wales, Australia)
Mental Health (Care and Treatment) (Scotland) Act 2003 (Scotland)
Mental Health (Compulsory Assessment and Treatment) Act 1992 (New Zealand)
Mental Health Services Act 1995 (Saskatchewan, Canada)
Mental Hygiene Law (New York, United States of America)
Medical Treatment Act 1998 (Victoria, Australia)
Patient Self-Determination Act 1990 (United States of America)
Powers of Attorney Act 1998 (Queensland, Australia)
Uniform Health-Care Decisions Act 1994 (United States of America)

European instruments

*Additional Protocol to the Convention on Human Rights and Biomedicine, on
Transplantation of Organs and Tissues of Human Origin*, agreed at Strasbourg,
24 January 2002
*Convention for the Protection of Human Rights and Dignity of the Human Being with
Regard to the Application of Biology and Medicine: Convention on Human Rights
and Biomedicine*, agreed at Oviedo, 4 April 1997.
*European Convention for the Prevention of Torture and Inhuman or Degrading
Treatment or Punishment 1987* (ETS No. 126)

International instruments

~

Introduction

Although the law may be far from our minds as we try to make healthcare decisions in circumstances which can be difficult and traumatic, in fact, the law plays a central role in the decision-making process. It provides the framework within which we deliberate; it tells us when we can make decisions for ourselves and when we cannot and it dictates what happens to us when our right to make our own decisions is removed. This book critically evaluates the law's engagement with the process of healthcare decision-making and explores ways in which this might be enhanced.

Since the latter part of the twentieth century, the law's approach to healthcare decision-making has centred on ensuring respect for the principle of individual autonomy. In this, the law reflects the predominant ethical status which has been accorded to the principle.[1] Thus, John Stuart Mill's famous aphorism that '[o]ver himself, over his own body and mind, the individual is sovereign'[2] might be seen as the defining summation of principle. This principle is given legal effect in Cardozo J's often-cited dictum that 'every human being of adult years and sound mind has a right to determine what shall be done with his own body'[3] Yet, the reality has always been more complex than citations of Mill or Cardozo might suggest. The status of autonomy within ethical discourse has been challenged for almost as long as the principle has been revered, while in a legal context the degree of respect accorded to the principle of autonomy has varied depending on the circumstances in which the principle is called into action. The principle has been most influential in respect of treatment refusal, especially where the refusal is based on adherence to religious beliefs. At the same time, however, in many jurisdictions the right of a capable patient to refuse treatment for a mental disorder has

---

[1] See O. O'Neill, *Autonomy and Trust in Bioethics* (Cambridge University Press, 2002), p. 2.

[2] J. S. Mill, *On Liberty* (London, 1859) in J. Grey (ed.) *On Liberty and Other Essays* (Oxford University Press, 1991), p. 14.

[3] *Schloendorff v. Society of New York Hospital* (1914) 211 NY 125, 128.

been decisively sidelined by mental health legislation. Where the right of autonomy is recognised, the law has relied on the requirement for capacity to act as gatekeeper for the application of the right. Thus, while respect for autonomy provides the principled foundation for the law's approach to decision-making, the question of whether or not each individual's decision will actually be respected is dependent on whether she meets the legal standard for capacity in respect of the decision in question.

The symbiotic relationship between the principle of autonomy and the requirement for capacity has a number of consequences for the law's response to healthcare decision-making. First, the law relies on capacity to deal with difficult cases on an individual basis. This has allowed the law to lend its support to autonomy with little analysis of what the principle actually means or of how conflicts with other principles should be resolved. The law's approach is effectively summarised by Lord Donaldson MR in *Re T (Adult: Refusal of Medical Treatment)*.[4] Setting out the applicable principle in the strongest terms, Lord Donaldson found that:

> An adult patient who … suffers from no mental incapacity has an absolute right to choose whether to consent to medical treatment, to refuse it or to choose one rather than another of the treatments being offered… This right of choice … exists notwithstanding that the reasons for making the choice are rational, irrational, unknown or even non-existent.[5]

However, His Lordship went on to note that the legal recognition of the right to consent to or refuse treatment 'merely shifts the problem … and calls for a very careful examination of whether, and if so the way in which, the individual is exercising that right'.[6]

Secondly, the law has treated autonomy as the principle-based part of the dyad, with capacity being treated as a simple matter of fact. Yet the capacity requirement is inherently normative. As Allen Buchanan and Dan Brock remind us, '[t]he proper standard of competence must be chosen; it cannot be discovered'.[7] Whether or not a person has capacity to make a particular decision depends on whether she reaches a designated standard in respect of specified abilities. What is required, both in respect of the standard to be reached and in respect of the necessary abilities, depends on the view of autonomy which we hold. This, in turn, depends on our view of the relationship between the individual and society and the point at which we believe societal duties to protect are implicated.

---

[4] [1992] 3 WLR 782.   [5] *Ibid.*, 786.   [6] *Ibid.*, 796.
[7] A. Buchanan and D. Brock. *Deciding for Others: The Ethics of Surrogate Decision Making* (Cambridge University Press, 1989), p. 47.

Normative factors also impact on the day-to-day operation of the capacity requirement. In reality, the law's requirement that capacity be assessed without reference to the nature of the decision the person proposes to make is almost impossible to meet.

Thirdly, the application of the capacity requirement sorts people into those whose voluntary decisions must be respected and those 'whose decisions, even if uncoerced, will be set aside and for whom others will act as surrogate decision-makers'.[8] Evidently, the impact of this sorting process is not neutral. People with capacity represent the norm. Those who do not are defined in contrast to this norm; they are, in this sense, the 'other'.[9] As a consequence, legal and ethical discourse in respect of people lacking capacity has been impoverished. Traditionally, the law has tended to ignore the issue of decision-making in this context, behaving as if this did not need a conceptual basis beyond a generalised adherence to an amorphous best interests standard. This position is beginning to change, driven in part by broader human rights agendas, including those set by the European Convention on Human Rights (ECHR) and the United Nations Convention on the Rights of Persons with Disabilities (CRPD).[10] Nonetheless, the legal consequences of a finding of incapacity remain significant.

The scope of the discussion

This book critiques the law's approach to healthcare decision-making and aspects of the liberal foundations upon which this has been based. In doing this, it focuses on three categories of people. These are adults with capacity, adults without capacity and adults who have been made subject to mental health legislation. The book does not attempt to address the particular issues which arise in respect of healthcare decision-making by and for children and young people. Although issues of autonomy, capacity and best interests arise in this context also, the unique nature of the relationship between parents and children gives rise to additional issues which cannot be discussed in sufficient depth in this work.[11] However,

---

[8] *Ibid.*

[9] The notion of 'othering' (defining people or groups as different from, and lesser than, a dominant group) is perhaps most closely associated with feminist theory, which identifies the way in which woman is seen as 'Other' in respect of a male norm: see S. de Beauvoir, *The Second Sex* (1949) Parshley, HM trans. (London: Penguin, 1972).

[10] (2006) General Assembly Resolution 61/106.

[11] There are various ways of conceptualising the relationship between children and parents. Recent developments have seen a move from notions of parental rights to children's

some aspects of law's approach in respect of children are relevant to the discussion at hand and these will be referred to where appropriate.

In terms of jurisdictions covered, the book focuses primarily on the law in England and Wales. The law in this jurisdiction reflects a range of significant recent developments in terms of case law, policy debate and legislative intervention. The Mental Capacity Act 2005 (MCA) is especially interesting for the purposes of the discussion here because of its efforts to formalise the concept of capacity and to facilitate new approaches to decision-making for people lacking capacity.[12] The protracted reform process which ultimately culminated in the Mental Health Act 2007 (MHA 2007) is also informative from both policy and legal perspectives.[13] In addition, parts of the book draw heavily on the legal position in the United States, which tends to adhere to a liberal autonomy-based model for decision-making in all circumstances, including incapacity and decisions in respect of treatment for a mental disorder. The book also includes discussion of aspects of the law of particular relevance to the arguments made from a number of other jurisdictions, including Australia, Canada, Ireland, New Zealand and Scotland.

Additionally, the book draws extensively on the jurisprudence of the European Court of Human Rights (ECtHR)[14] and on the domestic

rights: see J. Fortin, 'Children's Rights: Are the Courts Now Taking Them More Seriously?' (2004) 15 *King's College Law Journal* 253. However, additionally, as noted by J. Bridgeman, *Parental Responsibility, Young Children and Healthcare Law* (Cambridge University Press, 2007), p. 228, the issue of parental responsibility arises. For an approach to healthcare decision-making for children based on a conception of relational responsibilities, see Bridgeman, pp. 228–42.

[12] The MCA became operational over the course of 2007 with the main body of the Act coming into force on 1 October 2007. The MCA places on a statutory footing the law relating to capacity in respect of healthcare and welfare decisions and introduces a new framework for decisions in respect of property and financial affairs. The MCA also establishes a Court of Protection (MCA, s. 45) which has an equivalent status to the High Court (s. 47(1)). The MCA, s. 45(6) abolishes the office of the Supreme Court which had been called the Court of Protection. See generally R. Jones, *Mental Capacity Act Manual* (3rd edn) (London: Sweet and Maxwell, 2009); P. Bartlett, *Blackstone's Guide to the Mental Capacity Act 2005* (2nd edn) (Oxford University Press, 2008).

[13] The MHA 2007 amends the Mental Health Act 1983 in a number of respects including the introduction of 'supervised community treatment'. The MHA 2007 also amends the MCA, introducing measures covering admission to hospitals or care homes for people lacking capacity in circumstances where the admission constitutes a deprivation of liberty. The main part of the MHA 2007 came into force on 3 November 2008. See generally P. Fennell, *Mental Health: The New Law* (Bristol: Jordans, 2007).

[14] The United Kingdom ratified the ECHR in 1951 and extended the right of individual petition to the ECtHR in 1966. However, prior to domestic incorporation, national courts had no obligation to take account of the jurisprudence of the ECtHR.

application of the ECHR in the case law, which has developed in England and Wales since the commencement of the Human Rights Act 1998 (HRA).[15] The book also refers to other human rights instruments and, in particular, to the CRPD. As will be clear from the discussion, the CRPD is especially important in respect of decisions for patients lacking capacity and patients with a mental disorder. The CRPD entered into force on 3 May 2008, on receipt of its twentieth ratification. As of July 2010, the CRPD has been signed by 146 states and ratified by 88. Of the jurisdictions discussed in this book, the United Kingdom, Australia, Canada and New Zealand have ratified the CRPD while Ireland and the United States have signed the Convention but have not ratified it.[16] The CRPD is especially significant for the discussion in this book because it breaks down traditional distinctions between civil and political rights, which are usually negative, and social and economic rights which are usually positive.[17] An Optional Protocol operates alongside the CRPD. The effect of this is to allow individuals who consider that they have been the victims of a violation by a State Party of the provisions of the CPRD to directly petition the

---

[15] The HRA incorporated the ECHR into UK law with effect from 2 October 2000. The HRA requires courts or tribunals in determining a question which has arisen in connection with an ECHR right to take account of any judgment, decision, declaration or advisory opinion of the ECtHR (HRA, s. 2(1)). The method of incorporation adopted requires courts to interpret existing legislation 'in so far as is possible' in a way which complies with the ECHR (HRA, s. 3(1)). If this is not possible, a declaration of incompatibility may be made (HRA, s. 4(2)); however, a declaration of incompatibility does not affect the validity, continuing operation or enforcement of the provision (HRA, s. 4(6)). All proposed bills must include either a statement of compatibility with the ECHR by the relevant Minister or a statement that the Minister cannot state the Bill's compatibility but that the Government nonetheless wishes the House to proceed with the Bill (HRA, s. 19(1)). It is unlawful for 'public authorities' to act in a way which is incompatible with the ECHR unless they are statutorily bound to do so (HRA, s. 6(2)). For an overview of the HRA, see D. Feldman, *Civil Liberties and Human Rights in England and Wales* (2nd edn) (Oxford University Press, 2002), pp. 80–104; J. Wadham *et al.*, *Blackstone's Guide to the Human Rights Act 1998* (5th edn) (Oxford University Press, 2009).

[16] Other ratifying States include Italy, Spain, Sweden, South Africa and Mexico as well as a significant number of African and South American states.

[17] On the CRPD generally, see A. Hendricks, 'UN Convention on the Rights of Persons With Disabilities' (2007) 14 *European Journal of Health Law* 272; A. Lawson 'The United Nations Convention on the Rights of Persons With Disabilities: New Era or False Dawn?' (2006–2007) 34 *Syracuse Journal of International Law and Commerce* 563; D. MacKay, 'The United Nations Convention on the Rights of Persons With Disabilities' (2006–2007) 34 *Syracuse Journal of International Law and Commerce* 323; R. Kayess and P. French, 'Out of Darkness into Light? Introducing the Convention on the Rights of Persons With Disabilities' (2008) 8 *Human Rights Law Review* 1.

Committee on the Rights of Persons with Disabilities.[18] Of the jurisdictions discussed in this book, only Australia and the United Kingdom have acceded to the Optional Protocol.[19]

A final point relates to the terminology used in the book. First, in the interests of convenience, except where a specific gender-related point is under discussion, the book adopts the female pronoun throughout. Secondly, the book uses the term 'capacity' to mean both legal capacity and capacity in a more general sense. In this, it is consistent with the use of the term in the MCA but departs from the practice of some American commentators, who use the term 'competence' to describe legal capacity and the term 'capacity' for capacity in a general sense.[20] Thirdly, although, where possible, the book uses the term 'person,' it is sometimes necessary for clarity to use the term 'patient'. This is done with some discomfort, recognising the extent to which this usage serves to limit our view of the person who is currently in the position of patient.

The format for discussion

The issues arising are considered over six substantive chapters. In broad terms, the first two chapters are concerned with autonomy; the second two are concerned with capacity and the remaining two chapters are concerned respectively with decisions by and for people lacking capacity and with treatment for a mental disorder.

Chapter 1 investigates the principle of autonomy as a theoretical construct. This chapter differs from the rest of the book in that it makes limited reference to the law. Rather, its role is to lay down the theoretical foundations for the discussion to follow. By examining the diversity of views regarding the nature of autonomy, Chapter 1 shows that

---

[18] The Committee is established under Article 34 of the CRPD and is the key enforcement mechanism for the CRPD. States Parties that have ratified the CRPD must submit reports to the Committee within two years of entry into force of the CRPD for the State in question and every four years thereafter (Art. 35). The Committee may make such general recommmendations and suggestions on the reports submitted as it considers appropriate and these are forwarded to the State Party in question (Art. 36). For States which have acceded to the Optional Protocol, the Committee must consider any individual petition brought (provided the matter is considered admissible under Art. 2 of the Optional Protocol) and communicate its suggestions and recommendations, if any, to the State Party in question and to the petitioner (Art. 5 of the Optional Protocol).

[19] The Optional Protocol has been signed by 89 States and acceded to by 54. Among the acceding states are South Africa, Spain, Sweden, Mexico and many South American countries.

[20] See, for example, Buchanan and Brock, *Deciding for Others*.

autonomy is a more complex and nuanced concept than the law has typically assumed. The chapter explores the philosophical bases for respect for autonomy, identifying the predominant influence of Millian liberal principles of non-interference on modern legal conceptions of autonomy. The chapter also explores a range of critiques of autonomy, focusing in particular on critiques relating to the issue of agency and on critiques of the limited scope of a view of autonomy as non-interference. It uses the work of Joseph Raz[21] and of feminist 'relational' theorists[22] as the basis for an exploration of alternative conceptions of autonomy which focus on empowerment rather than non-interference. The chapter argues that these conceptions of autonomy can provide a better basis for the law's approach to the principle.

Chapter 2 explores the law's treatment of the autonomy principle. As will be evident from the discussion in this chapter, to date most legal discussion of autonomy has occurred in the context of treatment refusal. The right of autonomy has been conceptualised largely as a negative right to reject treatment choices made by professionals. There has been limited exploration of the question of limits on this right and relatively little legal discussion of a view of autonomy focused on empowerment. Chapter 2 argues that the ongoing status of autonomy in the law is dependent on the adoption of a more robust legal approach to the concept. This requires better legal analysis of both the issue of limits and of positive obligations to facilitate autonomy.

Chapter 3 explores normative aspects of the concept of capacity within an autonomy-based legal framework. It outlines the features of capacity as set out in the MCA and shows that these are largely in accordance with a liberal conception of the requirement. This chapter then identifies flaws in the liberal account of capacity. It argues that this account inappropriately conceptualises capacity as based solely on the workings of each individual's internal decision-making processes. People are seen as having or lacking capacity without reference to the context in which assessment takes place or to the factors external to the person, which impact on the

---

[21] In particular J. Raz, *The Morality of Freedom* (Oxford: Clarendon Press, 1986) and *Ethics in the Public Domain: Essays in the Morality of Law and Politics* (Oxford: Clarendon Press, 1994).

[22] C. Mackenzie and N. Stoljar, 'Autonomy Reconfigured' in C. Mackenzie and N. Stoljar (eds.) *Relational Autonomy: Feminist Perspectives on Autonomy, Agency, and the Social Self* (New York: Oxford University Press, 2000), p. 4, describe relational autonomy as an 'umbrella term' to describe a range of related perspectives that seek to recognise the socially embedded nature of the individual within a framework which retains respect for autonomy at its core.

assessment process. The chapter also argues that the liberal account of capacity fails to recognise the epistemological fallibility inherent in the operation of the capacity requirement and to deal with the normative consequences to which this gives rise. Accordingly, the chapter argues in favour of a relational approach to capacity and a more realistic approach to the role played by the nature of the decision made in the operation of the capacity requirement.

Chapter 4 provides a detailed evaluation of how capacity assessment operates in practice. It considers the components of the applicable standard under the MCA and identifies the tensions to which this standard gives rise when applied in practice and the resulting challenges faced by capacity assessors. This chapter also addresses the reality that, most of the time, legal capacity is not assessed by lawyers or courts but by healthcare professionals, most typically medical professionals. Chapter 4 explores the implications of this delegation of capacity assessment to the healthcare profession. While Chapter 4 makes a number of suggestions regarding how the capacity assessment process might be improved in practice, as with Chapter 3, a core conclusion emerging from Chapter 4 is that capacity is a less reliable 'sorting' mechanism than liberal theorists have assumed.

Chapter 5 is concerned with people who lack the capacity to make a healthcare decision and who, as a result, are sidelined by a framework focused on autonomy. The chapter identifies the flaws in the two traditional approaches to decision-making in this context, the best interests standard, which has been favoured in England and Wales, and the substituted judgment standard, which has been adopted in jurisdictions in the United States. It evaluates the efforts of the MCA to provide a blend of the two standards, which recognises the past and present wishes of the person lacking capacity within a framework that remains centred on best interests. Having assessed the possibilities offered by the MCA, Chapter 5 argues that the MCA cannot, of itself, provide a complete legal framework for decision-making. Consequently, the chapter explores the role of rights other than autonomy and assesses the potential contribution of the ECHR and the CRPD in this respect.

Chapter 6 evaluates the legal position in respect of treatment for a mental disorder. As the chapter shows, in many jurisdictions, including England and Wales, once a person has been brought within the ambit of mental health legislation, her right to refuse treatment for her mental disorder is significantly restricted, regardless of her decision-making capacity. Chapter 6 argues that this differential treatment is discriminatory and that it contributes to the stigmatisation of people with mental disorders. However, the chapter also draws on the legal position in the United States and Canada to argue that the difficult issues that arise in respect of treatment for a mental disorder cannot be addressed simply by extending a traditional right of autonomy as non-interference to this context. Instead, Chapter 6 argues in favour of legal measures to facilitate greater empowerment of patients with a mental disorder, regardless of whether or not they have decision-making capacity. This chapter also argues that the potentially abusive nature of treatment for a mental disorder requires a higher degree of protection for patients in this context.

The book concludes by identifying a number of key themes which have emerged from the discussion and exploring some of the broader implications of these for the future development of the law in respect of health-care decision-making.

1

Autonomy: variations on a principle

As originally used, the term 'autonomy', so central to bioethical debate, had nothing to do with health care or indeed with individuals. Rather, the term described the right of Greek city-states to self-government. With the Enlightenment, the principle of autonomy came to be associated with individuals as well as states and respect for autonomy now provides the philosophical underpinning for much of bioethics and law.[1] While this book is concerned with autonomy in the relatively limited sphere of decisions about treatment, the status to be accorded to individual autonomy is central to many bioethical debates, ranging from access to euthanasia and reproductive technology to the sale of organs or body parts.

Although the importance of autonomy to healthcare ethics and law is clear, what the principle actually means is less so. As Gerald Dworkin notes, '[a]bout the only features held constant from one author to another are that autonomy is a feature of persons and that it is a desirable quality to have'.[2] In fact, as this chapter shows, the concept of autonomy is more dynamic and complex than is sometimes appreciated in legal discussions of its role in healthcare decision-making. This chapter establishes the theoretical foundations for the legal discussion which follows in later chapters by exploring autonomy as a philosophical construct within ethical debate. This is important not least because, as Alasdair Maclean notes, the law tends to follow the dominant ethical arguments although with an extensive time lag.[3] The chapter begins with a brief overview of

[1] See D. Callahan, 'Can the Moral Commons Survive Autonomy?' (1996) 26 *Hastings Center Report* 41; C. Schneider, *The Practice of Autonomy* (New York: Oxford University Press, 1998), p. 3; P. Wolpe, 'The Triumph of Autonomy in American Bioethics: A Sociological View' in R. de Vries and H. Subedi (eds.) *Bioethics and Society: Constructing the Ethical Enterprise* (Upper Saddle River, NJ: Prentice Hall, 1998), p. 43; O. O'Neill, *Autonomy and Trust in Bioethics* (Cambridge University Press, 2002), p. 2.

[2] G. Dworkin, *The Theory and Practice of Autonomy* (New York: Cambridge University Press, 1988), p. 6.

[3] A. Maclean, *Autonomy, Informed Consent and Medical Law: A Relational Challenge* (Cambridge University Press, 2009), p. 215.

how, and why, the autonomy principle came to prominence in ethical discourse. It then examines the traditional underpinnings of the principle, exploring the Kantian linkage of autonomy to morality and objective conceptions of 'the good' and the classic liberal view of autonomy as based primarily on non-interference. It shows that the view of autonomy within healthcare ethics (and law) is derived primarily from Millian rather than Kantian principles. The chapter then explores the flaws in the traditional view of autonomy. While examining a range of critiques, particular emphasis is placed on the limited conception of the agent within traditional liberal discourse and the limited scope of a principle of non-interference.

Having identified flaws in the traditional liberal view of autonomy, the chapter presents an alternative account which views autonomy as 'a kind of achievement'.[4] Drawing on the work of Joseph Raz[5] and on arguments made by some 'relational' theorists, this account of autonomy is concerned with developing empowerment mechanisms which recognise the 'socially embedded' nature of the agent.[6] This is a richer, or as some commentators prefer to term it 'thicker', conception of autonomy than that currently enshrined by the law. As such, it offers possibilities for ongoing conceptual engagement with autonomy (and reminds us of the value of this endeavour).

Principle in practice: the elevation of autonomy in medical ethics

It is well known that, for much of the history of medicine, the principle of autonomy played no significant part in the operative ethical framework. Instead, the primary imperatives were doing good for the patient, the avoidance of harm and the protection of life.[7] As traditionally conceived, the first of these imperatives did not require consultation with the patient; the physician's view of what was good was the determining factor. This extreme form of beneficence, now often

---

[4] J. Raz, *The Morality of Freedom* (Oxford: Clarendon Press, 1986), p. 204.
[5] See in particular *The Morality of Freedom ibid.*; J. Raz, *Ethics in the Public Domain: Essays in the Morality of Law and Politics* (Oxford: Clarendon Press, 1994).
[6] C. Mackenzie and N. Stoljar 'Autonomy Reconfigured', in C. Mackenzie and N. Stoljar (eds.) *Relational Autonomy: Feminist Perspectives on Autonomy, Agency, and the Social Self* (New York: Oxford University Press, 2000), p. 4.
[7] Under the traditional Hippocratic Oath, the physician promised 'I will use my power to help the sick to the best of my ability and judgment; I will abstain from harming or wrongdoing any man by it': *Hippocratic Writings* J. Chadwick and W. N. Mann trans. (London: Penguin Books, 1950).

pejoratively referred to as paternalism, is described by Edmund Pelligrino and David Thomasma:

> Paternalism centres on the notion that the physician ... has better insight into the best interests of the patient than does the patient, or that the physician's obligations are such that he is impelled to do what is medically good, even if it is not 'good' in terms of the patient's own value system.[8]

The sanctity of life principle, which derives from the Judaeo-Christian tradition, regards life as having an intrinsic value unrelated to any individual's views regarding the value of her own life.[9] In its most extreme form (sometimes termed 'vitalism'[10]), adherence to this principle requires that life be preserved at all costs. A less extreme, and more commonly accepted, view of the principle acknowledges that there are instances in which life need not be preserved but still holds that human life has an 'intrinsic dignity which entitles it to protection from unjust attack'.[11] Proponents of this view may accept that, in John Keown's words, the sanctity of life principle does not require a person 'to administer or undergo a treatment which is not worthwhile'.[12] Nonetheless, on this view, respect for the sanctity of life principle requires that a decision regarding whether or not treatment is undergone is not made by the individual but is dictated by an objective assessment of what is worthwhile.

A shift in focus

These traditional ethical principles described above were, by and large, adhered to by doctors and accepted by patients with little discussion. As David Rothman points out, ethics was taught and learned 'at the bedside' on a case-by-case basis; in his words, it was 'as though medical decision making begins and ends (or, more precisely, should begin and end) with

---

[8] E. D. Pelligrino and D. C. Thomasma, *For the Patient's Good* (New York: Oxford University Press, 1988), p. 7.

[9] See the description of the principle in *Airedale NHS Trust v Bland* [1993] AC 789, 826 *per* Hoffmann LJ.

[10] See E. Keyserlingk, *Sanctity of Life or Quality of Life in the Context of Ethics, Medicine and Law* (Ottawa: Law Reform Commission of Canada, 1979), p. 12.

[11] J. Keown, 'Restoring Moral and Intellectual Shape to the Law After *Bland*' (1997) 113 *Law Quarterly Review* 481, 483.

[12] *Ibid.*, 485. Keown argues that a treatment is not worthwhile in this sense 'either because it offers no reasonable hope of benefit or because, even though it does, the expected benefit would be outweighed by burdens which the treatment would impose, such as excessive pain'.

the dyad of the doctor and the patient alone in the examining room'.[13] By the late 1960s, however, attitudes began to change.[14] Ethicists, especially in the United States, began to emphasise the importance of patient autonomy and to question the presumption that a doctor is in a better position to assess benefits for the patient than the patient herself.[15] Even more significantly, ethicists and other 'outsiders' (including judges, lawyers and legislators) began to establish a voice in defining 'the moral codes that were to guide physician behaviour'.[16]

There were several reasons why this kind of shift in attitude occurred at this time. Challenges to medical authority fitted comfortably within the broader suite of challenges to traditional authority which had become increasingly prevalent. Campaigns centred on race and civil rights and on women's rights drew attention to inherent inequities in society and the role of traditional authority in maintaining these. In addition, concerns more specific to the medical profession began to emerge. These included criticisms of treatment practices in respect of people with a mental disorder made by an influential anti-psychiatry movement[17] and the identification of a number of high-profile medical research abuses in the United States.[18] These matters attracted a good deal of public attention[19] and

---

[13] D. Rothman, *Strangers at the Bedside: A History of How Law and Bioethics Transformed Medical Decision Making* (New York: Basic Books, 1991), p. 9.

[14] *Ibid.*, p. 3, Rothman dates the crucial period of change (in the United States) as between 1966 and 1976.

[15] R. Veatch 'Autonomy's Temporary Triumph' (1984) 14 *The Hastings Center Report* 38, 38.

[16] Rothman, *Strangers*, p. 4. See also S. Toulmin 'How Medicine Saved the Life of Ethics' (1982) 25 *Perspectives in Biology and Medicine* 736.

[17] The anti-psychiatry 'movement' comprised a number of thinkers from different academic backgrounds and political perspectives. These included the English psychiatrist David Cooper (who coined the term in 1967); the Scottish psychiatrist R. D. Laing; and the American psychiatrist Thomas Szasz.

[18] These revelations made it clear that non-consensual experimentation could not be regarded simply as a historical aberration restricted to Nazi camps. Of particular significance was the publication of 'Ethics and Clinical Research' (1966) 274 *New England Journal of Medicine* 1354 (for discussion of the impact of this publication, see Rothman, *Strangers*, pp. 15–18) where Henry Beecher outlined 22 examples of medical experiments which risked the health or life of the subjects without the subjects' knowledge or consent.

[19] The anti-psychiatry message came to broad public attention through novels, including Ken Kesey's *One Flew Over the Cuckoo's Nest* (New York: Viking Press, 1962) and Sylvia Plath's *The Bell Jar* (London: Faber and Faber, 1971) and the film version of *One Flew Over the Cuckoo's Nest* (dir. Milos Forman). The Tuskegee Syphilis Trial, which first became public in 1972, received a good deal of publicity, not least because of its racial implications. The trial, which was carried out by the United States' Public Health Service,

contributed to growing public mistrust of the medical profession and an increased reluctance to accept medical views unquestioningly.

Responses in the ethics literature

In the United States, the official response to public concerns about research abuses came with the publication of the report of the National Commission for the Protection of Human Subjects of Biomedical and Behavioural Research (the Belmont Report) in 1978.[20] The report advocated the adoption of a principles-based approach in respect of the use of human subjects in research. Tom Beauchamp was instrumental in drafting the report[21] and he and James Childress adopted a similar approach in the first edition of *Principles of Biomedical Ethics*, which was published in 1979.[22] Now in its sixth edition,[23] this text is possibly the most influential text in medical ethics. Beauchamp and Childress proposed four governing principles for bioethics generally. These principles are autonomy, beneficence, non-malificence and justice. In the first edition of their book, Beauchamp and Childress expressly derived support for the autonomy principle from both Kantian deontology and Millian liberalism.[24] Merle Spriggs shows, however, that, with subsequent editions, the Kantian view of autonomy became less important while the utilitarian liberalism of Mill assumed greater significance.[25]

While Beauchamp and Childress have always maintained that no one of the four principles they identify should be seen as dominant, there is little doubt that autonomy came to be regarded, in Raanan Gillon's words,

ran from 1932 until 1972 and investigated the pathological evolution of syphilis if left untreated. The trial involved 399 poor black sharecroppers in Macon County, Alabama, who were not told the nature of their condition and were denied treatment: see J. Jones, *Bad Blood* (New York: Free Press, 1981).

[20] National Commission for the Protection of Human Subjects of Biomedical and Behavioural Research, *Ethical Principles and Guidelines for the Protection of Human Subjects of Research* (Washington: Department of Health, Education, and Welfare, 1979). Although first published in 1978, the report appears in the Federal Register dated 1979.

[21] See T. Beauchamp 'The Origins and Evolution of the Belmont Report' in J. Childress, E. Meslin and H. Shapiro (eds.) *Belmont Revisited: Ethical Principles for Research With Human Subjects* (Washington: Georgetown University Press, 2005), pp. 12–25.

[22] T. Beauchamp and J. Childress, *Principles of Biomedical Ethics* (1st edn) (New York: Oxford University Press, 1979).

[23] T. Beauchamp and J. Childress, *Principles* (6th edn) (New York: Oxford University Press, 2008).

[24] Beauchamp and Childress, *Principles* (1st edn), pp. 56–9.

[25] Spriggs, M. *Autonomy and Patients' Decisions* (Lanham, MD: Lexington Books, 2005), pp. 56–64.

as 'the first among equals'.[26] Indeed, by the 1994 edition of *Principles*, Beauchamp and Childress had acknowledged that 'autonomy rights have become so influential that it is today difficult to find affirmations of traditional models of medical beneficence'.[27] For some, including Gillon, this is the appropriate approach.[28] For others, the failure to engage with the other principles results in an impoverished ethical framework.[29] Nonetheless, as outlined by Robert Veatch, medical ethics came to be seen as 'a conflict between the old Hippocratic paternalism (having the physician do what he or she thought was best for the patient) and a principle of autonomy'.[30] Within a remarkably short time, autonomy had 'won the day'[31] and respect for patient autonomy became the central focus in relation to all medical interventions. This occurred especially quickly in the United States, where individual autonomy and freedom from external control had long been regarded as fundamental 'American' values.[32] The shift in ethical focus spread to other countries and, by the end of the twentieth century, autonomy had become the dominant value for healthcare ethics in most Western jurisdictions.

The role of autonomy in ethical guidance for professionals

The significance of autonomy (and the form of autonomy endorsed) came to be reflected in the ethical guidance for medical professionals.[33] In the first

[26] R. Gillon, 'Ethics Needs Principles – Four can Encompass the Rest – and Respect for Autonomy should be "First Among Equals"' (2003) 29 *Journal of Medical Ethics* 307.

[27] T. Beauchamp and J. Childress, *Principles of Biomedical Ethics* (4th edn) (New York: Oxford University Press, 1994), p. 272.

[28] See similar arguments in R. Veatch, *A Theory of Medical Ethics* (New York: Basic Books, 1981); T. Engelhardt, *The Foundations of Bioethics* (New York: Oxford University Press, 1986).

[29] See D. Callahan 'Autonomy: A Moral Good, Not a Moral Obsession (1984) 14 *The Hastings Centre Report* 40; E. Pelligrino 'The Four Principles and the Doctor-Patient Relationship: The Need for a Better Linkage' in R. Gillon (ed.) *Principles of Healthcare Ethics* (London: John Wiley & Sons, 1995); S. Holm 'Not Just Autonomy – the Principles of American Biomedical Ethics' (1995) 21 *Journal of Medical Ethics* 332. See also C. Foster *Choosing Life, Choosing Death: The Tyranny of Autonomy in Medical Ethics and Law* (Oxford: Hart Publishing, 2009), Chapter 2. For a critique of a principles-based approach to ethics more generally, see K. Clouser and B. Gert 'A Critique of Principalism' (1996) 15 *Journal of Medical Philosophy* 219.

[30] Veatch, 'Autonomy's Temporary Triumph', 38.   [31] *Ibid.*

[32] See W. Gaylin and B. Jennings *The Perversion of Autonomy: Coercion and Constraints in a Liberal Society* (Washington: Georgetown University Press, 2003), pp. 47–57.

[33] See generally J. Miola, *Medical Ethics and Medical Law: A Symbiotic Relationship* (Oxford: Hart Publishing, 2007), pp. 48–53.

edition of *Good Medical Practice*, published in 1995, the General Medical Council (GMC) mentioned autonomy under the heading 'Maintaining Trust' and included a requirement to 'respect the right of patients to be fully involved in decisions about their care' and to 'respect the right of patients to refuse treatment or take part in treatment or research'.[34] These rather bald statements represent the limits of the guide's discussion of autonomy (although this is perhaps unsurprising given that the substantive part of the document is itself only 13 pages long). The statements suggest a view of autonomy which locates decision-making in the professionals involved, leaving patients with the choice to reject these decisions or not. Autonomy is seen primarily as a matter of non-interference.

There has been an evident shift in focus in the most recent edition of *Good Medical Practice*, published in 2006. This contains a clear statement that the duties of a doctor include working in partnership with patients and respecting the patient's right to reach decisions with the doctor about their treatment and care.[35] This partnership approach is also evident in the current GMC guidance on consent.[36] Interestingly, by comparison, the American Medical Association (AMA) would seem to remain wedded to a 'non-interference' view of autonomy. The AMA Code of Medical Ethics states simply that '[t]he patient has the right to make decisions regarding the healthcare that is recommended by his or her physician. Accordingly, patients may accept or refuse any recommended treatment'.[37]

Autonomy: the philosophical antecedents

Modern autonomy theorists tend to rely on two philosophical foundations. The first is Immanuel Kant's deontological ethics; the second is the utilitarian liberalism of John Stuart Mill.[38] Sometimes, notwithstanding the differences in these philosophical approaches, both sources are relied on simultaneously.[39] An appreciation of the philosophical foundations and the differences between them is essential in order to understand the current approach to autonomy in healthcare ethics and law and to appreciate how understandings of the principle might develop in the future.

---

[34] *Good Medical Practice* (London: GMC, 1995), para. 11.
[35] *Good Medical Practice* (London: GMC, 2006).
[36] *Consent: Patients and Doctors Making Decisions Together* (London: GMC, 2008).
[37] *Code of Medical Ethics* (Chicago: American Medical Association, 2008–9), Opinion 10.01.
[38] For a much more detailed analysis of both sources than is attempted here, see Spriggs, *Autonomy and Patients' Decisions*, Chapters 1 and 2.
[39] See for example Beauchamp and Childress, *Principles* (1st edn).

A Kantian conception of autonomy

At first sight, the linkage between Kant's work and the principle of autonomy seems obvious, not least because Kant frequently employed the term 'autonomy'.[40] Gillon argues that Kant's fundamental principle of morality, or 'Categorical Imperative', is premised on the actions of an autonomous individual.[41] As expressed in 'The Formula of Universal Law', this Categorical Imperative is that 'I ought never to act except in such a way that I could also will that my maxim should become a universal law'.[42] Explaining the relevance of the Universal Law to individual autonomy in a healthcare context, Gillon argues:

> It is by both rationally recognising the validity of the moral law and willing or choosing to accept it for ourselves that we can be subject to the universal moral law and yet at the same time also authors of it.[43]

Thus, unless individuals have a choice about whether or not to accept a universal moral law, they cannot be bound by such a law. On this basis, Gillon argues that autonomy in the sense of individual freedom of choice is an essential component of Kantian ethics.

Disputing the linkage

Many Kantian scholars dispute the linkage between the Kantian conception of autonomy and a conception of autonomy as individual freedom of choice.[44] Onora O'Neill argues that, in setting out the Categorical

---

[40] See I. Kant, *Critique of Practical Reason* (1785) in M. Gregor (ed.) *Kant, Practical Philosophy* (Cambridge University Press, 1996).

[41] R. Gillon, *Philosophical Medical Ethics* (Chichester: John Wiley, 1985), p. 64. See also M. Charlesworth, *Bioethics in a Liberal Society* (Cambridge University Press, 1993), pp. 12–13.

[42] I. Kant, *Groundwork of the Metaphysics of Morals* (1785), p. 402, (from M. Gregor (ed.) *Kant: Groundwork of the Metaphysics of Morals* (*Cambridge Texts in the History of Philosophy*) (Cambridge University Press, 1997). Although there is only one Categorical Imperative, Kant formulated the universal law in three different ways. The other two are: 'Act in such a way that you treat humanity, whether in your own person or in the person of any other, always at the same time as an end and never merely as a means to an end' and 'Every rational being must so act as if he were through his maxim always a legislating member of the universal kingdom of ends'. See generally O. O'Neill, *Constructions of Reason: Explorations of Kant's Practical Philosophy* (Cambridge University Press, 1989); R. Sullivan, *An Introduction to Kant's Ethics* (Cambridge University Press, 1994).

[43] Gillon, *Philosophical Medical Ethics*, p. 64.

[44] See in particular O'Neill, *Autonomy and Trust*, pp. 83–6; J. Raz, *The Morality of Freedom*, p. 370; B. Secker 'The Appearance of Kant's Deontology in Contemporary Kantianism: Concepts of Patient Autonomy in Bioethics' (1999) 24 *Journal of Medicine and Philosophy* 43.

Imperative, Kant was not concerned with 'any special sort of act of choice, by which each *actually* chooses laws or principles for everyone else'. Rather, he was concerned to express a requirement regarding which principles '*could* be chosen by all, that is to say which principles are univeral*isable*, or *fit to be universal laws*'[45] Thus, Kant states that '[t]he concept of autonomy is inseparably connected with the idea of freedom and with the former there is inseparably bound the universal principle of morality, which ideally is the ground of all actions of rational beings'.[46] As summarised by Barbara Secker, the Kantian position is that while all rational people have the capacity to act autonomously, only those people who act morally (i.e. act in accordance with the Categorical Imperative) actually do so.[47] Self-legislation in the Kantian sense is therefore 'a self-enforced constraint'.[48] It is 'morality which we impose on ourselves'.[49] O'Neill uses the terms 'individual autonomy' and 'principled autonomy' to distinguish the two meanings of autonomy. Individual autonomy is autonomy in the sense which we associate with healthcare ethics and law; it is concerned with 'carving out some particularly independent trajectory in this world'.[50] Principled autonomy, on the other hand, is an action, the principle for which could be adopted by other people.[51]

Meir Dan-Cohen identifies a further distinction between the conception of autonomy as a choice (or 'choice autonomy') and 'will autonomy', the latter concept according more closely with the Kantian conception.[52] Will autonomy, he argues 'captures the sense of inevitability that is an important aspect of our moral experience'.[53] Thus, '[o]nce we realize what our moral duty in a situation is, we also appreciate that the moral course is in an important sense nonoptional'.[54] This view is clearly at odds with the free choice model. Dan-Cohen argues that the difference between choice autonomy and will autonomy lies not just in the absence of moral context from choice autonomy. Additionally, the Kantian conception of autonomy captures an 'inner necessity' or force (which he analogises to the experience of falling in love or the exercise of creative processes) that drives us to actions and which cannot be captured simply by representation as a choice among options.[55]

---

[45] O'Neill, *Autonomy and Trust*, p. 84, original emphasis.
[46] Kant, *Groundwork of the Metaphysics of Morals*, p. 71.
[47] Secker, 'The Appearance of Kant,' 47.
[48] Spriggs, *Autonomy and Patients' Decisions*, p. 17.   [49] *Ibid.*
[50] O'Neill, *Autonomy and Trust*, p. 85.   [51] *Ibid.*
[52] M. Dan-Cohen, *Harmful Thoughts: Essays on Law, Self, and Morality* (Princeton University Press, 2002), p. 135.
[53] *Ibid.*, p. 136.   [54] *Ibid.*   [55] *Ibid.*, pp. 136–7.

A Kantian conception of autonomy, therefore, is not about free choice but about the drive to appropriate or moral action. Thus, while, in O'Neill's caustic terms, autonomy's admirers within bioethics may 'crave and claim Kantian credentials,'[56] it would seem to be difficult to establish convincingly these credentials.

John Stuart Mill: the classic liberal view

In contrast to Kant, Mill 'hardly ever' used the term autonomy.[57] Yet, the principle of autonomy, as it has been given effect in healthcare ethics and law, derives in large part from Mill's utilitarian liberal vision.[58] In Mill's words, 'the only purpose for which power can be rightfully exercised over any member of a civilized community, against his will, is to prevent harm to others'.[59] The individual's 'own good, either physical or moral, is not a sufficient warrant'.[60] Thus, for Mill:

> The only part of the conduct of any one, for which he is amenable to society, is that which concerns others. In the part which merely concerns himself, his independence is, of right, absolute. Over himself, over his own body and mind, the individual is sovereign.[61]

Justifying the principle

Mill defended the principle of individual liberty on the utilitarian basis that it is through liberty that human individuality can develop. In his words,

> It is not by wearing down into uniformity all that is individual in themselves, but by cultivating it and calling it forth, within the limits imposed by the rights and interests of others, that human beings become a noble and beautiful object of contemplation.[62]

For Mill, allowing people a sphere of freedom had other instrumental benefits also. It encouraged originality and allowed persons of genius to develop.[63] It also recognised the essential differences between people and ensured that all people had the best chance to achieve happiness and moral growth.[64]

---

[56] O'Neill, *Autonomy and Trust*, p. 30.   [57] *Ibid.*

[58] See, in particular, Mill, *On Liberty* (London, 1859). For a detailed discussion of the linkage between Mill and this view of autonomy, see O'Neill, *Autonomy and Trust*, pp. 29–34.

[59] Mill, *On Liberty*, p. 14.   [60] *Ibid.*   [61] *Ibid.*   [62] *Ibid.*, p. 70.   [63] *Ibid.*, pp. 71–2.

[64] *Ibid.*, pp. 75–6.

Respect for the principle of individual autonomy remains central to modern liberal theorists. Ronald Dworkin echoes Mill in his defence of individual autonomy. In *Life's Dominion*, Dworkin argues that:

> Recognizing an individual right of autonomy makes self-creation possible. It allows each of us to be responsible for shaping our lives ... rather than be led along them, so that each of us can be, to the extent a scheme of rights can make this possible, what we have made of ourselves.[65]

For Ronald Dworkin, however, autonomy also has an intrinsic value. Thus, he argues, that '[f]reedom is the cardinal, absolute requirement of self-respect: no one treats his life as having any intrinsic, objective importance unless he insists on leading that life himself, not being ushered along it by others, not matter how much he loves or respects or fears them'.[66] As Alexander McCall Smith describes it, even if the non-autonomous individual avoids significant suffering in her life, it is commonly perceived that '[t]he moral texture of such a life is drab'.[67] In the healthcare context, this recognition means that, in Dworkin's words, '[w]e allow someone to choose death over radical amputation or a blood transfusion, if that is his informed wish, because we acknowledge his right to a life structured by his own values'.[68]

Other liberal theorists question the feasibility of alternatives to autonomy based on objective conceptions of the individual's good. Becky Cox White points out that, in spite of centuries of effort, all attempts have failed to develop a 'universally *shared* plausible list of things that are objectively good or evil'.[69] Even the seemingly uncontroversial values that are supported by healthcare professionals, such as life, health and the absence of pain, are not necessarily shared by patients.[70] Kim Atkins describes respect for autonomy as 'an acknowledgement of the limitations of our knowledge of other people'.[71] She argues that when we incorporate

[65] R. Dworkin, *Life's Dominion: An Argument About Abortion, Euthanasia, and Individual Freedom* (New York: Alfred A. Knopf, 1993), p. 224.

[66] *Ibid.*, p. 239. See also J. Feinberg *The Moral Limits of the Criminal Law, Vol 3: Harm to Self* (New York: Oxford University Press, 1986), pp. 44–7.

[67] A. McCall Smith, 'Beyond Autonomy' (1997) 14 *Journal of Contemporary Health Law and Policy* 23, 30.

[68] R. Dworkin, *Life's Dominion*, p. 239.

[69] B. Cox White, *Competence to Consent* (Washington DC: Georgetown University Press, 1994), p. 22, original emphasis.

[70] *Ibid.*

[71] K. Atkins, 'Autonomy and the Subjective Character of Experience' (2000) 17 *Journal of Applied Philosophy* 71. This article is one of the rare philosophical pieces relied upon by the courts, having been quoted by Dame Butler-Sloss P in *Re B (An Adult: Medical Treatment)* [2002] 2 All ER 449, 469–70.

autonomy into our world view, 'we accede to our fundamental fallibility and an epistemological humility'.[72]

Limits on autonomy

Within Mill's liberal account, autonomy is not accorded absolute respect. Respect for the principle is premised on 'all the persons concerned being of full age, and the ordinary amount of understanding'.[73] Mill also envisaged a limited degree of interference with freedom in order to establish that a person is aware of the consequences of her decision. Thus, in his famous wayfarer example, Mill describes a wayfarer approaching a dangerous bridge in circumstances in which it is uncertain whether she is aware of the danger. He states that it is permissible to stop the wayfarer to warn her of the dangers ahead but if, following the warning, the wayfarer still wishes to proceed, she should be permitted to do so.[74] Mill also recognised that interference with individual freedom could be justified in order 'to prevent harm to others'.[75] However, this justification does not allow a wholesale overriding of individual freedom. While acknowledging that 'no person is an entirely isolated being',[76] Mill argued that a person can be stopped from doing something only if, in doing that thing, she would 'violate a distinct and assignable obligation' to others.[77]

While the Millian account of autonomy is not without limits, once the right of autonomy does arise, it is accorded primary status in a hierarchy of values. Other values, such as beneficence or the sanctity of life, must be accorded subordinate status to the principle of autonomy because it is only in this way that the goal of sovereignty over one's own mind and body may be assured. This does not mean that these other values are meaningless or that they cannot co-exist with autonomy for most of the time. However, in a conflict between autonomy and other values, respect for autonomy dictates that decision-making power must be fully situated in the individual regardless of the consequences for the patient's welfare and even for her life. Thus, non-interference lies at the core of Mill's liberal philosophy.

However, non-interference was not the end of the matter. In Mill's words, '[t]here are good reasons for remonstrating with [an autonomous individual], or reasoning with him, or persuading him, or entreating him,

---

[72] Ibid., 75. In making this argument, Atkins draws on Thomas Nagel's work on the essential subjectivity of each individual: see 'What is it Like to be a Bat?' (1974) 83 The Philosophical Review 435.

[73] Mill, On Liberty, p. 84.   [74] Ibid., p. 107   [75] Ibid., p. 14.   [76] Ibid., p. 88.

[77] Ibid., p. 90.

but not for compelling him'.[78] This distinction which Mill makes between compulsion and other forms of interaction with the individual is significant; it suggests an understanding of autonomy which is more subtle than the 'take-it or leave-it' approach that is often associated with traditional liberalism. Nonetheless, the primary focus of this view of autonomy remains non-interference. As will be seen below, in this respect, the traditional liberal conception of autonomy has been subject to sustained critiques on a range of bases.

The limitations of traditional autonomy

Critics argue that the liberal conception of autonomy is reductionist in its conception of how people actually operate and that it is normatively inappropriate. Normative critiques of liberalism are most closely associated with communitarian[79] and feminist perspectives.[80] These critiques extend well beyond the healthcare context, with John Rawls' theory of political liberalism[81] providing the basis for much of the critical discussion. A comprehensive review of these critiques is not the concern of this book. Therefore, the focus of the discussion is on those critiques of particular relevance in the specific context of healthcare decision-making. Broadly speaking, these may be divided between critiques which are concerned with agency and those which are expressly normative. There is of course a significant overlap between the two sets of critiques; if a principle does not have a sound metaphysical grounding, this may well provide a normative reason for its rejection. The discussion below will begin by exploring the limited conception of the agent within traditional views of autonomy before proceeding to consider critiques which are more overtly normative.

---

[78] *Ibid.*, p. 14.

[79] This label is associated most closely with the political philosophers Alasdair MacIntyre, Michael Sandel, Charles Taylor and Michael Walzer. However, the label is applied by others (usually critics), rather than having been chosen by these theorists themselves: see S. Mulhall and A. Swift, *Liberals and Communitarians* (2nd edn) (Oxford: Blackwell Publishing, 1996).

[80] See summary of feminist critiques in Mackenzie and Stoljar (eds.) *Relational Autonomy*, pp. 5–12.

[81] As set out in J. Rawls, *A Theory of Justice* (Cambridge, MA: Harvard University Press, 1971); *Theory of Justice Revised Edition* (Cambridge, MA: Harvard University Press, 1999); *Political Liberalism* (New York: Columbia University Press, 1993); *Political Liberalism, Expanded Edition* (New York: Columbia University Press, 2005).

As will be seen, some of these critiques reveal important flaws in the traditional liberal view of autonomy. However, it should be noted at the outset that there is an element of the 'straw man' in respect of at least some of these charges.[82] As discussed above, Mill propounded a more sophisticated theory than simple non-interference and few modern liberal theorists would support the limited view of autonomy critiqued.[83] Yet, exploring these critiques is important, first because as will be seen in the next chapter, a simple view of autonomy as non-interference still pervades much legal discourse and an understanding of its limits is therefore essential and, secondly, because the critiques themselves need to be subject to critical evaluation if we are to develop an understanding of the possibilities and limits of the richer conception of autonomy which will subsequently be explored.

Autonomy, agency and the nature of the subject

Because respect for autonomy is centred on the individual subject as decision-maker or 'chooser of ends', it is essential to understand this subject and the presumptions made in respect of her agency.

The nature of the autonomous subject

In his communitarian critique of liberalism, Michael Sandel provides a critical analysis of the 'antecedently individuated'[84] liberal subject on both metaphysical and normative grounds. He argues that the liberal subject is individualistic, not necessarily in the sense of selfish or uncaring, but in the more fundamental sense that it is conceived as 'standing always at a certain distance from the interests it has'.[85] Thus, the liberal subject is separate (and separable) from her views, beliefs and interests. These are, in a sense, something she can take off or put on. A consequence of this is that '[n]o commitment could grip me so deeply that I could not understand myself without it'.[86] Sandel disputes this view of the subject on metaphysical grounds, arguing that 'community describes not just what [members of society] have as fellow citizens but also what they are, not a relationship

---

[82] A. Maclean, *Autonomy, Informed Consent and Medical Law*, p. 18.

[83] See, for example, the more nuanced views advanced in J. Rawls, *Political Liberalism*; R. Dworkin, *A Matter of Principle* (Oxford University Press, 1985); *Sovereign Virtue: The Theory and Practice of Equality* (Cambridge, MA: Harvard University Press, 2000).

[84] M. Sandel, *Liberalism and the Limits of Justice* (2nd edn) (Cambridge University Press, 1997), p. 62.

[85] *Ibid.*   [86] *Ibid.*

they choose (as in a voluntary association) but an attachment they discover, not merely an attribute but a constituent of identity'.[87]

Feminist theorists also identify the role of connection in the creation of the self, drawing especially on the role played by conditions of dependency which are inevitable aspects of childhood in the creation of one's moral personality. Annette Baier argues that 'our *understanding* of personality relates to its genesis, and, for us, that is in the conditions of biological life, in which one generation nurtures its successor generation, preparing it to take its place'.[88] In simple terms, we are who we are because of where we come from; we are inevitably 'socially embedded'.[89] Recognising this has consequences for the role of agency within liberal conceptions of autonomy.

Autonomy and agency

A presumption of agency underlies the liberal conception of autonomy. Our choices are autonomous because they are, in a fundamental sense, *our* choices. This is evident in the foundational accounts of autonomy within moral psychology. Gerald Dworkin's well-known account of autonomy is based on a hierarchical ordering of first- and second-order desires and a presumption of agency.[90] These premises are reflected in the two components of his account. First, he defines autonomy as 'a second-order capacity of persons to reflect critically upon their first-order preferences, desires, wishes and so forth and the capacity to accept or attempt to change these in light of higher-order preferences and values'.[91] Secondly, he includes a requirement for 'procedural independence'. This requires 'distinguishing those ways of influencing people's reflective and critical faculties which subvert them from those which promote and improve them'.[92] Gerald Dworkin identifies a number of potentially subverting

---

[87] *Ibid.*, p. 150. For a similar argument which draws on historical and inter-generational traditions in the constitution of identity, see A. MacIntyre *After Virtue: A Study in Moral Theory* (London: Duckworth, 1981).

[88] A. Baier, *Postures of the Mind: Essays on Mind and Morals* (Minneapolis: University of Minnesota Press, 1985), p. 85, original emphasis. See also A. Jaggar, *Feminist Politics and Human Nature* (Totowa, NJ: Rowman & Littlefield, 1983).

[89] Mackenzie and Stoljar (eds.) *Relational Autonomy*, p. 4.

[90] A broadly similar view of agency is offered by H. Frankfurt 'Freedom of the Will and the Concept of a Person' (1971) 68 *Journal of Philosophy* 5; G. Watson 'Free Agency' (1975) 72 *Journal of Philosophy* 202; J. Christman 'Constructing the Inner Citadel: Recent Work on the Concept of Autonomy' (1988) 99 *Ethics* 109. For a collection of broadly 'traditional' accounts of autonomy, see J. Christman (ed.) *The Inner Citadel: Essays on Individual Autonomy* (New York: Oxford University Press, 1989).

[91] G. Dworkin, *The Theory and Practice of Autonomy*, p. 20.   [92] *Ibid.*, p. 18.

conditions, including 'hypnotic suggestion, manipulation, coercive persuasion, subliminal influence'.[93]

The question arises as to whether decision-making agency of the type presumed by Dworkin and other traditional autonomy theorists is in fact possible. In considering this, it is perhaps best to begin by circumventing the long debated question of the relationship between determinism and free will.[94] 'Hard' determinists, who reject any (or almost any) role for free will, are rare.[95] So too are 'philosophically libertarian' theorists who reject any role for determinism and propound a theory of (more or less) complete free will.[96] The more widely accepted position, within Western philosophical discourse at any rate, is often described as compatibilist or 'soft' determinist, and suggests that determinism can be reconciled with notions of free will. The consequent discussion regarding how reconciliation might be achieved, while important, is not especially relevant to the current discussion. It is, however, important for the current discussion to investigate the empirical basis for presumptions about agency and how free one is in making decisions. It is therefore helpful to begin by considering some of the insights from behavioural theory in respect of how we make decisions.

Decision-making and behavioural theory

The way we approach decision-making has been the subject of a good deal of theoretical and empirical study by psychologists and behaviouralists.[97] Psychologists identify a number of heuristics (or problem-solving rules of thumb) which influence the ways in which people reach decisions.[98]

---

[93] *Ibid.*

[94] While this relationship has long been debated, famously by Thomas Hobbes, *Leviathan* (1651), and David Hume, *Enquiry Concerning Human Understanding* (1748), scientific advances in genetics and neuroscience have given new focus to discussions: see, in particular, the work of Patricia Churchland, *Neurophilosophy: Towards a Unified Science of the Mind-Brain* (Cambridge, MA: MIT Press, 1986); Paul Churchland, *Neurophilosophy at Work* (New York: Cambridge University Press, 2007); Daniel Dennett *Elbow Room: The Varieties of Free Will Worth Wanting* (Cambridge, MA: MIT Press, 1984).

[95] One of the few modern exponents of this view is T. Honderich, *How Free are You? The Determinism Problem* (2nd edn) (Oxford University Press, 2002).

[96] The most significant is perhaps R. Kane *The Significance of Free Will* (New York: Oxford University Press, 1996).

[97] See generally D. Koehler and N. Harvey (eds.) *Blackwell Handbook of Judgment and Decision Making* (Chichester: Wiley Blackwell, 2004); R. Thaler and C. Sunstein *Nudge: Improving Decisions About Health, Wealth, and Happiness* (New Haven: Yale University Press, 2008), Chapter 1.

[98] See especially the influential work of A. Tversky and D. Kahneman 'Availability: a Heuristic for Judging Frequency and Probability' (1973) 5 *Cognitive Psychology* 207;

The most relevant of these to decisions about health care are the heuristics of anchoring, availability and alternatives. Anchoring refers to the tendency in making a decision to focus (or anchor) on a particular value or piece of information and to measure or adjust the decision against this value or information. Thus, the way in which decisions are framed impacts on the choices made. This is illustrated in a healthcare context in a study of patient responses to a treatment decision where identical facts were presented in two different ways. Patients who were told 'of those who undertake this procedure, 90% are still alive after five years' were found to be more likely to agree to the procedure than patients who are told that, after five years, 10 per cent of people who undertake the procedure will have died.[99]

The 'availability' heuristic is linked to the ease with which examples of possible consequences are available or come to mind.[100] It is especially significant in dealing with probability and risk, both of which are clearly important factors in the task of healthcare decision-making. The application of this heuristic leads people to rate as more probable events which they can more easily imagine occurring. This may be because of heightened media exposure; it is well known for example that people are more likely to fear terrorist attacks or plane crashes than car crashes. Alternatively, a person's ease in imagining an event may be because of personal experiences. Thus, in making a decision about treatment, a person may over-rate the risk involved if a similar risk had materialised in respect of someone she knows. The 'alternatives' heuristic is linked to the number and types of alternative available to a person in making a choice. While increased alternatives can made choice easier, this can also lead to the deferral of decisions, to the choice of a default option, to the maintenance of the status quo[101] and to the choice of the most conservative option.[102] Thus, the addition of more alternatives does not necessarily make a person's choice easier or indeed improve the quality of the decision made.

Behavioural theory is important to our understanding of how decision-making works and raises especially interesting questions about the role of

'Judgment under Uncertainty: Heuristics and Biases' (1974) 185 *Science* 1124; 'The Framing of Decisions and the Psychology of Choices' (1981) 211 *Science* 453.

[99] See D. Redelmeier *et al.*, 'Understanding Patients' Decisions: Cognitive and Emotional Perspectives' (1993) 279 *Journal of the American Medical Association* 72.

[100] See Tversky and Kahneman 'Availability'.

[101] E. Shafir and R. LeBoeuf, 'Context and Conflict in Multiattribute Choice' in D. Koehler and N. Harvey (eds.), *Blackwell Handbook*, pp. 353–4.

[102] D. Redelmeier and E. Shafir, 'Medical Decision Making in Situations that Offer Multiple Alternatives' (1995) 273 *Journal of the American Medical Association* 302.

effective communication, the boundaries of manipulation and the appropriateness of surrogate decision-making. Conceptually, however, the insights derived from behavioural work do not significantly undermine the conception of decision-making freedom. Heuristics may bias our decisions in particular directions but, unless one operates on the basis of a particularly demanding view of agency, it would be difficult to argue that the ensuing decisions are not free.[103] However, if we broaden the context for consideration from the psychological to the social, a case may be made that at least some decisions which are not overtly the subject of subverting conditions (in the sense identified by Gerald Dworkin), cannot nonetheless, be categorised as those of wholly free agents.

Agency and social context

There is an extent to which, as sociologist Paul Wolpe argues, the idea of 'free choice' is 'socially constructed and situated'.[104] Wolpe notes some of the structural factors that may impede a person's ability to make free decisions about health care.[105] These include the power and prestige of the medical profession and the coercive influence of families and communities. In addition, class, race, education, cultural and religious factors all impact on the way in which people make decisions.[106] Furthermore, 'life circumstances, such as the need to get back to a job that will not tolerate long medical absences, coerce patients to make certain types of decisions'.[107]

Feminist theorists have been to the forefront in questioning the social and structural context in which individuals (and particularly women) make decisions and in identifying the impact of power relations and oppressive social factors on agency and decision-making freedom.[108] While early feminist work was concerned primarily with gender-based oppression, more recent work has focused on the diverse or 'intersectional' bases of oppression.[109] Attention is increasingly drawn to the role

---

[103] See C. Sunstein and R. Thaler, 'Libertarian Paternalism Is Not an Oxymoron' (2003) 70 *University of Chicago Law Review* 1159.

[104] Wolpe, 'The Triumph of Autonomy' in deVries and Subedi (eds.) *Bioethics and Society*, p. 54.

[105] *Ibid.* [106] *Ibid.* [107] *Ibid.*

[108] Identification of the impact of oppression on agency is most closely associated with radical feminist theorists: see especially the work of C. MacKinnon *Feminism Unmodified: Discourses on Life and Law* (Cambridge, MA: Harvard University Press, 1987).

[109] See K. Crenshaw 'Demarginalizing the Intersection of Race and Sex: A Black Feminist Critique of Antidiscrimination Doctrine, Feminist Theory and Antiracist Politics' [1989] *University of Chicago Legal Forum* 139.

of race, class, religion, social and cultural contexts in limiting agency. Applying feminist theory in a healthcare context, Celia Wells identifies the 'awkward questions' raised by the role of religion in some treatment refusal cases.[110] In some such cases, Wells suggests that it is arguable that 'the paternalism of law or of medicine is no more oppressive than that of religion or of marriage'.[111] Other feminist theorists identify the impact of 'Western' social norms on agency. Susan Sherwin questions the freedom of women's choices in respect of cosmetic surgery, reproductive technology, abortion, pre-natal genetic testing and hormonal replacement therapy[112] while Natalie Stoljar questions some decisions about contraception along similar lines.[113] Stoljar argues that decisions to avoid using contraception which are based on views that it is inappropriate for women to have an active sex life or to plan and initiate sex or that pregnancy and childbearing promote one's worthiness are informed by 'oppressive and misguided norms'.[114]

While an oppressive social environment may impact on an individual's agency, a focus on such factors alone fails to recognise the impact of health crises on agency more generally. Susan Dodds cites the example of a 'bastion of patriarchy' (male, white, able-bodied, tertiary-educated, professional) faced with a decision about treatment for prostrate cancer and shows the range of factors 'over which he has no control but which affect the quality of his care'.[115] Indeed, as she points out, the factors inculcated in him by his (privileged) enculturation may impede his decision-making freedom. He may accept invasive medical procedures because he considers that it would be 'weak or unmanly to accept his condition passively' or may be pushed towards risky experimental treatment because of a fear of dependency.[116] Thus, structural concerns about agency pervade

[110] C. Wells, 'Patients, Consent and Criminal Law' (1994) 16 *Journal of Social Welfare and Family Law* 65, 69.

[111] *Ibid*. See also C. Wells, 'On the Outside Looking In: Perspectives on Enforced Caesareans' in S. Sheldon and M. Thompson (eds.) *Feminist Perspectives on Health Care Law* (London: Cavendish Publishing, 1998), p. 255.

[112] 'A Relational Approach to Autonomy in Healthcare' in S. Sherwin (ed.) *The Politics of Women's Health: Exploring Agency and Autonomy* (Philadelphia: Temple University Press, 1998), pp. 27–8.

[113] N. Stoljar, 'Autonomy and the Feminist Intuition' in Mackenzie and Stoljar (eds.) *Relational Autonomy*.

[114] *Ibid*., p. 108. These motivations for the decision not to use contraception are taken from the study by K. Luker, *Taking Chances: Abortion and the Decision not to Contracept* (Berkeley: University of California Press, 1975).

[115] S. Dodds, 'Choice and Control in Feminist Bioethics' in Mackenzie and Stoljar (eds.) *Relational Autonomy*, p. 225.

[116] *Ibid*.

many aspects of healthcare decision-making, even if they are more acute in oppressive circumstances.

Traditional accounts of agency do not provide a framework within which to deal with the impact of social or structural contexts on agency. Accounts, such as that of Gerald Dworkin are, to use Marina Oshana's term, 'internalist'.[117] Thus, while Dworkin acknowledges that 'the choice of the kind of person one wants to become ... may be influenced by other persons or circumstances in such a fashion that we do not view those evaluations as being the person's own',[118] the subverting factors which he identifies as possible limits on agency do not include any reference to social context. A close reading indicates that this is not an accidental omission but is core to Dworkin's view of autonomy. This is clear in Dworkin's response to the classic liberal dilemma of whether a person can autonomously agree to become a slave. He argues:

> There is nothing in the idea of autonomy which precludes a person from saying: 'I want to be the kind of person who acts at the commands of others. I define myself as a slave and endorse those attitudes and preferences. My autonomy consists in being a slave.'[119]

Thus, for Gerald Dworkin, the circumstances and context leading to such a choice are irrelevant to the autonomous nature of the decision made. Unlike libertarian theorists,[120] Dworkin is not content with this outcome. Rather, he regards this as a limitation on the ethical value of autonomy and he acknowledges the need to seek other reasons, besides respect for autonomy, for why a person's voluntary agreement to become a slave does not make slavery morally acceptable.[121] For Dworkin, the answer to the moral questions lies in limited paternalism. He argues that '[t]he argument will have to appeal to some idea of what is a fitting life for a person and, thus, be a direct attempt to impose a conception of what is "good" on another person'.[122]

Agency and the embodied subject

Traditional conceptions of autonomy accord little significance to the embodied nature of the subject. Yet, all agents are essentially embodied.

---

[117] M. Oshana, 'Personal Autonomy and Society' (1998) 29 *Journal of Social Philosophy* 81, 83.

[118] G. Dworkin, *The Theory and Practice of Autonomy*, p. 18.   [119] *Ibid*, p. 129.

[120] See, famously, R. Nozick *Anarchy, State and Utopia* (New York: Basic Books, 1974), p. 33.

[121] See also Dan-Cohen, *Harmful Thoughts*, p. 157, who argues against voluntary slavery on the grounds of human dignity rather than autonomy.

[122] G. Dworkin, *The Theory and Practice of Autonomy*, p. 129.

Thus, arguing from a feminist perspective, Dodds points out that '[m]enstruation, pregnancy, childbirth, and breast-feeding, for example, are not activities in which participation can be chosen or rejected in the same way that, for example, purchasing a book, deciding to practice the piano, or building a bookshelf are chosen or rejected'.[123] Failure to recognise the patient as embodied also leads to a failure to appreciate the potentially coercive impact of illness on agency.

There have been surprisingly few efforts to investigate the impact of (serious) illness on decision-making. The work that does exist suggests that serious illness can have a profound impact on decision-making abilities. A pilot study by Eric Cassell *et al.* found that capable adults with serious illnesses performed equivalently to children under the age of 10 years in respect of a series of judgement tasks.[124] While these findings are preliminary in nature and should be approached with care,[125] they are, to a degree, supported by Carl Schneider's less scientific survey, which was based on his own interviews with patients as well as a range of empirical studies and literary and biographical accounts of illnesses.[126] Schneider concluded that a sick person may differ from her healthy self in fundamental ways, feeling 'frightened, discouraged, dull-witted, abstracted, uninterested and weary'.[127] When it come to decision-making, he points out that '[t]he more serious the decision, the likelier fear is to corrode concentration'.[128]

Although further empirical work is needed, these preliminary findings have important implications for how we think about agency in healthcare decision-making. Thus, for example, the elderly woman who says, 'I'm old and tired, so let me die' may be accurately representing her feelings but she may also be depressed at finding herself in hospital; she may be frightened of the future; or simply seeking reassurance.[129] The important

---

[123] 'Choice and Control' in Mackenzie and Stoljar (eds.) *Relational Autonomy*, p. 219. See also C. Mackenzie 'Abortion and Embodiment' (1992) 70 *Australian Journal of Philosophy* 136. For a critique of the law's failure to engage with embodiment, see R. Fletcher *et al.*, 'Legal Embodiment: Analysing the Body of Healthcare Law' (2008) 16 *Medical Law Review* 321.

[124] E. Cassell, A. Leon and S. Kaufman 'Preliminary Evidence of Impaired Thinking in Sick Patients' (2001) 134 *Annals of Internal Medicine* 1120.

[125] The study was small, consisting of only 63 patients and 28 people acting as controls. Further, the judgement tasks were those developed by psychologist Jean Piaget to measure cognitive development in children, and their applicability to adult healthcare decision-making is open to question.

[126] Schneider, *The Practice of Autonomy*, pp. xx–xi.   [127] *Ibid.*, p. 75.   [128] *Ibid.*, p. 56.

[129] See M. Wicclair, *Ethics and the Elderly* (New York: Oxford University Press, 1993), p. 55; B. Brody, *Life and Death Decision Making* (New York: Oxford University Press, 1988), Chapter 5.

point is that '[s]ickness, accidents and tragedy change people in different ways'[130] and that it may not always be appropriate simply to view a sick person as the same as her healthy self.

Addressing agency concerns

It is difficult to dispute the claim that individuals exist in social contexts and that they have physical bodies and it would seem reasonable to assume that these factors may impact on how people make healthcare decisions. The more difficult matter is where critiques of this kind should lead. This is an issue with which feminist theorists have had particular cause to engage, not least because some radical feminists have questioned whether, given the degree of oppression experienced by women, female agency (or 'a life out of which articulation [of a female perspective] might come'[131]) is in fact possible. An effort to resolve this conflict underlies feminist accounts of 'relational' autonomy.

John Christman argues that the factor which makes 'a conception of autonomy *uniquely* "relational" or "social" is that among its defining conditions are requirements concerning the interpersonal or social environment of the agent'.[132] Thus, relational approaches to autonomy require a broader investigation of the impact of social and structural factors on the agency of the decision-maker. Relational theorists respond in different ways to this challenge. Some accounts (sometimes described as 'procedural'[133]) are especially concerned with autonomy-building while remaining neutral as regards the content of individual decisions. Other accounts ('substantive' accounts) are not content-neutral but designate certain decisions or decisions made in certain circumstances as non-autonomous. The discussion to follow will focus on substantive accounts while procedural accounts of relational autonomy will be explored further as part of the discussion of autonomy as achievement in the last section of this chapter.

Substantive relational accounts of autonomy are, for the most part, concerned with the negative impact of social conditions on the attributes

---

[130] E. Cassell, 'Unanswered Questions: Bioethics and Human Relationships' (2007) 37 (5) *Hastings Center Report* 20, 23; M. Spriggs 'Autonomy in the Face of a Devastating Diagnosis' (1998) 24 *Journal of Medical Ethics* 123.

[131] MacKinnon, *Feminism Unmodified*, p. 39.

[132] J. Christman, 'Relational Autonomy, Liberal Individualism, and the Social Construction of Selves' (2004) 117 *Philosophical Studies* 143, 147. For a broader synthesis of key themes in relational autonomy, see J. Herring, 'Relational Autonomy and Rape' in S. Sclater *et al.* (eds.) *Regulating Autonomy: Sex, Reproduction and Family* (Oxford: Hart Publishing, 2009), pp. 56–8.

[133] Mackenzie and Stoljar (eds.) *Relational Autonomy*, pp. 19–21.

necessary for decision-making. Theorists identify as essential the possession of attributes variously described as self-trust,[134] self-respect[135] or self-worth.[136] Thus, for example, Carolyn McLeod and Susan Sherwin note the linkage between (female) addiction and experiences of violence or abuse. They argue that as abuse continues, self-trust is increasingly depleted as every decision which the abused person makes in an effort to avoid further abuse turns out to be ineffective.[137] Decisions made in such circumstances, they argue, cannot be considered fully autonomous.[138] Along similar lines, Stoljar argues that the 'feminist intuition' requires that 'preferences influenced by oppressive norms of femininity cannot be autonomous'.[139] Thus, for example, '[w]omen who accept the norm that pregnancy and motherhood increase their worthiness accept something *false*. And because of the internalization of the norm, they do not have the capacity to perceive it as false'.[140]

There are difficulties with addressing concerns about agency in this way. First, within current social contexts, freedom from oppressive social conditions requires, inevitably, freedom from society. Thus, these relational accounts would seem to have something in common with the derided individualistic stereotype of autonomy as independence and self-sufficiency.[141] Secondly, and of more practical concern, this approach has the effect of designating a good number of decisions as non-autonomous. To be fair, relational theorists do not necessarily suggest that non-autonomous decisions should be overridden.[142] Nonetheless, any widespread designation of decisions made in oppressive social conditions as non-autonomous presents an obvious difficulty for the redistribution of power within the healthcare context. While oppressive social conditions remain extant, this way of addressing concerns about agency would serve to perpetuate, and

---

[134] C. McLeod and S. Sherwin, 'Relational Autonomy, Self-Trust and Health Care for Patients who are Oppressed' in Mackenzie and Stoljar (eds.) *Relational Autonomy*.

[135] T. Hill, *Autonomy and Self-Respect* (Cambridge University Press, 1991).

[136] P. Benson 'Feeling Crazy: Self-Worth and the Social Character of Responsibility' in Mackenzie and Stoljar (eds.) *Relational Autonomy*, p. 72.

[137] McLeod and Sherwin, 'Relational Autonomy, Self-Trust' in Mackenzie and Stoljar (eds.) *Relational Autonomy*, p. 270.

[138] *Ibid.*, p. 271.

[139] Stoljar, 'Autonomy and the Feminist Intuition,' in Mackenzie and Stoljar (eds.) *Relational Autonomy*, p. 95.

[140] *Ibid*, p. 109, original emphasis.

[141] As pointed out by Christman, 'Relational Autonomy', 151.

[142] See, for example, McLeod and Sherwin's argument 'Relational Autonomy, Self-Trust', p. 271 regarding the pragmatic limitations of coercion in respect of treatment decisions by addicts.

indeed justify, a denial of decision-making power to people who live in oppressive circumstances. Furthermore, if, as argued above, it is recognised that illness itself is oppressive, this leaves open the possibility that a significant number of healthcare decisions of their nature cannot be categorised as autonomous. Thus, the recognition of a lack of agency could lead all too quickly back to a position of old-style paternalism.

For these reasons, there are serious difficulties with substantive relational accounts of autonomy. The procedural account of relational autonomy which is based on the enhancement of agency provides an alternative, and it will be argued, better way of dealing with concerns about agency. Before looking more closely at this, however, some of the normative concerns regarding the liberal conception of autonomy must be considered.

Normative critiques of autonomy

Although the role of autonomy in healthcare decision-making may be critiqued from a range of normative perspectives, this discussion will focus on evaluating three of the strongest arguments. The first relates to the moral status of the emblematic autonomous person; the second is concerned with the cost to other values arising from the elevation of autonomy above these values, while the third is concerned with the 'thinness' of autonomy as a 'take-it or leave-it' principle.

The moral status of the autonomous subject

Both communitarian and feminist critics have identified normative difficulties with the elevation of the liberal conception of the autonomous subject (as they see it). Communitarians dispute the view that the independent person (in Mary Ann Glendon's phrase, the 'lone rights-bearer'[143]) is an appropriate character around whom to build a moral theory.[144] Thus, Sandel contends that '[t]o imagine a person incapable of constitutive attachments ... is not to conceive an ideally free and rational agent, but to imagine a person wholly without character, without moral depth'.[145] In the

---

[143] M. A. Glendon, *Rights Talk: The Impoverishment of Political Discourse* (New York: Free Press, 1991), p. 47.

[144] While the feminist and communitarian critiques overlap in some respects, they derive from different bases and, more significantly, have different goals: see L. Barclay 'Autonomy and the Social Self' in Mackenzie and Stoljar (eds.) *Relational Autonomy*, pp. 61–8; E. Frazer and N. Lacey, *The Politics of Community: A Feminist Critique of the Liberal-Communitarian Debate* (London: Harvester Wheatsheaf, 1993).

[145] Sandel, *Liberalism and the Limits of Justice*, p. 179.

context of healthcare decisions, Daniel Callahan, one of the most influential ethicists sympathetic to the communitarian position,[146] argues:

> [Autonomy] buys our freedom to be ourselves, and to be free of undue influence by others, at too high a price. It establishes contractual relationships as the principal and highest form of relationships. It elevates isolation and separation as the necessary starting point of human commitments.[147]

In elevating isolation, decisions are taken out of context and issues of responsibility and concern for others become lost. As Margaret Brazier points out, respect for autonomy becomes simply a demand that 'I must be given what I want'.[148] Additionally, some feminist theorists dispute the moral worth of the individualistic conception of the self on gendered grounds, arguing that the elevation of individualistic values, such as autonomy, over care values reflects a fundamental devaluation of women's perspectives.[149]

At the core of this argument is the view that autonomy fails to address the normative consequences of social embeddedness. One way of doing this is through the recognition of patient responsibilities. Brazier provides one such account, noting that '[r]eciprocal ethical obligations extend into every area of our lives'.[150] Parents, for example, owe responsibilities to their children; (adult) children to their parents. The weight of each individual's responsibilities is 'conditioned by the individual's personal circumstances'.[151] This, Brazier concedes, is not fair, but, she argues, 'fairness is not a moral entitlement'.[152] In making decisions, including decisions about healthcare treatment, one is acting unethically if one fails to take account of these responsibilities.[153] Thus, she gives the example of the

---

[146] See D. Callahan, 'Individual Good and Common Good: A Communitarian Approach to Bioethics' (2003) 46 *Perspectives in Biology and Medicine* 496.

[147] Callahan, 'Autonomy: A Moral Good', 41.

[148] M. Brazier, 'Do No Harm – Do Patients Have Responsibilities Too?' (2006) 65 *Cambridge Law Journal* 397, 400.

[149] See C. Gilligan, *In a Different Voice: Psychological Theory and Women's Development* (Cambridge, MA: Harvard University Press, 1982); R. West, 'Jurisprudence and Gender' (1988) 55 *University of Chicago Law Review* 1. The question of whether women are inherently more drawn to care values is contested. For an argument that they are, see N. Noddings, *Caring: A Feminine Approach to Ethics and Moral Education* (Berkeley: University of California Press, 1984); V. Held, *Feminist Morality: Transforming Culture, Society and Politics* (Chicago: University of Chicago Press, 1993). For an alternative view, see A. Scales, 'The Emergence of Feminist Jurisprudence: An Essay' (1986) 95 *Yale Law Journal* 1373, 1381; C. MacKinnon *et al*, 'Feminist Discourse, Moral Values and the Law – A Conversation' (1985) 34 *Buffalo Law Review* 11, 74.

[150] 'Do No Harm', 402.   [151] *Ibid*.   [152] *Ibid*.   [153] *Ibid*.

widower who refuses surgery on a melanoma because of its impact on his looks and sexual allure and argues that he would be acting unethically if he acted without taking account of the consequences of his decision for his children.[154]

Recognising moral duties to take account of the interests of others is not antithetical to respect for autonomy. Indeed, as Brazier points out, '[i]t is the empowerment of patients which brings responsibilities'.[155] Yet, determining the extent of such duties is both contentious and difficult, especially in a legal context. An exploration of John Hardwig's argument in favour of a 'duty to die' based on principles of family-based ethics shows why this is the case. Hardwig suggests that a 'duty to die' arises from the 'deeply interwoven lives [which] debar us from making exclusively self-regarding decisions'.[156] Hardwig indicates that such a duty might arise where, by continuing to live, a person would impose a significant emotional, caregiving or financial burden on her family and loved ones; where a person is old; where a person has had a full and rich life; where a person's loved ones' lives are already impoverished or difficult; or where a person's loved ones have already made a significant contribution to making the person's life good.[157]

To be fair, Hardwig's extreme position in postulating a moral duty to die is not widely shared by communitarian ethicists.[158] However, this argument serves as a reminder that, by carefully situating the individual at the centre of her web of relationships, one risks losing the individual altogether. The possibilities for oppression in healthcare decision-making do not just emanate from healthcare professionals or healthcare structures. Hardwig's suggestions regarding when a duty to die would arise show that the more vulnerable a person, whether because of age, illness, disability or a debilitating condition, the greater the danger posed. The important point here is not that concern for others is normatively unimportant but that responsibilities in this respect fall differently on different

---

[154] *Ibid.* See also the account of moral responsibilities owed in the maternal-foetal context in R. Scott *Rights, Duties and the Body: Law and Ethics of the Maternal-Fetal Conflict* (Oxford: Hart Publishing, 2002), p. 87.

[155] Brazier, 'Do No Harm,' 401.

[156] J. Hardwig, 'Is there a Duty to Die?' (1997) 27 *Hastings Center Report* 34, 36.

[157] *Ibid.*, 38–9.

[158] For convincing rejections of Hardwig's argument from a (broadly speaking) communitarian perspective see D. Callahan, 'Our Burden Upon Others: A Response to John Hardwig' in J. Hardwig with N. Hentoff *et al. Is there a Duty to Die? and Other Essays in Medical Ethics* (New York: Routledge, 2000), pp. 139–44; M. Gunderson 'Being a Burden: Reflections on Refusing Medical Care' (2004) 34 *Hastings Center Report* 37.

people. Life may not be fair but unfairness may be accentuated by the demands we place on others.[159] For this reason, it is essential to interrogate the ways in which duties and responsibilities arise in a healthcare context and to proceed with considerable caution, especially if attempting to translate moral duties into a legal context.[160]

The cost to other values

A second basis for normative critique is the cost to other values arising from the endorsement of a liberal conception of autonomy. Onora O'Neill argues that the important value of trust between doctors and patients has been lost because of the liberal view of autonomy 'simply as independence from others'.[161] Contrasting the different features of trust and autonomy, she notes, '[t]rust flourishes between those who are linked to one another; individual autonomy flourishes where everyone has "space" to do their own thing'.[162] As O'Neill reminds us, '[t]rust is most readily placed in others whom we can rely on to take our interests into account, to fulfil their roles, to keep their parts in bargains'.[163] If we do not believe in our healthcare professionals' commitment to our welfare, our trust in them will be fatally undermined notwithstanding that our right of autonomy is respected.

It has also been argued that, because of its association with Western, liberal political philosophy, the endorsement of autonomy may have adverse implications for the values of pluralism, tolerance and the recognition of cultural difference and diversity.[164] Different cultures have different views of the individual and her relationship with society and these may not fit within the individualistic autonomy-based model.[165] Moreover, Callahan argues that the elevation of liberalism leads to the marginalisation of

---

[159] Note, for example, the gendered issues identified in K. George 'A Woman's Choice?: The Gendered Risks of Voluntary Euthanasia and Physician-Assisted Suicide' (2007) 15 *Medical Law Review* 1.

[160] As acknowledged by Brazier, 'Do No Harm,' 422.

[161] O'Neill, *Autonomy and Trust in Bioethics*, p. 24, original emphasis.

[162] *Ibid.*, p. 25.   [163] *Ibid.*

[164] See K. Gervais, 'Changing Society, Changing Medicine, Changing Bioethics' and B. Jennings, 'Autonomy and Difference: The Travails of Liberalism in Bioethics' in de Vries and Subedi (eds.) *Bioethics and Society*.

[165] See L. Blackhall *et al.*, 'Ethnicity and Attitudes Towards Patient Autonomy' (1995) 274 *Journal of American Medical Association* 820; F. Kitamura *et al.*, 'Image of Psychiatric Patients' Competency to Give Informed Consent to Treatment in Japan' (1999) 22 *International Journal of Law and Psychiatry* 45; M. Kara 'Applicability of the Principle of Respect for Autonomy: The Perspective of Turkey' (2007) 33 *Journal of Medical Ethics* 627

religious or conservative perspectives.[166] For those who feel alienated on these bases, the likely consequence is a further diminution in trust.

The significance of trust to medical practice is widely recognised[167] and the presence or absence of trust among patients is increasingly subject to empirical testing both in respect of individual relationships and of the profession more generally.[168] There is no indication from studies in the United Kingdom that there has been a significant diminution in trust in medical professionals since autonomy has assumed a greater role in healthcare ethics. In each of the annual IPSOS MORI polls commissioned by the Royal College of Physicians since 1983, medical professionals have consistently been identified as the profession which the public believes is most likely to tell the truth.[169] A cross-jurisdictional survey of patient attitudes also suggests that the public retains high levels of trust in the medical profession.[170] Even in the United States, where one might expect that an autonomy-based approach to healthcare would have had the greatest impact on trust, it would seem that the vast majority of patients continue to trust their doctors[171] (although there is evidence of diminution in trust in medicine as an institution).[172]

Of course, as Neil Manson and Onora O'Neill point out, generalised surveys tend to assume that trust is generic, undifferentiated and unrelated to evidence and are 'likely to ignore the discrimination and judgment that intelligent placing and refusal of trust requires'.[173] Furthermore, it may well be the case that the reason people continue to trust the medical profession is that most medical professionals do not operate on the basis of the kind of individualistic approach to autonomy criticised by O'Neill.[174]

---

[166] Callahan, 'Individual Good and Common Good,' 498.

[167] See D. Shore (ed.) *The Trust Crisis in Healthcare: Causes, Consequences, and Cures* (New York: Oxford University Press, 2007).

[168] See M. Hall *et al.*, 'Trust in the Medical Profession: Conceptual and Management Issues' (2002) 37 *Health Services Research* 1419.

[169] The percentage of the public who trust their doctors in this regard has risen from 82% in 1983 to 92% in 2008. See also M. Davies *Medical Self-Regulation: Crises and Change* (Aldershot: Ashgate, 2007), pp. 93–4.

[170] Z. Kmietovicz 'R.E.S.P.E.C.T – Why Doctors are Still Getting Enough of it' (2002) 324 *British Medical Journal* 11. The jurisdictions covered were the UK, France, Germany, Netherlands, Israel, Australia and the United States.

[171] See P. Norris 'Sceptical Patients: Performance, Social Capital and Culture' in Shore (ed.) *The Trust Crisis in Healthcare*, pp. 41–3.

[172] *Ibid.*, pp. 37–41.

[173] Manson and O'Neill, *Rethinking Informed Consent in Bioethics* (Cambridge University Press, 2007), p. 166.

[174] See empirical data on (American) doctors' approach to patient autonomy in R. E. Lawrence and F. A. Curlin 'Autonomy, Religion, and Clinical Decisions: Findings from a

Thus, empirical evidence of ongoing trust (insofar as this is meaningful) does not necessarily counter O'Neill's argument. However, the apparent resilience of the relationship between medical professionals and patients does suggest that the threat of autonomy to patient trust in the medical profession may be overstated.

A difficulty with the trust argument is that, as described earlier, the move to elevate autonomy came as a response to concerns regarding the trustworthiness of the medical profession. By seeking to empower patients, autonomy was seen as the answer to the problem of mistrust.[175] While this does not mean that an emphasis on the value of autonomy could not also be a cause of mistrust, it is important to remember that there was a perceived lack of trust before the shift to autonomy. Furthermore, even if respect for autonomy, as traditionally conceived within liberalism, does not enhance trust, it is difficult to see that a retreat from respect for the principle would do so. Are patients really going to trust their doctors more if they are told that they must cede decision-making powers to them? As Joel Feinberg reminds us, people who experience a violation of their autonomy feel more than mere irritation or frustration but rather feel that 'in some way they have been violated, invaded, belittled'.[176] Such feelings inevitably diminish rather than enhance trust.

A similar argument may be made in respect of diversity and pluralism. While it is true that a culturally chauvinistic application of autonomy could be alienating, it is not clear how a lack of respect for autonomy would facilitate diversity and pluralism. As Raz points out, the right to 'free religious worship' has 'stood at the cradle of liberalism'.[177] Raz argues that autonomy (as he conceives the principle) is valuable because it recognises and protects 'value pluralism'.[178] The basis for value (or moral) pluralism is 'not merely that incompatible forms of life are morally acceptable but that they display distinct virtues, each capable of being pursued for its own sake'.[179]

Certainly, as will be discussed in the next chapter, adherents of minority religions, such as Jehovah's Witnesses and Christian Scientists, have made important use of the legal right of autonomy in asserting their right to make healthcare decisions in accordance with their religious beliefs.

National Physician Survey' (2009) 35 *Journal of Medical Ethics* 214, which suggests that, while autonomy is influential on professionals, it does not guide medical professionals' decisions to the extent assumed in bioethics literature.

[175] See Wolpe, 'The Triumph of Autonomy', pp. 50–1.
[176] Feinberg, *The Moral Limits of the Criminal Law*, p. 27.
[177] Raz, *Morality of Freedom*, p. 251.   [178] *Ibid.*, p. 395.   [179] *Ibid*, p. 396.

The limited scope of non-interference

A third normative critique is that autonomy provides a basis for health-care ethics which is both intellectually and practically limited in what it offers. In Callahan's words, autonomy lacks the 'intellectual strength or penetration'[180] to deal with important ethical issues. It is, he says, 'a thin gruel for the future of bioethics'.[181] At the level of healthcare decision-making, O'Neill notes that '[w]hat is rather grandly called "patient autonomy" often amounts to a right to choose or refuse treatments on offer, and the corresponding obligation of practitioners not to proceed without patients' consent'.[182] While the individual's right to be left alone is protected, the traditional view of autonomy does little to ensure the delivery of appropriate treatment or adequate choice or options. Thus, autonomy, as a principle of non-interference, fails to shift the locus of power to the patient in a meaningful way.

The limits of the take-it-or-leave view are rather graphically illustrated in the following practitioner account of the death of a patient (in an Australian hospital):

> [A] young mother in [her] early 30's [sic] had an inoperable tumour at back of her nose and throat. In the end stages, this girl refused pain relief or sedatives. She did not want much medical intervention. It was the most distressing death I ever witnessed as she could not breathe and depended on a nasal tube as her only airway. This [was] frequently blocked and needed regular suctioning. It was very distressing for her, her family and staff. She was from a very poor social background and had little or no education. Staff tried to assist her as much as possible but it was an awful death for her.[183]

We do not, of course, know the options that were available to this woman. It may be the case that she had a range of options and chose freely to reject all of these. What is clear, however, is that the traditional view of autonomy does nothing to require the provision of these options. It protects the right to refuse treatment (and, in a case like this, to die in distress if one chooses); it does not require the provision of alternatives. Nor does the traditional view of autonomy require efforts to educate (within the limited context of the particular decision to be made) or engage with the patient, to create a space for her to make the decision which best serves

---

[180] Callahan, 'Individual Good and Common Good,' 499.   [181] *Ibid.*
[182] O'Neill, *Autonomy and Trust*, p. 37.
[183] C. Quinlan and C. O'Neill *Practitioners' Narrative Submissions* (Unpublished) (Dublin: Irish Hospice Foundation, 2008).

her needs. In this context, it is worth recalling Schneider's argument that respect for autonomy could become 'a welcome and acceptable way of passing on burdensome problems to patients'.[184] Thus, Schneider notes a study suggesting that doctors 'often seemed too ready to concede patients' "right to refuse" rather than to recognize the clinical problems that lay at the bottom of the refusal (e.g. poor or inconsistent communication) and to take steps to remedy them'.[185]

It might be suggested that this deficiency in autonomy could be addressed by placing greater reliance on other principles in healthcare ethics, such as beneficence or justice. Thus, respect for beneficence would require that healthcare professionals negotiate and seek to reach a consensus with the patient regarding the appropriate mode of treatment[186] and respect for justice would require that a range of options is available to patients.[187] On this basis, it might be argued that the appropriate response to the 'take-it-or-leave-it' critique is to accord greater significance to other principles. However, it might also be argued that the flaw lies not with the principle of autonomy but with the way in which the principle has been framed within (certain) ethical discourse. It will be argued below that the principle of autonomy can encompass the concept of meaningful choice and that this view of autonomy should be further developed.

The limitations of the traditional liberal view: some conclusions

The preceding section identified a number of concerns regarding the traditional liberal account of autonomy. These include concerns about agency and the failure of the traditional liberal view to address the impact of social context and embodiment on decision-making. The section also explored normative critiques, including the individualistic focus of traditional liberal conceptions of autonomy, the impact of respect for autonomy on other values and the thinness of the 'take-it-or-leave-it' view of autonomy as non-interference. These are powerful criticisms. One way of addressing the issues raised is to jettison the ideal of respect for autonomy, replacing it with the ideal of respect for care or responsibility-based principles which recognise the socially embedded nature of individuals. However, as was evident in the discussion above, the risks in doing this

---

[184] Schneider, *The Practice of Autonomy*, p. 5.
[185] *Ibid.*, quoting P. Appelbaum and L. Roth 'Patients who Refuse Treatment in Medical Hospitals' (1983) 250 *Journal of the American Medical Association* 1296, 1301.
[186] See Pelligrino and Thomasma, *For the Patient's Good*, Chapter 4.
[187] See Holm, 'Not Just Autonomy,' 335–6.

are considerable. Respect for autonomy keeps the individual at the centre of ethical discourse and in doing so provides some degree of protection against potentially oppressive forces. It may do this in a flawed and limited way but its contribution is nonetheless fundamental. For this reason, a better way of responding to these concerns is to recognise that they broaden the terrain for debate, requiring the opening up of some questions that had seemed settled.

Another way of dealing with concerns regarding the role of autonomy in healthcare ethics and law is to reconsider the nature of the autonomy principle and to ask whether autonomy can legitimately be conceptualised in ways that move beyond a focus on simple non-interference. The next section presents an account of autonomy as 'a kind of achievement'[188] and argues that this offers a better way of approaching the role of autonomy in respect of healthcare decision-making than the traditional liberal view. As will be seen, this account of autonomy does not purport to provide answers to all of the concerns discussed earlier but it does show the value of continuing engagement with the concept.

Autonomy as an 'achievement'

An account of autonomy as an 'achievement' draws on the work of Raz and on some relational theorists. The discussion identifies two aspects of autonomy as achievement: first, a view of autonomy which imposes positive obligations to ensure adequacy of choice, and secondly, autonomy-building as a means of addressing (to a degree at least) the issues in respect of agency identified above.

Autonomy and adequacy of choice

The view that respect for autonomy requires more than simple non-interference is closely associated with Raz's perfectionist liberal view of autonomy. The views of Raz may seem an odd choice as the basis for an alternative view of autonomy in healthcare law because he does not offer a rights-based conception of autonomy but rather posits autonomy as the value central to well-being and as 'a kind of achievement'. For this reason, Raz argues that 'in its full generality [autonomy] transcends what any individual has a right to'.[189] This does not mean that rights are irrelevant; Raz accepts that autonomy 'serves to justify and to reinforce various

---

[188] Raz, *The Morality of Freedom*, p. 204.   [189] *Ibid.*, p. 247.

derivative rights which defend and promote limited aspects of personal autonomy'.[190]

Raz's view of autonomy differs from the traditional liberal view in a number of ways.[191] First, for Raz, autonomy has an intrinsic moral value beyond the instrumental value prized by utilitarian liberals.[192] The roots of this moral value lie in Raz's conception of autonomy as the fundamental value for human well-being.[193] Raz defines well-being, in this sense, as how good or successful a person's life is, viewed predominantly (but not solely) from the person's own point of view.[194] A person's well-being 'consists in the successful pursuits of self-chosen goals and relationships'.[195] Thus, '[t]he ideal of personal autonomy is the vision of people controlling, to some degree, their own destiny, fashioning it through successive decisions throughout their lives'.[196]

Secondly, Raz does not regard autonomy as individualist. Indeed, he argues that 'the ideal of personal autonomy is incompatible with moral individualism'.[197] He rejects the view that an autonomous life can be seen simply as a 'life within unviolated rights' that 'create or protect opportunities'[198] but which leave it up to the individual how, and indeed whether, they exercise these opportunities.[199] On this basis, Raz rejects a view of autonomy as a 'right against coercion' which defeats 'all, or almost all, other considerations'.[200] He argues that 'the provision of many collective goods is constitutive of the very possibility of autonomy and it cannot be relegated to a subordinate role, compared with some alleged right against coercion, in the name of autonomy'.[201]

Thirdly, unlike theorists who favour a more classic liberal view, Raz argues that autonomy is 'valuable only if exercised in pursuit of the good'.[202] Thus, for Raz '[a]utonomous life is valuable only if it is spent in

---

[190] *Ibid.* On the distinction between core and derivative rights, see Raz, *ibid.*, pp. 168–70.

[191] The discussion in the text presents an abbreviated explanation of a complex body of work. For more detailed discussion of these aspects of Raz's work, see L. Green, 'Un-American Liberalism: Raz's "Morality of Freedom"' (1988) 38 *University of Toronto Law Journal* 317; Mulhall and Swift, *Liberals and Communitarians*, Chapter 10.

[192] Additionally, Raz rejects utilitarian justifications on several bases including the argument that some values are incommensurable: see L. Green *ibid.*, 321–2.

[193] This fundamental value derives from the nature of the society in which we live, which Raz (*Morality of Freedom*, p. 394) describes as a society 'whose social forms are to a considerable extent based on individual choice'.

[194] Raz, *Morality of Freedom*, p. 289.

[195] *Ibid.*, p. 370. Well-being is also linked to the pursuit of activities: see 'Duties of Well-Being' in Raz, *Ethics in the Public Domain*, p. 3.

[196] *Ibid.*, p. 369.   [197] *Ibid.*, p. 206.   [198] *Ibid.*, p. 204.   [199] *Ibid.*, pp. 204–5.

[200] *Ibid.*, p. 206.   [201] *Ibid.*, p. 207.   [202] *Ibid.*, p. 381.

the pursuit of acceptable and valuable projects and relationships'.[203] Raz denies that this represents as rigid a moral theory as it may appear because he argues that a moral theory that respects autonomy 'inevitably upholds a pluralistic view' of morality.[204] Furthermore, Raz points out that 'the fact that the state *considers* anything to be valuable or valueless is no reason for anything'.[205] On this basis, he argues that '[i]f it is likely that the government will not judge such matters correctly then it has no authority to judge them at all'.[206] Finally, unlike most modern liberals, Raz rejects a requirement for state neutrality.[207] Rather, he propounds a perfectionist view of liberalism,[208] arguing that 'it is the goal of all political action to enable individuals to pursue valid conceptions of the good and to discourage evil or empty ones'.[209] Thus, respect for autonomy 'permits and even requires governments to create morally valuable opportunities, and to eliminate repugnant ones'.[210]

It is evident from the preceding description that adequacy of choice is a fundamental component of Raz's perfectionist view of autonomy. Thus, at a basic level, Raz argues that '[a]utonomy cannot be achieved by a person whose every action and thought must be bent to the task of survival'.[211] Nor can a person be autonomous in the absence of meaningful or significant options.[212] Raz goes further, arguing that respect for autonomy requires that individuals have a choice between morally good options.[213] The important point here is not the number of options available but their variety.[214] It is clear that, applied in a healthcare context, this requirement does not deliver the consumerist freedom which Brazier caricatures as a position where '*My* choices about my healthcare should be met in full. What I want should be delivered'.[215] Such an approach is individualist, in a way in which Raz's view of autonomy is not. What the adequate choice

---

[203] *Ibid.*, p. 417. Raz illustrates this point (*ibid.*, p. 380) by reference to the 'autonomous wrongdoer', noting that our intuitions rebel against the notion that a wrongdoer is morally better if her actions are freely chosen.

[204] *Ibid.*, p. 381.   [205] *Ibid.*, p. 412, original emphasis.   [206] *Ibid.*

[207] Note, however, Mulhall and Swift's argument, *Liberals and Communitarians*, p. 315, that the difference between Raz and other liberals (including R. Dworkin and Rawls) in respect of State neutrality is not as significant as first appears.

[208] The term 'perfectionist' as used in this context refers to the neutrality or otherwise of the state: see Mulhall and Swift *ibid.*, pp. 25–33.

[209] Raz, *Morality of Freedom*, p. 133.   [210] *Ibid.*, p. 417.   [211] *Ibid.*, p. 379.

[212] *Ibid.*, p. 374.

[213] *Ibid.*, p. 379. Raz illustrates this with the example of a person who is allowed to choose or reject career options put to him but only at the cost of committing a murder each time an option is rejected. While the man has a choice, he has only one moral option.

[214] *Ibid.*, p. 375.   [215] Brazier, 'Do No Harm', 400, original emphasis.

argument does offer, however, is a basis upon which to interrogate the choices offered and how they are offered and a reason to reject the 'take-it-or-leave' view which (some) ethical and legal discourse presents as constituting respect for autonomy.

The notion that respect for autonomy requires adequacy of choice is shared by some relational theorists, who also provide more concrete examples of the kinds of question which arise when we look behind autonomy and investigate the adequacy of choices offered in respect of healthcare decision-making. Susan Sherwin points out that choice is inevitably constricted by institutional policy decisions.[216] For example, a hospital might offer mammograms on the first Friday of every month. Such decisions may (or may not) reflect discriminatory or biased practices which may not be obvious but which may mean that choice is more restricted for some people than for others.[217] Along similar lines, the need for patients to arrange for flexible work hours may not seem significant in setting institutional policy but may 'pose an insurmountable barrier to women in certain kinds of jobs'.[218] Thus, understanding where people are situated in a non-medical sense is essential if these people are to be offered a meaningful or adequate choice in a healthcare context.

It is also clear that adequacy of choice requires more in terms of communication than simply providing information about the decision to be made and leaving the patient to make up her own mind. Alasdair Maclean argues in favour of imposing positive obligations on healthcare professionals to facilitate understanding and good decision-making.[219] This requires dialogue with the patient in order 'to gain some understanding of the patient's perspective'.[220] Maclean also posits an obligation of 'mutual persuasion' which he describes as requiring both that healthcare professionals engage with the decision-making process and, 'if appropriate, sensitively challenge the resultant decision' and that the professional 'must be open to persuasion that their assessment is wrong'.[221] As will be seen in the next chapter, this goes beyond what the law currently requires. It is, however, more in line with the 'partnership' approach to healthcare decision-making which is contained in the GMC guidance, *Consent: Patients and Doctors Making Decisions Together*.[222]

---

[216] Sherwin (ed.) *The Politics of Women's Health*, pp. 26–7.   [217] *Ibid.*

[218] McLeod and Sherwin, 'Relational Autonomy, Self-Trust', pp. 267–8.

[219] Maclean, *Autonomy, Informed Consent and Medical Law*, p. 247.   [220] *Ibid.*

[221] *Ibid.*

[222] *Consent: Patients and Doctors Making Decisions Together* (London: GMC, 2008). However, the GMC is clear (para. 5) that, while doctors may recommend a particular

Agency, empowerment and autonomy-building

On the traditional view, autonomy is regarded as a feature of individual decisions or actions rather than as a way of being.[223] Insofar as the 'autonomous person' is thought about at all, it is taken for granted that an autonomous person is simply a person who makes autonomous decisions. This view is contested by Raz, who argues that '[a] person who has never had any significant choice, or was not aware of it, or never exercised choice in significant matters but simply drifted through life is not an autonomous person'.[224] This perspective is shared by many relational theorists. Jennifer Nedelsky speaks of 'becoming' autonomous, which she defines as being 'able to find and live in accordance with one's own law'.[225] This view of autonomy recognises that autonomy capacities or competencies can, depending on circumstances, be developed or thwarted. 'Capacities' in this sense must be distinguished from the legal requirement for capacity, which acts as gatekeeper for the right of autonomy and which will be discussed extensively in later chapters. However, there are underlying similarities. It will be argued in Chapter 3 that capacity in the legal sense can also be developed and, in Chapter 5, that even if people lack legal capacity, their capacity to engage in the decision-making process can, and should, be enhanced.

A number of theorists have put forward agency-building or empowerment as a way of addressing concerns about agency within liberalism.[226] Diana Meyers presents one of the most detailed accounts of this approach in respect of individual autonomy. Meyers argues that '[a]utonomous people must be able to pose and answer the question "What do I really want, need, care about, believe, value, etcetera?"; they must be able to act on the answer; and they must be able to correct themselves when they get the answer wrong'.[227] This, she argues, requires a range of skills. These

---

option which they believe to be best, 'they must not put pressure on the patient to accept their advice'.

[223] See Maclean's distinction, *Autonomy, Informed Consent and Medical Law*, p. 12, between the autonomous person, the autonomous act and the autonomous life.

[224] Raz, *Morality of Freedom*, p. 204.

[225] J. Nedelsky, 'Reconceiving Autonomy: Sources, Thoughts and Possibilities' (1989) 1 *Yale Journal of Law and Feminism* 7, 10.

[226] See especially M. Nussbaum and A. Sen (eds.) *The Quality of Life* (Oxford: Clarendon Press, 1993) and M. Nussbaum, *Women and Human Development: The Capabilities Approach* (Cambridge University Press, 2000).

[227] D. Myers, *Self, Society and Personal Choice* (New York: Columbia University Press, 1989), p. 76.

include obvious skills such as analytical and reasoning skills and the ability to resist pressures but also skills which may be less obvious. Thus, Meyers notes the need for introspective skills that sensitize individuals to their own feelings and desires; imaginative skills that enable individuals to envisage a range of possibilities; communication skills that enable individuals to get the benefit of others' views and, interpersonal skills that enable individuals to join forces to challenge and change social norms.[228] Meyers envisages all individuals as occupying a spectrum between minimally autonomous and fully autonomous and recognises that most people will fall somewhere in between.[229] Regardless of where on the scale a person falls, she argues that a goal of social development must be the enhancement of autonomy and the development of circumstances in which more people can become more fully autonomous.[230]

Susan Dodds applies the idea of developing autonomy skills in a healthcare context, noting the impact of healthcare providers' policies in this regard.[231] Thus, she argues that encouraging children and young people to participate in healthcare decision-making from an early stage and giving them the opportunity to ask questions, to voice their feelings and to take responsibility for aspects of their own care can help foster fuller autonomy in later life.[232] At the other end of the age spectrum, Dodds points out that nursing homes' policies and practices can either erode autonomy skills, leaving residents passive and 'atrophying their competence', or enhance their skills and enable them to retain autonomy competencies for as long as possible.[233] Thus, this approach requires policies and practices to be interrogated not just in terms of their impact on the current autonomy of individuals but also on the basis of whether and how they empower patients and develop future autonomy.

Perhaps more pertinent to the legal context, because of its focus on 'finding one's own law', the view of autonomy as empowerment also draws attention to issues of process. In setting out her reconception of autonomy, Jennifer Nedelsky notes the insights of administrative law and the potential of due process.[234] In the context of healthcare law, this approach to autonomy focuses on using the law to ensure the delivery of adequate participative processes which protect and facilitate the involvement

---

[228] 'Intersectional Identity and the Authentic Self' in Mackenzie and Stoljar (eds.) *Relational Autonomy*, p. 166.
[229] Myers, *Self, Society and Personal Choice*, p. 173.   [230] *Ibid.*, p. 189 ff.
[231] 'Choice and Control in Feminist Bioethics' in Mackenzie and Stoljar (eds.) *Relational Autonomy*, p. 229.
[232] *Ibid.*   [233] *Ibid.*, p. 230.   [234] Nedelsky, 'Reconceiving Autonomy', 26.

of individuals in decision-making. Again, this goes beyond the idea of autonomy as non-interference and requires the interrogation of decision-making processes in terms of whether they maximise and facilitate the shifting of power to the person who, ultimately, has to live with the decision made. As will be seen in later chapters, this is an issue not just in respect of people with capacity but in respect of all patients.

A view of autonomy as achievement offers more than the traditional liberal view. However, this account also has limitations. First, on this view, people are still divided into those who are autonomous and those who are not. While its focus on empowerment means that this view of autonomy blurs the boundaries between capable and incapable, it still does not provide a foundation for a legal and ethical framework within which to deal with decisions made by people who fall outside of the autonomy 'norm'. Secondly, in order to handle ethical issues, the law must 'technicalise' them, thereby translating ethical complexity into legal doctrine.[235] As discussed in the next chapter, one of the reasons autonomy as non-interference is so enthusiastically received by the law is the ease with which this particular ethical concept can be converted into legal doctrine. It is much more difficult to develop legal frameworks around an account of autonomy focused on empowerment. Further, as will be seen in later chapters, discussions of coercion become more complex within this kind of framework.

Conclusion

Autonomy is central to ethical discourse in respect of healthcare decision-making. However, its status and value are contested. This chapter has explored a number of concerns regarding the role of autonomy as an ethical principle in this context. In particular, it has emphasised concerns in respect of agency and the 'thinness' of the 'take-it-or-leave-it' view of autonomy as non-interference. However, it has also recognised that autonomy remains important because, in spite of its flaws, it still provides the most effective way of keeping the individual at the centre of ethical discourse and, in doing this, it provides some degree of protection against potentially oppressive forces. For this reason, it was argued that ongoing critical engagement with autonomy is a necessary part of the development

[235] See R. Fox, 'The Evolution of American Bioethics: A Sociological Perspective' in G. Weisz (ed.) *Social Science Perspectives on Medical Ethics* (Philadelphia: University of Philadelphia Press, 1990), p. 209.

of appropriate legal frameworks for healthcare decision-making. In this respect, it was suggested that a view of autonomy as empowerment provides a better way of thinking about autonomy than the traditional liberal view of autonomy as non-interference. The remaining chapters in the book will look at the practical application of the ethical principle of autonomy in the law. This begins in the next chapter with an analysis of how the legal right of autonomy has developed to date and some arguments regarding how the legal right might develop in the future.

2

Autonomy in the law

It is perhaps surprising that there is no express reference to a right of 'autonomy' (or 'self-determination') to be found in any of the leading bills of rights. Rather, the right is part of what Laurence Tribe calls, in respect of the United State Constitution, the 'invisible constitution'[1] While this does not diminish the degree of support the right enjoys (not least because the right also has a basis in the common law), it has meant that the ambit of the right receives relatively little legal analysis. Rather, the right tends to be invoked, often in a medical context, without any attempt to fit the right as applied within a broader analytical framework. Since Cardozo J's dictum in *Schloendorff* v. *Society of New York Hospital*,[2] the status of autonomy as a principle of non-interference has been largely uncontested in healthcare law. This is not least because, in many ways, respect for this form of autonomy sits comfortably with the law. Not only are the legal tools for enforcing this form of autonomy long established in the tort of trespass,[3] respect for the principle also allows courts to avoid engaging in judgments about the utility or morality of particular conduct and provides neat answers to difficult dilemmas.

This chapter considers the nature of the law's treatment of the principle of autonomy in the context of healthcare decision-making. It begins by outlining the sources of legal support for the principle. It then examines the application of the principle in individual cases where its primary contribution has been to provide a basis for a right to refuse treatment. As will be seen, this right has been subject to very few limits and the question of limits has received little legal analysis. This chapter argues that the law's reluctance to discuss the issue of limits has resulted in a

---

[1] L. Tribe, *The Invisible Constitution* (New York: Oxford University Press, 2008) argues that respect for autonomy represents the fundamental value underlying the United States' Constitution.
[2] (1914) 211 NY 125, 128.
[3] M. Brazier, 'Do No Harm – Do Patients Have Responsibilities Too?' (2006) 65 *Cambridge Law Journal* 397, 400.

conceptually under-developed understanding of autonomy and has contributed to the 'thinness' (and, ultimately, to the fragility) of the legal approach. The chapter ends by considering moves towards the imposition of positive legal obligations in respect of autonomy, which fit better with the empowerment-focused conception of autonomy discussed in the previous chapter.

Locating the legal right

As recognised by courts across the common law world, respect for the right of autonomy is deeply ingrained in the common law tradition.[4] In *United Pacific Railway Co* v. *Botsford*,[5] the United States Supreme Court stated that:

> No right is held more sacred, or is more carefully guarded by the common law, than the right of every individual to the possession and control of his own person, free from all restraint or interference of others, unless by clear and unquestionable authority of law.[6]

A similar approach is evident in Lord Reid's statement in *S* v. *McC (orse S) and M (DS intervener); W* v. *W*[7] that:

> English law goes to great lengths to protect a person of full age and capacity from interference with his personal liberty. We have too often seen freedom disappear in other countries not only by coups d'état but by gradual erosion: and, often it is the first step that counts. So it would be unwise to make even minor concessions.[8]

In addition to its common law basis, and notwithstanding the absence of express mention, the right of autonomy derives protection from written bills of rights. The longest established jurisprudence in this respect

---

[4] In addition to the cases discussed in the text, see *Ciarlariello* v. *Schacter* [1993] 2 SCR 119, 135 *per* Cory J (Supreme Court of Canada); *In re a Ward of Court* [1996] 2 IR 79, 156 *per* Denham J (Supreme Court of Ireland).

[5] (1891) 114 US 250.

[6] *Ibid.*, 251. This statement was endorsed by the US Supreme Court in *Cruzan* v. *Director, Missouri Department of Health* (1990) 497 US 261, 270 *per* Rehnquist CJ. See also *Washington* v. *Glucksberg* (1997) 521 US 702, 724 *per* Rehnquist CJ; 741 *per* Stevens J; *Stamford Hospital* v. *Vega* (1996) 236 Conn 646, 666; *Fosmire* v. *Nicoleau* (1990) 551 NE 2d 77, 80–1; *Matter of Christopher* (1998) 177 Misc 2d 352.

[7] [1972] AC 24.

[8] *Ibid.*, 43. See also *Sidaway* v. *Board of Governors of the Bethlem Royal Hospital* [1985] AC 871, 882 *per* Lord Scarman; 897 *per* Lord Bridge; 904 *per* Lord Templeman; *Re F (Mental Patient: Sterilisation)* [1990] 2 AC 1, 73 *per* Lord Goff.

emanates from the United States. However, there are few references to a right of autonomy (or self-determination) in early Supreme Court case-law in respect of health care. Thus, although, as recognised in *Planned Parenthood of Southeastern Pennsylvania* v. *Casey*,[9] a right of autonomy underpins decisions such as *Griswold* v. *Connecticut*[10] and *Roe* v. *Wade*,[11] the discussion in both cases centres on the right to privacy. In *Cruzan* v. *Director, Missouri Department of Health*,[12] the United States Supreme Court recognised a right to refuse medical treatment, which it regarded as being grounded in the individual's liberty interest.[13] Again, the Court did not make reference to a right of autonomy.[14] The language of auton-omy became apparent in the decision in *Planned Parenthood* v. *Casey*.[15] Here, a majority of the Supreme Court recognised, in the context of abor-tion rights, 'the right to make family decisions and the right to phys-ical autonomy'.[16] The terminology of autonomy was again evident in *Washington* v. *Glucksberg*,[17] although the main concern of the Supreme Court was to explain why a right of autonomy did not give rise to a right to physician-assisted suicide[18] rather than to elaborate on the nature of the right itself.

Superior courts in other jurisdictions have also recognised a constitu-tionally protected right of autonomy.[19] In Canada, the right of autonomy has been held to be part of the right to 'security of the person' as protected by section 7 of the Canadian Charter of Rights and Freedoms,[20] while in Ireland, autonomy has been held to be one of the unenumerated personal rights protected by Article 40.3.1 of the Irish Constitution.[21] A European Convention on Human Rights (ECHR)-derived right of autonomy was

---

[9] (1992) 505 US 833, 859–60 *per* O'Connor J.   [10] (1965) 381 US 479.

[11] (1973) 410 US 113.   [12] (1990) 497 US 261.

[13] The liberty interest is encompassed in the guarantee of due process contained in the Fourteenth Amendment, which provides that no State shall 'deprive any person of life, liberty, or property, without due process of law'.

[14] Contrast the more frequent references in decisions at State level: see, for example, the decisions of the Supreme Court of New Jersey in *Re Quinlan* (1976) 70 NJ 10 and *Re Conroy* (1985) 98 NJ 321.

[15] (1992) 505 US 833.   [16] *Ibid.*, 885.   [17] (1997) 521 US 702, 724.   [18] *Ibid.*, 732.

[19] See also the decision of the Victorian Civil and Administrative Tribunal (VCAT) in *Kracke* v. *Mental Health Review Board and Others* [2009] VCAT 646 that the right to autonomy is implicit in a number of rights in the Victorian Charter of Human Rights and Responsibilities.

[20] See *Rodriguez* v. *British Columbia (AG)* [1993] 3 SCR 519.

[21] See *In Re a Ward of Court* [1996] 2 IR 79; *North Western Health Board* v. *HW and CW* [2001] 3 IR 622; *Fitzpatrick and Another* v. *K and Another* [2008] IEHC 104; see M. Donnelly, 'The Right of Autonomy in Irish Law' (2008) 14 *Medico-Legal Journal of Ireland* 34.

first recognised in *Pretty* v. *United Kingdom*.[22] The European Court of Human Rights (ECtHR) affirmed that the right of autonomy comes within the protection of Article 8, stating that 'the notion of personal autonomy is an important principle underlying the interpretation of [the Article's] guarantees'.[23] The ECtHR found that Article 8 permitted the refusal of medical treatment even if this would lead to the death of a patient[24] and that the imposition of treatment on a capable, adult patient without consent 'would quite clearly interfere with a person's physical integrity in a manner capable of engaging the rights protected under art 8(1) of the Convention'.[25] This position was affirmed in *Tysiac* v. *Poland*[26] where, significantly, the ECtHR recognised that respect for autonomy imposed positive obligations on a State.[27] The implications of this for the legal development of an empowerment-focused conception of autonomy are discussed below. Prior to this, however, it is necessary to consider the primary way in which the right of autonomy has been given legal effect in respect of healthcare decisions. This is through the requirement for consent to treatment and a corresponding right to refuse treatment.

A right in action: autonomy, consent and the right to refuse

The principal legal mechanism through which the right of autonomy has been delivered is through the requirement for consent to medical treatment.[28] Ruth Faden and Tom Beauchamp cite the 1767 decision in *Slater* v. *Baker and Stapleton*[29] as the first judicial recognition of the requirement

---

[22] (2002) 35 EHRR 1, para. 61.

[23] *Ibid.* The Court confirmed this principle in *Goodwin* v. *United Kingdom* [2002] ECHR 2978/02, para. 90; *I* v. *United Kingdom* [2002] ECHR 2979, para. 70.

[24] This contrasts with the narrow view which had been taken in *R (Pretty)* v. *DPP* [2002] 1 AC 800. Lord Bingham, 821, and Lord Steyn, 835, both regarded Art. 8 as protecting autonomy in life but not in relation to the ending of life.

[25] *Pretty* v. *United Kingdom* (2002) 35 EHRR 1, para. 63. See also *Jehovah's Witnessess of Mascow* v. *Russia* [2010] ECHR 302/02, para. 136.

[26] (2007) 45 EHRR 42, para. 107.   [27] *Ibid.*

[28] The inevitability of the link between respect for autonomy and a requirement for consent has been disputed: see J. S. Taylor, 'Autonomy and Informed Consent: A Much Misunderstood Relationship' (2004) 38 *The Journal of Value Inquiry* 383; N. Manson and O. O'Neill, *Rethinking Informed Consent in Bioethics* (Cambridge University Press, 2007), pp. 16–22. For a rebuttal of these arguments, see A. Maclean, *Autonomy, Informed Consent and Medical Law: A Relational Challenge* (Cambridge University Press, 2009), pp. 41–5. For a critique of over-reliance on consent as a solution to all ethical problems, see R. Brownsword, 'The Cult of Consent: Fixation and Fallacy' (2004) 15 *Kings College Law Journal* 223; Manson and O'Neill, *Rethinking Informed Consent*, pp 68–96.

[29] (1767) 2 Wils KB 359.

for consent to medical treatment.[30] The plaintiff in this case hired the defendant doctors to remove bandages from his fractured leg. In spite of the plaintiff's protests, the doctors re-fractured the leg and placed it in an experimental brace to stretch it while the new fracture healed. The doctors were held to have acted improperly because 'a patient should be told what is about to be done to him, that he may take courage and put himself in such a situation as to enable him to undergo the operation'.[31]

The legal linkage between respect for autonomy and the requirement for consent became established in a series of early twentieth century American decisions in the tort of battery.[32] However, as subsequent case law has shown, the fact of consent does not, of itself, provide legal justification in respect of all medical interventions. Superior courts across the common law world have rejected autonomy-based arguments in favour of a right to assisted suicide.[33] The fact of consent may also not provide the basis for the lawful amputation of healthy limbs.[34] Thus, in practical terms, the most prominent consequence of the right of autonomy in respect of healthcare decision-making has been the legal recognition of a right to refuse treatment.

A right to refuse treatment

While the foundations for the autonomy-based requirement for consent were laid in *Schloendorff* in 1914, it was not until the 1960s that patients began to seek court approval in advance for treatment refusal.[35] The decision in the New York case of *Erickson* v. *Dilgard*[36] would appear to be

---

[30] R. Faden and T. Beauchamp, *A History and Theory of Informed Consent* (New York: Oxford University Press, 1986), p. 116.

[31] (1767) 2 Wils KB 359, 361.

[32] See *Mohr* v. *Williams* (1905) 95 Minn 261; *Pratt* v. *Davies* (1906) 224 Ill 300; *Rolater* v. *Strain* (1913) 39 Okla 572; *Schloendorff* v. *Society of New York Hospital* (1914) 211 NY 125. See further A. McCoid, 'A Reappraisal of Liability for Unauthorised Medical Treatment' (1957) 41 *Minnesota Law Review* 381, 387–93.

[33] See *R (Pretty)* v. *DPP* [2002] 1 AC 800; *Pretty* v. *United Kingdom* (2002) 35 EHRR 1; *Washington* v. *Glucksberg* (1997) 521 US 702; *Vacco, Attorney General of New York* v. *Quill* (1997) 521 US 793; *Rodriguez* v. *British Columbia (AG)* [1993] 3 SCR 519. See generally, P. Lewis, *Assisted Dying and Legal Change* (Oxford University Press, 2007), Chapter 2.

[34] However, the issue has not been judicially determined: see T. Elliott, 'Body Dysmorphic Disorder, Radical Surgery and the Limits of Consent' (2009) 17 *Medical Law Review* 149, 175.

[35] In fact, there were relatively few actions in battery in the intervening years: see A. McCoid, 'A Reappraisal of Liability,' 393–402. Note the Canadian cases of *Marshall* v. *Curry* [1933] 3 DLR 260; *Murray* v. *McMurchy* [1949] 2 DLR 442.

[36] (1962) 44 Misc 2d 27. *Cf* the earlier case of *Martin* v. *Industrial Accident Commission* (1956) 147 Cal App 2d 137 where the Court recognised *obiter* that a person was free to refuse a blood transfusion.

the first time that the right of a patient to refuse treatment in advance was explicitly recognised.[37] Like many of the early cases, this case concerned the refusal of a blood transfusion by a Jehovah's Witness[38] and was decided on the basis of religious freedom, which is protected by the First Amendment to the United States Constitution.[39]

As jurisprudence in the United States developed, patients began to establish a right to refuse treatment based on the right of autonomy or self-determination.[40] Typically, these patients were elderly and suffering from terminal conditions.[41] In later cases, the right to refuse was extended to patients who were not terminally ill[42] and to patients who no longer had legal capacity.[43] The right to refuse treatment was affirmed by the United States Supreme Court in *Cruzan* v. *Director, Missouri Department of Health*,[44] with the majority stating that it proceeded on the basis of a presumption that the 'United States Constitution would grant a competent person a constitutionally protected right to refuse lifesaving hydration and nutrition'.[45] The Court rejected the view, which had been favoured by most courts at state level, that the right to refuse treatment was grounded

[37] Legislation permitting the compulsory sterilisation of people on the basis inter alia of criminality was held to be unconstitutional by the United States Supreme Court in *Skinner* v. *Oklahoma* (1942) 316 US 535. However this decision was based on the equal protection clause in the Fourteenth Amendment to the United States Constitution and on the right to reproduce, rather than on the right of autonomy.

[38] The prohibition on blood transfusions is based on a literal interpretation of biblical commands such as 'Only flesh with its soul – its blood – you must not eat' (Genesis 9: 3,4) and 'Keep abstaining from … blood and from things strangled and from fornication' (Acts 15:28, 29): see further Watch Tower Biblical and Tract Society of Pennsylvania, *Family Care and Medical Management for Jehovah's Witnesses* (New York: Watch Tower Biblical and Tract Society, 1995), pp. 3–5.

[39] See also *In re Brooks' Estate* (1965) 32 Ill 2d 361; *Matter of Melideo* (1976) 88 Misc 2d 974; *St Mary's Hospital* v. *Ramsey* (1985) 465 So 2d 666; *Wons* v. *Public Health Trust* (1989) 541 So 2d 96. See Anon, 'Medical Technology and the Law' (1990) 103 *Harvard Law Review* 1520, 1643–6.

[40] See for example *Re Quackenbush* (1978) 156 NJ Super 282; *Salz* v. *Perlmutter* (1978) 362 So 2d 160; *Re Yetter* (1973) 62 Pa D and C 2d 619; *Lane* v. *Candura* (1978) 376 NE 2d 1232.

[41] The plaintiff in *Re Quackenbush* was 72 years old and suffering from gangrene; the plaintiff in *Salz* v. *Perlmutter* was 73 years old and suffering from Lou Gehrig's disease, which resulted in his ongoing dependence on a respirator; the plaintiff in *Re Yetter* was in her sixties and suffering from cancer.

[42] *Bouvia* v. *Superior Court* (1986) 179 Cal App 3d 1127.

[43] *Re Quinlan* (1976) 70 NJ 10. As discussed further in Chapter 5, in these circumstances the right was to be exercised by surrogate decision-makers acting on the basis of what the person would have wanted had she had capacity.

[44] (1990) 497 US 261.   [45] *Ibid.*, 279.

in the right to privacy, holding it instead to be grounded in the right to liberty.[46] For the majority, this constituted a downgrading of the status of the right because the right of privacy is a fundamental right which may not be interfered with without a compelling reason whereas the liberty interest may be balanced against state interests.[47]

The approach adopted by the United States courts was subsequently endorsed in other jurisdictions.[48] In *Malette* v. *Shulman*,[49] the Court of Appeal of Ontario relied on the common law right of autonomy in making a substantial award of damages in battery where the defendant doctor had administered a blood transfusion to an unconscious Jehovah's Witness, notwithstanding the refusal instructions set out in a card she carried and her daughter's confirmation that these instructions represented her mother's continued wishes. In the view of the Court,

> The doctrine of informed consent is plainly intended to ensure the freedom of individuals to make choices concerning their medical care. For this freedom to be meaningful, people must have the right to make choices that accord with their own values, regardless of how unwise or foolish those choices may appear to others.[50]

Although recognised *obiter* in earlier cases,[51] the right to refuse treatment was first applied in England and Wales in the Court of Appeal decision in *Re T (Adult: Refusal of Medical Treatment)*.[52] Like the early North American cases, *Re T* concerned the refusal of a blood transfusion by a young woman who had been brought up as a Jehovah's Witness (although she had not been practising her religion prior to her illness).[53] The Court of Appeal unanimously recognised a right to refuse treatment, which

---

[46] *Ibid.*

[47] The minority *ibid.*, 302 *per* Brennan J (with whom Marshall and Blackmun JJ joined) confirmed the applicability of the liberty interest, although they regarded the liberty interest in a case such as this as a fundamental one that could not be outweighed by the interests of the state.

[48] In addition to the jurisdictions discussed in the text, see Ireland: *In Re a Ward of Court* [1996] 2 IR 79; *Western Health Board* v. *HW and CW* [2001] 3 IR 622; *JM* v. *The Board of Management of St Vincent's Hospital* [2003] 1 IR 321; *Fitzpatrick* v. *K* [2008] IEHC 104; Western Australia: *Brightwater Care Group Inc* v. *Rossiter* [2009] WASC 229.

[49] (1990) 67 DLR (4th) 321 (Ont CA).

[50] *Ibid.*, para. 19. See also *Nancy B* v. *Hôtel-Dieu de Québec* (1992) 86 DLR (4th) 385; *Rodriguez* v. *British Columbia (AG)* [1993] 3 SCR 519; *BD* v. *Stone and Eastern Regional Health Integrated Authority* (2006) NLTD 161.

[51] See *Re F (Mental Patient: Sterilisation)* [1990] 2 AC 1, 55 *per* Lord Brandon; *In re R (A Minor) (Wardship: Medical Treatment)* [1992] Fam 11.

[52] [1992] 3 WLR 782.   [53] *Ibid.*, 788.

Lord Donaldson MR described as 'absolute'.[54] Lord Donaldson MR noted the patient's 'right to self-determination – his right to live his own life how he wishes'.[55] Although this conflicted with society's interest in 'upholding the concept that all human life is sacred', his Lordship concluded that 'in the ultimate the right of the individual is paramount'.[56] The right to refuse treatment was affirmed by the House of Lords in *Airedale NHS Trust* v. *Bland*[57] and applied in a number of subsequent cases.[58] Lord Donaldson's description of the right as 'absolute' was reiterated by Butler-Sloss LJ in *Re MB (An Adult: Medical Treatment)*.[59]

The practical consequences of the recognition of the right to refuse were expanded in *St George's Healthcare NHS Trust* v. *S*,[60] where the Court of Appeal, for the first time, awarded damages in trespass (as well as granting declaratory relief) to a woman who had had a caesarean section performed on her without her consent.[61] The decision was also notable because of the Court's finding that the existence of a judicial declaration permitting the treatment did not provide a defence to the tort of trespass. The declaration had been obtained in circumstances of startling procedural inadequacy, due largely to the behaviour of the healthcare trust,[62] and, in such circumstances, the declaration could not provide a defence.

In addition to judicial statements of a right to refuse medical treatment, legislation in a number of jurisdictions contains an explicit statement of the right. The Australian Capital Territories Human Rights Act 2004,[63] the Victorian Charter of Rights and Responsibilities[64] and the New Zealand Bill of Rights[65] all contain prohibitions on medical treatment (and experimentation) without consent.

---

[54] *Ibid.*, 786.   [55] *Ibid.*, 796.   [56] *Ibid.*

[57] [1993] AC 789, 864 *per* Lord Goff; 857 *per* Lord Keith.

[58] See *inter alia Re C (Adult: Refusal of Medical Treatment)* [1994] 1 WLR 290; *Re AK (Medical Treatment: Consent)* [2001] 1 FLR 129; *Re B (Adult: Refusal of Medical Treatment)* [2002] 2 All ER 449. Cf. *Secretary of State for the Home Department* v. *Robb* [1995] 2 WLR 722 where the Family Division of the High Court held in the context of a hunger strike that the right of self-determination of a convicted prisoner took priority over any countervailing interests of the state.

[59] [1997] 2 FCR 541, 549. See also *R (on the application of SH)* v. *Mental Health Review Tribunal* [2007] EWHC 884 (Admin), [35] *per* Holman J.

[60] [1998] 3 WLR 936. See R. Bailey-Harris, 'Pregnancy, Autonomy and the Refusal of Treatment' (1998) 114 *Law Quarterly Review* 550.

[61] In *Re T* [1992] 3 WLR 782, 803, Staughton LJ had expressed doubts regarding whether an English court would make an award of damages in such circumstances.

[62] See description at [1998] 3 WLR 936, 947.   [63] Section 10 (2).

[64] Section 10 (c) of the Charter of Human Rights and Responsibilities Act 2006.

[65] Bill of Rights Act 1990, ss. 10, 11.

Treatment refusal: behind the rhetoric

While recognising a right to refuse treatment, courts have been careful as regards how this right has been applied in practice. *Re T (Adult: Refusal of Medical Treatment)* is representative of most early decisions before the courts in England and Wales in that it combines a strong statement of the right to refuse with a finding that the right did not apply in the circumstances before the court. While in *Re T* this was because of undue influence (by the young woman's mother) and lack of accurate information,[66] the most common reason that the right has been held not to apply is because of the patient's lack of capacity.[67] Thus, capacity has acted as a safety-valve, allowing courts to endorse the right to refuse treatment while, at the same time, avoid applying it in practice. The role and use of capacity in this way is discussed further in Chapter 4.

In some more recent cases, however, the courts have tended towards a more vigorous approach to the application of the right. In *Re B (Adult: Refusal of Medical Treatment)*,[68] Dame Butler Sloss P made an order permitting a 43-year-old paralysed woman to have artificial ventilation removed notwithstanding that this would lead to her death.[69] Dame Butler-Sloss favoured the 'personal autonomy of the severely disabled patient' over concerns expressed by the medical professionals caring for the patient.[70] Dame Butler-Sloss took a similarly robust approach in *Re W*,[71] upholding the right of a capable prisoner who had an untreatable psychopathic disorder (and who therefore was not subject to compulsion under the Mental Health Act 1983) to refuse treatment even though the prisoner's injuries were self-inflicted and the prisoner was using the situation to force his transfer to hospital.

---

[66] At the time of the patient's written refusal, it had appeared unlikely that a blood transfusion would be required and her medical carers had given the patient assurances in this regard.

[67] See in particular the body of cases discussed in Chapter 3 in which women refused to have medically indicated caesarean sections. On the early jurisprudence, see J. Harrington, 'Privileging the Medical Norm: Liberalism, Self-Determination and Refusal of Treatment' (1996) 16 *Legal Studies* 348, 358–62.

[68] [2002] 2 All ER 449.

[69] Additionally, the Court made a nominal award of damages in respect of prior interference with the woman's right to refuse the treatment. The applicant had sought nominal damages only [2002] 2 All ER 449, 455.

[70] *Ibid.*, 472. Ms B's doctors (*ibid.*, 463) could not 'bring themselves to contemplate that they should be a part of bringing Ms B's life to an end'.

[71] [2002] MHLR 411.

Alasdair Maclean suggests that a possible explanation for conflicting judicial findings in respect of the right to refuse may be an (unspoken) judicial 'desire to avoid the death of a life that the judge sees as worthwhile'.[72] He argues that lives may be seen as not worthwhile in this sense, either because they are not worth living for the person involved[73] or, more contentiously, because of the anti-social or burdensome nature of the individuals involved.[74] Maclean suggests that this may provide an explanation for the decisions to uphold the right to refuse treatment of a long-term criminally detained patient with a mental disorder in *Re C (Adult: Refusal of Medical Treatment)*[75] and of a prisoner in *Re W*[76] and to uphold the right to refuse food of a prisoner in *Secretary of State for the Home Department* v. *Robb*.[77] Were the suggestion of a semi-eugenic basis for decisions about refusals true, it would represent an alarming judicial departure from the ethical principle that lives should be valued equally.[78] It is likely, however, that any unspoken desires may relate more to an assessment of the risk of death rather than a valuation of the underlying lives. It is noteworthy, for example, that, by the time of the decision, the life of the patient in *Re C* was not in immediate danger and that the refusal in question would become relevant only if C's medical condition recurred.[79] Similarly, in *Re W*, Dame Butler-Sloss P noted that W 'is not in any way at the point of death'.[80] She also noted that the applicant had previously resiled from threats to hang himself.[81] Furthermore, as explored in the next section, judicial decisions are likely to reflect broader concerns in respect of agency, which may result in different approaches being taken to the right to refuse treatment in practice.

---

[72] A. Maclean, 'Advance Directives and the Rocky Waters of Anticipatory Decision-Making' (2008) 16 *Medical Law Review* 1, 5. See also Maclean, *Autonomy, Informed Consent and Medical Law*, pp. 210–11.

[73] As, for example, was the case in *Re B (Adult: Refusal of Medical Treatment)* [2002] 2 All ER 449: see Maclean *ibid.*, 5–6.

[74] Maclean *ibid.*, 6, argues that the decision to permit the forced feeding of the notorious Moors murderer, Ian Brady, in *R* v. *Collins and Ashworth Hospital Authority ex parte Brady* [2000] Lloyds Rep Med 355 is not anomalous in this respect on the basis that Brady's crimes were so heinous that it was symbolically important that he should not be allowed to avoid his punishment, even by causing his own death.

[75] [1994] 1 WLR 290.   [76] [2002] MHLR 411.   [77] [1995] 2 WLR 722.

[78] See the distinction drawn in A. Buchanan and D. Brock, *Deciding for Others: The Ethics of Surrogate Decision Making* (Cambridge: Cambridge University Press, 1989), pp. 123–4, between quality of life assessments based on the individual's own assessment of her life and those based on the assignment of value to a person's life.

[79] [1994] 1 WLR 290, 293.   [80] [2002] MHLR 411, [32].   [81] *Ibid.*

Dealing with concerns about agency

As emerged from the discussion in the previous chapter, questions in respect of agency arise in at least some situations in which the right to refuse treatment is implicated. Courts have developed a number of legal mechanisms to deal with such questions, including the operation of a requirement for voluntariness and the utilisation of a presumption in favour of life. However, these have been employed sparingly in practice, when compared with the widespread judicial reliance on the capacity requirement.

Voluntariness, agency and the right to refuse

The requirement that consent to and refusal of medical treatment must be voluntarily given and free from coercion is long established. In England and Wales, the requirement was affirmed in *Freeman* v. *Home Office*.[82] This case was concerned with allegations made by a prisoner that he had been physically restrained and that medical treatment had been forcibly imposed on him. Both the trial judge and the Court of Appeal held that there was no evidence to support this contention. The Court of Appeal rejected the argument that the very fact of imprisonment rendered a patient unable to give a voluntary consent. However, it accepted that some situations, including the provision of medical treatment in a prison setting, require a closer examination of consent for the purposes of establishing voluntariness.[83] In recognising that conditions can be inherently coercive, the Court might be described as showing the beginnings of a relational approach to autonomy. However, this approach has not been developed in later cases involving prisoners[84] and, as will be seen below, there has been little enthusiasm in other cases for a social or relational approach to the voluntariness requirement.

In *Re T (Adult: Refusal of Medical Treatment)*, notwithstanding the Court of Appeal's strong endorsement of an autonomy-based right to refuse treatment, the Court held that the patient's refusal of a blood transfusion was not binding because she had been unduly influenced by her mother.[85] In the words of Lord Donaldson MR:

> The real question in each such case is 'Does the patient really mean what he says or is he merely saying it for a quiet life, to satisfy someone else or

[82] [1984] 2 WLR 130 (QB); [1984] 2 WLR 802 (CA).

[83] *Ibid.*, 813. See generally M. Somerville, 'Refusal of Medical Treatment in "Captive" Circumstances' (1985) 63 *Canadian Bar Review* 59.

[84] See, for example, the approach of Kay J in *R* v. *Collins and Ashworth Hospital Authority ex parte Brady* [2000] Lloyds Rep Med 355.

[85] [1992] 3 WLR 782, 795 *per* Lord Donaldson; 803 *per* Butler-Sloss LJ; 804 *per* Staughton LJ. The patient's mother was a Jehovah's Witness and both the patient's initial oral refusal

because the advice and persuasion to which he has been subjected is such
that he can no longer think and decide for himself?' In other words, 'Is it
a decision expressed in form only, not in reality?'[86]

Lord Donaldson MR identified certain classes of relationship as more
likely to raise a possibility of undue influence. He noted that 'the influence
of parents on their children and of one spouse on the other can be, but is
by no means necessarily, much stronger than would be the case in other
relationships'.[87] Lord Donaldson also noted the power of persuasion based
upon religious belief and that religious arguments deployed by a person
in a close relationship would have added force. This, he said, 'should alert
the doctors to the possibility – no more – that the patient's capacity or will
to decide has been overborne'.[88]

Surprisingly, given the way in which Lord Donaldson MR expressed
his 'real question', the issue of undue influence has rarely come before
the courts since *Re T*. The most significant case is *Mrs U* v. *Centre for
Reproductive Medicine*.[89] In this case, the applicant sought to overturn her
husband's signed refusal of consent to the posthumous use of his sperm
on the basis that this refusal had been made as a result of undue influence by a staff member at the fertility clinic, which the couple had been
attending. In the High Court, Dame Butler-Sloss P accepted that the staff
member in question would have been a 'formidable' presence and that
there was clearly pressure on the applicant's husband to refuse his consent.[90] However, applying Lord Donaldson's test from *Re T*, she found that
it was not possible to conclude that this pressure was such that 'an able,
intelligent, educated man of 47, with a responsible job and in good health'
had had his will overborne to such an extent that he 'no longer thought
and decided for himself'.[91] This finding was upheld by the Court of
Appeal. Hale LJ noted that the 'whole scheme' of the Human Fertilisation
and Embryology Act 1990 'lays great emphasis upon consent'.[92] She

and her later written refusal came after she had spent a period alone with her mother. At
the hearing, the patient's mother declined to give evidence of what had passed between
her and her daughter during these times (789) and the patient was unconscious and
unable to give evidence.

[86] *Ibid.*, 797.   [87] *Ibid.*   [88] *Ibid.*

[89] [2002] EWHC 36 (Fam) (*sub nom Centre for Reproductive Medicine* v. *U*); [2002] EWCA
Civ 565 (CA). See S. Pattinson, 'Undue Influence in the Context of Medical Treatment'
(2002) 5 *Medical Law International* 305. Note also comments of Holman J in *R (on the
application of SH)* v. *Mental Health Review Tribunal* [2007] EWHC 884 (Admin), [35].

[90] [2002] EWHC 36 (Fam), [25]. This was clinic policy. Dame Butler-Sloss P accepted that
the applicant's husband had been persuaded to change his original consent to the posthumous use of his sperm because of his belief that the couple's fertility treatment would
be interrupted if the consent form were not changed.

[91] *Ibid.*, [28].   [92] [2002] EWCA Civ 565, [21].

differentiated the circumstances of this case from undue influence in other circumstances, including in respect of the determination of the law-fulness of medical treatment'.[93] There are, she noted, 'other justifications for performing life-saving medical treatment apart from the possession of a lawful consent' while there is 'no other justification for continuing to store human sperm'.[94]

There is little support in *Centre for Reproductive Medicine* for a rela-tional or social approach to concerns about agency. Although Dame Butler-Sloss P acknowledged the great desire of the couple to have a child,[95] neither she nor the Court of Appeal was open to the argument that this would have impeded agency to such a degree as to undermine the decision made. This approach is in interesting contrast to a decision of the Irish High Court in *JM v. The Board of Management of St Vincent's Hospital*.[96] This case, which came before the Court in circumstances of considerable urgency, concerned an application by the patient's hus-band for a declaration that a blood transfusion should be administered to his unconscious wife notwithstanding the fact that, while conscious, she had refused this treatment. The woman's condition was now life-threatening and the Court heard evidence that, without the transfusion, she would die.

Finnegan P proceeded on the basis of a right to refuse treatment which is protected under Article 40.3.1 of the Constitution of Ireland.[97] The evidence presented by the applicant in favour of intervention was that '[t]he notice party is African. Part of her culture is that she adopts the reli-gion of her husband upon marriage'.[98] The woman had, in fact, become a Jehovah's Witness on her marriage, having started studying to do so approximately seven months prior to the case arising.[99] Responding to this evidence, Finnegan P found that the woman's refusal of treatment had happened 'because of her cultural background and her desire to please her husband and not offend his sensibilities'. She was 'preoccupied with her husband ... rather than with whether to have the treatment and her own welfare'. He considered that, if the woman were now lucid, she would agree with the decision and would be comforted by her husband's attitude.[100] Noting that there was a 60 per cent chance that the woman would survive if the transfusion were administered and that the woman had a child and a loving husband, he described his decision as 'easy'.[101]

---

[93] *Ibid.*, [25].   [94] *Ibid.*   [95] [2002] EWHC 36 (Fam), [25].   [96] [2003] 1 IR 321.
[97] *Ibid.*, 324.   [98] *Ibid.*
[99] Evidence was also given, *ibid.*, 325, that the woman had wavered in reaching the deci-sion, saying initially that she would take the blood and then changing her mind.
[100] *Ibid.*   [101] *Ibid.*

In truth, the issues raised by this case are far from easy. The decision shows both the dangers of taking a social or relational approach to agency and the dangers of not doing so. On the one hand, the woman had, very shortly before becoming unconscious, indicated her ongoing desire to refuse the treatment.[102] At this time, she was acting in full awareness of the possible consequence of the refusal and there were no false reassurances that the need for a transfusion was unlikely to arise. Nor was there any suggestion that the women lacked decision-making capacity or that she had been subject to undue influence in reaching her decision. In fact, her husband gave evidence that he had told his wife that it was her decision and that she should not decide because of him.[103] It is therefore very difficult to find any basis, consistent with existing legal doctrine, for a decision to override the woman's refusal.

Yet, if the evidence is to be believed, the woman's primary motivation was to please her husband, something which had been culturally inculcated into her. Her death would clearly not accord with this motivation. Furthermore, on the evidence presented, her decision seems to lack the degree of independent thought which we associate with autonomous decision-making.[104] Suggestions from the previous chapter about building autonomy-competencies are of little use in this kind of situation (although they might help to prevent such situations developing). However, the need for procedural adequacy, which was also identified as relevant to patient empowerment, is relevant. In this case, for example, the woman in question was a notice party to the proceedings rather than a defendant; she was not legally represented and the application was opposed only by legal counsel for the treating doctor. While independent representation might not have made the court's task easier (in fact, it would likely have increased the difficulty), it would at least have provided the court with a more accurate understanding of the implications of the decision and a more defensible basis for decision-making.

In light of the difficulties which the approach taken in this case reveals, it is perhaps understandable that the courts in England and Wales have chosen not to involve themselves too closely in social aspects of agency. Instead, the courts have preferred to deal with agency issues through the application of a presumption in favour of life.

---

[102] *Ibid.*   [103] *Ibid.*

[104] See, for example, R. Dworkin, *Life's Dominion: An Argument About Abortion, Euthanasia, and Individual Freedom* (New York: Alfred A. Knopf, 1993), pp. 239–40.

Presumptions, doubts and the exercise of autonomy

Having set out an 'absolute' right to refuse treatment in *Re T (Adult: Refusal of Medical Treatment)*, Lord Donaldson MR continued by noting that '[i]n case of doubt, that doubt falls to be resolved in favour of the preservation of life for if the individual is to override the public interest, he must do so in clear terms'.[105] His Lordship gave little further indication regarding the factors which cause a situation to fall into the category of 'cases of doubt'. In *Re T* itself, the patient had been given misleading, reassuring information by her doctors regarding the consequences of an advance refusal of blood products, and it would seem that she did not know she was exercising her right to refuse in a situation where the refusal could realistically lead to her death. Because the patient was unconscious when the case came before the Court, it was not possible to ascertain what she would have done if she had known the level of risk involved and, accordingly, the case may fairly easily be categorised as one of doubt.

The category of 'cases of doubt' was not discussed further in *Re T*[106] and the issue was not taken up in subsequent decisions until the decision of Munby J in *HE v. A Hospital NHS Trust*.[107] This case concerned an application by the father of a 24-year-old woman, AE, for a declaration that a blood transfusion should be administered to the woman, who was now unconscious, notwithstanding her advance written refusal of such treatment on the basis of her religious beliefs as a Jehovah's Witness. Medical evidence suggested that, without a blood transfusion, AE would die within the next 24 hours. The applicant presented a number of facts as evidence in support of his claim that the hospital should override his daughter's advance refusal. Of most relevance to the current discussion was the fact that AE had recently become engaged to a Turkish man and, as a condition of her marriage, she had agreed that she would reject her faith as a Jehovah's Witness and would revert to being a Muslim.[108] AE had not attended any Jehovah's Witness services since her engagement and had promised her fiancé that she would not do so. Two months prior

---

[105] [1992] 3 WLR 782, 796.

[106] Lord Donaldson MR's categorisation received little attention from commentators, although see K. Mason, 'Master of the Balancers; Non-Voluntary Therapy Under the Mantle of Lord Donaldson' (1993) 2 *Juridical Review* 115.

[107] [2003] EWHC 1017 (Fam).

[108] AE had originally been brought up a Muslim; however, following the separation of her parents, AE and her brother lived with their mother, ceased to practise as Muslims and were brought up as Jehovah's Witnesses.

to her current illness, she had informed her family of her intention to marry her fiancé and had said that she would not allow anything to get in her way and that she would follow her fiancé's Muslim faith.[109]

Munby J found that the presumption in favour of life was a determining factor in dealing with the uncertainties to which this kind of case give rise. First, he noted that there is a presumption in favour of life which causes the burden of proof to fall on the person seeking to uphold an advance refusal of treatment in a life-threatening situation.[110] Emphasising Lord Donaldson MR's reference to 'cases of doubt',[111] he found that proof of the validity of the advance refusal and of its continuing applicability must be clear and convincing and '[w]here, as here, life is at stake, the evidence must be scrutinised with especial care'.[112] Secondly, an advance refusal of treatment will not survive a 'material change of circumstance'.[113] If an argument is made that a material change of circumstances arises, the evidential burden falls on the person who seeks to argue that the advance refusal is no longer applicable.[114] However, once it is established that there is some reason for doubt, the burden shifts back to the person seeking to uphold the advance refusal to prove that the refusal is still operative.[115] As Sabine Michalowski points out, this approach to the burden of proof means that, especially in life-threatening situations, advance treatment refusals are inherently unreliable.[116]

In the circumstances of the case before him, Munby J found that he did not have to resort to reliance on a presumption in favour of life. Rather, he decided on the basis of 'the essential, and ultimately, compelling' evidence that AE had not merely decided to reject her faith as a Jehovah's Witness but 'had actually implemented that decision, by discontinuing her previously frequent attendance at religious meetings and services'.[117] AE's 'abandonment and rejection of her faith' deprived the directive of any continuing validity and effect.[118] Munby J considered that, even if he was wrong in reaching this conclusion on the facts, his finding in favour of intervention could still be justified because the evidence presented raised 'real doubts, not fanciful doubts or mere speculation' which, according to the presumption in favour of life, had to be resolved in favour of the preservation of life.[119]

---

[109] [2003] EWHC 1017 (Fam), [13]. Additionally, AE had said that she did not want to die and had not mentioned her refusal form during a previous stay in hospital.

[110] *Ibid.*, [23].   [111] *Ibid.*, [27].   [112] *Ibid.*, [24].   [113] *Ibid.*, [29].   [114] *Ibid.*, [43].   [115] *Ibid.*

[116] S. Michalowski, 'Advance Refusals of Life-Sustaining Medical Treatment: The Relativity of the Absolute Right' (2005) 68 *Modern Law Review* 958, 981.

[117] [2003] EWHC 1017 (Fam), [49].   [118] *Ibid.*   [119] *Ibid.*, [50].

There is an argument that Munby J's decision in *HE* is a straightforward application of judicial paternalism. Alasdair Maclean argues that 'given that [AE] was a young woman with a potentially worthwhile life ahead, her father's evidence provided a way around the need to respect her refusal'.[120] However, this underplays the difficulty of the agency issues arising. On the one hand, as Maclean notes, the written directive 'remained the most authoritative indication of [AE's] wishes'[121] and although AE has stopped attending religious services, she had not destroyed her treatment refusal form.[122] On the other hand, the case leaves genuine doubts about what AE would have wished to happen. These doubts derive in part at least from the social context in which AE lived and from the possibility that, for reasons that may (or may not) have arisen from gender-related oppression, her primary goal was to please her fiancé. Thus, although the desire to please may have led in the opposite direction, this case is like the Irish case of *JM v. The Board of Management of St Vincent's Hospital*[123] in raising questions about women's agency. Munby J's reliance on the presumption in favour of life provides a more established legal framework within which to deal with questions of this kind than the approach taken in *JM*. However, it must be recognised that this comes at a cost to the overall status of the right of autonomy, one which may be especially felt by women. Furthermore, this approach allows the social, cultural and philosophical attributes of agency to be hidden behind a legal façade. For this reason, as was argued in Chapter 1, there is a need for greater engagement with issues of agency and the development of mechanisms to minimise the possibilities of these kinds of cases arising.

Limiting the legal right

As noted above, the earliest jurisprudence on treatment refusal emanates from the United States. In the relevant cases, the right to refuse treatment tended to be balanced against the interests of others. Thus, the right was found to be limited in a range of circumstances, based, for the most part, on obligations which the patient was found to owe to other people. Accordingly, applications asserting a right to refuse treatment

---

[120] Maclean, 'Advance Directives and the Rocky Waters', 7.   [121] *Ibid.*, 7.

[122] In this respect, it is significant that the circumstances arising were unlikely to have come as a surprise to AE as she had a congenital heart defect and had known since childhood that she would need surgical intervention at some point and she had been aware of the seriousness of her condition on entering hospital.

[123] [2003] 1 IR 321.

were denied because the exercise of the right would affect fetal interests;[124] because the exercise would leave the applicant's minor children without a parent;[125] and because the exercise of the right would leave the applicant's family reliant on state support.[126] In *Superintendent of Belchertown* v. *Saikewicz*,[127] the Supreme Judicial Court of Massachusetts identified four relevant state interests which could limit the right to refuse treatment. These were the preservation of life; the protection of the interests of innocent third parties; the prevention of suicide; and the maintenance of the ethical integrity of the medical profession.[128]

A shift in focus in United States law

As the law developed, courts in the United States became less inclined to allow the right to refuse treatment to be overridden in the interests of others.[129] Thus, in *Fosmire* v. *Nicoleau*, the New York Court of Appeals dismissed the argument that the state's interest in protecting the welfare of children requires that parents' right to refuse treatment be accorded a lesser degree of protection.[130] The comparative weakness of the state's interest in the preservation of life was made clear in *Thor* v. *Superior Court*.[131] In this case, the Supreme Court of California rejected the applicant's petition for permission to tube feed a quadriplegic prisoner who was refusing food and medical treatment, leading to a risk of his death. The Court considered that there was no countervailing state interest in the preservation of life sufficient to justify granting the order. It also rejected the argument that, where a patient is not in chronic pain such as to make life hopeless and intolerable (as in the earlier case of *Bouvia* v.

---

[124] See *Jefferson* v. *Griffin Spalding County Hospital* (1981) 274 SE 2d 457; *Raleigh Fitkin-Paul Morgan Memorial Hospital* v. *Anderson* (1964) 42 NJ 421; *In re Jamaica Hospital* (1985) 128 Misc 2d 1006; *Crouse Irving Memorial Hospital, Inc* v. *Paddock* (1985) 127 Misc 2d 101.

[125] See *In the Application of President and Directors of Georgetown College Inc* (1964) 118 App DC 90; *Holmes* v. *Silver Cross Hospital* (1972) 340 F Supp 125. In a number of other cases, the absence of dependant children was cited as a relevant factor in allowing individuals to exercise their right to refuse treatment: see *Re Yetter* (1973) 62 Pa D&C 2d 619; *Salz* v. *Perlmutter* (1978) 362 So 2d 160.

[126] See *United States* v. *George* (1965) 239 F Supp 752. Compare *Norwood Hospital* v. *Munoz* (1991) 564 NE 2d 1017.

[127] (1977) 370 NE 2d 417.   [128] *Ibid.*, 425.

[129] This is notwithstanding the approach of the US Supreme Court in *Cruzan* v. *Director, Missouri Department of Health* (1990) 497 US 261 where a majority viewed the right to refuse treatment as part of the liberty interest which had to be balanced against state interests.

[130] (1990) 551 NE 2d 77.   [131] (1993) 855 P 2d 375.

Superior Court),[132] she is entitled to a proportionately smaller measure of control over bodily intrusions.[133]

There has also been a shift in attitude in respect of possible fetal harm.[134] In *Re AC*, the District of Columbia Court of Appeals stated that it would require 'an extraordinary case indeed' before a court would be justified in overriding a patient's wishes and ordering the performance of a major surgical intervention such as a caesarean section,[135] while in *Baby Boy Doe*, the Appellate Court of Illinois held that 'a competent woman's choice to refuse medical treatment as invasive as a caesarean section during pregnancy must be honoured, even in circumstances where the choice may be harmful to the fetus'.[136] Although as Rosamund Scott points out, a question mark still remains about treatment which could not be characterised as invasive, it would seem that the right of a pregnant woman to refuse most forms of medical treatment is firmly established.[137]

England and Wales: limits on an 'absolute' right?

As described above, in the first detailed discussion of treatment refusal by the English courts, Lord Donaldson MR described the right to refuse as 'absolute'.[138] However, he immediately contradicted this by setting out one 'possible qualification' where viable fetal life was at risk.[139] His Lordship also noted the 'very strong public interest in preserving the life and health of all citizens'.[140] Subsequent case law has yet to set a limit on the right to refuse treatment. Although Lord Donaldson's possible limit based on fetal interests was applied in *In re S (Adult: Refusal of Treatment)*,[141] this approach was dismissed by the Court of Appeal, first in an *obiter* statement in *Re MB (An Adult: Medical Treatment)*,[142] and then in *St George's Healthcare NHS Trust v. S*.[143]

---

[132] (1986) 179 Cal App 3d 1127.   [133] (1993) 855 P 2d 375, 385.

[134] Note, however, the 2004 decision by state prosecutors in the State of Utah to prosecute for murder a woman who refused a caesarean section, allegedly for cosmetic reasons, leading to the death of one of the twins she was carrying. In April 2004, the woman was sentenced to 18 months probation, having pleaded guilty to the lesser charge of child endangerment. See commentary in M. Miller, 'Refusal to Undergo a Caesarean Section: A Woman's Right or a Criminal Act?' (2005) 15 *Health Matrix* 383.

[135] (1990) 573 A 2d 1235, 1252. For a critique of the Court's reasoning (although not its conclusion), see R. Scott, *Rights, Duties and the Body: Law and Ethics of the Maternal-Fetal Conflict* (Oxford: Hart Publishing, 2002), pp. 117–19.

[136] (1994) 632 NE 2d 326, 329. See the similar finding in respect of a blood transfusion in *Re Fetus Brown* (1997) 294 Ill App 3d 159.

[137] Scott, *Rights, Duties and the Body*, p. 141.

[138] *Re T (Adult: Refusal of Medical Treatment)* [1992] 3 WLR 782, 786.   [139] *Ibid.*, 786.

[140] *Ibid.*, 799.   [141] [1993] Fam 123.   [142] [1997] 2 FCR 541, 556.   [143] [1998] 3 WLR 936.

In *St George's Healthcare*, the Court of Appeal set out in detail why fetal interests did not limit the right of autonomy of a pregnant woman. Although Judge LJ, speaking for the Court, did not ultimately dispute that the fetus lacked legal personality under the law of England and Wales, he acknowledged that '[w]hatever it is, a foetus is not nothing; if viable it is not lifeless and it is certainly human'.[144] Furthermore, he rejected the argument that the fetus and the mother could be considered as the same and that 'in refusing treatment which would benefit the foetus a mother is simply refusing treatment for herself'.[145] Rather, the focus of the judgment was on the significance of the right of autonomy. Judge LJ noted Lord Reid's 'salutary warning' in respect of the dangers of making minor concessions with respect to the right.[146] Asking 'how can a forced invasion of a competent adult's body against her will even for the most laudable of motives (the preservation of life) be ordered without irremediably damaging the principle of self-determination?',[147] his Lordship concluded that, 'while pregnancy increases the personal responsibilities of a woman it does not diminish her entitlement to decide whether or not to undergo medical treatment'.[148]

The issue of parental duties to children has not come before the English courts although in light of the strength of the endorsement of individual autonomy in *St George's Healthcare*, it is difficult to see how any attempt to rely on such a limiting factor might succeed.[149] The applicability of a limit based on the preservation of life or on the concerns of the medical

---

[144] *Ibid.*, 952.   [145] *Ibid.*, 953.   [146] *Ibid.*, 951.   [147] *Ibid.*, 953.

[148] *Ibid.*, 957. Note the complex position in Ireland where a fetus (or 'unborn' as described in Article 40.3.3 of the Constitution of Ireland) has a constitutionally protected right to life which the State is obliged 'with due respect to the equal right to life of the mother … to respect, and, as far as practicable, by its laws to defend'. It is arguable that this constitutional provision might require a limit on a pregnant woman's autonomy if fetal life were put at risk by the decision. However, it should be noted that the Supreme Court has shown some discomfort with allowing the right to life of the unborn to trump all of a pregnant woman's rights other than the right to life: see *Society for the Protection of Unborn Children (Ireland) Ltd* v. *Grogan (No 5)* [1998] 4 IR 343, 375 *per* Denham J; 389–90 *per* Keane J. See generally G. Hogan and G. Whyte, *JM Kelly: The Irish Constitution* (4th edn) (Dublin: Lexis Nexis Butterworths, 2003), p. 1523.

[149] Note the *ex tempore* decision of the High Court of Ireland in *Re K*, unreported, Abbott J, 22 September 2006, which granted permission to transfuse blood to a woman who refused blood on religious grounds on the basis that the woman's death would leave her infant child with no parent in the State to care for him (the woman having recently arrived in Ireland from the Democratic Republic of Congo). The case was reopened in *Fitzpatrick and Another* v. *K and Another* [2008] IEHC 194 (in an action brought by the hospital seeking clarification of its legal position) and the Court held that the woman had lacked decision-making capacity and that the decision to grant permission for the transfusion

profession was rejected in *Re B (Adult: Refusal of Medical Treatment)*.[150] Dame Butler-Sloss P favoured the 'personal autonomy of the severely disabled patient' over concerns expressed by the medical professionals caring for Ms B.[151] However, the case is short on analysis and the priority accorded to Ms B's autonomy is asserted but, unlike the approach taken in *St George's*, it is not substantiated by reference to any reasoning in respect of the other (subordinate) interests at stake.[152]

From the forgoing, it would seem that in England and Wales, while the right to refuse treatment is perhaps not absolute, the courts are certainly reluctant to interfere with the right. Additionally, as will now be discussed, legislators in England and Wales have declined to include measures for the imposition of treatment in legislation in respect of infectious diseases.

Treatment refusal, public health and infectious diseases

The legal framework governing infectious diseases in England and Wales is set out in the Public Health (Control of Disease) Act 1984 (PHA) as amended. The focus of the legislation is on the removal of people with certain (serious) infectious diseases ('notifiable diseases')[153] from the community and on the restriction of some kinds of behaviour in order to prevent the spread of disease. Under the amendments introduced by the Health and Social Care Act 2008, the Health Minister may introduce regulations imposing a wide range of restrictions including restrictions on international travel[154] or on the holding of a public event or gathering.[155] Other provisions, of more interest to the current discussion, are personal in their impact. Thus, the Minister may introduce regulations permitting a 'special restriction or requirement' which may be imposed by an order of a Justice of the Peace.[156] The relevant measures include that a person who is or may be infected with a notifiable disease may be required to

---

could be justified on this basis. Laffoy J declined to offer what would have been an advisory opinion on the balance between competing interests of parent and child.

[150] [2002] 2 All ER 449.   [151] *Ibid.*, 472.

[152] For discussion of the interests of medical professionals in such cases, see Brazier, 'Do No Harm,' 417–20; and of family members and of the state in the preservation of life, R. Huxtable, 'A Right to Die or is it Right to Die?' (2002) 14 *Child and Family Law Quarterly* 341.

[153] Details regarding the diseases to which the legislation applies are set out in the Schedule to the Public Health (Infectious Diseases) Regulations 1988, SI 1546/1988.

[154] PHA, s. 45B inserted by Health and Social Care Act 2008, s. 129.

[155] PHA, s. 45C(4)(b).

[156] PHA, s. 45C(4)(d). Additionally, a Justice of the Peace may make orders in respect of 'things': s. 45H and 'premises': s. 45I. Before the powers outlined in the text arise, the Justice of the Peace must be satisfied that the person is or may be infected or contaminated;

submit to medical examination.[157] She may also be removed to a hospital or other suitable establishment and detained in such an establishment.[158] She may be kept in isolation or quarantine and 'disinfected or decontaminated' and be required to wear protective clothing.[159] A person in this situation may also be required to submit to monitoring and reporting in respect of her health[160] and made subject to restrictions about where she goes and with whom she has contact and she may be required to abstain from working or trading.[161] An initial order for detention or quarantine may not exceed 28 days. However, the order may be extended by periods of up to 28 days on review.[162]

While permitting the introduction of these potentially highly restrictive measures, the PHA states clearly that a person cannot be required to undergo 'medical treatment'.[163] This is no surprise given that, in its review of the PHA (which preceded the 2008 Act) the Department of Health started from the position that it should not be possible to require a person to undergo treatment, or vaccination or other prophylaxis.[164] The review noted that '[c]ompulsory treatment powers are generally not a feature of legislation in the United Kingdom' and that an adult with capacity normally has the right to refuse treatment even if that treatment is in their best interests. This, of course, omits to mention that compulsory treatment powers are central to mental health legislation. As regards what constitutes treatment, the review noted that 'most people would see procedures that involve taking medication internally (for example, by injection or by swallowing tablets) as "treatment"'.[165]

Gaps in the law's approach

The preceding discussion shows that, outside of the context of treatment for a mental disorder, the law in England and Wales has been slow

that the infection or contamination is one which presents or which could present significant harm to human health; that there is a risk that the person might infect or contaminate others and that it is necessary to make the order in order to remove or reduce the risk: s. 45G(1).

[157] PHA, s. 45G(2)(a).   [158] PHA, s. 45G(2)(b), (c).   [159] PHA, s. 45G(2)(d), (e), (f).

[160] PHA, s. 45G(2)(h). The person may also be required to provide information and answer questions about her health or other circumstances: s. 45G(2)(g) and about a 'related party' who may have been infected or contaminated: s. 45G(4).

[161] PHA, s. 45G(2)(j), (k).   [162] PHA, s. 45F(8).   [163] PHA, s. 45E(1).

[164] *Review of Parts II, V and VI of the Public Health (Control of Disease) Act 1984: A consultation on proposals for changes to public health law in England* Gateway Ref. 7742 (London: Department of Health, 2007), para. 5.11.

[165] *Ibid.*, para 5.12.

to recognise limits in respect of the right to refuse treatment. This may be, in part, because the applicants in the relevant cases were unusual or exceptional people.[166] For less 'exceptional' people, as discussed in the next chapter, the right to refuse treatment has been moderated in practice through the enthusiastic application of the capacity requirement. As a result, there has been little analysis of the question of limits. This lack of analysis leaves gaps in the law's approach. There has been little discussion of the relevance of degrees of invasiveness or of possible obligations to persuade and no discussion of the relationship between the right of autonomy which is protected in respect of treatment and other threats to autonomy, including the loss of liberty. These issues are significant and the failure to engage with them may ultimately weaken the force of the law's endorsement of autonomy.

Interrogating invasiveness

It is well known that even the slightest pin-prick can constitute a battery if performed without consent and that, from a legal perspective centred solely on autonomy, the pin-prick is no less serious than major invasive surgery. There are good reasons why the law adopts this approach. As Raz points out, '[o]ften coercion is wrong primarily because it is an affront or an insult and not so much because of its more tangible consequences'.[167] Yet, in focusing on all interventions, the other consequences of bodily invasion are lost, as are the reasons, besides a breach of autonomy, why bodies need to be protected from invasion. The consequences of this omission are most evident in legal discourse in respect of people found to lack capacity. As discussed in Chapter 5, for much of its history, the law has treated even extreme physical invasions of people lacking capacity as unproblematic, provided that the basis for the invasion met an often amorphous best interests standard.[168]

The law's reluctance to discuss degrees of invasiveness also closes off any scope for discussion of balance. It is not enough simply to state a 'slippery slope' argument about the dangers of making 'minor concessions'

---

[166] Ms B was described by Butler-Sloss P ([2002] 2 All ER 449, 473) as a 'splendid' person with courage, strength of will and determination. The claimant in St George's Healthcare was unusual in the clarity and vigour with which she pursued her rights: see A. Morris, 'Once Upon a Time in a Hospital … The Cautionary Tale of St George's Healthcare NHS Trust v. S, R v. Collins and Others ex parte S [1998] 3 All ER 673' (1999) 7 Feminist Legal Studies 75, 83.

[167] Raz, The Morality of Freedom (Oxford: Clarendon Press, 1986), p. 156.

[168] See, for example, Re MB (An Adult: Medical Treatment) [1997] 2 FCR 541, 556.

with vague references to practices in other countries.[169] There has been relatively little analysis regarding how, and whether, even as a theoretical proposition, minor (non-invasive) interferences with autonomy might be justified. One valuable contribution is Rosamund Scott's analysis of the reasons why a 'beneficial pill' (a hypothetical pill without side-effects, which would benefit the fetus without harming the woman) should not be administered to a pregnant woman without her consent.[170] Scott makes the consequentialist argument that permitting any form of interference with women's autonomy could lead to a diminution in trust and to a consequent 'maternal flight' from care.[171] She also recognises the equality issues raised by compelled treatment of pregnant women[172] and the symbolic meanings implicit in the use of coercion with women 'being the *vehicles* to maternal health'.[173] These are strong arguments. However, they are, as Scott acknowledges, 'predominantly contextual,' requiring consideration 'not only of the unique position of women and the way their bodies are implicated … but also of the possible vulnerability of some women, which may be increased when pregnant'.[174] Different situations give rise to different issues of balance. It may well be the case that the tidiness of the 'no concessions' approach is preferable to the messiness of balancing. Without closer analysis of this question, however, the law's approach to limits on the right of autonomy is incomplete and its endorsement of autonomy is not convincing.

Treatment refusal and persuasion

A second gap in the law's approach relates to the issue of persuasion as an alternative means of dealing with situations in which the right of autonomy must be balanced against other factors. As described in the previous chapter, while defending a principle of non-interference in all but a very limited set of circumstances, Mill was clear that '[t]here are good reasons for remonstrating with [an autonomous individual], or reasoning with him, or persuading him, or entreating him'.[175] Thus, persuasion has an established foundation within the liberal tradition. The viability or otherwise of such an alternative has received little judicial attention, although in *Re B (Adult: Refusal of Medical Treatment)*, Dame Butler-Sloss P did

---

[169] S v. McC (orse S) and M (DS intervener); W v. W [1972] AC 24, 43 per Lord Reid.
[170] Scott, *Rights, Duties and the Body*, pp. 369–83.   [171] *Ibid.*, pp. 369–71.
[172] *Ibid.*, pp. 375–81.   [173] *Ibid.*, p. 382, original emphasis.   [174] *Ibid.*, p. 383.
[175] J. S. Mill, *On Liberty* (London, 1859) in Grey, John (ed.) *On Liberty and Other Essays* (Oxford University Press, 1991), p. 14.

'diffidently' suggest to the applicant that if she reconsidered her decision, 'she would have a lot to offer the community at large'.[176]

Scott argues in favour of persuasion, rather than coercion, as the mechanism to deal with treatment refusal by pregnant women.[177] She argues that, in some oppressive situations, a woman may not 'have had the chance to learn to exercise autonomy responsibly,' perhaps because she has not 'had the occasion to cultivate the degree of self-trust requisite for her to acquire and use autonomy skills competently'.[178] In such circumstances, Scott advocates 'sympathetic discussion and counselling' in the face of a decision to refuse treatment.[179] Alasdair Maclean argues in favour of a more general obligation to facilitate good decision-making and advocates a model of 'mutual persuasion'.[180] This is based on both a professional duty to seek the patient's reasons and a moral obligation on patients 'to engage in the dialogue, to reflect on and to explain their decisions, as far as possible'.[181]

There are risks in recognising a legal duty to persuade. It is all too easy to move from persuasion to what is effectively an overriding of the will of the person and a denial of her right to make the decision. Both Scott and Maclean are conscious of the dangers. In the specific context of pregnant women, Scott argues that 'heavy duty persuasion' should be restricted to situations where the treatment refused does not involve significant pain or risks and to situations where the reasons for the refusal are 'insufficiently serious', 'trivial', 'irrational/inappropriate and purposeless' or 'non existent'.[182] Maclean argues that a duty to persuade 'must be restricted to the use of rational argument and should avoid any manipulative tactics such as deception, bullying or undue exploitation of the patient's guilt'.[183] Whether these boundaries could be maintained in practice is unclear. Questions also arise regarding whether a legal duty can legitimately be imposed in respect of a concept like persuasion, which is essentially amorphous and difficult to bring within a rigorous evidentiary framework. For these reasons, the most reasonable way to deal with the issue of persuasion in a legal context may well be through the development of obligations in respect of communication. As discussed further below, there are at least some legal moves in the direction of imposing positive

---

[176] [2002] 2 All ER 449, 473.   [177] Scott, *Rights, Duties and the Body*, pp. 236–45.

[178] *Ibid.*, p. 374.   [179] *Ibid*, p. 375.

[180] Maclean, *Autonomy, Informed Consent and Medical Law*, p. 247.   [181] *Ibid.*, p. 248.

[182] Scott, *Rights, Duties and the Body*, p. 243.

[183] Maclean, *Autonomy, Informed Consent and Medical Law*, p. 249.

obligations in this regard and this might provide a more legally defensible way of dealing with the issue of 'persuasion'.

Autonomy and liberty: dealing with conflicts

Within a traditional liberal approach, some restrictions on liberty are justifiable on the basis of protecting the interests of others.[184] Margaret Brazier and John Harris argue, 'the interests of others are prejudicially affected by disease to a greater extent than is the case with much of the overt violence which is the everyday business of the criminal law'.[185] As was clear from the discussion above, the protection of the right to refuse treatment for an infectious disease may operate alongside quite substantial restrictions on liberty in other respects. The question which arises is whether coerced treatment should be treated, as the review of the PHA concluded, as inherently different from other forms of coercion and what the broader consequences of this are for individual liberty.[186]

Although the review of the PHA did not attempt to justify its conclusion, there are a number of possible arguments as to why coerced treatment is different to other forms of coercion. First, it might be argued that medical treatment is more invasive. In many cases, this will be the case, not least because medical treatment involves taking something into one's body and because of the force required to impose treatment on a resistant patient. In other cases, however, the non-treatment alternative may be equally, if not more, invasive. For many people, being locked up or restricted in movement, or even being required to remove their clothing and be 'disinfected or decontaminated' may be more invasive than taking medication. Secondly, a consequentialist argument might be made that people would be less likely to seek medical help if they feared the imposition of treatment. This is a real concern but it arises with equal force in respect of any forcible intervention. The prospect of restrictions on movement is not any more likely to make someone seek medical help than the prospect of being forced to take medication. Thirdly, there is a practical argument that coerced medication requires ongoing monitoring and is difficult to enforce. Again, this has force. Yet, as discussed in Chapter 6, this did not trouble the legislature in England and Wales when introducing 'supervised community treatment' for people with mental disorders.

---

[184] See Mill's statement of the harm principle, *On Liberty*, p. 14.

[185] M. Brazier and J. Harris, 'Public Health and Private Lives' (1996) 4 *Medical Law Review* 171, 177.

[186] The issues here are complex and have received relatively little consideration within ethical discourse: see M. Selgelid, 'Ethics and Infectious Disease' (2005) 19 *Bioethics* 272.

Furthermore, restrictions on movement or contact are not necessarily any easier to monitor than taking medication. On the basis of these arguments, coercion in respect of treatment would not seem, in principle, to be greatly different from other forms of coercion. The significant issue is the invasiveness of the intervention and not whether this is couched in terms of 'treatment' or otherwise.

A consequence of the decision to regard the right to refuse treatment as unassailable while permitting an individual's autonomy to be over-ridden in other respects is the creation of a potential conflict between the right to refuse treatment and broader autonomy and liberty rights of the individual. The effect of this conflict may be seen in the decision of the High Court of Ireland in *S* v. *Health Service Executive*.[187] The woman at the centre of this case had a highly infectious, antibiotic-resistant form of tuberculosis. She had been detained for over 11 months in a negatively pressurised room in a hospital, which was guarded at all times by a security guard. As with the PHA, the relevant Irish legislation permits detention but not involuntary treatment.[188] The woman had refused treatment for her condition and it was accepted that 'the reality of the position is that the patient is going to die [in hospital] unless she consents to treatment'.[189] Although the woman was initially regarded as having decision-making capacity, during the period of her detention her mental health deteriorated and, following the hearing, the matter of her capacity was referred to the President of the High Court for further investigation.

This was an unusual case, not least because the underlying legislation is procedurally inadequate to an extraordinary degree.[190] Nonetheless, the essential conflict between respect for autonomy in the context of treatment and respect for liberty in a broader sense can arise even within a more modern and rights-based legislative framework. In essence, the question (which, as will be seen in Chapter 6, also arises in respect of treatment for a mental disorder) is whether coerced treatment can ever be justified in order to allow a person to regain her liberty. In other words, can a breach of autonomy in a narrow sense be justified on the basis of

---

[187] [2009] IEHC 106.   [188] Health Act 1947, s. 38.

[189] [2009] IEHC 106, p. 39 of transcript.

[190] The Health Act 1947, s. 38 contains no mechanism for legal review prior to detention and no mechanism for automatic review of detention (although it does permit the detained person to petition the Minister for Health). Surprisingly, the Act was upheld as constitutional (the question of ECHR compliance not being considered). For a critique of the decision, see M. Donnelly, 'Public Health and Patient Rights: S v. HSE' (2009) 15 *Medico-Legal Journal of Ireland* 66.

protecting autonomy in a broader one? The classic liberal answer to this question is straightforward. If a sufficient case for risk-based detention is made,[191] then the person should be detained in order to protect the interests of others but her right to refuse treatment should not be overridden. In essence, she has a choice; she can accept the treatment and be released or refuse the treatment and accept the consequences of detention.

There are two difficulties with this argument. First, it fails to recognise the coercive context in which a person acts where she agrees to accept the treatment in order to avoid detention or other restrictions on liberty. As Raz argues, a 'person may force another by changing the circumstances surrounding that other person's choice'.[192] Such a person 'subjects the will of another to his own and thereby invades that person's autonomy'.[193] The subsequent decision cannot be described as autonomous. Secondly, this argument fails to take account of the possible impact of detention on agency and decision-making capacity. Eventually, as happened in *S* v. *HSE*, a detained person may reach the point of losing capacity and treatment will be imposed on her because it is in her best interests, leaving her (theoretical) right of autonomy intact. In these circumstances, it is difficult to see how a person's autonomy can be said to be protected in any real sense.

The thinness of the liberal view of autonomy as non-interference is apparent in this kind of situation. The difficult issues arising can only be dealt with through measures which have no place within the traditional liberal view. In particular, issues of communication and persuasion arise, as do issues of advocacy, procedural fairness and representation. It would seem that, in *S* v. *Health Service Executive*, for example, the relationship of trust between the woman and the healthcare providers was virtually non-existent. The background provided in the judgment shows why this came to be the case. Edwards J noted that 'nobody seems to [have been] in charge of the non-medical facets of the case'.[194] He also noted the lack of information provided to the woman and the 'box-ticking' approach taken to informing the woman of her legal rights.[195] Thus, long before the question of coercion arises, it is essential in cases such as this that mechanisms are developed to deliver on autonomy as a positive right and not simply as a right of non-interference. As will become clear in the discussion below,

---

[191] This leaves aside the important question of how risk is assessed and the relationship between risk and rights: see T. Murphy and N. Whitty, 'Is Human Rights Prepared?: Risk, Rights and Public Health Emergencies' (2009) 17 *Medical Law Review* 219, 232–44.

[192] Raz, *The Morality of Freedom*, p. 154.   [193] *Ibid.*

[194] [2009] IEHC 106, p. 72 of transcript.   [195] *Ibid.*, p. 71 of transcript.

the law has some distance to travel in this direction. However, arguably, the first tentative steps are being taken.

Autonomy and positive obligations

In the decision of the Court of Appeal in *R (Burke)* v. *General Medical Council*, Lord Phillips MR noted that:

> [T]he right to refuse treatment gives the patient what appears to be a positive option to choose an alternative. In truth the right to choose is no more than a reflection of the fact that it is the doctor's duty to provide a treatment that he considers to be in the interests of the patient and that the patient is prepared to accept.[196]

It was argued in the previous chapter that this represents an overly limited conception of autonomy and that a more appropriate view of autonomy requires more than a simple take-it-or-leave approach centred on treatment refusal. For the latter conception to have any application in the law, autonomy will have to be regarded as a claim-right, to use the Hohfeldian term,[197] imposing positive obligations either on the State or on healthcare professionals to facilitate the exercise of autonomous choice. As will be seen below, there is a small, but arguably growing, body of jurisprudence which expands the scope of the legal right of autonomy beyond a principle of non-interference and which provides a basis for further development of autonomy as a positive right. The discussion below will begin by looking at ECtHR jurisprudence in this respect and will then consider duties imposed by the law of tort in respect of the provision of information, which is an essential attribute of a positive right of autonomy.

Autonomy as a positive right in the European Court of Human Rights

Although, as David Feldman notes, most of the rights protected by the ECHR are negative, non-interference rights,[198] a growing feature of the jurisprudence of the ECtHR has been the recognition of positive rights,

---

[196] [2005] EWCA (Civ) 1003, [51].

[197] A 'claim-right' is a right which avails against a person or group of persons, creating a duty or obligation in them: see W. N. Hohfeld 'Some Fundamental Legal Conceptions as Applied in Judicial Reasoning' (1913) 23 *Yale Law Journal* 16, 32.

[198] D. Feldman, *Civil Liberties and Human Rights in England and Wales* (2nd edn) (Oxford University Press, 2002), p. 53.

which place obligations on the State to take positive actions to protect individuals. In *X and Y* v. *The Netherlands*,[199] the ECtHR found that the effective protection of a person's private life under Article 8 could entail the imposition of positive obligations on the State.[200] As noted above, in *Pretty* v. *United Kingdom*,[201] the ECtHR recognised a basis in Article 8 for the protection of autonomy.[202] The applicant in *Pretty* formulated her arguments in favour of a right to assisted suicide as implicating both positive and negative rights.[203] However, the formulation of autonomy which she relied upon was autonomy in the classic sense of non-interference; in this instance, she sought the removal of the criminal law sanction which prevented her husband providing assistance to her in ending her life. Although the ECtHR was 'not prepared to exclude that this constitutes an interference with [the applicant's] right to respect for private life' as protected by Article 8,[204] it found that a restriction on assisted suicide could be justified under Article 8 (2) as interference 'necessary in a democratic society'.[205] Shortly afterwards, in *Goodwin* v. *United Kingdom*,[206] the ECtHR conceptualised the right of autonomy as established in *Pretty* as a right of protection for 'the personal sphere of each individual'.[207] In *Goodwin*, this right was regarded as justifying the imposition of a positive requirement on states to provide an appropriate means of recognising the changed legal status of post-operative transsexuals.[208]

The positive obligations arising from the right of autonomy were considered in a healthcare context in *Tysiac* v. *Poland*.[209] The applicant in this case successfully argued that the absence of a comprehensive framework to protect her right to a lawful abortion constituted a breach of her rights under Article 8. The ECtHR held that '[w]hile the State regulations on abortion relate to the traditional balancing of privacy and the public interest, they must – in the case of a therapeutic abortion – be also assessed against the positive obligations of the State to secure the physical integrity of mothers-to-be'.[210] The ECtHR elaborated on the nature of the positive obligations

---

[199] (1986) 8 EHRR 235.

[200] For discussion of positive obligations under Art. 8 (until 2004), see A. Mowbray *The Development of Positive Obligations under the European Convention on Human Rights* (Oxford: Hart Publishing, 2004), pp. 127–88.

[201] (2002) 35 EHRR 1.   [202] *Ibid.*, para. 61.

[203] The applicant argued that Arts. 2 and 3 of the ECHR imposed positive obligations on the State to permit her to choose to end her life.

[204] (2002) 35 EHRR 1, para. 67.   [205] *Ibid.*, para. 78.   [206] (2002) 35 EHRR 447.

[207] *Ibid.*, para. 90.   [208] *Ibid.*, para. 93.   [209] (2007) 45 EHRR 42.

[210] *Ibid.*, para. 107. Abortion is permitted under Polish law up until 12 weeks into the pregnancy if there is a threat to the life or health of the woman, as certified by a medical

owed which, it stated, may include 'the adoption of measures designed to secure respect for private life ... including both the provision of a regulatory framework of adjudicatory and enforcement machinery protecting individuals, rights and the implementation, where appropriate, of specific measures'.[211] As with negative rights, the ECtHR found that a fair balance had to be struck between the competing interests of the individual and those of the community as a whole.[212] The ECtHR emphasised the significance of process in delivering rights that are 'practical and effective' and found that, while Article 8 contains no explicit procedural requirements, it is important for the effective enjoyment of the rights guaranteed by the Article that 'the relevant decision-making process is fair and such as to afford due respect to the interests safeguarded by it'.[213] In the case in question, the ECtHR noted that there was no procedural framework under which a woman who disagreed with medical opinion regarding the risk of continuing her pregnancy could assert her rights.[214] It also noted that any remedial measures available to the applicant were of a retroactive and compensatory character and found that these did not afford the applicant a mechanism to vindicate her right to respect for her private life in advance.[215]

In recognising that 'States cannot fulfil their duties under the Convention by simply remaining passive,'[216] the ECtHR approach to autonomy moves legal understandings of the principle beyond simple non-interference. It also shows that the imposition of positive obligations in respect of autonomy does not mean that, to quote Brazier, '[w]hat I want should be delivered'[217] but that a fair balance must be struck between individual rights and societal interests. The question of what constitutes a fair balance in such circumstances is not, and cannot be, easily resolved.[218] Nonetheless, by recognising the possibility of positive obligations, the jurisprudence of the ECtHR presents a better foundation for the law in respect of autonomy than the traditional legal approach to autonomy as simply a matter of non-interference.

---

professional. The applicant argued that her request for an abortion due to the risk posed to her eyesight was rejected following a brief and unsatisfactory meeting with an ophthalmologist and that there was no appropriate mechanism for appeal or review of this decision.

[211] *Ibid.*, para. 110.   [212] *Ibid.*, para. 111.   [213] *Ibid.*, para. 113.   [214] *Ibid.*, para. 121.

[215] *Ibid.*, para. 125.

[216] A. Mowbray 'The Creativity of the European Court of Human Rights' (2005) 5 *Human Rights Law Review* 57, 78

[217] Brazier, 'Do No Harm,' 400.

[218] See Mowbray, 'The Creativity of the European Court of Human Rights', 78 on the different responses of the ECtHR to the balancing required in individual cases.

Information and communication: obligations in the law of tort

A second mechanism by which positive obligations in respect of autonomy might be delivered is through the law of tort. As will be seen, the most feasible role for the law of tort in this regard is through the imposition of positive duties to provide information and to facilitate communication. Adequate information is essential for the exercise of the right of autonomy as is effective communication between the healthcare provider and the patient. The context for the imposition of obligations through the law of tort is quite different from ECHR-based obligations. First, the ECtHR jurisprudence discussed above was concerned with the obligations of the State or of a public authority. The scope of tort-based obligations is broader, arising in any situation in which a duty of care applies. Secondly, in tort, whether or not an obligation arises will depend on the imposition of liability for negligence, most usually on an individual healthcare professional. Thus, an obligation is recognised only in the context of a professional's failure to meet it. For reasons discussed further below, this makes the law of tort far from ideal as a mechanism for developing conceptions of a positive right of autonomy. Before considering the difficulties, however, it is necessary to look at how the law of tort has dealt with two related but distinct concepts. The first is information provision and the second is the broader concept of communication which, as will be seen below, differs from information provision in a number of key respects. As will become clear, the law's focus on the first matter has obscured the need for legal discussion in respect of the second.

Information provision

It is by now well established that failure to provide certain information in advance of obtaining consent to medical treatment creates liability in the law of tort. In the United States, the duty to disclose information had its origins in the patient's right of autonomy. Thus, in *Canterbury* v. *Spence*, Robinson J found that '[t]rue consent to what happens to one's self is the informed exercise of a choice, and that entails an opportunity to evaluate knowledgeably the options available and the risks attendant upon each'.[219] In England and Wales, the origins of the duty to disclose may be found in the professional duties owed by a medical professional to a patient rather

---

[219] (1972) 464 F 2d 772, 780.

than in the facilitation of patient rights.[220] Regardless of the origins of the legal position, courts in both jurisdictions (and indeed across the common law world) have found that the failure to provide information in advance of treatment provides a basis for an action in negligence rather than battery.[221] However, the difference in origin led to the adoption of differing standards of care, with courts in the United States,[222] as well as in Canada[223] and Australia,[224] basing the relevant standard on what the reasonable patient would want to know and those in England and Wales basing the standard on what the reasonable professional would consider appropriate to disclose.[225] While the reasonable patient standard is more closely associated with respect for autonomy, the distinction between the two standards has become increasingly blurred.[226] Thus, in *Wyatt* v. *Curtis*, Sedley LJ noted that, 'what is substantial and what is grave are questions on which the doctor's and the patient's perception may differ, and in relation to which the doctor must therefore have regard to what may be the patient's perception'.[227]

More significant, perhaps, has been the approach to autonomy taken by the House of Lords in *Chester* v. *Afshar*.[228] In this case, the majority was prepared to override the requirement that a plaintiff must establish that, but for the failure of the defendant to provide a warning in respect of surgery, she would not have undergone the surgery.[229] Instead, the majority

---

[220] See A. Maclean, 'The Doctrine of Informed Consent: Does it Exist and Has it Crossed the Atlantic?' (2004) 24 *Legal Studies* 386, 404–6.

[221] See *Canterbury* v. *Spence* (1972) 464 F 2d 772 (US); *Chatterton* v. *Gerson* [1981] QB 432 (EW).

[222] *Canterbury* v. *Spence* (1972) 464 F 2d 772.   [223] *Reibl* v. *Hughes* (1980) 114 DLR 3d 1.

[224] *Rogers* v. *Whittaker* (1992) 109 ALR 625.

[225] *Sidaway* v. *Governors of Bethlem Royal Hospital* [1985] AC 871. The Irish courts also leaned in the direction of the reasonable professional standard: see *Walsh* v. *Family Planning Services* [1992] 1 IR 496; *Bolton* v. *Blackrock Clinic* unreported Supreme Court, 23 January 1997. However, in *Fitzpatrick* v. *White* [2007] IESC 51, the Supreme Court clearly endorsed a reasonable patient standard.

[226] The blurring, insofar as it has happened, is attributable primarily to the application of the decision of the House of Lords in *Bolitho* v. *City and Hackney Health Authority* [1998] AC 232 in the context of the duty to disclose in *Pearce* v. *United Bristol Healthcare Trust* [1998] EWCA (Civ) 865.

[227] [2003] EWCA Civ 1779, [16].

[228] [2004] UKHL 41. See S. Devaney, 'Autonomy Rules OK' (2005) 13 *Medical Law Review* 102. For a less enthusiastic response, see K. Mason and D. Brodie, 'Bolam, Bolam – Wherefore art thou *Bolam*?' (2005) 9 *Edinburgh Law Review* 398.

[229] The difficulties posed by the causation requirement are well documented: see G. Robertson, 'Informed Consent Ten Years Later: The Impact of *Reibl* v. *Hughes*' (1991) 70 *Canadian Bar Review* 423; M. Jones, 'Informed Consent and Other Fairy Stories' (1999) 7 *Medical Law Review* 103, 121–3.

held for the plaintiff on the basis that, had she known about the risk in question, she would not have gone ahead with the surgery at the time she did.[230] The speeches of the majority are striking in the number of times they refer to autonomy. Having quoted from Ronald Dworkin's well-known elucidation of the basis for the right of autonomy,[231] Lord Steyn justified the departure from established principle on the basis of the vindication of the plaintiff's 'right of autonomy and dignity'.[232] In a similar vein, Lord Hope started with the proposition that 'the law which imposed the duty to warn on the doctor has at its heart the right of the patient to make an informed choice as to whether, and if so when and by whom, to be operated on'.[233] Although *Chester* was not directly concerned with the nature of the legal duty to disclose information, such was the move towards autonomy-derived rhetoric that, in its wake, Mason and Laurie concluded that, 'the question is no longer "is the doctrine of informed consent coming to the United Kingdom?" but, rather, "what can we do to improve on the American model?"'[234] Thus, on both sides of the Atlantic, it may now be said that there is a positive obligation derived from respect for autonomy that certain information must be given to patients in advance of treatment.

While the existence of an autonomy-derived obligation to disclose information would seem to be established, the extent of the information which must be disclosed remains unclear. As is well known, regardless of the applicable standard, the vast bulk of the case law in respect of the duty to disclose has related to the disclosure of risks involved in a procedure. However, there has been some expansion of the category of relevant information. In *Birch* v. *University College London Hospital NHS Trust*, Cranston J found a duty to disclose alternatives to the proposed treatments

---

[230] Lord Steyn [2004] UKHL 41, [24] described this as a 'narrow and modest departure from traditional causation principles' while Lord Bingham, [9] (dissenting) described it as 'a substantial and unjustified departure from sound and established principle'. For a defence of the majority position, see J. Stapleton, 'Occam's Razor Reveals an Orthodox Basis for *Chester* v. *Afshar*' (2006) 122 *Law Quarterly Review* 426.

[231] *Ibid.*, [18] quoting R. Dworkin, *Life's Dominion: An Argument About Abortion, Euthanasia, and Individual Freedom* (New York: Alfred A Knopf, 1993), p. 224. The full quote may be found in Chapter 1, p. 20.

[232] *Ibid.*, [24].

[233] *Ibid.*, [86]. The dissenting judges, Lords Bingham and Hoffman, did not comment on autonomy but based their dissent on the appropriate application of causation principles.

[234] K. Mason and G. Laurie, *Mason and McCall Smith's Law and Medical Ethics* (7th edn) (Oxford University Press, 2006), p. 410. See Maclean's more tentative conclusions in *Autonomy, Informed Consent and Medical Law*, p. 176.

and to provide information in respect of the comparative risks arising.[235] There would also seem to be support for a duty to disclose information about the consequences of treatment refusal.[236]

Lord Hope's *obiter* statement in *Chester* that a patient has a right to be informed 'as to whether, and if so when and by whom, to be operated on'[237] lends some support to a duty to disclose the identity of the person who will perform the surgery.[238] As Brazier and Cave note, in practice within the NHS system, consent forms expressly state that no assurance is given that any particular doctor will operate.[239] However, it is unclear whether the simple fact of the inclusion of such a provision in a form without any verbal reference would be considered a sufficient defence to an action if Lord Hope's comments are accepted by a later court. Lord Hope's comments might also provide indirect support for an argument that doctors have a duty to disclose information in respect of their own professional competence or any unusual features or attributes they might have which may be relevant to the patient's decision to consent. Such obligations have been recognised in some jurisdictions in the United States.[240] However, there is, as yet, little support for these kinds of disclosure obligations in England and Wales.[241]

The disclosure of other kinds of information has tended to remain outside the ambit of the legal duty, even in the context of broader disclosure obligations which have been imposed by courts in the United States. In *Arato v. Avedon*,[242] the applicant argued that the defendant had a legal

---

[235] [2008] EWHC 2237 (QB), [77]. See R. Heywood, 'Medical Disclosure of Alternative Treatments' (2009) 68 *Cambridge Law Journal* 30. For similar findings, see the Canadian case of *Haughian* v. *Paine* (1987) 37 DLR (4th) 624 (Sask CA) and the Californian case of *Cobbs* v. *Grant* (1972) 8 Cal 2d 229.

[236] See *Re T (Adult: Refusal of Medical Treatment)* [1992] 3 WLR 782, 798; see also the Californian case of *Truman* v. *Thomas* (1980) 611 P 2d 902.

[237] [2004] UKHL 41, [86].

[238] This would be in line with decision of the New Jersey Supreme Court in *Perna* v. *Pirozzi* (1983) 92 NJ 446. Contrast the view of the Supreme Court of Ireland in *Walsh* v. *Family Planning Services* [1992] 1 IR 496.

[239] M. Brazier and E. Cave, *Medicine, Patients and the Law* (4th edn.) (London: Penguin, 2007), p. 119.

[240] *Faya and Rossi* v. *Almaraz* (1993) 620 A 2d 327. The Maryland Court of Appeals found that a doctor's failure to inform patients of his human immunodeficiency virus status before performing surgery on them constituted a battery (even though the risk of transmission of the virus from surgeon to patient was very low).

[241] There has been no support for fiduciary-based disclosure in such circumstances: see *Sidaway* v. *Governors of Bethlem Royal Hospital* [1985] AC 871, 884; *R* v. *Mid-Glamorgan FHSA ex parte Martin* (1993) 16 BMLR 81 (HC).

[242] (1993) 858 P 2d 598.

obligation to let her deceased husband know his limited prospects of recovery, arguing that, had he known this, he would not have undergone the rigours of an unproven therapy but would have chosen to get his business affairs in order.[243] The Supreme Court of California Court rejected the finding of the Californian Court of Appeal that 'a physician is under a duty to disclose information material to the patient's *nonmedical* interests'.[244] Yet, as George Annas points out, patients need to know this information 'not only because it is the patient's body, but, more important, because it is the patient's life'.[245]

In summary, it would seem that the law is gradually, though not inexorably, moving in the direction of positive autonomy-derived obligations to provide a more comprehensive range of information to patients in making treatment decisions. As was argued in the previous chapter, however, the goal of developing individual agency requires much more than simply the provision of information. The next section will consider the legal treatment of the broader issue of communication within the context of delivering on this goal.

Communication

Neil Manson and Onora O' Neill argue that much of current thinking about informed consent 'rests upon a *distorted* conception of the nature and significance of information and communication'.[246] This approach sees information as something which is stored, contained or possessed and which is then transmitted, passed on or disclosed.[247] They argue that this 'radically downplay[s] the importance of the rich set of background commitments and competencies that are essentially involved in the activity of communication'[248] and fails to recognise that the recipients of information are agents 'with complex sets of practical and cognitive commitments by which they shape their response to others' communications'.[249] They argue that, in contrast to this approach, effective communication recognises the significance of context, of shared background knowledge, of awareness of the inferences which the other party may draw, and of knowledge of each other's commitments and competences.[250]

---

[243] *Ibid.*, 601–2. The deceased had failed to do this which had led to a failed business and to substantial real estate and tax losses after his death.

[244] *Ibid.*, 599, original emphasis.

[245] G. Annas, *Some Choice: Law, Medicine and the Market* (New York: Oxford University Press, 1998), p. 60.

[246] Manson and O'Neill, *Rethinking Informed Consent*, p. 26, original emphasis.

[247] *Ibid.*, pp. 36–7.   [248] *Ibid.*, p. 39.   [249] *Ibid.*, p. 47.   [250] *Ibid.*, pp. 56–7.

There are strong indications from empirical data that communication in the sense described by Manson and O'Neill is lacking to a significant degree in healthcare decision-making. In study after study, patients have indicated that they do not understand the consent form they are signing and that they quickly forget even the most basic information relating to the procedures consented to.[251] As summarised by Michael Jones, '[w]hatever the reason, many doctors are not good at communicating with patients and there are numerous studies in medical journals which demonstrate that in reality many if not most patients remain completely uninformed'.[252]

Although the law has, for the most part, not been concerned with the issue of communication, there have been some recent moves to recognise that the professional's duty does not end with simple disclosure without reference to the manner in which the disclosure is made.[253] Thus, in *Deriche* v. *Ealing Hospital NHS Trust*,[254] Buckley J accepted expert evidence that the defendant should have ensured that the claimant 'had fully understood the nature of the risk' (for her unborn child in respect of her infection with chickenpox) by illustrating the possible harm and the severity of this by reference to some of the four known problems which might arise.[255] Additionally, Buckley J seemed to consider that it was not enough to rely on another doctor's notes but that it was necessary to investigate the extent of the patient's understanding.[256] The Supreme Court of

---

[251] See, for example, J. Bergler *et al.*, 'Informed Consent: How Much Does the Patient Understand?' (1980) 27 *Clinical Pharmacology and Therapeutics* 435; B. R. Cassileth *et al.*, 'Informed Consent – Why are its Goals Imperfectly Realized?' (1980) 302 *New England Journal of Medicine* 896. See also the studies cited in M. Jones, 'Informed Consent and Other Fairy Stories', 125–7, and M. Donnelly, *Consent: Bridging the Gap Between Doctor and Patient* (Cork University Press, 2002), pp. 32–3.

[252] M. Jones, 'Informed Consent and Other Fairy Stories,' 130.

[253] See Maclean, *Autonomy, Informed Consent and Medical Law*, p. 177. Note also the rather oblique reference to a need for the patient to be made to 'appreciate fully what was in store for him' in the decision of the Supreme Court of Ireland in *Walsh* v. *Family Planning Services* [1992] 1 IR 496, 534–5.

[254] [2003] EWHC 3104 (QB).

[255] *Ibid.*, [34]. Note, however, that the plaintiff was not successful in her action because she did not convince the Court that she would have acted differently if she had been aware of the risk.

[256] See Maclean, *Autonomy, Informed Consent and Medical Law*, p. 178. Contrast, however, the decision in *Al Hamwi* v. *Johnston and Another* [2005] EWHC 206 where Simon J rejected the argument that there was a positive obligation to ensure that a patient understood information: see Maclean, *ibid.*, pp. 179–80; J. Miola, 'Autonomy Rued OK' (2006) 14 *Medical Law Review* 108.

Ireland has recognised the significance of the timing of the disclosure of information.[257] The Court considered that

> There are obvious reasons why, in the context of elective surgery, a warning given only shortly before an operation is undesirable. A patient may be stressed, medicated or in pain in this period and may be less likely for one or more of these reasons to make a calm and reasoned decision in such circumstances.[258]

These cases may suggest the beginnings of a broader duty to communicate but it is still a long way from a legal requirement for the kind of nuanced and complex communication that Manson and O'Neill describe as being necessary. This is not surprising. As will be discussed below, there are structural reasons why reliance on the law of tort to deliver on positive obligations in respect of autonomy is unlikely to lead to a significant shift in this direction.

Positive obligations in the law of tort: the problems

The preceding discussion shows that the law of tort has, to a degree, imposed positive duties that help deliver on a positive right of autonomy. For a number of reasons, however, the imposition of duties through the law of tort is not an effective way of developing the law in this area. First, actions in tort are inherently self-starting; they require an individual to initiate proceedings. This is something which patients who are most in need of mechanisms for empowerment may find most difficult to do. This also means that the law develops in a piecemeal fashion with inevitable gaps and without any kind of systematic normative overview.[259] Secondly, actions in tort are inevitably confrontational; the patient's right is established only at a cost both financially (albeit usually indemnified by insurers) and in terms of the reputation of the defendant. As Mason and Laurie point out, in such circumstances, '[i]t is not only justice to the patient that is at stake'.[260] Thirdly, as Maclean notes, the law of tort is limited in the flexibility of its remedies. The courts have no power to require practices to change and no remedies beyond an award of damages.[261] Fourthly, when

---

[257] *Fitzpatrick* v. *White* [2008] 3 IR 551.
[258] *Ibid.*, 565. In the circumstances of the case in question, however, the Court found that there was no evidence that the plaintiff had been stressed, anxious, sedated or in pain and accordingly, the timing of the warning was not considered to a breach of the duty of care.
[259] See M. Jones, 'Informed Consent and Other Fairy Stories,' 106; Maclean, *Autonomy, Informed Consent and Medical Law*, p. 214.
[260] Mason and Laurie, *Mason and McCall-Smith*, p. 410.
[261] Maclean, *Autonomy, Informed Consent and Medical Law*, p. 214.

one moves from hard facts, such as whether specified information was given, into the murkier waters of assessing the effectiveness of communication, the evidentiary difficulties faced by both claimants and defendants are considerable. Fifthly, legal actions in tort are often less effective at changing underlying patterns of behaviour than at developing ways of showing compliance with legal rules.[262] Sixthly, tort law itself is subject to broader shifts in policy. Maclean points out previous oscillations in the law of negligence from pro-plaintiff to pro-defendant and notes the possibility of a similar swing in the wake of *Chester* and in light of concerns regarding growth of a 'compensation culture'.[263]

There have been several suggestions regarding alternative ways of dealing with these kinds of issues. One is that the relationship between doctor and patient should be recognised as fiduciary in nature with attendant obligations.[264] Peter Bartlett situates his argument in this respect in the context of the move of medicine from a public service mentality (which, of course, characterised the system in the United Kingdom to a much greater extent than in many other jurisdictions) into the world of markets and competition.[265] He argues that the issue is not simply one of status as fiduciary but rather it is necessary 'to identify how specific applications of fiduciary law can assist in creating a coherent structure of regulation of the medical profession'.[266] A second possibility, put forward by Mason and Brodie is to allow for an award of damages based on an invasion of autonomy (which they envisage as a lesser award than damages in negligence).[267] A third alternative, advanced by Alasdair Maclean, is the introduction of legislation in respect of consent. Maclean suggests that 'any amount of "tinkering" with the common law will inevitably be inadequate'.[268] He argues that the introduction of legislation, combined with a code of practice and the appointment of an independent regulator, would enable the law to be 'both proactive and flexible'.[269] Such a measure

---

[262] See the practice of 'consenting' patients (deputising a junior doctor to have the consent form signed) described in *Learning from Bristol: The Report of the Public Inquiry Into Children's Heart Surgery at the Bristol Royal Infirmary 1984–1995* (2001), Cm 5297(1)), p. 295.

[263] Maclean, *Autonomy, Informed Consent and Medical Law*, pp. 215–16.

[264] As argued by M. Brazier, 'Patient Autonomy and Consent to Treatment: The Role of the Law?' (1987) 7 *Legal Studies* 169, 190–1; A. Grubb, 'The Doctor as Fiduciary' (1994) 47 *Current Legal Problems* 311; P. Bartlett, 'Doctors as Fiduciaries: Equitable Regulation of the Doctor-Patient Relationship' (1997) 5 *Medical Law Review* 193.

[265] Bartlett, 'Doctors as Fiduciaries', 223–4.   [266] *Ibid.*

[267] Kenyon and Brodie, '*Bolam, Bolam*', 305–6.

[268] Maclean, *Autonomy, Informed Consent and Medical Law*, p. 217.   [269] *Ibid.*

would also have an important symbolic effect which, Maclean argues, 'would serve to emphasise the relative value the community places in autonomy, self-determination and health'.[270]

Of these three alternatives, perhaps the most feasible in the immediate term is the development of a stand-alone action in respect of a breach of autonomy (which might run alongside an action in negligence in some cases). In this respect, the action for a breach of ECHR rights under section 8 of the HRA may offer a possible avenue for future development, in respect of actions by public authorities at any rate.[271] This allows for a remedy, including an award of damages, in respect of any act (or proposed act) of a public authority which a court finds is (or would be) unlawful.[272] However, while this alternative may provide a broader scope for engagement with autonomy than tort actions, it is still open to the criticism that it requires individuals to initiate the action and accordingly results in piecemeal legal development.

Conclusion

Although the view of autonomy as non-interference is well entrenched in the law, it has been relatively little analysed at the level of principle. This results in a legal framework which offers little beyond a right to refuse treatment. It has been argued in this chapter that the courts' failure to provide a close analysis of the right to refuse treatment and to engage with the question of limits on the right results in an impoverished understanding of the right. A more rigorous treatment of the question of limits would point to the need for a deeper understanding of autonomy and the interrogation of the legal framework from a perspective of patient empowerment rather than simply non-interference.

This chapter showed that there are some moves, emanating from the ECtHR and, to a lesser extent, from the law of tort, to recognise positive obligations in respect of autonomy. However, while worthwhile in themselves, these developments are unlikely to deliver dramatic enhancement

---

[270] *Ibid.*

[271] It is generally accepted that healthcare professionals, including general practitioners in private practice, are 'public authorities' in respect of NHS functions: see House of Lords House of Commons Joint Committee on Human Rights, *The Meaning of Public Authority under the Human Rights Act* HL Paper 39; HC 382.

[272] HRA, s. 8(1). In order for an award of damages to be made, the court must be satisfied that the award is necessary to afford just satisfaction to the person involved taking account of all the circumstances, including any other relief or remedy granted: HRA, s. 8(3).

of patient autonomy. Once one attempts to move beyond a simple principle of non-interference, the possibilities for what can be achieved through the law will always be restricted. This does not diminish the importance of the legal contribution nor the need to think about ways in which positive obligations might develop. However, it does serve as a valuable reminder that the law is just a part of the development of an appropriate framework for healthcare decision-making.

Finally, this chapter has argued that, even within the limited view of autonomy as non-interference, the legal reality has been rather different from that which the rhetoric of autonomy would suggest. As will be seen in the next chapter, most patients are not permitted to make decisions that appear contrary to their best interests or indeed to the interests of others or of society. Instead, these issues have been dealt with through the operation of the capacity requirement, which serves as a gatekeeper for the right of autonomy.

3

Capacity: the gatekeeper for autonomy

The previous chapter showed that, while the law may reject 'hard' pater-nalism, 'soft' paternalism (intervention on the basis of incapacity) remains a fundamental component of the law's approach to healthcare decision-making.[1] As several commentators have pointed out, the operation of the capacity requirement may conceal 'hard' paternalism or favour societal interests over those of the individual in a way which may, in fact, be more damaging to a person's autonomy in practice that an overt recognition of limits on the right.[2] Accordingly, an understanding of capacity is essen-tial in order to appreciate what the principle of autonomy means at a con-ceptual level and how it operates in individual cases.

In adopting any principles in respect of capacity, the law makes norma-tive choices.[3] In the words of the United States President's Commission:

> [A] conclusion about a patient's decisionmaking capacity necessarily reflects a balancing of two important, sometimes competing object-ives: to enhance the patient's well-being and to respect the person as a self-determining individual.[4]

---

[1] For the distinction between 'soft' and 'hard' paternalism, see J. Feinberg, 'Legal Paternalism' (1977) 1 *Canadian Journal of Philosophy* 106.

[2] See J. Harrington, 'Privileging the Medical Norm: Liberalism, Self-Determination and Refusal of Treatment' (1996) 16 *Legal Studies* 348, 358–62; M. Brazier, 'Hard Cases Make Bad Law' (1997) 23 *Journal of Medical Ethics* 341, 343; R. Scott, *Rights, Duties and the Body: Law and Ethics of the Maternal-Fetal Conflict* (Oxford: Hart Publishing, 2002), pp. 161–2; see also Law Commission, *Report on Mental Incapacity* Report No. 231 (London: HMSO, 1995), pp. 39–40.

[3] See A. Buchanan and D. Brock, *Deciding for Others: The Ethics of Surrogate Decision Making* (New York: Cambridge University Press, 1989), p. 47; L. Kopelman, 'On the Evaluative Nature of Competency and Capacity Judgments' (1990) 13 *International Journal of Law and Psychiatry* 309; M. Gunn, 'The Meaning of Incapacity' (1994) 2 *Medical Law Review* 8, 14.

[4] President's Commission for the Study of Ethical Problems in Medicine and Biomedical and Behavioural Research, *Making Health Care Decisions: A Report on the Ethical and Legal Implications of Informed Consent in the Patient-Practitioner Relationship* (Washington DC: US Superintendent of Documents, 1982), p. 57.

This chapter examines the normative choices which have been made by the law in respect of capacity. It outlines the features of the current legal standard for capacity in England and Wales as set out in the Mental Capacity Act 2005 (MCA) and evaluates these in terms of consistency with the liberal principle of autonomy, which is recognised as providing the basis for the law in respect of healthcare decision-making. The discussion here is concerned with questions of principle, leaving a more detailed discussion of how the law actually operates in practice to Chapter 4. The evaluation shows that, at a level of principle, the law's approach to capacity is, for the most part, consistent with its endorsement of individual autonomy. The chapter then identifies several limitations in this approach to capacity and argues that, because of these limitations, capacity is a less effective gatekeeper for the right of autonomy than is presumed by the law. However, the chapter also concludes that capacity is still a better gatekeeper than alternative concepts such as vulnerability or lack of insight.

Capacity in the law: the normative choices made

Although a capacity requirement in one form or another is core to the liberal view of autonomy, liberal theorists have dedicated relatively little attention to a consideration of the concept. Theorists offer different views as regards what abilities a person should have in order for a right of autonomy to arise. In *On Liberty*, Mill premised the principle of non-interference on 'all the persons concerned being of full age, and the ordinary amount of understanding'.[5] He expanded on this in his wayfarer example, arguing that, having stopped the wayfarer approaching a dangerous bridge to inform her of the dangers ahead, further intervention is unacceptable unless the wayfarer is 'a child, or delirious, or in some state of excitement or absorption incompatible with the full use of the reflecting faculty'.[6] Ronald Dworkin's account of capacity is premised on the view that the autonomous individual has 'the ability to act out of genuine preference or character or conviction or a sense of self'.[7] For other liberals, a requirement for rationality is more to the fore. John Rawls' account of justice as fairness

---

[5] J. Mills (London, 1859) in Grey, John (ed.) *On Liberty and Other Essays* (Oxford University Press, 1991), p. 84.

[6] *Ibid.*, p. 107.

[7] R. Dworkin, *Life's Dominion: An Argument About Abortion, Euthanasia, and Individual Freedom* (New York: Alfred A Knopf, 1993), p. 225.

is premised on individuals having the capacity to act as 'free and equal rational beings'.[8]

The normative choices made in respect of capacity extend beyond the abilities required. As may be seen below, they concern all aspects of the surrounding framework, including the scope of decisions covered, the use of presumptions and the factors considered relevant to the assessment.

A functional, decision-specific test

The MCA favours a functional, task-specific, approach to capacity.[9] Thus, the relevant question is not whether a person has capacity in a general sense but whether she has the capacity to make a specific decision. This approach seeks to maximise the circumstances in which the right of autonomy is protected. In recommending the adoption of this approach to capacity, the Law Commission noted that any alternative based on an individual's status (for example, the fact that she had been admitted to wardship) would be 'quite out of tune with the policy aim of enabling and encouraging people to take for themselves any decision which they have the capacity to take'.[10]

This approach is also consistent with respect for the rights to privacy, autonomy and bodily integrity protected under Article 8 of the European Convention on Human Rights (ECHR)[11] and respect for the right to fair procedures arising under Article 6.[12] It also accords with Article 12 of the United Nations Convention on the Rights of Persons with Disabilities

---

[8] J. Rawls, *Theory of Justice* (Cambridge, MA: Harvard University Press, 1971), p. 516. See also the role accorded to rationality in J. Harris, *The Value of Life* (London: Routledge and Keegan Paul, 1985), p. 201; D. Beyleveld and R. Brownsword, *Human Dignity in Bioethics and Biolaw* (Oxford University Press, 2002), p. 117.

[9] MCA, s. 2(1). A functional approach had also long been accepted at common law in most instances: see *Banks* v. *Goodfellow* (1870) LR 5 QB 549 (testamentary capacity); *Boughton* v. *Knight* (1873) LR 3 P & D 64 (capacity to contract); *Jenkins* v. *Morris* (1880) 14 Ch D 674 (capacity to execute a lease); *Roe* v. *Nix* [1893] P 55 (functional approach to testamentary capacity adopted notwithstanding admission to wardship); *Re Park's Estate, Park* v. *Park* [1953] 2 All ER 1411 (testamentary capacity and capacity to marry). However, Part VII of the Mental Health Act 1983 and the Enduring Powers of Attorney Act 1985 (both of which were repealed by the MCA) permitted global findings of incapacity to make decisions about property and affairs.

[10] Law Commission, *Report on Mental Incapacity*, p. 33.

[11] See *R* v. *C* [2009] UKHL 42, [27] *per* Baroness Hale.

[12] See *Winterwerp* v. *Netherlands* [1979] 2 EHRR 387; *Shtukaturov* v. *Russia* [2008] ECHR 44009/05; *Masterman-Lister* v. *Brutton & Co* [2002] EWCA Civ 1889, [29] *per* Kennedy LJ; [74] *per* Chadwick LJ. See P. Bartlett *et al.*, *Mental Disability and the European Convention on Human Rights* (Leiden: Martinus Nijhoff, 2007), Chapter 6; M. Keys, 'Legal Capacity

(CRPD), which requires that Member States must ensure that measures relating to the exercise of legal capacity 'are proportional and tailored to the person's circumstances, apply for the shortest time possible and are subject to regular review by a competent, independent and impartial authority or judicial body'.[13] A functional approach is also an aspect of best practice as set out in the Council of Europe Recommendation Concerning the Legal Protection of Incapable Adults.[14] This approach also draws support from empirical studies which show that, in practice, many people who lack capacity in respect of some aspects of their lives are still able to make some decisions for themselves.[15]

A presumption of capacity

The law's endorsement of autonomy requires a presumption in favour of capacity. Such a presumption is long established at common law[16] and is now statutorily endorsed in the MCA.[17] The current law also leaves no scope for a presumption of continuance (i.e. a presumption that once an individual has been found to lack capacity, she continues to do so),[18] which continued to operate under the law of England and Wales until it was rejected by the Court of Appeal in *Masterman-Lister* v. *Brutton & Co.*[19]

Law Reform in Europe: An Urgent Challenge' in G. Quinn and L. Waddington (eds.) *European Yearbook of Disability Law* (Oxford: Hart Publishing, 2009).

[13] Article 12 (3).

[14] *Recommendation No R (99) 4 of the Committee of Members to Member States on Principles Concerning the Legal Protection of Incapable Adults* (adopted 23 February 1999), Principle 3.

[15] See W. Suto *et al*, 'Capacity to Make Financial Decisions among People With Mild Intellectual Disabilities' (2005) 49 *Journal of Intellectual Disability Research* 199. On capacity of patients with mental disorders, see P. Appelbaum and T. Grisso, 'The MacArthur Treatment Competence Study I: Mental Illness and Competence to Consent to Treatment' (1995) 19 *Law and Human Behaviour* 105; J. Bellhouse *et al.*, 'Capacity-Based Mental Health Legislation and its Impact on Clinical Practice: 2) Treatment in Hospital' (2003) *Journal of Mental Health Law* 24; G. Owen *et al.*, 'Mental Capacity to Make Decisions on Treatment in People Admitted to Psychiatric Hospitals: Cross Sectional Study' (2008) 337 *British Medical Journal* 40.

[16] See L. Shelford, *Practical Treatise on the Law Concerning Lunatics, Idiots, and Persons of Unsound Mind* (Philadelphia: J. S. Littell, 1833), p. 23; *Re T (Adult: Refusal of Medical Treatment)* [1992] 3 WLR 782, 796.

[17] MCA, s. 1(2).

[18] For an application of the presumption of continuance, see *Cartwright* v. *Cartwright* (1793) 1 Phillim 100; *White* v. *Driver* (1809) 1 Phillim 84.

[19] [2002] EWCA Civ 1889, [17].

The relevant abilities: understanding,
reasoning and authenticity

The identification of the abilities necessary for capacity is important for both practical and principled reasons.[20] At the level of principle, there must be a connection between the abilities required for capacity and the underlying justifications for respect for autonomy. At a practical level, the greater the range of abilities required, the greater the number of people who will be found to lack capacity. The MacArthur Treatment Competence Study showed that the implications of this are especially significant for patients with mental illnesses.[21] The study tested patients with mental illnesses (schizophrenia and depression) and physical illness (angina) in respect of understanding, reasoning ability and appreciation (which is essentially an ability to reach authentic or consistent decisions). When patients were tested for understanding only, approximately 28 per cent of patients with schizophrenia were found to lack capacity.[22] However, when all three abilities were tested, approximately 50 per cent of patients with schizophrenia were found to lack capacity.[23] This difference in impact was confirmed by the results obtained in respect of patients with depression.[24] For patients with physical illness, the abilities tested had a less obvious impact, although there was an increase in the number of patients found to lack capacity when all three abilities were tested.[25]

---

[20] See the early effort to identify relevant abilities in L. Roth, A. Meisel and C. Lidz, 'Tests of Competency to Consent to Treatment' (1977) 134 *American Journal of Psychiatry* 279, where the effort is described (283) as equivalent to 'a search for the holy grail'.

[21] The study is reported in Appelbaum and Grisso, 'The MacArthur Treatment Competence Study I; T. Grisso *et al*, 'The MacArthur Treatment Competence Study II: Measures of Abilities Related to Competence to Consent to Treatment' (1995) 19 *Law and Human Behaviour* 127; T. Grisso and P. Appelbaum, 'The MacArthur Treatment Competence Study III: Abilities of Patients to Consent to Psychiatric and Medical Treatments' (1995) 19 *Law and Human Behaviour* 149.

[22] See Grisso and Appelbaum, 'The MacArthur Treatment Competence Study III', 149, 168.

[23] *Ibid.*

[24] *Ibid.* If anything, the results were more dramatic in this context – 5.4 per cent of patients with depression were found to lack capacity on the basis of a test for understanding alone, while almost 25 per cent of patients were categorised as lacking capacity when tested across the three categories.

[25] *Ibid.*, 7.3 per cent of patients with physical illness (angina) were found to lack capacity based on the understanding test and 12.2 per cent were found to lack capacity when measured across the three categories.

The common law test for capacity, set out by the Court of Appeal in *Re MB (An Adult: Medical Treatment)*,[26] is largely replicated in the MCA.[27] A person is defined as lacking capacity in relation to a matter 'if at the material time he is unable to make a decision for himself in relation to the matter because of an impairment of, or a disturbance in the functioning of, the mind or brain'.[28] A person is unable to make a decision if she is unable:

(a) to understand the information relevant to the decision,
(b) to retain that information,
(c) to use or weigh that information as part of the process of making the decision, or
(d) to communicate her decision (whether by talking, using sign language or any other means).[29]

Chapter 4 will explore in detail what these broad statements have been found to mean in practice and will show that a number of aspects of the test for capacity come under strain when applied. However, it would seem, at a level of principle, that the abilities required map loosely onto the ability to understand, to reason (in the sense of processing information logically) and to reach decisions free from compulsion or other inhibiting factors. As will be seen below, the normative choices made by the law in identifying these abilities as relevant are consistent with respect for the liberal principle of autonomy.

Capacity as understanding

Although the ability to understand information relating to the decision to be made is almost universally regarded as a minimum requirement for capacity, few commentators regard this ability as sufficient. Michael Jones and Kirsty Keywood present one of the few arguments in favour of a view of capacity based solely on understanding.[30] They contend that this approach is 'more respectful of patient autonomy and more consistent

---

[26] (1997) 2 FCR 541, 553–4.
[27] Note that, as discussed further in Chapter 6, the Mental Health Act 1983 adopts a different standard for capacity to consent to treatment for a mental disorder.
[28] MCA, s. 2(1).   [29] MCA, s. 3(1).
[30] M. Jones and K Keywood, 'Assessing the Patient's Competence to Consent to Medical Treatment' (1996) 2 *Medical Law International* 107. See also C. Culver and B. Gert, 'The Inadequacy of Incompetence' (1990) 68 *The Milbank Quarterly* 619, 620 (although capacity as conceived by these commentators does not play the same gate-keeping role which it plays under the law).

with established legal principles'.[31] For this reason, they argue that the patient 'whether mentally disabled or otherwise, who is able to understand the treatment issues, should be competent to consent [to] or to reject medical treatment'.[32]

The difficulty with a test for capacity based solely on understanding is that it is premised on a limited conception of the way in which people make decisions. It does not attempt to address the factors that may impede a person in applying information to her own situation. Thus, it cannot recognise the effect of compulsion (whether internal, arising from some forms of mental illness, or external, arising from pressures placed on a patient) on an individual's capacity to make decisions. Referring to the specific instance of the anorexic patient, Jones and Keywood argue that such a patient should not be found to lack capacity simply because 'we cannot understand why she chooses not to eat and because we believe her choice to be irrational'.[33] It is true that assessors' failure to understand a decision does not mean that the person who makes the decision lacks capacity. However, the criticism skates over the issue of how compulsive disorders should be dealt with and is directed instead at critiquing the view of capacity as requiring individuals to be able to make rational decisions.

Capacity and rationality

In order to assess the relationship between capacity and rationality, it is necessary to distinguish between two different manifestations of rationality. First, there is the view of rationality as objectively defensible; and, secondly, there is the view of rationality as a logical process of reasoning. The first view of rationality would require individuals whose capacity is questioned to have the ability to make objectively reasonable or 'good' decisions. Such an account is difficult to reconcile with the liberal account of autonomy endorsed by the law. Mill defended the principle of non-interference, not on the basis of the objective defensibility of individuals' decisions, but because, through liberty, individuality can develop.[34] Recourse to 'objective' standards, whether on the basis of objective conceptions of 'the good' or on any other basis, would appear to be inconsistent with the liberal acknowledgement of the individual's 'right to a life structured by his own values'.[35] Feminist commentators have identified

[31] *Ibid.*, 134.   [32] *Ibid.*, 137.   [33] *Ibid.*   [34] Mill, *On Liberty*, p. 70.
[35] R. Dworkin, *Life's Dominion*, p. 239. A similar argument may be made about the Kantian view of rationality as morality as described in O. O' Neill, *Autonomy and Trust in Bioethics* (Cambridge University Press, 2002), p. 85.

another difficulty with a requirement for rationality in this sense, pointing out that 'women have long been portrayed and perceived as irrational, as incapable of objectivity or of engaging in reasoned decisionmaking'.[36]

The second view of rationality is process-focused. On this view, as described by the United States President's Commission, decision-making capacity requires 'the ability to reason and to deliberate about one's choices'.[37] The ability to 'manipulate information rationally' is also fundamental to the influential capacity assessment mechanism, the MacArthur Competence Assessment Tool for Treatment (the MacCAT-T) developed by Thomas Grisso and Paul Appelbaum.[38] The President's Commission and the authors of the MacCAT-T are careful to distinguish an approach that is based on the ability to reason from an approach which decides capacity on the basis of whether the decision made is a rational one. Grisso and Appelbaum note that it is possible to work through an irrational belief in a logical or rational way. It is also possible to process information in a logical and rational way but still reach a conclusion that is eccentric or unpopular.[39] Case law on capacity provides examples of both situations. The American case of *In re Maida Yetter*[40] concerned a woman who refused surgery for breast cancer because she argued that it would interfere with her ability to have children and with her career as a movie actress. This was incorrect because the woman was 60 years old and did not have a career as an actress. However, if the premises upon which she had made her decision had been true, her conclusions might well have followed logically. An example of logical reasoning leading to an unpopular conclusion may be found in *St George's Healthcare NHS Trust* v. *S*,[41] where, notwithstanding the substantial risk posed to fetal life, the patient refused a caesarean section because of her belief in letting nature take its

---

[36] S. Stefan, 'Silencing the Different Voice: Competence, Feminist Theory and Law' (1993) 47 *University of Miami Law Review* 763, 772. See S. Miles and A. August, 'Courts, Gender and the Right to Die' (1990) 18 *Law, Medicine and Healthcare* 85; The depth of the linkage between gender and rationality is explored in G. Lloyd, *The Man of Reason: 'Male' and 'Female' in Western Philosophy* (London: Metheun Publishing, 1984).

[37] President's Commission, *Making Healthcare Decisions*, p. 57. See the similar test suggested by Buchanan and Brock, *Deciding for Others*, p. 23.

[38] The MacCAT-T is described in detail in T. Grisso and P. Appelbaum, *Assessing Competence to Consent: A Guide for Physicians and Other Health Professionals* (New York: Oxford University Press, 1998). The MacCAT-T is discussed in more detail in Chapter 4. See also P. Appelbaum, 'Assessment of Patients' Competence to Consent to Treatment' (2007) 357 *New England Journal of Medicine* 1834.

[39] Grisso and P. Appelbaum, *Assessing Competence*, p. 53.

[40] (1973) 62 Pa D & C 2d 619.   [41] [1998] 3 WLR 936.

course. In both of these examples, the person could be said to have the ability to reason even if the decision made was not rational.[42]

It is, of course, one thing to say that a test based on rationality is about the process employed rather than the conclusion reached but quite another to ensure that a person is not deemed to lack reasoning ability simply because she makes an irrational decision. Nonetheless, leaving aside the practical question of application, a requirement for reasoning ability would seem, at a level of principle, to be consistent with Mill's reference to 'full use of the reflecting faculty' and with Ronald Dworkin's requirement for an 'ability to act out of genuine preference or character or conviction or a sense of self'.[43] It is difficult to see how a person could be said to act out of a sense of self if she cannot make logical deductions regarding the consequences of her decisions.

However, a focus on reasoning ability on its own fails to capture fully the liberal ideal of acting out of a sense of self. One reason for this is that a focus on reasoning fails to take account of the importance of affective (or emotional) factors in the decision-making process. Louis Charland argues that, in traditional work on capacity, emotion has wrongly been regarded as a negative factor which limits a person's ability to make decisions.[44] Charland draws on broader developments in emotion theory, and in particular on the work of Antonio Damasio,[45] to show the positive contribution of emotion to decision-making. Damasio's study investigated the effect of damage to the part of the brain that deals with emotions (the ventromedial region of the frontal lobe) on individuals' cognition, memory and behaviour. The study found that although people who had

---

[42] The applicant in *Re Maida Yetter* (1973) 62 Pa D & C 2d 619 could have run into difficulties in meeting the standard for the ability to understand. However, in the case in question, she was held to have capacity because she had other reasons for refusing the surgery unconnected to her delusions, given that her aunt had died following similar surgery some years previously.

[43] R. Dworkin, *Life's Dominion*, p. 225.

[44] L. Charland, 'Is Mr Spock Mentally Competent?: Competence to Consent and Emotion' (1998) 5 *Philosophy, Psychiatry and Psychology* 67; 'Appreciation and Emotion: Theoretical Reflections on the MacArthur Treatment Competence Study' (1999) 8 *Kennedy Institute of Ethics Journal* 359. See also M. Somerville, 'Refusal of Medical Treatment in '"Captive" Circumstances' (1985) 63 *Canadian Bar Review* 59, 65–8; K. Glass, 'Refining Definitions and Devising Instruments: Two Decades of Assessing Mental Competence' (1997) 20 *International Journal of Law and Psychiatry* 5, 20–3. See also the evidence presented by A. Zigmond on behalf of the Royal College of Psychiatrists to the Joint Committee on the Draft Mental Health Bill (*First Report of the Joint Committee on the Draft Mental Health Bill* (HL Paper 79–1; HC 95–1) (London: The Stationery Office, 2005), para. 153.

[45] See A. R. Damasio, *Descartes' Error: Emotion, Reason and the Human Brain* (New York: Grosset/Putnam, 1994).

suffered this damage could understand and memorise without difficulty, they were unable to plan for the future, could not maintain healthy relationships and behaved in self-destructive ways.[46] Thus, people may be able to perform perfectly in tests based on understanding and rationality but 'without emotions they appear unable to cope successfully with real life decision making'.[47] One reason for this, as identified by Becky Cox White, is that emotions help people to recognise a conflict in their first-order desires.[48] For example, a patient who wants to refuse life-saving treatment but who also wants to continue to live will be aware of the conflict through 'negative felt and cognitive emotions'.[49] These emotions motivate people to assess and evaluate their desires and to monitor their evaluation.[50] In other words, for most people, it is only if a decision 'feels' wrong that they will re-examine the basis on which the decision is made.

Charland suggests that mechanisms need to be developed to 'operationalize and test' how emotions contribute to capacity.[51] The difficulty with this, as Paul Appelbaum notes, is that emotional experience has an 'intrinsically subjective nature'.[52] Some people are more emotionally literate than others. While acknowledging that a capacity to feel emotions may contribute to 'good' decision-making,[53] Appelbaum argues that the difficulties with testing for emotions may lead to unreliable measurement, which in turn will lead to high error rates in capacity assessment with 'many people unfairly excluded from making treatment decisions'.[54] Cox White puts forward an alternative, and in some ways more feasible, way of dealing with affective abilities. She argues that, rather than requiring a general standard of affective ability, emotion should be relevant to establishing the consistency or authenticity of a person's actions. She argues

---

[46] Depressive illnesses can have broadly similar impacts on emotional ability: see C. Elliot, *Bioethics, Culture and Identity: A Philosophical Disease* (New York: Routledge, 1999), Chapter 5; A. Rudnick, 'Depression and Competence to Refuse Psychiatric Treatment' (2002) 28 *Journal of Medical Ethics* 155.

[47] Charland, 'Is Mr Spock Mentally Competent?,' 73.

[48] B. Cox White, *Competence to Consent* (Washington DC: Georgetown University Press, 1994), p. 132.

[49] *Ibid.*   [50] *Ibid.*

[51] Charland, 'Appreciation and Emotion,' 372. For a similar argument, see T. Breden and J. Vollmann, 'The Cognitive-Based Approach of Capacity Assessment in Psychiatry: A Philosophical Critique of the MacCAT-T' (2004) 12 *Health Care Analysis* 273.

[52] P. Appelbaum, 'Ought We to Require Emotional Capacity as a Part of Decisional Competence?' (1999) 8 *Kennedy Institute of Ethics Journal* 377, 385.

[53] *Ibid.*, 386.

[54] *Ibid.*, 385. See also the concerns raised by Somerville, 'Refusal of Medical Treatment', 67 and Glass, 'Refining Definitions', 22–3.

that 'a person who usually perceives and attends to his emotions but in a particular situation is doing neither, is not competent'.[55] Thus, rather than measuring the individual against the 'right' emotional response, she is measured against her own general responses to emotional matters. While this is more persuasive than a general affective requirement, as will be seen below, there are still difficulties with this kind of subjective test.

Capacity as consistency/authenticity

A focus on consistency or authenticity adopts a subjective approach to capacity, requiring that the individual have the ability to measure her decision against her own view of what is important. There is a clear link between this view of capacity and the liberal understanding of the right of autonomy. If autonomy is to be respected because it 'allows each of us to be responsible for shaping our lives',[56] it is consistent to expect the autonomous individual to have the capacity to make the value choices necessary to do this. Thus, Ronald Dworkin regards autonomy as protecting 'people's general capacity to lead their lives out of a distinctive sense of their own character, a sense of what is important to and for them'.[57] Whether patients have a right of autonomy turns on 'the degree of their general capacity to live a life in that sense'.[58] Dworkin does not 'assume that competent people have consistent values or always make consistent choices, or that they always lead structured, reflective lives'.[59] Expanding on his view of capacity in the context of people with dementia, Dworkin argues that:

> [I]f [a person's] choices and demands, no matter how firmly expressed, systematically or randomly contradict one another, reflecting no coherent sense of self and no discernable even short-term aims, then he has presumably lost that capacity that it is the point of autonomy to protect.[60]

While, in general terms, there is a clear link between an authenticity-based view of capacity and the liberal principle of autonomy, this leaves open the question of what degree of authenticity or consistency should be necessary in order to establish capacity. In describing the authenticity requirement, the President's Commission considered that the individual must have reasonably stable values and be able to make 'reasonably consistent choices'.[61] However, as Ruth Faden and Tom Beauchamp point out, most people do not engage reflectively with their motivations and

---

[55] Cox White, *Competence to Consent*, p. 137.   [56] R. Dworkin *Life's Dominion*, p. 224.
[57] *Ibid.*, p. 224.   [58] *Ibid.*, pp. 224–5.   [59] *Ibid.*, p. 224.   [60] *Ibid.*
[61] President's Commission, *Making Healthcare Decisions*, p. 58. See also Buchanan and Brock, *Deciding For Others*, pp. 23–5.

CAPACITY: THE GATEKEEPER FOR AUTONOMY

imposing such a requirement would lead 'many familiar acts of consenting and refusing [not] to qualify as autonomous'.[62] Faden and Beauchamp also note that patients are not always consistent when confronted with the stresses of serious illness.[63] They suggest that a more reasonable view would focus on an absence of impediments to the patient's decision-making ability. Thus, they argue that this aspect of capacity should be understood as 'independence from control by neurotic compulsions, addictions, and related self-alienating psychiatric disorders'.[64]

Faden and Beauchamp's watered down conception of authenticity clearly falls some distance short of the liberal ideal of autonomous decision-making. Yet, more demanding alternatives require people whose capacity is in question to show that they can achieve a standard of decision-making over and above the norm. Thus, respect for the liberal principle of autonomy seems to pull in two directions. Faden and Beauchamp's conception is, on balance, probably more consistent with respect for autonomy because its achievability minimises the circumstances in which people are denied the right of autonomy and because its relative simplicity in application minimises the chance of errors occurring. However, this still involves according autonomous status to decisions that could not have been made in accordance with the liberal ideal.

The irrelevance of outcome

Respect for the liberal principle of autonomy requires that external factors, including the outcome or nature of the decision reached and the degree of risk assumed, are irrelevant to the determination of capacity. As discussed in Chapter 1, respect for autonomy is premised on allowing each individual to determine for herself what is good. Therefore, whether or not a person's decision complies with other people's perception of 'the good' is irrelevant to whether the person has capacity. In the words of the Law Commission, according a role to the nature of the decision reached is inappropriate because it 'penalises individuality and demands conformity at the expense of personal autonomy'.[65]

This position has been routinely affirmed by the courts[66] and is also given legislative effect in the MCA, which states that a person is 'not to be

---

[62] R. Faden and T. Beauchamp, *A History and Theory of Informed Consent* (New York: Oxford University Press, 1986), p. 265.
[63] *Ibid.*, p. 266.   [64] *Ibid.*, p. 268.
[65] Law Commission, *Report on Mental Incapacity*, p. 33.
[66] See *Austen v. Graham* (1854) 8 Moo PCC 282 (testamentary capacity); in a healthcare context see *Re MB (An Adult: Medical Treatment)* [1997] 2 FCR 541, 554 *per* Butler-Sloss

treated as unable to make a decision merely because he makes an unwise decision'.[67] MCA backing for this position is enhanced by the inclusion of a causal threshold in the legislative definition of capacity. The MCA states that 'a person lacks capacity in relation to a matter if at the material time he is unable to make a decision for himself in relation to the matter because of an impairment of, or disturbance in the functioning of, the mind or brain'.[68] This causal threshold seeks to ensure that 'unimpaired' patients will not have their capacity questioned because of the decisions they make.[69] It will be argued below that, notwithstanding these efforts, the removal of outcome from the capacity assessment process will always be partial at best. However, at the level of principle, there is no evidence of inconsistency between the law's approach and the liberal principle it endorses.

The role of risk

The operation of a variable standard for capacity depending on the level of risk to which the decision gives rise has been favoured in *obiter* comments in a number of decisions relating to healthcare.[70] In *Re T (Adult: Refusal of Medical Treatment)*, Lord Donaldson MR considered that

> [T]he doctors should consider whether at that time [the patient] had a capacity which was commensurate with the gravity of the decision which he purported to make. The more serious the decision, the greater the capacity required.[71]

Lord Donaldson MR did not indicate why he thought that a variable standard was appropriate. However, his adoption of the standard is consistent with his injunction, elsewhere in *Re T*, that, '[i]n case of doubt,

---

LJ; *St George's Healthcare NHS Trust* v. *S* [1998] 3 WLR 936, 957 *per* Judge LJ; *Bolton Hospitals NHS Trust* v. *O* [2003] 1 FLR 824, 827 *per* Dame Butler-Sloss P.

[67] MCA, s. 1 (4).   [68] MCA, s. 2(1).

[69] See the Law Commission's justifications (*Report on Mental Incapacity*, p. 34) for its recommendation that a threshold approach to capacity should be adopted.

[70] The variable standard has also been recognised outside the healthcare context: see *Re Beaney* [1978] 1 WLR 770, where Nourse QC, sitting as a Deputy High Court Judge, adopted a variable standard in determining whether a person had the capacity to make a gift.

[71] [1992] 3 WLR 782, 796. Later in his judgment, Lord Donaldson repeated this requirement in slightly different language. In summarising his conclusions, his Lordship noted (799) that 'What matters is whether at that time the patient's capacity is reduced below the level needed for a refusal of that importance, for refusals can vary in importance. Some may involve a risk to life or of irreparable damage to health. Others may not.'

that doubt falls to be resolved in favour of the preservation of life'.[72] Thus, while affirming the patient's right to refuse treatment, his Lordship was keen to ensure that mechanisms were in place to protect patients from the consequences of the exercise of this right and the employment of a variable standard for capacity was an aspect of this protection.

A variable standard was also endorsed in *Re MB (An Adult: Medical Treatment)*.[73] Butler-Sloss LJ stated that, '[t]he graver the consequences of the decision, the commensurately greater the level of competence is required to take the decision'.[74] Dame Butler-Sloss P again indicated her support for the variable standard in *Re B (Adult: Refusal of Medical Treatment)* where she held the applicant's capacity to be 'commensurate with the gravity of the decision she may wish to make'.[75] A variable standard has also been endorsed by the Irish High Court, where the adoption of the standard was linked with the protection of the right to life under the Constitution of Ireland. In *Fitzpatrick and Another* v. *K and Another*, Laffoy J found that a refusal of treatment is 'in effect a waiver of the patient's right to life' and, accordingly, that it must 'reach a particularly high threshold before it can be considered a valid refusal'.[76]

Although some commentators have suggested alternative interpretations,[77] it is difficult to see how Lord Donaldson MR's comments can mean anything other than that he (and the courts which have endorsed his comments) intended a higher degree of capacity to be required for decisions that involve a higher level of risk.[78] The comments are of course *obiter* and the matter has not been considered in any

---

[72] *Ibid.*, 796.   [73] [1997] 2 FCR 541.   [74] *Ibid.*, 553.

[75] [2002] 2 All ER 449, 472. The variable standard has also been mentioned as applicable on a number of other occasions: see *St George's Healthcare NHS Trust* v. *S* [1998] 3 WLR 936, 958 *per* Judge LJ; *Re AK (Medical Treatment: Consent)* [2001] 1 FLR 129, 135 *per* Hughes J; *R (on the application of B)* v. *Dr SS and Dr AC* [2006] EWCA Civ 28, [49] *per* Phillips CJ.

[76] [2008] IEHC 104, at p. 19 of the transcript.

[77] See A. Grubb, *Kennedy and Grubb Medical Law* (3rd edn) (London: Butterworths, 2000), p. 627, who suggests that Lord Donaldson simply meant that 'the courts will give the most careful scrutiny to the process of reaching such decisions, in particular where the patient's life is at stake.' See also M. Gunn *et al.*, 'Decision-Making Capacity' (1999) 7 *Medical Law Review* 269, 273, who argue that Lord Donaldson's statement is 'a reflection of the greater complexity of the decision to be made'.

[78] This is the interpretation taken by G. Richardson, 'Autonomy, Guardianship and Mental Disorder: One Problem, Two Solutions' (2002) 65 *Modern Law Review* 702, 705; K. Stern, 'Competence to Refuse Life-Sustaining Medical Treatment' (1994) 110 *Law Quarterly Review* 541, 545; the Report of the Expert Committee *Review of the Mental Health Act 1983* (Department of Health, HMSO, 1999), pp. 90–1; Consultation Paper of the Law Reform Commission, *Vulnerable Adults and the Law: Capacity* (LRC CP 37–2005) (Dublin: Law Reform Commission, 2005), para. 7.18.

depth by the courts.[79] There has been surprisingly little discussion of the variable standard in policy documents. In one of its early consultation papers, the Law Commission expressed 'some difficulty with the idea that there should be a "greater capacity" as opposed to an ability to understand more, or more significant, information' depending on the nature of the decision.[80] It is not entirely clear what the Law Commission intended, as the matter was not discussed in any detail in the Consultation Paper and is not mentioned at all in the Law Commission's final report. In the specific context of treatment for a mental disorder, the variable standard was endorsed by the Report of the Expert Committee on the Mental Health Act 1983[81] and by the Review of the Mental Health (Scotland) Act 1984,[82] although without detailed discussion in either report.

The MCA does not mention the variable standard, although the Code of Practice to the MCA states that '[i]f a decision could have serious or grave consequences, it is even more important that a person understands the information relevant to the decision'.[83] Peter Bartlett argues that the MCA does not support a variable standard.[84] This is on the basis that section 3(4) of the MCA states that the information relevant to a decision includes 'information about the reasonably foreseeable consequences' of deciding one way or another or of failing to reach the decision. Bartlett suggests that this 'would seem to include reasonably foreseeable risks and benefits flowing from the various decisions possible, or of failing to make a decision'.[85] He argues that because this section requires an understanding of all possible options, 'it follows that the standard of capacity is the same, no matter what choice [a person] makes'.[86] As will be seen,

[79] There does not appear to be judicial endorsement of the standard in the United States: certainly, there is no mention in the survey of the law in J. Berg et al., 'Constructing Competence: Formulating Standards of Legal Competence to Make Medical Decisions' (1996) 48 *Rutgers Law Review* 345, 352–62.

[80] Law Commission, Consultation Paper No. 129, *Mentally Incapacitated Adults and Decision-Making: Medical Treatment and Research*, (London: HMSO, 1993), pp. 18–19.

[81] *Expert Committee Review of the Mental Health Act 1983* (London: Department of Health, HMSO, 1999), p. 90. For commentary on this aspect of the report, see N. Eastman and R. Dhar, 'The Role and Assessment of Mental Incapacity: A Review' (2000) 13 *Current Opinion in Psychiatry* 557.

[82] *Report of the Review of the Mental Health (Scotland) Act 1984: New Directions* (Chair: Rt Hon Bruce Millan) (Edinburgh: Scottish Executive, 2001), p. 57.

[83] Mental Capacity Act 2005: Code of Practice (London: The Stationery Office, 2007), para. 4.19.

[84] P. Bartlett, *Blackstone's Guide to the Mental Capacity Act 2005* (2nd edn) (Oxford University Press, 2008), p. 51.

[85] *Ibid.*   [86] *Ibid.*

as a matter of logic, Bartlett is correct. However, his assessment may be overstating the effect of section 3(4). After all, the Court of Appeal in *Re MB* identified the relevant information to be understood as including information 'as to the likely consequences of having or not having the treatment in question'[87] while at the same time endorsing a standard for capacity whereby '[t]he graver the consequences of the decision, the commensurately greater the level of competence is required to take the decision'.[88]

The basis for a variable standard

Although not referred to in any of the relevant case law, the justifiability of a variable standard for capacity has been the subject of extensive debate among philosophers. The idea of a variable standard for capacity, depending on the level of risk involved, was first advanced by James Drane in the form of 'sliding scale model' for capacity.[89] Under this model, the level of capacity required varies according to the risks and benefits of the patient's decision. The lowest level of capacity is required for medical decisions 'that are not dangerous and are objectively in the patient's best interest'[90] and the highest level of capacity is required where the patient's decision is contrary to her best medical interests, for example, where the patient refuses effective treatment for an acute illness. In determining risk and benefit, Drane uses 'reasonable' or objective outcomes. In contrast, Buchanan and Brock's sliding scale is based on a subjective assessment of risk and benefit which is concerned with 'the expected effects of a particular treatment option in forwarding the patient's underlying and enduring aims and values, to the extent that these are known'.[91] The variable standard was endorsed by the United States' President's Commission (although without detailed consideration).[92] It was also adopted by Thomas Grisso and Paul Appelbaum as part of the MacCAT-T.[93]

The effect of the adoption of a variable standard based on risk is that a patient may be deemed capable of consenting to a treatment while, at the same time, lacking the capacity to refuse the same treatment. In this

---

[87] *Ibid.*, 553–4.   [88] *Ibid.*, 553.

[89] J. Drane, 'The Many Faces of Competency' (1985) 15 *Hastings Center Report* 17.

[90] *Ibid.*

[91] Buchanan and Brock, *Deciding for Others*, p. 52. For example, in calculating the risk/benefit ratio for a practising Jehovah's Witness who refuses a life-saving blood transfusion, account should be taken of factors beyond the patient's best medical interests, including her concern to avoid eternal damnation.

[92] President's Commission, *Making Health Care Decisions*, p. 57.

[93] Grisso and Appelbaum, *Assessing Competence*, p. 24.

respect, the standard appears both illogical and asymmetrical. As Mark Wicclair argues:

> [N]o matter what [the patient] finally decided, the decision she faced was: to accept or forego life-extending measures. Insofar as a choice between these options requires an ability to comprehend and to weigh the consequences of *both*, it seems odd to maintain that accepting treatment calls for significantly less decision-making ability than refusing treatment.[94]

In Ian Wilks' colourful analogy, the standard appears reminiscent of show-elections in totalitarian regimes; the voter has the right to vote but no choice.[95]

A number of commentators have tried to argue that, despite appearances, the variable standard is not, in fact, asymmetrical or illogical. Mark Wicclair suggests that a variable standard reflects the greater complexity of more risky decisions.[96] He illustrates this argument with reference to an example that Buchanan and Brock use in order to illustrate the intuitive appeal of a variable standard. The example refers to a five-year-old child and postulates that most people would be happy to allow her to decide what to have for lunch but not how to invest a large sum of money.[97] Wicclair develops the example, arguing that the choice of lunch is neither complex nor risky unless, for example, the child is allergic to a certain food. In this instance, the choice becomes more risky but it also becomes more complex because a wider range of factors have to be understood and appreciated.[98] He argues that it is the latter factor which justifies the intuitive appeal of the variable standard.

However, serious or high-risk decisions are not necessarily more complex. For example, the choice faced by a Jehovah's Witness between saving her life and facing damnation through the acceptance of a blood transfusion might well be stark and difficult, but it cannot be described as especially complicated. Equally, low risk decisions may be quite complex, perhaps requiring careful weighing up of finely balanced factors. In short, complexity and risk are two different concepts which sometimes overlap but sometimes do not and any attempt to justify a variable standard on the basis of complexity is unconvincing.

[94] M. Wicclair, 'Patient Decision-Making Capacity and Risk' (1991) 5 *Bioethics* 91, 103–4, original emphasis.
[95] I. Wilks, 'The Debate Over Risk-Related Standards of Competence' (1997) 11 *Bioethics* 413, 418.
[96] Wicclair, 'Patient Decision-Making Capacity,' 96–7.
[97] Buchanan and Brock, *Deciding for Others*, p. 60.
[98] Wicclair, 'Patient Decision-Making Capacity,' 96–7.

A second argument is that decision-making processes can legitimately be differentiated according to the decisions reached. Dan Brock argues that:

> [T]he two choices to consent or refuse will be based on different processes of reasoning or decisionmaking; the overall processes of reasoning must be different if for no other reason than that they result in different choices.[99]

This does not seem very convincing, however. The different conclusions reached may mark a difference in values rather than in the underlying reasoning process. Wilks presents a more detailed, although no more convincing, version of this argument. He argues that the process of decision-making involves two separate tasks: 'the task of making a yes-decision, and the task of making a no-decision'[100] and that different capacities are necessary for each task, depending on the level of risk involved. As an example, he posits two tightrope walkers, one of whom never falls and the other of whom sometimes falls. He then specifies the task of walking the tightrope, in the first instance, with a safety net and, in the second, with the safety net removed without the walker's knowledge. He argues that the first walker remains capable regardless of the removal of the net but that the second walker's capacity is changed, not because her ability has changed, but because of an external factor, namely the increase in risk levels caused by the removal of the net.[101] There are several problems with this argument. First, Wilks confuses the individual's capacity to do something with whether she should be permitted to do the thing in question. As Gita Cale notes, unless the walker notices the absence of the net and panics, her capacity is not changed by the absence of the net; it is simply that we feel a greater need to protect her.[102] Secondly, as Tom Buller argues the notion of separate 'yes' and 'no' decisions is unconvincing.[103] As Buller points out, in order for a decision to be 'legitimately regarded as a *bona fide* decision, [the patient] must recognize that there are other options available to him, and it must be possible for [the patient] to change his mind and accept the proposed treatments'.[104] Thus, every 'yes' decisions encompasses a 'no' decision and vice versa.

---

[99] D. Brock, 'Decisionmaking Competence and Risk' (1991) 5 *Bioethics* 107, 112.

[100] Wilks, 'The Debate Over Risk-Related Standards,' 422.   [101] *Ibid.*, 419.

[102] G. Cale, 'Risk-Related Standards of Competence: Continuing the Debate Over Risk-Related Standards of Competence' (1999) 13 *Bioethics* 132, 140–1.

[103] T. Buller, 'Competence and Risk-Relativity' (2001) 15 *Bioethics* 93, 105–6.

[104] *Ibid.*, 106.

Ultimately, it is difficult to defend the variable standard against a change of asymmetry on the grounds of either complexity or different decision-making processes. The only possible justification for a variable standard therefore is the normative one that, in Buchanan and Brock's words, the standard allows 'a better and more sensitive balance between the competing values of self-determination and well-being that are to be served by a determination of competence'.[105] Whatever the normative case to be made for this argument (a question discussed further in the next section), it is undoubtedly inconsistent with prioritisation of the legal right of autonomy. Thus, insofar as it has endorsed a variable standard for capacity, this represents the one respect in which there is a dissonance between the law's approach to capacity at a conceptual level and its endorsement of the liberal principle of autonomy.

Limitations of the 'liberal account' of capacity

The preceding discussion shows that the law's approach to capacity is, with the exception of some *obiter* endorsements of a variable standard for capacity, consistent with the law's endorsement of the liberal principle of autonomy. This section identifies a number of limitations of this account of capacity (which it terms the 'liberal account'). It argues that this account fails to recognise the relational nature of capacity; that it ignores the normative and practical consequences of uncertainty in the respect of the assessment of capacity; that it presumes tasks to be neatly separable in a way which is not always sustainable; and that it encounters difficulties in dealing with some kinds of mental disorder. Some suggestions are made as regards how these limitations might be addressed although, as will be clear, solutions to the issues arising are not always straightforward.

Capacity: a relational phenomenon

Core to the liberal account of capacity is the presumption that a person who has capacity to make a decision can be distinguished from a person who does not, with the only issue being the basis upon which such distinctions are made. Yet, the reality is more complex. Just as a focus on agency in Chapter 1 shows the range of structural and other factors that impede autonomous decision-making, a closer look at capacity reveals

---

[105] Buchanan and Brock, *Deciding for Others*, p. 64. See similar justification offered by the President's Commission, *Making Healthcare Decisions*, p. 60; Drane, 'The Many Faces of Competency', 21.

impediments to a person's ability to meet the standard for capacity. Leaving aside, for the present, issues of assessor bias (which are examined in Chapter 4), a range of factors may create impediments to capacity. A nervous or intimidated patient or a person with limited education may have difficulty understanding information, especially if it is explained in unfamiliar language.[106] More structural impediments may arise from the physical environment in which a person finds herself. Conditions of passivity in nursing homes can atrophy residents' capacities,[107] which is turn may accelerate the loss of decision-making abilities associated with dementia or other age-related illness.[108]

Impediments may also be gender-based or racially or ethnically derived. For example, a person who has always assumed a particular gendered role within a marriage may find it difficult to act outside of this role if his or her spouse dies.[109] In respect of race and ethnicity, a study of rates of incapacity among psychiatric patients in a London hospital found proportionately higher numbers of black and minority (in particular African Caribbean) patients to lack capacity.[110] Although they did not comment in detail on why this was likely to be the case, the authors of the

[106] A link between lower levels of education and incapacity was found in V. Raymont et al., 'Prevalence of Mental Incapacity in Medical Inpatients and Associated Risk Factors: Cross-Sectional Study' (2004) 364 Lancet 1421; J. G. Wong et al., 'Decision Making Capacity of Inpatients With Schizophrenia in Hong Kong' (2005) 193 Journal of Nervous and Mental Disease 316; L. Roth et al., 'Competency to Decide About Treatment or Research' (1982) 5 International Journal of Law and Psychiatry 279.

[107] See C. Lidz and R. Arnold, 'Institutional Constraints on Autonomy' (1990) 14 Generations 65; C. Lidz et al., The Erosion of Autonomy in Long-Term Care (New York: Oxford University Press, 1992).

[108] Old age is the demographic variable most closely associated with findings of incapacity: see D. Okai et al., 'Mental Capacity in Psychiatric Patients: Systematic Review' (2007) 191 British Journal of Psychiatry 291, 294.

[109] B. Secker, 'Labelling Patient (In)Competence: A Feminist Analysis of Medico-Legal Discourse' (1999) 30 Journal of Social Philosophy 295, 303, gives the example of a woman who has never engaged with financial matters who finds herself lacking the capacity to manage her financial affairs after her husband's death. An alternative example is that of the man who has never engaged with matters of health or lifestyle, leaving such concerns to his wife. In such a situation, the man may well lack the capacity to make certain kinds of healthcare decisions.

[110] Cairns et al., 'Prevalence and Predictors of Mental Incapacity in Psychiatric In-Patients' (2005) 187 British Journal of Psychiatry 379, 383. This reflects other research which found that a proportionally higher number of black and ethnic minority patients were involuntarily admitted to psychiatric facilities: see S. Wall et al., Systematic Review of Research Relating to the Mental Health Act 1983 (London: Department of Health, 1999). For similar findings in the United States, see S. Stefan, 'Race, Competence Testing and Disability Law: A Review of the MacArthur Competence Research' (1996) 2 Psychology, Public Policy and Law 31.

study noted the role played by 'contextual and environmental factors' in whether or not a person has capacity.[111] A United States-based anthropological study found that African American patients with mental illnesses were less likely to describe their illness in medical terms and more likely to ascribe it in 'socio-situational terms'.[112] This, in turn, led to higher findings of incapacity based on a lack of understanding by the patients of their illness. The authors suggest that these patterns may 'reflect the alienation and marginalization of this group, expressed through the rejection of white, middle class, professionally conceived and delivered psychiatric diagnosis and treatment'.[113]

Constructing capacity

On this view, capacity is seen, to a degree at least, as a constructed state which can be enhanced or diminished depending on the surrounding circumstances. Thus, just as a relational account of autonomy requires the development of 'autonomy competencies', a relational account of capacity requires that attempts be made to enhance each individual's decision-making capacity and to address impediments to the attainment of capacity. The view that capacity can (and should) be developed is reflected, in different ways, in other philosophical approaches to the concept. As might be expected, it is core to feminist accounts of capacity.[114] It is also implicit in a hermeneutic approach to capacity. As described by Roger Lundin '[h]ermeneutics presupposes an interactive, relational, intersubjective self'.[115] A hermeneutic approach emphasises the importance of dialogue and the transformative effect of engagement with other people. Hermeneutic ethics does not presume an absolute truth but rather focuses on each individual creating her own meaning through a process of engagement. Key to a hermeneutic enquiry is 'the commitment to generate questions that aim for engagement rather than alienation'.[116] In this

---

[111] Cairns *et al.*, 'Prevalence and Predictors of Mental Incapacity in Psychiatric In-Patients,' 384.

[112] S. Estroff *et al.*, 'Everybody's Got a Little Mental Illness: Accounts of Illness and Self Among People With Severe Persistent Mental Illness' (1991) 5 *Medical Anthropology Quarterly* 331, 357.

[113] *Ibid.*

[114] See S. Sherwin, *No Longer Patient: Feminist Ethics and Health Care* (Philadelphia: Temple University Press, 1992), pp. 156–7; E. Maeckelberghe, 'Feminist Ethic of Care: A Third Alternative Approach' (2004) 12 *Health Care Analysis* 317.

[115] R. Lundin *et al.*, *The Promise of Hermeneutics* (Cambridge: Paternoster Press, 1999), p. 134.

[116] J. Clegg, 'Practice in Focus: A Hermeneutic Approach to Research Ethics' (2004) 32 *British Journal of Learning Disabilities* 186, 186.

respect, the 'issue is not so much how to *assess* capacity, but how to *develop* it through interaction and dialogue'.[117]

This view of capacity is consistent with therapeutic jurisprudence. As described by Bruce Winick '[t]herapeutic jurisprudence suggests the need for an assessment of the therapeutic impact of legal rules'.[118] In relation to capacity, Winick notes the possible adverse psychological effects for a patient arising from a finding of incapacity.[119] As well as the social stigma, he points to effects such as learned helplessness[120] and lack of motivation, and argues that, if an individual is diagnosed as lacking capacity in one regard, this may contribute to a diminution of capacity in other regards. For this reason, Winick argues that capacity assessment should be viewed as 'a teaching or helping process'.[121]

This view of capacity is also consistent with the approach taken by the CRPD. Article 12(2) states that 'States Parties shall recognize that persons with disabilities enjoy legal capacity on an equal basis with others in all aspects of life'.[122] Although, on one reading, this could be seen as requiring a prohibition on capacity-based distinctions, as Amita Dhanda shows, it is unlikely that the final Article is intended to operate in this way.[123] However,

[117] L. Benaroyo and G. Widdershoven, 'Competence in Mental Health Care: A Hermeneutic Perspective' (2004) 12 *Health Care Analysis* 295, 298, original emphasis.

[118] B. Winick, 'The Right to Refuse Mental Health Treatment: A Therapeutic Jurisprudence Analysis' (1994) 17 *International Journal of Law and Psychiatry* 99, 100. On therapeutic jurisprudence generally, see D. Wexler and B. Winick, *Essays in Therapeutic Jurisprudence* (Durham, NC: Carolina Academic Press, 1991); D. Wexler and B. Winick (eds.) *Law in a Therapeutic Key: Developments in Therapeutic Jurisprudence* (Durham, NC: Carolina Academic Press, 1996). For a critique of therapeutic jurisprudence, see C. Slogobin, 'Therapeutic Jurisprudence: Five Dilemmas to Ponder' (1995) *Psychology, Public Policy and Law* 1933; S. Behnke and E. Saks, 'Therapeutic Jurisprudence: Informed Consent as a Clinical Indication for the Chronically Suicidal Patient With Borderline Personality Disorder' (1998) 31 *Loyola of Los Angelus Law Review* 945, 978–81.

[119] B. Winick, 'The Side Effects of Incompetency Labelling and the Implications for Mental Health Law' (1995) 1 *Psychology, Public Policy and Law* 6.

[120] See M. Seligman, *Helplessness: On Depression, Development and Death* (San Francisco: Freeman, 1975), who argues that when an individual comes to believe that she cannot change her situation, she ceases to try to do so.

[121] B. Winick, 'The MacArthur Treatment Competence Study: Legal and Therapeutic Implications' (1996) 2 *Psychology, Public Policy and Law* 137, 151.

[122] For an account of earlier iterations of Art. 12 and the surrounding debate, see A. Dhanda, 'Legal Capacity in the Disability Rights Convention: Stranglehold of the Past or Lodestar for the Future?' (2006–2007) 34 *Syracuse Journal of International Law and Commerce* 429, 438–56.

[123] *Ibid.*, 460–1. This conclusion is supported by the interpretations taken by States Parties in contributions to the General Assembly: see, in particular, the Canadian final statement to the General Assembly: see Dhanda *ibid.*, 455–6.

the Article does require that States 'take appropriate measures to pro-vide access by persons with disabilities to the support they may require in exercising their legal capacity'.[124] In this respect, the provision of advo-cacy, mentoring and other ways of developing capacity (and, as discussed further in Chapter 5, of supporting decision-making by people lacking capacity) becomes not just a general policy goal but a requirement under international law.

What can be achieved?: empirical data

The arguments outlined above are supported by empirical data which show that greater engagement on the part of the assessor (or other med-ical personnel) may increase the capacity of the person assessed, in some circumstances at least. Grisso and Appelbaum's comparative study of cap-acity in people with physical and mental illnesses found that all patient groups (and the non-patient control group) manifested considerably bet-ter understanding of information relating to their treatment after the information was broken down into separate parts and disclosed to them for a second time than had been manifested when the information was disclosed whole for the first time.[125] This finding is confirmed by Gunn *et al.*'s study of levels of understanding in patients with a range of mental disorders. This study investigated the levels of understanding in respect of a routine blood test among four groups of adult participants: one with chronic schizophrenia, one with a learning disability at the lower end of the mild disabilities range, one with (at least moderate) dementia and a final control group drawn from the general population.[126] The study found a marked improvement in the levels of understanding achieved by patients with mental illness and learning disabilities when information was made more accessible by being broken down into smaller blocks.[127] Interestingly, for patients with dementia, rendering information more accessible in this way did not impact on findings of capacity at all.[128]

The above studies were concerned with the ability to understand. Of the abilities needed for capacity, this is the ability which is most likely to benefit from assistance. Empirical data are needed regarding whether similar improvements might be found in respect of the ability to use and

---

[124] Art. 12(3). See also Art. 24(1), which requires States Parties to provide an educational system and lifelong learning directed to '[t]he development by persons with disabilities of their personality, talents and creativity, as well as their mental and physical abilities, to their fullest potential'.

[125] See Grisso and Appelbaum, 'The MacArthur Treatment Competence Study III', 173.

[126] Gunn *et al.*, 'Patient Decision-making Capacity', 270.   [127] *Ibid.*, 280.   [128] *Ibid.*

weigh relevant information. However, while the findings do not suggest that capacity can always be developed, they do show that some patients, particularly patients with mental illnesses and intellectual disabilities, can cross the line and be found capable because of the way in which they are treated in advance of the assessment.

Delivering on the relational approach

The relational view of capacity requires a shift in focus away from testing the internal workings of the individual's mind and instead requires that account be taken of all the factors, both structural and personal, which prevent the individual from having capacity. It also means that the capacity assessor may no longer be viewed as an objective outsider who tests the patient and decides whether she is capable or not but as an essential part of the process of developing her capacity.

One of the most striking innovations in the MCA is the extent to which the Act attempts to incorporate mechanisms to enhance individuals' capacity. Section 1(3) sets out the underlying principle that a person is not to be treated as unable to make a decision unless 'all practicable steps' to help the person have been taken without success, and section 3(2) states that a person is not to be regarded as unable to understand relevant information if 'he is able to understand an explanation of it given to him in a way that is appropriate to his circumstances'. The accompanying Code of Practice also provides guidance for assessors in this respect.[129] These are important legislative steps. However, the MCA is limited in what it can deliver. Both statutory requirements leave considerable latitude regarding how the matter of practicability or appropriateness is to be determined. More significantly, as discussed further in Chapter 4, the MCA does not provide any effective mechanisms to enforce these requirements. Assessors are told what to do but not *required* in a meaningful sense to do it.

Recognition of a relational approach to capacity also requires a focus on advocacy and education as well as research into developing better mechanisms to assist people in developing capacity. In terms of advocacy, the establishment under the MCA of the Independent Mental Capacity Advocate Service is an important development.[130] However, the service is of little assistance in the present context because the advocate is appointed only where the person has already been found to lack capacity.[131]

---

[129] See Code paras. 2.6–2.9 and Chapter 3.
[130] MCA, ss. 35–41. This service which is available, inter alia, in respect of decisions regarding the provision of serious medical treatment is discussed in detail in Chapter 5.
[131] MCA, s. 37(1).

Although, once appointed, advocates may challenge decisions which have been made, including the decision that the person lacked capacity, this possibility arises only after the decision as to incapacity has been taken.[132] Thus, while the service may help people overturn inappropriate assessments, it contributes relatively little as a capacity-development mechanism. This position is, of course, entirely consistent with the liberal account of capacity; a person with capacity does not need an advocate because she can make her own decisions. On a relational view, however, the provision of some degree of support in advance of the determination of capacity could enhance the capacity of the person assessed, and thereby provide a greater degree of protection for the autonomy of the individual involved.

Outcome, risk and uncertainty

As described above, a core aspect of the liberal account of capacity is the view that the decision which a person proposes to make is irrelevant to the assessment of her capacity. On this view, capacity is an internal matter which is assessed without reference to external factors such as the outcome of the decision made. However, it is highly unlikely that this approach actually operates in practice. As the Law Commission noted, prior to the introduction of the MCA, an 'outcome-based' approach to capacity 'is almost certainly in daily use'.[133] Outcome and risk would also seem to have a subliminal influence on judicial assessments. As discussed in the previous chapter, in cases in which the courts have upheld a person's right to refuse treatment, they have tended to note the relatively low level of risk of this actually happening in the case in question.[134] While judges have not explicitly accorded any significance to this factor in their deliberations, writing extra-judicially, Thorpe LJ has described judicial motivations (in the context of caesarean sections). Thorpe writes that:

> Whatever emphasis legal principle may place upon adult autonomy with the consequent right to choose between treatments, at some level the judicial outcome will be influenced by the expert evidence as to which treatment affords the best chance of the happy announcement that both mother and baby are doing well.[135]

---

[132] Mental Capacity Act (Independent Mental Capacity Advocates) (General) Regulations 2007 (SI 1832/2007), Reg. 7.

[133] Law Commission, *Report on Mental Incapacity*, pp. 39–40.

[134] *Re C (Adult: Refusal of Medical Treatment)* [1994] 1 WLR 290, 293; *Re W* [2002] MHLR 411, [32].

[135] Thorpe LJ, 'The Caesarean Section Debate' [1997] *Family Law* 663, 664.

It is unlikely that this position will be changed in any significant way by the inclusion of a statement in the MCA that a person is 'not to be treated as unable to make a decision merely because he makes an unwise decision'.[136] A similar position was routinely endorsed by the courts prior to the introduction of the MCA and, as the Law Commission noted, this seemed to have had little impact on the use of the outcome-based approach in practice. It is also unlikely that any significant change will result from the inclusion in the MCA of a causal threshold based on an 'impairment' of the mind or brain.[137] As described above, the purpose of this was to ensure that 'unimpaired' patients were afforded maximum decision-making freedom. However, the relevant provision is stated in such an imprecise way as to provide little protection for patients who make unusual or high-risk decisions.[138] Thus, the fact that a patient proposes to make this kind of decision is likely to suggest an impairment of the mind or brain which in turn will lead to her capacity being investigated. Furthermore, the limited protection provided to 'unimpaired' patients by the inclusion of the requirement is bought at the cost of associating incapacity with mental disorders and intellectual disability.[139] This creates an increased likelihood that assessors will find patients with these conditions to lack decision-making capacity simply on the basis of their underlying condition and not as a result of a rigorous application of the functional test.

There are a number of reasons why outcome cannot be wholly removed from the capacity assessment process. As will be argued below, there are inherent difficulties in applying a test for capacity in respect of some kinds of mental disorders. Furthermore, as will be shown in Chapter 4, capacity assessors who are healthcare professionals face normative and practical challenges in applying a test for capacity, especially in circumstances where a finding of capacity will lead to the death or a significant deterioration in the health of the person assessed. But perhaps the primary reason

---

[136] MCA, s. 1(4).   [137] MCA, s. 2(1).

[138] A similar argument was made in relation to the 'mental disorder' threshold first recommended by the Law Commission in *Mentally Incapacitated Adults and Decision-Making: A New Jurisdiction* Consultation Paper No. 128 (London: HMSO, 1993), paras. 3.10–3.14: see D. Carson, 'Disabling Progress: The Law Commission's Proposals on Mentally Incapacitated Adults' Decision-Making' (1993) 15 *Journal of Social Welfare and Family Law* 304, 313; P. Fennell, 'Statutory Authority to Treat, Relatives and Treatment Proxies' (1994) 2 *Medical Law Review* 30, 36.

[139] While the association is less because the term 'mental disorder' is not used in the MCA, it is difficult to see that the new terminology creates sufficient distance (or indeed how any terminology could do so) between mental disorder and an 'impairment' of the mind or brain.

that outcome remains a feature of the assessment process is the inherent uncertainty in respect of conclusions reached about capacity. As the Irish judge Black J once noted, a court 'possesses no X-ray contrivance that can lay bare the workings of the human mind'.[140] Both case law and empirical studies discussed in Chapter 4 confirm the proposition that conclusions about capacity are epistemologically fallible.

The epistemological fallibility of conclusions about capacity has two consequences. First, in circumstances of uncertainty, the pull towards an objectively verifiable basis for a decision is inevitably strong. An 'unreasonable' conclusion is highly likely to be viewed as evidence of incapacity.[141] Similarly, if in doubt, there are obvious attractions in achieving what would seem objectively to be the least harmful result. Secondly, as discussed below, there are normative consequences. Respect for autonomy means something different when there is uncertainty regarding whether or not a decision is autonomous.

The liberal account of capacity tends to ignore the consequences of epistemological fallibility. Instead, it operates on the basis that by simply stating that outcome should play no role in assessments of capacity, this will, in fact, occur. In practice, this may well pose a significant threat to individual autonomy, all the more so because the role afforded to outcome is unspoken and patients are denied the opportunity to provide contrary evidence or counter arguments. However, while the failure to acknowledge the issue of uncertainty is a limitation of the liberal account of capacity, as will be seen below, this is not an easy matter to address.

Dealing with uncertainty

One way of dealing with epistemological fallibility is through the use of a variable standard for capacity. Liberal theorist Joel Feinberg justifies the adoption of a variable standard on this basis.[142] Feinberg suggests two rules of thumb to determine the standard to be applied. First, the more

---

[140] *Provincial Bank* v. *McKeever* [1941] IR 471, 485.

[141] As argued (in the context of testamentary and contractual capacity) by M. Green, 'Proof of Mental Incompetency and the Unexpressed Major Premise' (1944) 53 *Yale Law Journal* 271.

[142] J. Feinberg, *The Moral Limits of the Criminal Law: Vol III: Harm to Self* (New York: Oxford University Press, 1986), pp. 118–19. The variable standard suggested by Feinberg relates to the broader concept of 'voluntariness' rather than to capacity. He describes (p. 107) the conditions for a 'perfectly voluntary' decision as follows: the chooser is 'competent'; she does not choose under coercion or duress; she does not choose because of more subtle manipulation; she does not choose because of ignorance or mistaken belief; she does not choose in circumstances that are temporarily distorting.

risky the conduct, the greater the degree of voluntariness required and, secondly, the more irrevocable the risked harm, the greater the degree of voluntariness required if it is to be permitted.[143] The basis for the second rule of thumb is that, once an irrevocable harm has occurred, it is too late to reverse it. A mistake in judging voluntariness can never be corrected. Feinberg notes the distinction between harm and irrevocability. The death of a terminally ill person in great pain may not be as harmful as the death of a young, fit person, but both deaths are equally irrevocable. For this reason, Feinberg argues that 'the voluntariness of decisions to terminate one's own life or to assume substantial risks of accidental death must be determined, other things being equal, by stringent standards'.[144]

Feinberg contends that, although the variable standard he advocates can look like hard paternalism, his justification for the standard is, in fact, consistent with his underlying liberal philosophy. In his words, 'the defining purpose of the soft paternalist is to prevent people from suffering harm that they have not truly chosen to suffer'.[145] Buchanan and Brock point out that, in making this argument, Feinberg presumes that greater moral harm is done by inappropriately allowing someone to risk her life or health than by inappropriately limiting her freedom to act.[146] In this respect, Feinberg undeniably favours the principles of beneficence and the sanctity of life over the principle of autonomy.

From a legal perspective, there are some attractions in Feinberg's position. Although to date, legal discourse in respect of healthcare decision-making has afforded little overt recognition to beneficence (outside of situations of incapacity), there has been clear legal recognition of the significance of the sanctity of life principle. As Lord Hoffman noted in *Airedale NHS Trust* v. *Bland*, the view that human life has an intrinsic value is, in one form of another, 'part of almost everyone's intuitive values'.[147] As his Lordship also noted, in the case of a conflict with autonomy 'one or other principle must be sacrificed'.[148] Lord Hoffman confirmed that, in such circumstances, autonomy clearly 'trumps' the sanctity of life.[149]

---

[143] *Ibid.*, pp. 118–19.   [144] *Ibid.*, p. 120.   [145] *Ibid.*, p. 119.

[146] Buchanan and Brock, *Deciding for Others*, pp. 44–7. See also the arguments of J. deMarco, 'Competence and Paternalism' (2002) 16 *Bioethics* 231, 238–9.

[147] [1993] AC 789, 826. Respect for the sanctity of life provides the basis for Art. 2 of the ECHR, described by the ECtHR in *Pretty* v. *United Kingdom* (2002) 35 EHRR 1, para. 37 as 'one of the most fundamental provisions of the Convention'.

[148] [1993] AC 789, 827.

[149] *Ibid.* There are divergent views regarding the impact of *Bland* on the sanctity of life principle more generally. For arguments (from very different normative perspectives) that the decision significantly undercuts the principle, see J. Keown, 'Restoring Moral and

However, as Munby J has pointed out, the priority accorded to autonomy presumes a straight contest which is free from doubt in respect of the patient's capacity (or, where an advance directive is involved, in respect of the validity of the directive).[150] When there is doubt, the balance is different and the normative conflict is no longer straightforward. In such circumstances, according priority to autonomy over the sanctity of life would involve eroding the sanctity of life principle, not on the basis of respect for an autonomous decision but on the basis of respect for a decision which might or might not be autonomous. The justification for the erosion of the sanctity of life principle in such circumstances is less than in respect of a clearly autonomous decision. A reasonable case may be made that, if the sanctity of life principle is to retain any meaning at all, this would seem a reasonable context for it to play a role.

If this normative position is accepted, it could justify the use of a variable standard for capacity, one which requires greater levels of capacity where there is a risk to life. This would also have the advantage of providing a more transparent framework for capacity assessment and, in this way, might address the practical consequences arising from uncertainty which were discussed above. If the unspoken role of outcome was more overt, it might be easier to combat. Thus, a formal application of the variable standard would require proof that a decision constitutes a risk to life, so that the higher standard of capacity would be required. As Genevra Richardson points out, a mere statement that a decision is high risk does not demonstrate that this is in fact the case.[151] In this regard, risk should be measured in the light of a consideration of the alternatives to the proposed treatment and not as a simple proposition. For example, the assessment would include an examination of whether a patient is prepared to consent to a treatment that is not optimal but which carries a lower level of risk than outright treatment refusal.[152] This would mean that medical evidence would have to deal directly with questions of risks, benefits

Intellectual Shape to the Law after *Bland*' (1997) 113 *Law Quarterly Review* 481; P. Singer, *Rethinking Life and Death: The Collapse of Our Traditional Ethics* (New York: OUP, 1994), p. 75. For an alternative argument, see A. McGee, 'Finding a Way through the Ethical and Legal Maze: Withdrawal of Medical Treatment and Euthanasia' (2005) 13 *Medical Law Review* 357 (see Keown's ripose, 'A Futile Defence of *Bland*: A Reply to Andrew McGee' (2005) 13 *Medical Law Review* 393).

[150] *R (Burke)* v. *General Medical Council and Others* [2004] EWHC 1879 (Admin), [76].

[151] Richardson, 'Autonomy, Guardianship and Mental Disorder', 721.

[152] For example, in *Re C (Adult: Refusal of Medical Treatment)* [1994] 1 WLR 290, the applicant was prepared to accept antibiotic treatment for his gangrenous foot but refused to countenance an amputation.

and alternatives before a court could determine the applicable standard for capacity. This would move the matter of alternatives to the proposed treatment to play a more central role in the process.

However, the formalisation of a variable standard has not been attempted in practice. A sophisticated model for incorporating risk, based on a subjective assessment of risk and the introduction of complex evidence of risks and benefits, could prove difficult to apply in a court setting and even more difficult in circumstances where capacity is informally assessed by non-legal professionals. Thus, the adoption of a variable standard could simply reify a paternalistic approach to capacity without any benefits in terms of transparency and accountability. Nonetheless, the point remains that, if the law on capacity is to develop a more meaningful conceptual framework, some way of dealing with the consequences of epistemological fallibility must be employed and the variable standard may represent one way of doing this.

Atomised tasks and the functional approach

As noted above, a functional, task-specific approach is an essential component of the liberal account of capacity. This approach presumes that the task of decision-making is divisible into atomised units, in relation to each of which an individual's inherent capacity may be measured at the point in time when the decision comes to be made. This premise is sustainable in relation to certain healthcare decisions, such as, for example, consent to a surgical intervention. However, it is not universally true. Some decisions are multi-faceted or are intrinsically linked to each other, while others are not temporally specific but are ongoing. In both contexts, and especially in the second, the operation of the functional test encounters difficulties.

The functional test and the definition of a 'task'

In most aspects of everyday living, tasks do not separate neatly into isolated units. Inevitably, judgements have to be made regarding where one task ends and another begins. For example, in a healthcare context, does the decision to consent to surgery include the decision to consent to aspects of after-care? As is evident from the discussion in *Bailey* v. *Warren*,[153] drawing boundaries around tasks can present a serious challenge. In this case, the Court of Appeal had to determine whether the task

---

[153] [2006] EWCA Civ 51.

of making a settlement regarding liability following an accident was separate to the task of agreeing quantum. Interestingly, Hallett LJ (who took
a narrow view of what the 'task' involved)[154] and Arden LJ (who adopted
a broader definition of 'task')[155] both relied on 'common sense' to support their conclusions.[156] In fact, the issue is more one of policy than of
common sense. The more narrowly a task is defined, the more decision-
making power is allowed to remain with the person whose capacity is at
issue. However, a narrow definition of 'task' can also involve elements of
artificiality, and requires ongoing capacity assessment in a way that is neither practical nor especially useful.[157]

Temporally separable tasks and fluctuating capacity

Many healthcare decisions relate to ongoing treatment rather than
one-off procedures. The functional approach is more difficult to apply
in such cases. This is especially true given that, in the words of the Law
Commission, people 'may have levels of capacity that vary from week to
week or even from hour to hour'.[158] In practical terms, fluctuating capacity is unlikely to cause difficulties where the person whose capacity is at
issue is content to abide by the original decision (whether this was made
by the person herself while she had capacity or made by others in her best
interests while she lacked capacity). However, difficulties arise where a
person wishes to depart from a decision to provide treatment based on her
best interests made while she lacked capacity. If, on an application of the
functional test, she has the necessary capacity, then, on the application of
basic liberal legal principles, there should be nothing to prevent her from
refusing the treatment. In such circumstances, however, a pattern can
develop whereby decisions taken while capable lead to subsequent incapacity. This is followed by the imposition of treatment, recovery, refusal of
treatment and so on.

The nature of the difficulty is evident in *Re G (An Adult) (Mental
Capacity: Curt's Jurisdiction)*.[159] In this case, an interim order had been
made limiting contact between a woman with a history of mental illness

---

[154] *Ibid.*, [73]–[74].   [155] *Ibid.*, [122].

[156] Arden LJ's broader approach also enjoyed the support of Ward LJ *ibid.*, [177].

[157] Munby J's decision in *In the Matter of MM* [2007] EWHC 2003 (Fam) might be seen
as coming close to the line. Munby J found that a woman had the capacity to consent
to sexual intercourse with a (specific) person although she did not have the capacity to
consent to contact with that person: see Munby J's defence of this aspect of his decision,
ibid., [95].

[158] Law Commission, *Report on Mental Incapacity*, para. 3.5.

[159] [2004] EWHC 2222 (Fam).

and her parents on the basis that her father had a negative impact on her mental health. At the time of the interim order, the woman had lacked the capacity to make a decision and the order was made on the basis of her best interests. Following a period during which the order limited contact with her father, the woman's mental health improved, she regained capacity and then wished to see her father again. The evidence suggested that if the contact restrictions were lifted, she would lose capacity again. Similar issues arose in *Re R (A Minor) (Wardship: Medical Treatment)*,[160] which concerned a young woman who fluctuated between psychotic and lucid periods. During these lucid periods, she refused to take antipsychotic medication, thus leading to the onset of a psychotic period.

The judges in both cases declined to operate a temporally-specific functional approach to capacity. In *Re G*, Bennett J rejected the view that the court's jurisdiction 'would be entirely dependent on the shifting sands of whether G did, or did not, have the requisite capacity at the time of the final hearing'.[161] In determining capacity, he concluded that the 'focal point' of the inquiry must be the situation which had led to the woman being taken into care and, on this basis, he held that she lacked capacity to consent to contact with her father.[162] Similarly, in *Re R*, Lord Donaldson MR suggested that the test for capacity needed to be 'modified in the case of fluctuating mental disability to take account of that misfortune'.[163] His Lordship did not give any indication regarding how this modification might take place and his comments were *obiter* as the case was decided not on the basis of the young woman's fluctuating capacity but on the basis of her age.[164]

Dealing with fluctuating capacity

The issue of fluctuating capacity draws attention to the question of temporal separation of tasks. As with defining the decision-making task, the way in which the boundaries are drawn is a matter of policy. A temporally narrow definition of the task of decision-making creates the possibility of a cycle of refusal followed by diminished capacity and imposed treatment. A temporally broad definition of the decision-making task, along the lines adopted by Bennett J in *Re G*, determines current capacity on the

---

[160] [1991] 4 All ER 177.   [161] [2004] EWHC 2222 (Fam), [91].   [162] *Ibid.*, [112].
[163] [1991] 4 All ER 177, 187.
[164] The Court of Appeal held that the right of young people aged less than 18 years to refuse treatment was limited and could be subject to parental and court intervention on the basis of best interests: see M. Brazier and C. Bridge, 'Coercion or Caring: Analysing Adolescent Autonomy' (1996) 16 *Legal Studies* 84.

basis of prior factors. Neither option appears to be especially attractive. The first option delivers inadequate protection in respect of both autonomy and beneficence. The patient's decision is routinely overridden while, at the same time, the therapeutic benefit of any treatment provided is reduced by the interruptions to treatment every time she regains capacity. On the other hand, the approach of Bennett J leaves no space for the possibility of recovery.

Some issues in respect of fluctuating capacity might be resolved by better negotiation and communication with patients, especially during the periods when they have legal capacity. This may lessen the possibility of rejection of treatment and prevent the development of the cycle described above. More widespread availability of advance care directives might also enhance patients' trust in the process. Furthermore, as discussed in Chapter 5, the MCA definition of best interests requires the 'past and present' views of the patient to be taken into account.[165] Thus, the fact that a patient has routinely refused treatment while she had capacity must surely be a relevant factor in determining whether treatment could be provided when she lacks capacity. However, while these steps might diminish the extent of the problems arising in the context of fluctuating capacity, they do not solve it.

The most likely context in which the issue of fluctuating capacity will arise is in respect of patients with a mental disorder. As a result, the difficult question of how to deal with fluctuating capacity in respect of healthcare decisions is very often avoided by the patient being brought within the ambit of the Mental Health Act 1983 (MHA). As discussed further in Chapter 6, the application of this legislation results in a wholesale overriding of the patient's right of autonomy. In their exploration of the case for the introduction of a capacity-based approach to treatment for a mental disorder, the Report of the Expert Committee addressed the difficulties posed by fluctuating capacity. The Committee rejected the view that a person who has a fluctuating condition would have to develop 'florid symptoms of psychosis' before treatment could be imposed.[166] Instead, the Committee considered that the determination of capacity should take account of whether 'there was a clear history of relapse and positive response to treatment'.[167] This approach takes account of external factors which are irrelevant on a liberal account of capacity. However, it also provides a better framework for dealing with the issue of fluctuating capacity

---

[165] MCA, s. 4(6).   [166] *Review of the Mental Health Act 1983*, para 7.13.
[167] *Ibid.*, para. 7.14.

than recourse to the MHA. Accordingly, it is perhaps the best approach to take in these circumstances.

Authenticity and egosyntonicity

As discussed above, the concept of authenticity is core to the liberal account of capacity. The MCA affords legal recognition to this concept through the requirement for an ability 'to use or weigh' information in making a decision.[168] This requirement is derived from a Law Commission recommendation that a 'decision based on a compulsion, the overpowering will of a third party or any other inability to act on relevant information as a result of mental disability is not a decision made by a person with decision-making capacity'.[169] Although the Law Commission had dropped its earlier use of the term 'true' choice to describe this requirement,[170] in essence, this is still what the provision requires. In the context of mental disorders, the Review of the Mental Health Act 1983 described the premise behind the notion of 'true' choice as follows:

> A person may lack capacity, where, although intellectually able to understand and apply the information, that person nonetheless reaches a judgment which s/he would not have reached in the absence of the disorder. Such a judgment can be said to be primarily the product of the disorder and not to reflect the person's true preferences.[171]

An account of capacity based on authenticity works well in many situations. In situations where the incapacity arises as a result of panic, for example, there is usually a fairly obvious course that the individual would have pursued had it not been for her panic.[172] It is also likely to work effectively where a person experiences compulsions that are inconsistent with her self-perception. Thus, for example, Ruth Faden and Tom Beauchamp recount the experience of one woman whose obsessive germ fixation led to almost continual hand washing which she did not wish to do but which she was unable to prevent herself from doing.[173] However, not all disorders are experienced as alien or inconsistent with a person's self-perception. With egosyntonic disorders, the disorder becomes part of a person's identity or self and is not something which she sees as a thing apart. In such

[168] MCA, s. 3(1).   [169] Law Commission, *Report on Mental Incapacity*, p. 39.
[170] See Law Commission, Consultation Paper No. 129, pp. 20–1.
[171] *Review of the Mental Health Act 1983*, pp. 88–9.
[172] See *Re MB (An Adult: Medical Treatment)* [1997] 2 FCR 541, 554; *Bolton Hospitals NHS Trust v. O* [2003] 1 FLR 824, [14].
[173] Faden and Beauchamp, *History and Theory of Informed Consent*, p. 267.

circumstances, a person may not have 'true preferences' outside of her illness or current situation which can be referred to in order to challenge the authenticity of her current decision. Rather, her illness may be a core part of who she is.

As the work of Tan *et al.* shows, this is a possible consequence of some compulsive diseases, including anorexia nervosa.[174] Drawing on interviews with 10 young women aged between 13 and 22 years with a diagnosis of anorexia nervosa and with seven of their mothers,[175] Tan *et al.* show that some of the young women identified their illness as key to their identity.[176] As Tan *et al.* describe it, the issue of personal identity was not just related to obvious factors such as weight or shape but 'to a set of values about life in general that the participants had'.[177] For these young women, many of whom had developed anorexia in early adolescence, the 'anorexia identity' was 'not merely a caricature or degeneration of their former selves but something quite distinct, with new and additional features such as a strong drive to achieve, preoccupation with food, and control of themselves'.[178] These factors made it difficult for the young women to contemplate or imagine a life without anorexia. Tan *et al.* point out that the effect of treatment could be seen to 'eradicate the disorder and thereby "kill" the person they felt they were, replacing it with a different person'.[179] As discussed further in Chapter 6, the imposition of compulsory treatment in such circumstances raises complex ethical issues that cannot be resolved simply by reference to whether or not the person with anorexia has legal capacity.

For present purposes, the important point is the difficulties which egosyntonic disorders pose for a liberal account of capacity as requiring

---

[174] See J. Tan, 'The Anorexia Talking' (2003) 362 *Lancet* 1246; J. Tan *et al.*, 'Anorexia Nervosa and Personal Identity: The Accounts of Patients and Their Parents' (2003) 26 *International Journal of Law and Psychiatry* 533; J. Tan *et al.*, 'Competence to Refuse Treatment in Anorexia' (2003) 26 *International Journal of Law and Psychiatry* 697; J. Tan *et al.*, 'Competence to Make Treatment Decisions in Anorexia Nervosa: Thinking Processes and Values' (2006) 13 *Philosophy, Psychology and Psychiatry* 267. Similar issues arise with some personality disorders and some forms of depression: see A. Rudnick, 'Depression and Competence to Refuse Psychiatric Treatment' (2002) 28 *Journal of Medical Ethics* 155.

[175] For methodology, see Tan *et al.*, 'Anorexia Nervosa and Personal Identity,' 538.

[176] Tan *et al.*, 'Anorexia and Personal Identity,' 539; Tan *et al.*, 'Competence to Make Treatment Decisions,' 276.

[177] Tan *et al.*, 'Competence to Make Treatment Decisions', 276.

[178] Tan *et al.*, 'Anorexia Nervosa and Personal Identity, 544.

[179] Tan *et al.*, 'Competence to Make Treatment Decisions, 276; Tan *et al.*, 'Anorexia Nervosa and Personal Identity,' 542.

an ability to make true or authentic decisions. In some circumstances, a healthcare decision is simultaneously a 'true' preference arising from a part of the patient's identity and an 'untrue' preference arising from her underlying condition.[180] In practical terms, the difficulty of separating true from false selves means that assessors are likely to reach conclusions in respect of capacity based on the nature or outcome of the decision the patient proposes to make. For patients with a mental disorder, this may lead inevitably to a finding of incapacity.

Alternatives to capacity

Given the limitations of the liberal account of capacity identified in the previous section, a question arises as to whether an alternative way of 'sorting' decisions might be legally and ethically more defensible. As will be seen below, there are alternatives to capacity as a way of sorting decisions. Two alternatives which have been receiving some attention are vulnerability and impaired decision-making. An exploration of these alternatives shows that they give rise to even more difficulties than a capacity-based approach. Accordingly, it will be argued that capacity remains the best way of sorting healthcare decisions but that its limitations must be recognised.

Vulnerability as an alternative to capacity

A standard for protection based on vulnerability has, as Dunn *et al.*[181] show, played an increased role in the exercise of the court's inherent jurisdiction in recent years.[182] In the leading judicial authority in respect of the standard, *Re SA (Vulnerable Adult with Capacity: Marriage)*, Munby J held that the inherent jurisdiction may be invoked 'wherever a vulnerable adult is, or is reasonably believed to be, for some reason deprived of the capacity to make the relevant decision, or disabled for some reason from giving or expressing a real and genuine consent'.[183] In the case in question,

---

[180] Tan *et al.*, 'Anorexia Nervosa and Personal Identity,' 544–5.

[181] M. Dunn *et al.*, 'To Empower or to Protect? Constructing the "Vulnerable Adult" in English Law and Public Policy' (2008) 28 *Legal Studies* 234, 236–8.

[182] The 'inherent jurisdiction' was recognised by the House of Lords in *Re F (Mental Patient: Sterilisation)* [1990] 2 AC 1 and serves essentially the same role as the *parens patriae* jurisdiction which was abolished in England and Wales in 1959.

[183] [2005] EWHC 2942 (Fam), [79]. In reaching this conclusion, Munby J relied on the decisions in *Re G (An Adult: Mental Capacity) (Court's Jurisdiction)* [2004] EWHC 2222 (Fam) and *Re SK (Proposed Plaintiff) (An adult by way of her litigation friend)* [2004] EWHC 3202 (Fam).

Munby J invoked the jurisdiction in respect of a young woman (SA) and granted an order to prevent SA's family from taking her to Pakistan where there was a possibility that she might be coerced into a marriage arranged by her parents.[184] SA was assessed as having the legal capacity to marry.[185] However, she was described as being in the borderline range of ability in terms of intelligence;[186] she was also profoundly deaf and unable to communicate orally.[187]

Munby J set out a description of a 'vulnerable adult' in terms which he acknowledged were considerably broader than incapacity:[188]

> I would treat as a vulnerable adult someone who, whether or not mentally incapacitated, and whether or not suffering from any mental illness, or mental disorder, is or may be unable to take care of him or herself, or unable to protect him or herself against significant harm or exploitation, or who is deaf, blind or dumb, or who is substantially handicapped by illness, injury or congenital deformity.[189]

He held that SA was 'a vulnerable adult who there is every reason to believe may, by reason of her disabilities, and even in the absence of any undue influence or misinformation, be disabled from making a free choice and incapacitated or disabled from forming or expressing a real or genuine consent'.[190]

A vulnerability standard along the lines advanced by Munby J is problematic for a number of reasons. Dunn *et al.* point out some of these difficulties. First, because vulnerability is construed in a way which is 'tied to the personal, social, economic and cultural circumstances within which individuals find themselves at different points in their lives', it has the potential to be extraordinarily wide in its 'scope and application'.[191] Secondly, while the assessment of capacity has become task-specific, a vulnerability approach 'reawakens the ghost' of an approach to capacity based on status.[192] A person may be deemed vulnerable (and deprived of decision-making freedom) simply on the basis of her disability. Thirdly, cases based on vulnerability 'raise the possibility that a judgement that a person has the capacity to make an autonomous decision will be considered an inconvenient truth' which may be ignored as the focus for discussion shifts to other matters.[193]

---

[184] *Ibid.*, [18]. The young woman was not opposed to an arranged marriage, nor was she opposed to the cultural mores within which she and her family operated; however, she wished to choose from a range of people identified by her family and she wished to continue to live in the United Kingdom.
[185] *Ibid.*, [11]. [186] *Ibid.*, [8]. [187] *Ibid.*, [4]. [188] *Ibid.*, [76]. [189] *Ibid.*, [82].
[190] *Ibid.*, [124]. [191] Dunn *et al.*, 'To Empower or to Protect', 241. [192] *Ibid.*, 244.
[193] *Ibid.*, 247.

It is difficult to see how a standard based on vulnerability, as defined by Munby J, could be consistent with the CRPD. The denial of decision-making power to a person because she is 'deaf, blind or dumb' would seem to run contrary to the requirement in Article 12(2) that 'persons with disabilities [should] enjoy legal capacity on an equal basis with others in all aspects of life'. In focussing on intervention rather than empowerment, a vulnerability-based standard serves to reinforce the difficulties that a person may be encountering. It provides no means for a person to escape from an oppressive context and reduces the possibility of imaginative engagement with other ways of dealing with the issues arising from this oppressive context. There is also an argument that a focus on vulnerability leads to a failure to engage more closely with some of the more difficult questions in respect of capacity. In *Re SA*, for example, while SA was held to have the capacity to marry, she was also found to lack the capacity to conduct litigation.[194] Accordingly, her ability to leave her marriage was clearly impeded. In the specific context of the possible marriage in question (an arranged marriage in a foreign jurisdiction), this might be seen as an essential component of the contract.[195] A significant question here is whether one is concerned with a capacity to marry in the abstract or the capacity to marry in the specific context in question. Although Munby J has tended to favour a more abstract approach,[196] in *R* v. *C*, the House of Lords rejected such an approach in respect of consent to sexual relations.[197] For the purposes of the current discussion, the important point is that questions like this need to be addressed as part of the development of an appropriate legal framework in respect of the complex concept of capacity. A focus on vulnerability impedes such development by offering an easier alternative to courts.

In brief, a standard based on vulnerability lacks both rigour and a sufficiently established conceptual basis. Whatever the case for the use of a standard in other contexts,[198] it is difficult to see that a standard based on vulnerability can be justified in the respect of healthcare decisions.

---

[194] *Ibid.*, [16].

[195] On the role of a right of exit in such circumstances, see M. Enright, 'Choice, Culture and the Politics of Belonging: The Emerging Law of Forced and Arranged Marriage' (2009) 72 *Modern Law Review* 331.

[196] See also *In the Matter of MM* [2007] EWHC 2003 (Fam) where Munby J favoured a general approach to capacity to consent to sexual relations.

[197] [2009] UKHL 42, [24]. Although the House of Lords was concerned with the issue of consent as defined in the Sexual Offences Act 2003, the tenor of Baroness Hale's comments suggests a broader disagreement with this aspect of Munby J's approach: see J. Herring, '*R* v. *C*: Sex and Mental Disorder' (2010) 126 *Law Quarterly Review* 36.

[198] See J. Herring, 'Protecting Vulnerable Adults: A Critical Review of Recent Case Law' (2009) 21 *Child and Family Law Quarterly* 498, who suggests that there might be a basis

'Significantly impaired' decision-making

A second possible alternative to capacity is a standard based on 'significantly impaired' decision-making, which has been suggested in the context of treatment for a mental disorder. This standard was recommended in the Review of the Mental Health (Scotland) Act 1984[199] and given effect in the Mental Health (Care and Treatment) (Scotland) Act 2003, which requires that a patient's ability to make decisions must be 'significantly impaired' before a treatment order can be made.[200] This standard was also favoured by the Joint Committee in its discussions regarding the Draft Mental Health Bill 2004.[201] The Committee relied on evidence provided by Dr Anthony Zigmond from the Royal College of Psychiatrists regarding the distinction between this standard and one based on capacity.

Dr Zigmond made two arguments as to why this standard was preferable to one based on capacity. First, he argued that '[t]he notion that there is a particular cut off point one side of which somebody lacks capacity, the other side they retain capacity, is of itself wrong'.[202] In this, Dr Zigmond is undoubtedly correct. However, the difficulty here is not with whether the basis for the binary division is called 'incapacity' or 'impaired decision-making'. A standard based on impaired decision-making does the same thing as a standard based on capacity; it divides people into those whose right to autonomy is respected and those whose right is not. Simply calling the dividing point a different name does not solve any of the problems of the artificiality of the divide. Rather, more substantive steps are required to minimise the impact of the artificiality of the binary division in practice.

Dr Zigmond's second argument related to the definition of capacity. He argued that:

> One of the acknowledged difficulties with the current definition of 'incapacity' is that it relies almost entirely on a person's ability to think, what we call cognitive ability, and we recognise that in the field of mental health, of course, emotions play a large part, and so at a very practical clinical level we think that the notion of impaired decision-making by reason of

---

for intervention on the basis of vulnerability in respect of living arrangements in circumstances in which Art. 3 of the ECHR (protection from inhuman and degrading treatment) arises.

[199] *Report of the Review of the Mental Health (Scotland) Act 1984*, p. 57. This test was seen as 'less legalistic' and easier to apply in practice than a test based on capacity.

[200] Section 64 (5)(d).

[201] *First Report of the Joint Committee on the Draft Mental Health Bill*, Recommendation 26.

[202] *Ibid.*, para. 153.

mental disorder would be much easier for people to understand and relate to patients with mental health problems.[203]

In fact, as was argued above, the test for legal capacity encompasses more than cognitive abilities. Therefore, the problem identified by Dr Zigmond is possibly less to do with the actual legal standard for capacity and more an aspect of a failure to communicate the standard to professionals on the ground. As will be seen in the next chapter, this represents a significant problem for this aspect of the law in practice.

A standard based on impaired decision-making runs into similar difficulties in respect of precision and rigour to those identified in respect of a standard based on vulnerability. This vagueness makes the standard based on impaired decision-making even more susceptible to imprecise application than a capacity-based standard. Thus, the likelihood of patients being found to have significantly impaired decision-making ability where they disagree with medical advice may well be even greater than it is under a standard based on capacity.

The need for clear guidance regarding what is meant by 'significantly impaired' decision-making was recognised in the context of the Scottish legislation.[204] The term is not defined in the Mental Health (Care and Treatment) (Scotland) Act 2003 but some indication as to what it means may be found in the accompanying Code of Practice.[205] This states that, in assessing impaired decision-making, similar factors will be taken into account as in respect of an assessment of incapacity.[206] The difference between the two standards identified by the Code is that 'arguably,' impaired decision-making arises from a disorder of the mind 'resulting in a decision being made on the basis of reasoning coloured by a mental disorder'. In contrast, incapacity is described as implying 'actual impairments or deficits which prevent or disrupt the decision-making process'.[207] It is difficult to be sure exactly what the Code means by this distinction and how impaired decision-making differs from the application of a test based on capacity to 'use and weigh' information relevant to the decision. The lack of clarity regarding what is meant by the standard diminishes

---

[203] *Ibid.*

[204] See *Mental Health (Care and Treatment) (Scotland) Act 2003 Consultation Report on Draft Code of Practice and Regulations Policy Proposals* (Edinburgh: Scottish Executive Social Research, 2005).

[205] *Mental Health (Care and Treatment) (Scotland) Act 2003 Code of Practice, Vol II, Civil Compulsory Powers* (Edinburgh: Scottish Executive, 2005); see also Scottish NHS Education for Frontline Staff: available at www.nes.scot.nhs.uk.

[206] *Ibid.*, para. 22.   [207] *Ibid.*, para. 23.

the contribution of legal review of assessments. It is difficult to see how an assessment that a person's decision-making ability is 'significantly impaired' can be reviewed if there is no clear legal standard upon which to base the review.

For these reasons, and notwithstanding its limitations, capacity would seem to offer a better mechanism for sorting decisions than alternatives based on vulnerability or significantly impaired decision-making.

Conclusion

The capacity requirement is central to the exercise of the right of autonomy. This chapter has evaluated the legal standard for capacity in England and Wales and shown that, at the level of principle, the approach to capacity is largely in accordance with the law's endorsement of the liberal principle of autonomy. The chapter has also identified the limitations of a 'liberal account' of capacity. It has argued that a liberal account fails to recognise the relational nature of capacity and the practical and normative consequences of the epistemological fallibility of capacity assessment. It has also identified the limitations of this approach in circumstances where tasks cannot be neatly individuated and in circumstances where an ongoing mental disorder has had a profound impact on an individual's identity and self-perception.

In spite of the limitations identified, however, a standard based on capacity would still seem to offer the best option in respect of sorting health-care decisions. Although there is still a good deal of work to be done in this regard, there is a better chance of developing a rigorous legal framework around the concept of capacity than there is in respect of alternatives based on vulnerability or significantly impaired decision-making. However, a better legal framework for capacity would serve only to diminish rather than to remove the limitations which arise from a binary sorting of decisions. This becomes especially clear in the discussion of the operation of capacity assessment in practice in the next chapter.

4

Capacity assessment in practice

In *Re B (Adult: Refusal of Medical Treatment)*, Dame Butler-Sloss P described the test for capacity as 'clear and easily to be understood by lawyers'.[1] In fact, as this chapter shows, while the outline of the legal test may be stated with ease, what the test actually means is far from clear. Lord Phillips CJ was perhaps nearer the mark when he described capacity as 'an important, but by no means straightforward concept under English law'.[2] The lack of clarity increases the likelihood of assessors including their own views regarding the appropriateness of the patient's decision as part of the assessment of whether or not she has capacity. The legal test, however, represents just one part of the overall framework for capacity assessment in practice. The kind of process employed in testing for capacity is crucial both in ensuring accurate assessments and in developing the capacity of the person assessed, as is required under the Mental Capacity Act 2005 (MCA).[3] In this respect, formal judicial determinations of capacity comprise a very small proportion of such determinations. For the most part, the law has delegated the function of assessing capacity to non-judicial assessors. These are primarily healthcare professionals, and in most serious cases involving healthcare decisions, they are likely to be medical professionals. Furthermore, even when capacity is judicially determined, judicial conclusions are heavily reliant on expert evidence from professionals.

This chapter examines capacity assessment in practice.[4] It begins by breaking down the elements of the MCA test for capacity, setting out the abilities required and analysing the tensions to which the test gives rise when applied in practice. The chapter then looks at the small number of contexts in which formal capacity assessments take place, the procedures

---

[1] [2002] 2 All ER 449, 455.
[2] *R (on the application of B)* v. *Dr SS and Dr AC* [2006] EWCA Civ 28, [49].
[3] MCA, s. 1(3).
[4] This chapter draws on M. Donnelly, 'Assessing Capacity under the Mental Capacity Act 2005: Delivering on the Functional Approach?' (2009) 29 *Legal Studies* 464.

employed when this occurs and the role of expert evidence. The chapter then moves to consider informal capacity assessments, which comprise the vast majority of assessments. Drawing on empirical data, it explores the challenges experienced by non-legal assessors in carrying out the task of assessing capacity according to a legal standard and it evaluates the effect of delegation on capacity assessments in practice. It concludes by suggesting a number of ways in which a better approach to informal assessment might be delivered, although it also argues that these will diminish rather than remove the problems which have been identified.

Components of the capacity requirement

The MCA standard for capacity to make healthcare decisions centres on three sets of abilities: understanding, retention, and using and weighing information.[5] These abilities were also central to the test for consent to medical treatment at common law[6] and, therefore, pre-MCA case law continues to be relevant.

In addition, the MCA includes a requirement that a person must have the ability to communicate her decision (whether by talking, using sign language or by any other means).[7] The inability to communicate presents a practical rather than a philosophical justification for overriding patient autonomy. A person who lacks the ability to communicate may have the capacity to make fully autonomous decisions. However, if these decisions cannot be communicated, they cannot be given effect. For this reason, it is essential that every effort be made to establish communication. This is something which would seem to be possible in even quite severe cases. Thus, in *Re AK (Medical Treatment: Consent)*,[8] a young man with advanced motor neurone disease was able to communicate by a slight blinking movement.[9] Given the rarity of complete inability to communicate, findings of incapacity on this basis are likely to be highly unusual. One of the few examples of such a finding is the decision of the New Zealand High Court in *Auckland Area Health Board v. Attorney General*,[10] where the inability to communicate of a patient with an extreme form of

---

[5] MCA, s. 3(1).   [6] *Re MB (An Adult: Medical Treatment)* (1997) 2 FCR 541, 553–4.
[7] MCA, s. 3(1)(d).   [8] [2001] 1 FLR 129.
[9] In this, the case bears similarities to the experiences recounted by J.-D. Bauby, *The Diving Bell and the Butterfly* (Paris: A. Knopf, 1997).
[10] [1993] 1 NZLR 235. Contrast the Canadian case of *Nancy B v. Hotel Dieu de Quebec* (1992) 86 DLR (4th) 385 where a young woman with this disease was still able to communicate her wishes.

Guillain–Barré (or locked-in) syndrome provided the basis for a finding of incapacity.

The ability to understand information

The ability to understand information is the most straightforward of the abilities required for capacity. However, even in this context, there is a lack of clarity regarding the boundaries of the requirement, both in terms of what the person must be able to understand and in terms of how understanding might be assessed. As will be seen, this lack of clarity reflects a broader philosophical uncertainty regarding what respect for autonomy actually requires.

Understanding what?: the relevant information

Delimiting the amount of information that must be understood presents an interesting dilemma when viewed through the lens of the law's endorsement of autonomy. On the one hand, it might be argued that the amount of information should be limited in order to minimise the numbers of people found to lack capacity on this basis and to reduce the possibility of 'information overload' and confusion.[11] Furthermore, because information about risks may create feelings of stress and panic, perhaps especially in a person of borderline capacity, it might seem reasonable that information about risk should be limited in order to avoid this. On the other hand, outside of the capacity context, the 'delivery' of respect for autonomy through the doctrine of informed consent depends, in theory at least, on people understanding quite substantial amounts of information, especially in respect of risks. Thus, the underlying goal of protecting patients' autonomy causes the law to be pulled simultaneously in opposite directions.

In setting out the requirement for the ability to understand 'information relevant to the decision', the MCA defines 'relevant information' as including information about the reasonably foreseeable consequences of '(a) deciding one way or another, or (b) failing to make the decision'.[12] However, the MCA does not place outer boundaries around the information that must be understood. The accompanying Code of Practice provides more detail, although given the broad range of circumstances in

[11] See M. Gunn, 'The Meaning of Incapacity' (1994) 2 *Medical Law Review* 8, 24.
[12] MCA, s. 3(4). Contrast the Adults With Incapacity (Scotland) Act 2000, s. 1(6), which does not specify any information.

which the MCA is applicable, this inevitably lacks precision.[13] Thus, the Code recommends that time be taken to explain anything that might help the person to make a decision. It advises assessors not to give any more information than a person needs on the basis that this might be confusing, although it also cautions against omitting to supply important information. The Code also suggests that information should be given about risks and benefits and foreseeable consequences of making or not making the decision and that, where there is a choice, similar information must be given about all the options.[14]

A review of the case law shows very few findings of incapacity on the basis of a lack of understanding alone.[15] Accordingly, there is limited judicial guidance regarding the boundaries of 'relevant' information. In *R* v. *Mental Health Act Commission, ex parte X*,[16] Stuart Smith J was clear that a patient does not have to have a technical understanding of the 'precise physiological process involved' in a treatment decision. However, in *London Borough of Ealing* v. *KS and Others*,[17] in finding the patient to lack capacity, Wood J noted her inability to explain the meaning of the word 'cyst' as well as her failure to 'grasp' that, if the cyst were found to be malignant, her ovary might have to be removed. It is difficult to see how the failure to understand the word 'cyst' could be determinative, especially given that English was not the woman's first language and that she had earlier indicated an understanding that a lump would be removed.[18] However, because Wood J accepted the expert evidence without close scrutiny,[19] there is little analysis of the ways in which the woman had failed to meet the standard for capacity.

In *R (on the application of B)* v. *Dr SS and Dr AC*, the Court of Appeal made it clear that the test for understanding goes beyond simple understanding of information at an abstract level ('if a person does not have this treatment, it is likely that she will die') and requires an ability to appreciate the information in a more personal context ('if I do not have this treatment, it is likely that I will die').[20] It would seem that this requires that the patient

[13] Mental Capacity Act 2005: Code of Practice (London: The Stationery Office, 2007), para. 3.9.

[14] *Ibid.*

[15] Patients who have failed to meet the standard for understanding have generally also failed to meet the standard in respect of the other requirements for capacity: see, for example, *Tameside and Glossop Acute Services Trust* v. *CH* [1996] 1 FCR 753, 771.

[16] (1988) 9 BMLR 77.   [17] [2008] EWHC 636 (Fam), [84].

[18] *Ibid.*, [83].   [19] *Ibid.*, [84].

[20] [2006] EWCA Civ 28, [34]. On the meaning of 'appreciation,' see P. Fennell, 'Informal Compulsion: The Psychiatric Treatment of Juveniles under Common Law' (1992) 4

believes that the information is relevant in her own context. In the case in question, the applicant refused to accept that he had a mental illness or that he was in need of treatment and he was held to lack capacity on this basis.[21]

In this context, the question of what must be appreciated arises. In *Re E (A Minor) (Wardship: Medical Treatment)*, Ward J found that a 15-year-old Jehovah's Witness, who wished to refuse a life-saving blood transfusion, lacked capacity because

> [H]e has no realisation of the full implications which lie before him as to the process of dying. He may have some concept of the fact that he will die, but as to the manner of his death and to the extent of his and his family's suffering I find that he has not the ability to turn his mind to it nor the will to do so.[22]

This decision was clearly motivated by the policy concern that the court 'should be very slow to allow an infant to martyr himself'.[23] The high (possibly unachievable) degree of appreciation required shows the essential malleability of the appreciation requirement in achieving this aim.

The decision in *Re E* may have been distorted by the paternalistic approach favoured by the courts in the 'retreat from *Gillick*'.[24] Whether a similar approach is likely in respect of adults of borderline capacity is unclear. What is clear, however, is that the appreciation requirement has the potential to require a much higher standard of decision-making from people of borderline capacity than most people whose capacity is not at issue manage to achieve.

Testing for understanding

The first applications of the understanding requirement were not concerned with whether a person actually understood information but rather with whether, at a more abstract level, a person had the ability to

Journal of Social Welfare and Family Law 311, 324; A. Buchanan and D. Brock, *Deciding for Others: The Ethics of Surrogate Decision-Making* (New York: Cambridge University Press, 1989), p. 24.

21 *Ibid.* Contrast the decision of the Supreme Court of Canada in *Starson* v. *Swayze* (2003) SCC 32, discussed further in Chapter 6.

22 [1993] 1 FLR 386, 391.

23 *Ibid.*, 394.

24 G. Douglas, 'The Retreat from *Gillick*' (1992) 55 *Modern Law Review* 569. Although reported in 1993, the decision in *Re E (A Minor) (Wardship: Medical Treatment)* was handed down in September 1990 and preceded the Court of Appeal decision in *Re W (A Minor) (Medical Treatment: Court's Jurisdiction)* [1992] 3 WLR 758, which held that a capable minor's refusal of treatment could be overridden on the basis of the minor's best interests.

understand.[25] Correspondingly, testing for understanding tended to be general in nature.[26] The classic capacity testing mechanism, the Mini-Mental State Examination (MMSE), is an example of this approach.[27] The test is based on a series of questions intended to test orientation, memory, concentration, language and visual-spatial ability.[28] Patients who perform well on these general cognitive measures are considered to have capacity while those who do not are referred for further assessment.[29] As Peter Bartlett and Ralph Sandland point out, the difficulty with this kind of measure is that, while it may measure cognitive function at a general level, 'it is at best difficult to see how the cognitive function correlates with capacity'.[30] Further, Gunn et al. note that this approach to capacity may have an adverse impact on some patients with learning difficulties, who may have difficulty dealing with abstract concepts but may be quite capable of understanding information related to their own concrete situation.[31]

General cognitive testing is inconsistent with the functional approach to capacity which is adopted in the MCA.[32] Accordingly, the focus has shifted from assessment of the ability to understand to assessment of actual understanding.[33] The well-known capacity-testing mechanism, the MacArthur Competence Assessment Tool for Treatment (the MacCAT-T), includes

---

[25] See, for example, *R v. Mental Health Act Commission ex p. X* (1988) 9 BMLR 77.

[26] See V. Abernethy, 'Compassion, Control and Decisions About Competency' (1984) 141 *American Journal of Psychiatry* 53, 57; L. Roth et al., 'Tests of Competency to Consent to Treatment' (1977) 134 *American Journal of Psychiatry* 279, 281–2.

[27] See M. Folstein et al., 'Mini Mental State – A Practical Method for Grading the Cognitive State of Patients for the Clinician' (1975) 12 *Journal of Psychiatric Research* 189. For a summary of the most widely used tests, see T. Grisso, *Evaluating Competencies: Forensic Assessments and Instruments* (2nd edn) (Dordrecht: Kluwer Academic, 2002), Chapter 9; L. Dunn et al., 'Assessing Decisional Capacity for Clinical Research or Treatment: A Review of Instruments' (2006) 163 *American Journal of Psychiatry* 1323.

[28] Among the tasks to be performed are writing a sentence, copying a drawing and spelling words backwards.

[29] Scoring is out of a total of 30; it is recommended that patients who score below 23 should be referred for further assessment.

[30] P. Bartlett and R. Sandland, *Mental Health Law: Policy and Practice* (3rd edn) (Oxford University Press, 2007), p. 514.

[31] M. J. Gunn et al., 'Decision-Making Capacity' (1999) 7 *Medical Law Review* 269, 305.

[32] See also *Practice Note (Declaratory Proceedings: Medical and Welfare Decisions for Adults Who Lack Capacity)* [2002] 1 WLR 325, 327, which expressly discounted expert evidence in respect of capacity based on 'global psychometric test results'.

[33] See Gunn, 'The Meaning of Incapacity', 18; P. Appelbaum and T. Grisso, 'The MacArthur Treatment Competence Study I: Mental Illness and Competence to Consent to Treatment' (1995) 19 *Law and Human Behaviour* 105, 109; Gunn et al., 'Decision-Making Capacity', 304.

a test for actual understanding as one of three test measures.[34] The relevant test measure, called 'Understanding Treatment Disclosures (UDT), requires the assessor to provide the patient with information relating to the disorder, the treatment proposed, and the risks and benefits. The assessor then tests the patient's understanding through questions that require a description of the information provided in the patient's own words and through the patient's response to statements that must be identified as being 'the same as' or 'different to' the information.[35] Even if this specific mechanism is not employed, it is difficult to see how any mechanism for testing actual understanding could do other than require evidence that the patient understands the information provided. Given that many patients whose capacity is not at issue do not understand information about their treatment,[36] this requires more from patients whose capacity is in question than most patients achieve. Thus, patients who meet the very broadly defined causal requirement in the MCA by having an impairment in the functioning of the mind or brain[37] operate at an immediate disadvantage when compared with people without such an impairment.

A requirement for actual understanding also makes the patient reliant on healthcare professionals to provide information in such a way as to enable her to understand it.[38] Deliberate or unintentional failure to communicate on the part of the professionals may result in a finding of incapacity.[39] It is this relationship of dependence which led to the inclusion in the MCA of the requirements to take all practicable steps to assist a person and to provide an explanation in a way appropriate to the person's circumstances.[40] However, as discussed further below, the lack of

---

[34] Details of the test are outlined in T. Grisso and P. Appelbaum, *Assessing Competence to Consent: A Guide for Physicians and Other Health Professionals* (Oxford University Press, 1998).

[35] *Ibid.*, p. 187.

[36] See inter alia the studies quoted in M. Jones, 'Informed Consent and Other Fairy Stories' (1999) 7 *Medical Law Review* 103, 125–7.

[37] MCA, s. 2(1).

[38] See A. Grubb, *Kennedy and Grubb Medical Law* (3rd edn) (London: Butterworths, 2000), p. 616.

[39] For examples of deliberate decisions not to communicate information, see *Re E (A Minor)* (Wardship: Medical Treatment) [1993] 1 FLR 386 and *Re L (Medical Treatment: Gillick Competency)* [1998] 2 FLR 810. Both cases involved minors and this may have been a relevant factor in the approach taken. In both cases, the courts approved the doctors' decisions not to spell out in detail to the young people the manner of death they faced if they did not consent to the treatment and then held the young people to lack capacity on the basis that they did not understand the manner of death faced.

[40] MCA, ss. 1(3) and 3 (2).

meaningful enforcement mechanisms limits the potential impact of these provisions.

The ability to retain information

The requirement that a patient must have the ability to retain information is in line with research which suggests that '[i]f information has not been "stored" in a manner that facilitates recall at the time one is making a decision, the relevant information is not available [to the patient]'.[41] Given the large number of people with dementia, which is often associated with memory loss,[42] it may seem surprising that the issue of retention of information has received very little attention in the case law on capacity.[43] However, this may be because patients with dementia tend to be more compliant with treatment decisions and therefore the issue of capacity does not reach the courts.

Because the issue of retention has not been discussed by the courts, there is little clarity regarding how the requirement might apply. The MCA states that a person is not to be regarded as unable to make a decision because she can retain information 'for a short period only'.[44] In this respect, the legislation is attempting to ensure that people with longer term memory difficulties (typically people with early dementia) are not found to lack capacity on this ground alone. However, the vague way in which the legislation is phrased does not relate the ability required to the function to be performed. The Code to the MCA offers some clarification, stating that the person must be able to 'hold the information in their mind long enough to use it to make an effective decision'.[45] This period will vary, depending on the circumstances of the case in question. While more in line with the purpose of the retention requirement, the variability increases the malleability of the test.

As with the understanding requirement, the retention requirement presents a dilemma in terms of how best to respect individual autonomy.

---

[41] Grisso and Appelbaum, *Assessing Competence to Consent*, p. 41.

[42] J. Herring, 'Losing It? Losing What? The Law on Dementia' (2009) 21 *Child and Family Law Quarterly* 3, 3, notes that in the United Kingdom alone, 683,597 people have dementia, a figure expected to reach one million in the next decade.

[43] The issue is mentioned (along with other issues) in *London Borough of Ealing* v. *KS and Others* [2008] EWHC 636 (Fam), [84].

[44] MCA, s. 3(3).

[45] Code, para. 4.20.

While the adoption of a minimal retention requirement protects patient autonomy by preventing patients with early dementia from being found to lack capacity, it also limits the patient's opportunity to change her mind. If a patient cannot remember the basis on which she made a decision, she will have difficulty in revisiting the decision or even in recalling that she made the decision in the first place.[46] This is not especially problematic for one-off decisions, such as consent to surgery (provided the time-span between the consent and the surgery is sufficiently short) but it is a problem for decisions which are ongoing in effect. This raises the question of whether patients with memory difficulties should be reminded of basic information and asked if they still agree with their original decision. While attractive in theory, it could be distressing and confusing for many patients with retention difficulties to be asked to revisit treatment decisions. Once again, the dissonance between the ideal of autonomous decision-making and the reality of people's lives is evident.

The ability to use and weigh information

An inability to use and weigh information has provided the basis for most of the determinations of incapacity encountered in the case law (although, in many of these cases, treatment was actually authorised on a basis other than the patient's incapacity).[47]

The 'use and weigh' test applied

The 'use and weigh' test, as it has been applied by the courts, has focused on the factors that prevent a person from making a decision. Case law in respect of this ability indicates that a person may be unable to 'use and weigh' information for reasons arising from an underlying mental disorder or for more transitory reasons arising from a current medical condition. In terms of underlying disorders, the courts have recognised that a patient may lack the

---

[46] The Code *ibid.*, suggests the use of aids, such as videos and voice recorders, to assist longer-term retention.

[47] In some cases, treatment was authorised because the patient was a minor (and therefore any refusal of treatment could be overridden on the basis that the treatment was in her best interests): see *Re R (A Minor) (Wardship: Medical Treatment)* [1991] 4 All ER 177; *Re W (A Minor) (Wardship: Medical Treatment)* [1992] 3 WLR 758. In other case, treatment was authorised because the patient came within the ambit of the Mental Health Act 1983: see *South West Hertfordshire Health Authority v. KB* [1994] 2 FCR 1051; *F v. Riverside Health Trust* (1993) 20 BMLR 1 (overturned on other grounds in *Riverside NHS Mental Health Trust v. Fox* [1994] 1 FLR 614); *B v. Croydon Health Authority* [1995] 2 WLR 294; *Tameside and Glossop Acute Services Trust v. CH* [1996] 1 FLR 762.

ability to use and weigh information because she suffers from a psychosis[48] or personality disorder[49] which leads to false beliefs. In this respect, the 'use and weigh' requirement incorporates the requirement, which Thorpe J identified in *Re C (Adult: Refusal of Medical Treatment)*,[50] that a person must have the ability to believe the information provided.

Among the false beliefs which have been recognised by the courts[51] have been the patient's belief that she is not ill;[52] that proposed treatment will do harm rather than good;[53] that the proposed treatment is not intended to promote her welfare[54] and that facts are true which are not.[55] Although the matter has not yet come before the courts, it is probable that a patient with severe depression could also come within the ambit of the test if she rejected anti-depressive medication because she did not believe that any treatment could alleviate her symptoms[56] as would an anorexic patient's view that further refusal of food would not lead to her death.[57] False beliefs, which were unrelated to an underlying illness or psychosis, were regarded as impeding capacity in the Irish case of *Fitzpatrick and Another* v. *K and Another*, where Laffoy J held that the claimant's belief that her anaemia could be treated through the administration of Coca-Cola and tomatoes rendered her unable to weigh information relevant to her decision to decline a blood transfusion.[58]

---

[48] *Re D (Medical Treatment: Mentally Disabled Patient)* [1998] 2 FLR 22.

[49] *R* v. *Collins and Another, ex p. Brady* (2000) 58 BMLR 173; *NHS Trust* v. *T* [2004] EWHC 1279 (Fam).

[50] [1994] 1 WLR 290, 295.

[51] Note also the example given by Baroness Hale in *R* v. *C* [2009] UKHL 42, [24] of a person who believes that she has been commanded by God to have sexual intercourse.

[52] *B* v. *Dr SS, Dr G and Secretary of State for the Department of Health* [2005] EWHC 1936 (Admin).

[53] *NHS Trust* v. *T* [2004] EWHC 1279 (Fam) (the patient believed that blood was evil).

[54] *R (on the application of B)* v. *Haddock and Others* [2005] EWHC 921.

[55] In *Trust A and Trust B* v. *H (An Adult Patient)* [2006] EWHC 1230 (Fam), the patient believed that she did not have children and that the proposed operation would interfere with her ability to have children.

[56] T. Grisso and P. Appelbaum, 'The MacArthur Treatment Competence Study III: Abilities of Patients to Consent to Psychiatric and Medical Treatments' (1995) 19 *Law and Human Behaviour* 149, 163–4 found that approximately 14 per cent of patients with depression had difficulties appreciating the potential value of treatment proposed in their situations.

[57] For accounts of disbelief in this context, see J. Tan *et al.*, 'Competence to Make Treatment Decisions in Anorexia Nervosa: Thinking Processes and Values' (2006) 13 *Philosophy, Psychology and Psychiatry* 267, 271–72.

[58] [2008] IEHC 104. Laffoy J adopted the test in *Re C (Adult: Refusal of Medical Treatment)* [1994] 1 WLR 290, 295 as the applicable test for capacity under Irish law. The test as adopted did not include a causal requirement for an impairment of the functioning of the mind or brain.

Patients have also been found to lack the ability to use and weigh information because, in the words of Butler-Sloss LJ in *Re MB (An Adult: Medical Treatment)*, the pressures of the situation are such that '[o]ne object may be so forced upon the attention of the invalid as to shut out all others that might require consideration'.[59] Among the relevant pressures, as set out by Lord Donaldson MR in *Re T (Adult: Refusal of Medical Treatment)*, are 'confusion or other effects of shock, severe fatigue, pain or drugs'.[60] In *Re MB*, Butler-Sloss LJ recognised the possible relevance of these factors. However, she noted that they must operate 'to such a degree that the ability to decide is absent'.[61] Fear or panic may also be disabling factors if they 'paralyse the will and thus destroy the capacity to make a decision'.[62] In *Re MB* itself, the patient's phobic fear of needles was found to render her incapable of making the decision to refuse the proposed caesarean section.[63] Similarly, in *Bolton Hospitals NHS Trust v. O*, the patient, who suffered from post-traumatic stress disorder arising from her previous caesarean sections, panicked and withdrew her consent to a caesarean section on four separate occasions.[64] Dame Butler-Sloss P held the woman to lack capacity because her inability 'to see through the consequences of the act was inhibited by the situation of panic in which she found herself'.[65]

Courts have also found that a compulsion to refuse treatment may derive from an underlying mental disorder. In *Re W (A Minor) (Medical Treatment: Court's Jurisdiction)*,[66] Lord Donaldson MR disputed Thorpe J's earlier finding that a young woman with anorexia nervosa had capacity because she was able to understand the relevant information. In Lord Donaldson's view, Thorpe J had not taken sufficient account of the fact that it was a feature of anorexia nervosa that it creates 'a compulsion to refuse treatment or only to accept treatment which is likely to be ineffective'.[67] He described this attitude as 'part and parcel of the disease' and noted that 'the more advanced the illness, the more compelling it may become'.[68] This kind of compulsion was again recognised in *Re C (Detention: Medical Treatment)*, where Wall J found that C, a young woman who had anorexia nervosa, lacked the capacity to use and weigh

---

[59] [1997] 2 FCR 541, 554.

[60] [1992] 3 WLR 782, 796. See also *Norfolk and Norwich Healthcare (NHS) Trust v. W* [1997] 1 FCR 269; *Rochdale Healthcare (NHS) Trust v. C* [1997] 1 FCR 274. In both cases, the stress and pain of labour were found to be incapacitating factors.

[61] [1997] 2 FCR 541, 554.

[62] *Ibid.*   [63] *Ibid.*   [64] [2002] EWHC 2871.

[65] *Ibid.*, [15].   [66] [1992] 3 WLR 758.   [67] *Ibid.*, 769.   [68] *Ibid.*

information and that she was able selectively to ignore or distort information to suit her immediate purposes in a way which was largely unconscious and which she was unable to control.[69]

Tensions in the 'use and weigh' test

Notwithstanding the body of jurisprudence described above, what is actually required by a 'use and weigh' test remains in some respects unclear.
This is in part because most of the decisions have cited the absence of
the ability rather than attempting to set out in any detail what the ability
entails. A number of issues are problematic: first, the issue of belief; secondly, the issue of undue influence; and thirdly, the role of rationality.

(i) The role of belief   In *Re C (Adult: Refusal of Medical Treatment)*,[70]
Thorpe J set out a three-part test for capacity which included a requirement for the ability to believe information relevant to the decision in
question. Although a requirement for belief was not expressly included in
the common law test in *Re MB (An Adult: Medical Treatment)*[71] or in the
MCA test, it is clear from subsequent case law that the ability to use and
weigh encompass this.

The appropriate role for belief in the test for capacity is problematic in
light of the law's endorsement of autonomy. Beliefs are, in many instances,
inaccessible to those who do not share them. Yet, while some beliefs may
seem reasonable to outside observers, even if the beliefs are not shared,
others may seem unreasonable or unacceptable. Thus, for example, while
religious beliefs may lack a basis in provable fact, most outsiders are prepared to recognise a religious believer's acceptance of the tenets of her
faith. On the other hand, the belief of the patient in *State of Tennessee,
Department of Human Services* v. *Northern* that there was nothing wrong
with her feet although they were 'disfigured, coal black, crusty, cracking,
oozing, and rancid' seems inherently unreasonable.[72] While we may categorise beliefs as reasonable or not at an instinctual level, finding a justifiable basis for this is more difficult. Why is it reasonable for a Jehovah's
Witness to believe that she faces damnation for accepting a blood transfusion and not for a patient to believe that proposed treatment is not
intended to promote her welfare? Or, if religion is treated as a special case,

---

[69]   [1997] 2 FLR 180, 196.   [70]   [1994] 1 WLR 290.
[71]   [1997] 2 FCR 541, 554.
[72]   (1978) 563 SW 2d 197, 214. The patient was held to lack capacity because she lacked com-
       prehension of her situation.

why should a belief that nature should take its course be regarded as reasonable[73] while a belief that one is not ill is regarded as unreasonable?[74]

There is clearly no easy answer to this. The English courts have tried to reduce the impact of the difficulty by linking lack of belief to an underlying condition. Thus, in *Re C (Adult: Refusal of Medical Treatment),*[75] Thorpe J upheld the applicant's right to make an advance refusal of amputation on the basis that the applicant 'in his own way' believed the evidence that he could die without an amputation if his gangrene returned.[76] Thorpe J quoted expert evidence that there was not a direct link between the plaintiff's persecutory delusions and his beliefs regarding his present condition.[77]

When the belief requirement was assimilated into the use and weigh requirement in *Re MB*, the focus of the court was also on the source of the disbelief. Butler-Sloss LJ approved the view that, if a compulsive disorder or phobia 'stifles belief in the information presented to [the patient] then the decision may not be a true one'.[78]

By focusing on the source of the disbelief, rather than on whether the disbelief is reasonable or not, the English courts may avoid some of the difficulties with assessing the relative value of beliefs. However, because the MCA includes a causal threshold that requires that a person must have an impairment of the functioning of the mind or brain before the question of capacity can arise,[79] the very fact that the issue of capacity has arisen at all means that she has an underlying impairment. Therefore, in reality, courts are unlikely to be able to avoid making a value judgement regarding the quality or reasonableness of the patient's belief. This

---

[73] As in *St George's Healthcare NHS Trust* v. *S* [1998] 3 WLR 936.

[74] As in *B* v. *Dr SS, Dr G and Secretary of State for the Department of Health* [2005] EWHC 1936 (Admin).

[75] [1994] 1 WLR 290.

[76] In fact, as Bartlett and Sandland, *Mental Health Law*, p. 523, point out, Thorpe J's conclusion on this point is questionable in light of the evidence that Mr C believed that his life would be saved by divine intervention in such an event.

[77] [1994] 1 WLR 290, 292. See the similar conclusion reached by the Supreme Court of Ohio in *Re Milton* (1987) 505 NE 2d 255. Here, the appellant refused treatment for cancer on the basis of her firm belief in faith healing and, in particular, in the healing powers of a Reverend Jenkins, to whom she had the delusional belief that she was married. Notwithstanding her delusional belief in respect of the marriage, the majority of the Court held that her belief in faith healing stood 'on its own, without regard to any delusion' and she was therefore permitted to refuse the treatment.

[78] [1997] 2 FCR 541, 554.

[79] MCA, s. 2(1).

means that if the beliefs of a patient with a mental disorder or an intellectual disability are not seen as reasonable in the eyes of the assessor, those beliefs are almost inevitably going to be regarded as evidence of her lack of capacity. Thus, although at a theoretical level assessors are required to make determinations without making value judgements, when the test is applied to real people, this kind of neutrality is in fact impossible.

(ii) The role of undue influence   A second issue that is difficult to resolve satisfactorily within the framework of the use and weigh requirement relates to the role of undue influence. As is evident from the discussion in Chapter 2, the issue of undue influence does not just arise in the context of capacity. However, in a number of cases, the English courts have linked the two concepts.[80] In *Re T (Adult: Refusal of Medical Treatment)*, Lord Donaldson MR identified the patient's strength of will and the relationship of the patient to the persuader as relevant factors in determining if a patient's decision has been vitiated by undue influence.[81] Lord Donaldson noted that the presence of these factors should 'alert the doctors to the possibility – no more – that the patient's capacity *or* will to decide has been overborne'.[82]

The concepts were again linked in *Re MB* where, in setting out factors which might cause a patient to lack capacity, Butler-Sloss LJ noted that '[o]ne object may be so forced upon the attention of the invalid as to shut out all others that might require consideration'.[83] This statement is in fact a quote from a case relating to undue influence[84] and the statement could clearly be equally applicable to compulsion arising from external actors as well as that arising from internal sources. Hedley J took a similar approach in *Re Z: A Local Authority* v. *Mr Z and the Official Solicitor*,[85] noting that the presumption of capacity may be rebutted in a situation where the person has been 'unduly influenced by the views of others or by undue concern for the burden … imposed on others'.[86] The Law Commission

---

[80] For a discussion of the linkage between these concepts (in the context of contractual and testamentary capacity), see M. Green, 'Fraud, Undue Influence and Mental Incompetency: A Study in Related Concepts' (1943) 43 *Columbia Law Review* 176.

[81] [1992] 3 WLR 782, 797.   [82] *Ibid.*, emphasis added.   [83] [1997] 2 FCR 541, 554.

[84] The quote is from the testamentary capacity case of *Banks* v. *Goodfellow* (1870) LR 5 QB 549, 569 *per* Lord Cockburn CJ, who in turn was quoting from the earlier decision of *Harwood* v. *Baker* (1840) 3 Moo PC 282, which concerned undue influence in respect of a testamentary disposition.

[85] [2004] EWHC 2871 (Fam).

[86] *Ibid.*, [14]. The case in question was concerned with whether the claimant could travel to Switzerland in order to avail of euthanasia (where the procedure was lawful), hence Hedley J's focus on the issue of concern for the burden the condition imposed on others.

also saw a role for undue influence in the test for capacity. In its *Report on Incapacity*, the Law Commission stated that '[t]here are also some people who, because of a mental disability, are unable to exert their will against some stronger person who wishes to influence their decisions or against some *force majeure* of circumstances'.[87] This led the Law Commission to conclude that a decision lacked capacity if it was based on the 'overpowering will of a third party'.[88]

While the inclusion of undue influence within the test for capacity serves to address a genuine concern that some people of borderline capacity may be less able to resist if pressure is applied,[89] treating undue influence as an aspect of capacity means that a patient, who would be capable of making a decision if she had not encountered a particular set of pressures, will be found to lack capacity solely on the basis of the behaviour of external actors. By focusing on the patient's incapacity rather than on the pressures brought to bear on her, attention is shifted away from the real cause of the problem, which in some instances could be alleviated if addressed.

(iii) Rationality and the role of reasons for decisions   As discussed in Chapter 3, it is a fundamental premise of the liberal account of capacity that people do not have to reach rational or reasonable decisions in order to have capacity.[90] However, as also discussed in that chapter, this does not preclude a role for reasoning ability. The ability to process information, or reason, is an essential part of the ability to use and weigh information. As described by Munby J in *R (Burke)* v. *The General Medical Council and Others*, capacity is 'dependent on having the ability, whether or not one chooses to use it, to function rationally'.[91] However, assessors might easily confuse a requirement for reasoning ability with a requirement that the person reach a reasonable decision.

---

[87] Law Commission, *Report on Incapacity*, p. 38.

[88] *Ibid*, p. 39.

[89] See also the approach to consent taken in *R (on the application of E)* v. *Criminal Injuries Compensation Appeals Panel* [2003] EWCA Civ 234. Here, the Court of Appeal concluded that the applicant's vulnerability, his low IQ and his young age were all factors that should be taken into account in considering whether his consent to sexual relations with a fellow prisoner was valid or was a result of coercion.

[90] See *Re T (Adult: Refusal of Medical Treatment)* [1992] 3 WLR 782, 796 *per* Lord Donaldson MR; *Bolton Hospitals NHS Trust* v. *O* [2003] 1 FLR 824, 827 *per* Dame Butler-Sloss P.

[91] [2004] EWHC 1879 (Admin), [42]. Munby J defined this as 'having the ability to understand, retain, believe and evaluate (i.e. process) and weigh the information which is relevant to the subject-matter'.

The decision in *South West Hertfordshire Health Authority* v. *KB*[92] shows this confusion in action. In this case, Ewbank J held that a woman with anorexia nervosa lacked the capacity to use and weigh information on the basis that the woman regarded it as unlikely that she would die if she refused food because she was aware that, if she came close to death, she was likely to be resuscitated by her doctors under the emergency provisions of the Mental Health Act 1983. This accurate assessment of the situation shows a high level of reasoning ability, notwithstanding that the woman's decision to allow matters to reach this point might well be said to be irrational.

One reason for courts' difficulties in separating the ability to reason from the rationality of the decision reached relates to the mechanisms for assessing reasoning ability. Given the move from general to specific evaluations, it is difficult to see how reasoning ability can be measured without requiring a person to reveal the reasons for her decision. Thus, for example, the MacCAT-T test measure for reasoning ability, which is entitled 'Thinking Rationally About Treatment' (TRAT), assesses a person's reasoning processes by requiring her to state reasons for her decision, which are then marked on the basis of consequential reasoning, comparative reasoning, generating consequences and logical consistency.[93] Even if this rather demanding standard were not required, some degree of disclosure of reasons is essential in order to make an assessment of reasoning ability. Such a requirement seems to run contrary to Lord Donaldson MR's statement that 'the patient's right of choice exists whether the reasons for making that choice are rational, irrational, unknown or even non-existent'.[94] However, it is difficult to see any way around this. In practical terms, this once again shows the distinction between patients who are found to have an impairment of the functioning of the mind or brain and those who are not so found. For people who fall into the first category, whether because of mental disorder, intellectual disability or for some other reason, there is no right to make decisions for 'non-existent' reasons. Instead, if a person cannot produce good reasons for her decision, the fact that she reaches an irrational decision is highly likely to be regarded as evidence of an irrational or illogical reasoning process.

---

[92] [1994] 2 FCR 1051.
[93] Grisso and Appelbaum, *Assessing Competence to Consent*, pp. 187–8.
[94] *Re T (Adult: Refusal of Medical Treatment)* [1992] 3 WLR 782, 796.

The abilities in summary

The preceding analysis of the abilities required for capacity shows the malleability of the test for capacity. It also illustrates the difficulty in applying the capacity requirement in a way that prioritises patient autonomy when respect for patient autonomy may lead the test simultaneously in opposing directions. It is also clear that the test for capacity is not, and cannot be, a test for something wholly internal. The extent to which patients can achieve capacity is dependent on the behaviour of external actors, and especially on assessors. In the light of this, it is necessary to look more closely at process of capacity assessment, beginning with the relatively rare instances where capacity is judicially determined.

Judicial determinations, process and the role of expert evidence

Empirical research shows that the nature of the process employed in reaching a decision is crucial to the quality of the decision reached.[95] Research also shows that the process employed may have important consequences for the way in which people respond to a decision reached about them, even if they do not agree with the decision.[96] Perhaps the most significant contributor to an effective process in this sense is the (meaningful) participation in the process of the individual to whom the decision relates.[97] Participation in the process may also enhance individual well-being and self-esteem in a broader sense.[98] For these reasons, a 'good' assessment process, premised on 'honesty, informedness, transparency and patience', must be an essential aspect of the law in respect of capacity.[99]

---

[95] See D. J. Galligan, *Due Process and Fair Procedures* (Oxford: Clarendon Press, 1996).

[96] See T. Tyler, *The Social Psychology of Procedural Justice* (New York: Plenum, 1988); T. Tyler, *Why People Obey the Law* (New Haven: Yale University Press, 1990). In the context of mental health admissions, see J. Peay, *Tribunals on Trial* (Oxford; Clarendon Press, 1989), pp. 44–5; D. Dennis and J. Monahan (eds.) *Coercion and Aggressive Community Treatment: A New Frontier in Mental Health Law* (New York: Plenum Press, 1996), p. 24; I. Freckelton, 'Mental Health Review Tribunal Decision-Making: A Therapeutic Jurisprudence Lens' (2003) 10 *Psychiatry, Psychology and Law* 44.

[97] See Galligan, *Due Process and Fair Procedures*, pp. 131–2.

[98] B. Winick, 'The Right to Refuse Mental Health Treatment: A Therapeutic Jurisprudence Analysis' (1994) 17 *International Journal of Law and Psychiatry* 99, 100

[99] I. Freckelton, 'Involuntary Detention Decision-Making, Criteria and Hearing Procedures: An Opportunity for Therapeutic Jurisprudence in Action' in K. Diesfeld and I. Freckelton (eds.) *Involuntary Detention and Therapeutic Jurisprudence: International Perspectives on Civil Commitment* (Aldershot: Ashgate, 2003), p. 337.

The process for formal assessment

In a set of guidelines issued by the Court of Appeal, appended to its decision in *St George's Healthcare NHS Trust* v. *S*, the Court suggested that a formal adjudication of capacity by the courts should take place only 'if there remains a serious doubt about the patient's competence, and the seriousness or complexity of the issues' requires it.[100] The *Practice Note (Declaratory Proceedings: Medical and Welfare Decisions for Adults Who Lack Capacity)*,[101] issued in the wake of the guidelines, identified two situations in which intervention always requires court approval. These are cases involving non-consensual sterilisation and cases involving the discontinuance of artificial hydration and nutrition for a person in a vegetative state.[102] The current *Practice Note* also includes certain termination of pregnancy cases.[103] The *Practice Note* also suggests that 'any serious treatment decision … where there are doubts and difficulties over the assessment of either the patient's capacity or best interests should be referred to the court'.[104]

This approach to judicial involvement is echoed in the Code to the MCA. The Code states that a judicial determination will occur only in 'rare' circumstances.[105] It suggests that an application to the Court of Protection regarding capacity to make a particular decision may be necessary where a person wants to challenge a decision that she lacks capacity, where professionals disagree about a person's capacity to make a serious decision, or where there is a dispute, perhaps among family members, regarding whether a person has capacity.[106]

The procedural framework

The applicable procedural framework for capacity assessment is set out in the Court of Protection Rules 2007[107] and the Practice Directions

---

[100] [1998] 3 WLR 936, 969. The Court noted that, should this arise, evidence must also be provided regarding whether the person also lacks the capacity to manage her own affairs, including the appointment of a legal representative. If this is the case, it may be necessary to appoint a litigation friend for the purposes of the hearing.

[101] [2002] 1 WLR 325. This Practice Note is included as an Annex to *Practice Direction (Declaratory Proceedings: Incapacitated Adults)* [2002] 1 WLR 325.

[102] *Ibid.,* 326.

[103] *Practice Note: Declaratory Proceedings: Medical and Welfare Decisions for Adults who Lack Capacity* [2006] 2 FLR 373, [5].

[104] *Ibid.,* [6]. In *Re F*, Case No 11649371, 28th May 2009, Judge Marshall QC found that the threshold for the Court of Protection to accept jurisdiction should not be set too high. The 'proper test' for engagement of the court, ([44]) is 'whether there is evidence giving good cause for concern that P may lack capacity in some relevent regard'.

[105] Code, para. 8.16.   [106] Code, para. 8.16.

[107] SI 1744/2007, as amended by the Court of Protection (Amendment) Rules 2009, SI 582/2009.

issued by the Court of Protection.[108] In line with the HRA, the Court of Protection Rules seek to provide a 'human rights-compliant process'[109] for capacity assessment. The overriding objective of the Rules is to enable the Court 'to deal with a case justly, having regard to the principles contained in the [MCA]'.[110] The Rules cover all aspects of the judicial capacity assessment process (as well as the other functions of the Court of Protection). Thus, they set out the documents to be used, mechanisms for service of documents, and notification requirements as well as the applicable procedures in respect of hearings, admissions, evidence and depositions, and the role of experts. There are also provisions in respect of disclosure, litigation friends and change of solicitor, as well as costs, appeals and enforcement. Of particular interest to the current discussion is the efforts which the Rules make to facilitate participation by the person in respect of whom the assessment is made. A person whose capacity is at issue must be served notice of any matter or document,[111] including any application or appeal or the withdrawal of an application or appeal. She is entitled to attend the hearing[112] and is entitled to a 'litigation friend' during the proceedings.[113]

In addition to her own participation in the process, a person whose capacity is formally assessed is entitled to legal representation.[114] However, there is not an automatic entitlement to free legal representation. Whether a person is entitled to free representation depends on whether her situation comes within the funding criteria laid down by the Legal Services Commission.[115] In summary, the relevant Scheme provides legal aid for

[108] These may be accessed at the website of the Office of the Public Guardian (www.public-guardian.gov.uk).

[109] See *Explanatory Memorandum to the Court of Protection Rules 2007* No 1744 (L 12), para. 7.2.

[110] r. 3(1).   [111] r. 40.   [112] r. 90(2).

[113] r. 141. A person may act as litigation friend for someone if she can fairly and competently conduct proceedings on behalf of that person and if she has no interests adverse to those of the person (r. 142). The Official Solicitor may also be appointed as litigation friend (r. 143).

[114] On the importance of quality legal representation, see M. Perlin, 'Fatal Assumption: A Critical Evaluation of the Role of Counsel in Mental Disability Cases' (1992) 16 *Law and Human Behaviour* 39; M. Perlin, 'Is it More Than "Dodging Lions and Wastin' Time"? Adequacy of Counsel, Questions of Competence, and the Judicial Process in Individual Right to Refuse Treatment Cases" (1996) 2 *Psychology, Public Policy and Law* 114, 120; T. Carney, *et al.*, 'Advocacy and Participation in Mental Health Cases: Realisable Rights or Pipe-dreams?' (2008) 26 *Law in Context* 125.

[115] The Commission is established under the Access to Justice Act 1999. Under s. 6(8) of the Act, the Lord Chancellor may order the Commission to fund the provision of specified services. From the commencement of the MCA, the Lord Chancellor issued an authorisation under s. 6(8) ordering that certain applications to the Court of Protection should be funded.

decisions in respect of medical treatment, including psychological treatment, where the Court considers an oral hearing to be necessary.[116] Among the examples offered by the Legal Services Commission of circumstances in which legal aid would be made available are where it is proposed to withdraw artificial hydration and nutrition; where there is a proposal to sterilise a person without capacity; and certain termination of pregnancy cases. The Commission guidance also suggests that in '[m]any, but not all, cases' which the current *Practice Note* indicates should be subject to a court hearing, the entitlement to legal aid will be triggered.[117]

Beyond formal process

Formal statements of rights to participation and access to legal representation are important first steps in developing an appropriate capacity assessment process. However, the delivery of an appropriate process requires more than this. Indeed, a formal process may serve as a barrier to genuine participation by the person involved, alienating her from the decision made.[118] This is illustrated in Anne Vittoria's investigation of the operation of judicial adult guardianship hearings in Kansas.[119] Vittoria found that the hearings were 'perfunctory, with little or no input from the potential ward even if he or she is present'.[120] Lawyers acting for the possible ward tended to keep her to the margins of the hearing and were afraid to allow her to speak. In the words of one lawyer quoted, if she 'allowed the proposed ward to speak, he would just end up proving his "problem" to the judge when he opened his mouth'.[121] Vittoria found that alliances developed between judges and other professionals, which created a distance between these professionals and the person whose capacity was being assessed. Professionals were referred to by their formal titles while the person was often called by her first name or treated as if

---

[116] See Legal Services Commission, *Guidance on Mental Capacity Cases* (October 2007), [3], available at www.legalservices.gov.uk.

[117] *Ibid.*, [4]. For list, see text to note 104 above.

[118] See P. Bartlett, 'A Matter of Necessity: Enforced Treatment under the Mental Health Act' (2007) 15 *Medical Law Review* 86, 91; M. Donnelly, 'Assessing Legal Capacity: Process and the Operation of the Functional Test' [2007] 2 *Judicial Studies Institute Journal* 141, 161–8; M. Donnelly, 'Treatment Reviews: Legalism, Process and Rights Protection' in B. McSherry and P. Weller (eds.) *Rethinking Rights-Based Mental Health Law* (Oxford: Hart Publishing, 2010) pp. 282–3.

[119] A. Vittoria, 'The Elderly Guardianship Tribunal Hearing: A Socio-Legal Encounter' (1992) 6 *Journal of Aging Studies* 165.

[120] *Ibid.*, 167.

[121] *Ibid.*, 184.

she were not present at all. In brief, although formal procedural protections were in place, the subjects of the hearings were generally marginalised by the hearing process.

Terry Carney and David Tait's investigation of tribunal-based guardianship hearings in Australia offers a different picture of the formal hearing process.[122] This study found that tribunal members sought to incorporate the person whose guardianship was under consideration into the process, making efforts to welcome her and to explain the nature of the hearing[123] and to involve her at various stages in the process.[124] The tribunal members also sought to develop alliances between them and the person.[125] As a result, lawyers were sometimes made to feel marginalised, especially if they were hired by relatives rather than by the person herself,[126] and medical evidence was carefully scrutinised, at times to the chagrin of doctors who were displeased to see their professional judgements treated as no more authoritative than the evidence of their patients.[127] Carney and Tait measured the success of the tribunal approach using a number of standards, including whether the people involved were satisfied with the process and its ultimate outcome. In about half the cases, people (including carers) were happy with the process and the outcomes and, in another third, they were partly satisfied.[128] While this does not provide definitive evidence regarding the validity of the process, the model described by Carney and Tait would appear to have a better chance of enhancing patient capacity than the judicial model described by Vittoria. Accordingly, Carney and Tait's model would seem to be more in line with the relational approach to capacity advocated in the previous chapter.

These studies suggest that developing an appropriate procedural framework for capacity assessment is not a straightforward matter. Different imperatives may suggest different requirements. For example, while legal

---

[122] T. Carney and D. Tait, *The Adult Guardianship Experiment* (Annandale, NSW: Federation Press, 1997). The study relates to tribunals in New South Wales and Victoria, which, at the time of the study, were three-member bodies. Subsequently, the Victorian Guardianship Tribunal has become a one-member tribunal and has been incorporated into the Victorian Civil Appeals Tribunal (VCAT). Carney and Tait's findings therefore must be understood in the light of the tribunal structures of their time.

[123] *Ibid.*, p. 118.

[124] This included (*ibid.*, pp. 119–20) asking the person's views at different points and summarising medical evidence and giving the person the opportunity to comment on this.

[125] *Ibid.*, pp. 120–1. Tribunal members also tried (pp. 118–19) to minimise the impact of negative images emerging from professional evidence by stressing the similarities between the person and the tribunal board members.

[126] *Ibid.*, p. 122. [127] *Ibid.*, p. 123. [128] *Ibid.*, p. 156.

representation may fulfil the fair procedures requirement, it may also have the effect of alienating the individual from the process. What these studies clearly show, however, is the importance of broader engagement with the formal assessment process[129] and the need for empirical investigation of the way in which the Court of Protection operates. If the law is to take seriously its commitment to protecting autonomy, including the obligations arising under Article 12 of the United Nations Convention on the Rights of Persons with Disabilities (CRPD), it must find a means of operating formal capacity assessment in a way which maximises the capacity of the individual involved.[130] In this context, it now falls to consider the role of expert evidence and how this fits within a process centred on assessing and developing capacity.

The role of expert evidence

Courts have long relied heavily on expert medical evidence regarding capacity.[131] A survey of case law from England and Wales indicates that the vast majority of judicial decisions regarding capacity are based on psychiatric evidence regarding the patient's compliance with the legal test for capacity. This judicial approach is now formalised in the current *Practice Note*, which states that '[m]edical evidence as to capacity is required in every case, generally from a psychiatrist'.[132]

Judicial responses to expert evidence

In the case law prior to the MCA, when uncontradicted expert evidence was presented to the court, the court's ultimate decision almost invariably

---

[129] Both studies draw on the work of sociologist Erving Goffman on the theory of encounters: see E. Goffman, *The Presentation of Self in Everyday Life* (New York: Doubleday, Anchor, 1959).

[130] This may include judicial education as regards the best means of ensuring these values are upheld: see A. J. Shaddock *et al.*, 'Communicating With People With an Intellectual Disability in Guardianship Board Hearings: An Exploratory Study' (1999) 24 *Journal of Intellectual and Developmental Disability* 279.

[131] See L. Shelford, *Practical Treatise on the Law Concerning Lunatics, Idiots, and Persons of Unsound Mind* (Philadelphia: J. S. Littell, 1833), p. 40; M. Krasik, 'The Lights of Science and Experience: Historical Perspective on Legal Attitudes Toward the Role of Medical Expertise in Guardianship of the Elderly' (1989) 33 *American Journal of Legal History* 201.

[132] [2006] 2 FLR 373, [15]. For people with learning difficulties, the *Practice Note* suggests that the evidence of a psychologist may suffice. This *Practice Note* show a more directive approach than the previous one [2002] 1 WLR 325, [7], which described medical evidence as 'generally' required. Note, however, the view of the Court of Appeal in *G* v. *E* [2010] EWCA Civ 822, [61] that 'it would simply be unreal to require psychiatric evidence in every case' and that in cases of chronic conditions, 'credible expert evidence' of a psychologist would suffice.

accorded with that of the medical expert.[133] The dearth of reported decisions from the Court of Protection makes it difficult to assess if this has changed since the commencement of the MCA. However, if Wood J's acceptance of the doctor's 'compelling and unchallenged evidence which establishes lack of capacity' in *London Borough of Ealing* v. *KS and Others*[134] is indicative, it may well be that the MCA has had little impact in this respect.

As the law in this area has developed, it has become apparent that medical experts' evidence regarding capacity may be in conflict, in some cases quite spectacularly.[135] In these cases, judges have had to decide between competing views. It is difficult to point to a pattern in terms of preferred evidence and, obviously, it is impossible to assess conclusions without knowing the detail of the evidence as presented. It is noteworthy, however, that some judges appear to prefer the evidence of independent experts who do not have an immediate relationship with the person whose capacity is at issue.[136] This preference, insofar as it exists, could be seen as favouring the objective perspective of an outsider to the situation. However, it could also be argued that it fails to take account of the greater levels of knowledge that come from more intimate connections with the person whose capacity is being assessed.

Difficulties with judicial reliance on expert evidence

Judicial reliance on the evidence of medical experts has often been the subject of critical comment and, in a public lecture delivered in 2001, Lord

---

[133] One notable exception is the decision in *Rochdale Healthcare (NHS) Trust* v. *C* [1997] 1 FCR 274 where, in circumstances of extreme urgency, Johnson J disregarded the views of the consultant obstetrician that a woman, who refused to consent to a caesarean section, had legal capacity and found the woman to lack capacity.

[134] [2008] EWHC 636 (Fam), [84]. The case concerned capacity to marry as well as capacity to consent to medical treatment and, for this reason, was heard by the Family Court rather than the Court of Protection.

[135] For a sample of some disagreements, see *Re C (Adult: Refusal of Medical Treatment)* [1994] 1 WLR 290, 293; *R (Wilkinson)* v. *Broadmoor Special Hospital Authority* [2002] 1 WLR 419, 425; *Re JT (Adult: Refusal of Medical Treatment)* [1998] 2 FCR 662, 665; *B* v. *Dr SS, Dr G and Secretary of State for the Department of Health* [2005] EWHC (Admin) 1936, [190].

[136] In *Re C (Adult: Refusal of Medical Treatment)* [1994] 1 WLR 290, 293, Thorpe J preferred the evidence of psychiatrists appointed by the legal teams to that of the psychiatrist who had treated the applicant for almost 18 months and who had gained his 'trust and confidence'. In *Re JT (Adult: Refusal of Medical Treatment)* [1998] 2 FCR 662, 664, Wall J preferred the evidence of a psychiatrist who had met the patient twice to that of a nurse sister employed by the hospital who appeared to have an ongoing professional relationship with the patient.

Woolf acknowledged that courts had, in the past, treated 'the medical profession with excessive deference'.[137] Writing from an American perspective, Thomas Grisso outlines some of the problems with the quality of expert evidence in the context of capacity assessment. First, the expert may be ignorant of the law and consequently fail to provide relevant testimony. Grisso uses the example of the expert who gives 'diagnostic testimony' as conclusive evidence of incapacity; for example, where the expert gives evidence that someone has a mental disorder such as schizophrenia and then concludes on this basis that she lacks capacity in respect of a particular decision.[138] Secondly, the expert may be primarily concerned with persuading the court to accept her view and may therefore fail to present accurately the true complexity of a situation.[139] Thirdly, experts may not take sufficient care in formulating the evidence they present. In Grisso's words:

> Examiners sometimes may not obtain sufficient information about the examinee, in terms of quantity, type, or reliability of the observations, in order to reach certain conclusions credibly. In other instances, adequate data regarding the examinee may be available, but the interpretative meanings of the data in relation to the information needs of the court cannot be supported credibly by past research in psychiatry and psychology.[140]

Some US legal commentators are scathing in their critiques of the expert evidence given in capacity hearings in the context of refusal of treatment for a mental disorder.[141] Ansar Haroun and Grant Morris argue that some psychiatrists provide evidence in a way that is essentially deceptive.[142] They

---

[137] Woolf L, 'Are the Courts Excessively Deferential to the Medical Profession?' (2001) 9 *Medical Law Review* 1, 1. However, Lord Woolf argued that the position had begun to change for the better and that the balance was now 'about right'.

[138] Grisso, *Evaluating Competencies*, p. 12.

[139] *Ibid.*, p. 15. See T. Gutheil and H. Bursztajn, 'Clinicians' Guidelines for Assessing and Presenting Subtle Forms of Patient Incompetence in Legal Settings' (1986) 143 *American Journal of Psychiatry* 1020, 1020, who advise psychiatrists on strategies for the presentation of evidence in relation to a patient whose capacity is not obviously impaired so as to ensure that 'the inexperienced assessor or judge' is not 'taken in'.

[140] Grisso, *Evaluating Competencies*, p. 17.

[141] See S. Stefan, 'Leaving Civil Rights to the "Experts": From Deference to Abdication Under the Professional Judgment Standard' (1992) 102 *Yale Law Journal* 639; D. Bersoff, 'Judicial Deference to Nonlegal Decisionmakers: Imposing Simplistic Solutions on Problems of Cognitive Complexity in Mental Disability Law' (1992) 46 *Southern Methodist University Law Review* 329; M. Perlin, 'Pretexts and Mental Disability Law: The Case of Competency' (1993) 47 *University of Miami Law Review* 625; G. Morris, 'Judging Judgment: Assessing the Competence of Mental Patients to Refuse Treatment' (1995) 32 *San Diego Law Review* 343

[142] A. M. Haroun and G. H. Moss, 'Weaving a Tangled Web: The Deceptions of Psychiatrists' (1999) 10 *Journal of Contemporary Legal Issues* 227.

argue that this deceptive behaviour includes a failure to obtain informed consent for an assessment of capacity,[143] a failure to acknowledge bias[144] and a failure to appraise courts of the true levels of their uncertainty in their opinions.[145] While it cannot be assumed that these critiques would apply in other cultural and legal climates, they do show the need for a review of the quality of expert evidence relied on.

On the basis of the reported decisions in England and Wales, there is some variation in terms of the detail in which the expert evidence is recounted by the courts.[146] This may well reflect different judicial attitudes to the role of the evidence in question. If experts' views are to be accepted without question, there may be little need to spend time elaborating on what those views are. The reported decisions also suggest that there is little or no judicial recognition of the educative and enhancement aspects of the capacity assessment process. Even in the cases with detailed expositions, the experts' views are simply recounted without any reference to the issue of whether a person might have been assisted in reaching the standard for capacity.

Improving the evidence process

It is difficult to assess the quality of expert evidence relied on by the courts without better empirical data. For this reason, an essential first step to improving the evidence process is the accumulation of empirical data regarding what actually happens in practice. A second step is the development of a systematic method of evaluating the quality of expert evidence. With the exception of certain remarks of Dame Butler-Sloss,[147] there is little judicial guidance for experts in formulating appropriate evidence. The Court of Protection Rules provide some assistance in this regard. The Rules state that expert evidence must be given in a written report[148] and that the Court may give directions as to the matters to be covered in

---

[143] *Ibid.*, 231.   [144] *Ibid.*, 232.   [145] *Ibid.*, 234.

[146] Compare the detailed descriptions given by Dame Butler-Sloss P in *Re B (Adult: Refusal of Medical Treatment)* [2002] 2 All ER 449, 462–70; by Thorpe J in *Re C (Adult: Refusal of Medical Treatment)* [1994] 1 WLR 290, 295; and by Charles J in *B* v. *Dr SS, Dr G and Secretary of State for the Department of Health* [2005] EWHC (Admin) 1936, [190] with the limited discussion in the early caesarean section cases, see for example, *Tameside and Glossop Acute Services Trust* v. *CH* [1996] 1 FCR 753.

[147] In *Re B (Adult: Refusal of Medical Treatment)* [2002] 2 All ER 449, 470, Dame Butler-Sloss P drew particular attention to the evidence of one expert, noting that the evidence 'may be of assistance for clinicians in the future'.

[148] SI 1744/2007, r. 124.

the report.[149] The Court may direct a discussion between experts, requiring them, where possible, to reach an agreed opinion on the relevant issues.[150] The Court may also direct the experts, following a discussion between them, to prepare a report for the Court, setting out the issues on which they agree and those on which they disagree, together with a summary of their reasons for disagreeing.[151]

The process for admitting evidence under the Rules allows the Court of Protection to make a valuable contribution to improving the standard of capacity assessment by requiring assessors to elucidate more fully the way in which they reach conclusions about capacity. In this respect, special care is required in relation to the way in which the Court uses directions seeking expert agreement. Evidence must not be allowed to become reduced to a form of 'horse-trading', where experts reach compromises and present an agreed front to the Court. If the Court is to make an impact, it is essential that it produces a body of written decisions, which give guidance to professionals and which are available for consideration and critique. While the general expectation under the Court of Protection Rules is that hearings before the Court will be held in private,[152] the Court may authorise the publication of information about proceedings or the publication of the full text or a summary of the judgment or order.[153] Publication of capacity judgments needs to be done on a systematic basis if the expertise which, it is hoped, will develop in the Court is to be fully utilised and the impact of a more rigorous approach is to be widely felt. In this respect, detail is important. It is not enough simply to summarise the finding as regards capacity. In order to develop knowledge among assessors and among people who wish to challenge assessments, detailed critical engagement with the assessment process is needed, especially in the early days of the MCA. As will be discussed below, this is especially significant given that the MCA is premised on the extensive delegation of capacity assessment to non-lawyers.

Delegation of capacity assessment under the MCA

The functional approach to capacity adopted by the MCA requires a separate assessment of capacity for each decision a person proposes to make. Given the administrative challenges to which this gives rise, it is unsurprising that the MCA delegates the function of capacity assessment.

---

[149] r. 126.   [150] r. 128(1).   [151] r. 128(3).   [152] r. 90.

[153] r. 91. The Court has done this on a number of occasions. To date, there is little guidance regarding capacity emerging from the case law: however, see *Re F*, Case No 11649371, 28th May 2009 on operation of presumption of capacity.

Reliance on assessors to whom the function of capacity assessment has been delegated can only be justified, however, if the assessors have the skills and knowledge necessary to carry out the task. As Bartlett and Sandland remind us, decisions taken under the MCA are given statutory authority. In such circumstances, they ask 'can, or should, the state really turn its back on how these decisions are made?'[154]

Who are the assessors?

The MCA does not directly address the question of who should act as assessor, leaving this to be dealt with in the accompanying Code. As noted above, the Code envisages that a judicial determination of capacity will occur only in 'rare' circumstances.[155] In respect of other decisions, the identity of the assessor will vary depending on the nature of the decision. For most 'day-to-day' decisions, the Code states that capacity will be assessed by the person who, at the time the decision comes to be made, is directly concerned with the care of the person whose capacity is in question.[156] Thus, a family member may decide whether or not a person has the capacity to consent to being dressed or a care worker may decide whether a person can agreed to be bathed.[157] If a doctor or healthcare professional proposes treatment or examination, the Code states that she should assess the person's capacity to consent to this.[158]

For more 'complex' decisions, the Code states that a 'formal' assessment by a (non-legal) professional may be required.[159] This kind of assessment may also be required where someone challenges an original finding of lack of capacity, where family members disagree, or where there is a conflict of interest between the original assessor and the person assessed.[160] The professional in question may simply be the person's general practitioner.[161] However, the Code notes that, if the person has a particular condition or disorder, it may be appropriate to consult a specialist such as a consultant psychiatrist or psychologist or another professional, perhaps a speech and language therapist, with experience in the field in question.[162] However, while making some moves towards a multi-disciplinary approach, it is evident that the Code envisages that most professional capacity assessors will continue to be healthcare professionals, and most probably doctors.

---

[154] Bartlett and Sandland, *Mental Health Law*, p. 575.
[155] Code, para. 8.16. [156] *Ibid.*, para. 4.38.
[157] *Ibid.* [158] *Ibid.*, para. 4.40.
[159] *Ibid.*, para. 4.42. [160] *Ibid.*, para. 4.53.
[161] *Ibid.*, para. 4.51. [162] *Ibid.*

Where the capacity assessment arises in circumstances that involve a possible deprivation of liberty (by admission to a hospital or care home),[163] a specific regulatory framework applies.[164] In these circumstances, the capacity assessor is appointed by the designated 'supervisory body'[165] and must fulfil the criteria set out in the Mental Capacity (Deprivation of Liberty) Regulations 2008.[166] Eligible assessors include mental health professionals, social workers, nurses, occupational therapists and psychologists.[167]

Assessing capacity: what the MCA expects

The MCA is rather circumspect regarding what is expected from assessors. It does, however, expressly state that a person is to be assumed to have capacity[168] and that she is not to be treated as unable to make a decision merely because she makes an unwise decision.[169] The MCA also states that a lack of capacity cannot be established merely by reference to a person's age or appearance, or to 'a condition of his, or an aspect of his behaviour, which might lead others to make unjustified assumptions about his capacity'.[170] The Code gives more detailed guidance regarding the steps to be taken in assessing capacity.[171] Strikingly, however, it does not expressly state that consent to the assessment must be sought. Rather, the Code

---

[163] A deprivation of liberty is defined in accordance with Art. 5 of the ECHR and the case law arising under the Article; further guidance is found in the *Mental Capacity: Deprivation of Liberty Safeguards Code of Practice* (London: The Stationery Office, 2008).

[164] This follows the amendment of the MCA by s. 50 of the Mental Health Act 2007, which inserts ss. 4A, 4B and 16A into the MCA. This amendment was necessary to address the consequences of the decision in *HL* v. *United Kingdom* (2004) 40 EHRR 761. Under the MCA, s. 4A, a person may be deprived of liberty through admission to a hospital or care home only where the admission is authorised by a court order or by the relevant 'supervisory body' in accordance with the procedures laid down in Sch. A1 to the MCA.

[165] If the proposed admission is to a care home, the relevant supervisory body is the local authority; if to a hospital in England, the relevant body is the relevant primary care trust; if to a hospital in Wales, it is the Welsh Ministers or a local health board: MCA, Sch. A1, Pt. 4.

[166] Mental Capacity (Deprivation of Liberty: Standard Authorisations, Assessments and Ordinary Residence) Regulations 2008, SI 1858/2008.

[167] *Ibid.*, Reg. 6.   [168] MCA, s. 1(2).   [169] MCA, s. 1(4).

[170] MCA, s. 2(3). The Code, para. 4.8 notes the deliberate choice of the term 'appearance', which is intended to cover the physical characteristics of certain conditions, for example Down's syndrome, and other aspects of a person's appearance, such as skin colour, tattoos and body piercings. The term 'condition' is also intended to be interpreted in a wide-ranging way (Code, para. 4.9) to include physical disabilities, illnesses related to age, temporary conditions and extrovert behaviour.

[171] See, in particular, Code, paras. 4.36 and 4.45.

suggests that the assessor should '[m]ake every effort to communicate with the person to explain what is happening'.[172] This seems rather a weak statement within a framework that is supposed to centre on developing capacity. It is difficult to see how a patient can be facilitated in developing her decision-making capacity if she is not even aware that the process of assessment is taking place.

The issue of consent to assessment is, in fact, difficult in the light of the statutory presumption of capacity.[173] The Code to the MCA states that, if a person lacks the capacity to consent or to refuse an assessment of capacity, the assessment may go ahead provided that the person does not object to the assessment and that the assessment is in her best interests.[174] However, the Code also states that 'nobody can be forced to undergo an assessment of capacity'.[175] This is entirely consistent with the statutory presumption of capacity. It means, however, that a person can effectively prevent intervention (regardless of whether or not she would have been found to lack capacity) since, if she cannot be assessed, there is no evidence to rebut the presumption of capacity and treatment cannot be provided.[176] It is perhaps for this reason that the Code skates over the issue of consent to the assessment in the way it does.

Enforcing the MCA requirements

Section 5 of the MCA provides the primary mechanism for enforcing the statutory requirements in respect of assessment. This section provides a statutory protection from liability for any person who does an act in connection with the care or treatment of another person lacking capacity, provided that 'reasonable steps' have been taken to establish whether the person lacks capacity in relation to the matter in question. In this respect, the Code becomes significant. Although there are no specific sanctions for failure to comply with the Code, section 42(5) of the MCA states that, if it appears to a court or tribunal conducting any criminal or civil proceedings that a provision of the Code or a failure to comply with the Code is relevant to the question considered, the provision or failure must be taken into account in deciding the question.

---

[172] Code, para. 4.45.
[173] MCA, s. 1(2). Although, note the flexible approach to the presumption taken in *Re F*, Case No 11649371, 28th May 2009.
[174] Code, para. 4.58.   [175] *Ibid.*, para. 4.59.
[176] The Code, para. 4.59 notes that, if there are serious worries about a person's mental health, it may be possible to admit the person under the Mental Health Act 1983, although it also states that simply refusing an assessment of capacity in no way constitutes sufficient grounds for assessment under the Mental Health Act 1983.

The Code suggests a variation in standard regarding what constitutes 'reasonable steps', depending on the identity of the assessor. Thus, the Code states that carers 'do not have to be experts in assessing capacity'.[177] However, it goes on to state that, if someone challenges a carer's assessment, she must be able to describe the steps she has taken in assessing capacity and to show that she has objective reasons for reaching her conclusion.[178] In contrast, according to the Code, 'a doctor assessing somebody's capacity to consent to treatment must demonstrate more skill than someone without medical training'.[179] Peter Bartlett argues that the basis for a differential standard for doctors and other assessors is not obvious on the face of the statute.[180] Noting the move towards a multi-disciplinary approach, he suggests that '[i]f [capacity] determinations are not just a medical matter, why should the courts expect doctors to be better at them than other people?'[181] While probably largely reflective of reality, the Code's singling out of doctors is potentially misleading. The important point is not that doctors should be better at capacity assessment than non-doctors but that professionals in any discipline who act as assessors should be held to a higher standard than non-professionals. Assessing capacity is a professional activity that requires assessors to use 'some special skill or competence'.[182] Professionals carrying out this function should be obliged to understand the statutory standard in detail and be able to show a sufficient degree of competence in applying this knowledge to individual cases. As will be seen below, professional assessors appear to encounter difficulties in respect of both aspects.

Assessing the assessors

The law has effectively handed over the task of assessing capacity to non-lawyers. In considering the impact of this, two questions come to mind. First, do assessors have the necessary skills and knowledge to carry out the task? Secondly, can assessors perform a value-neutral, unbiased assessment of capacity as required under the MCA[183] and the Code?[184] It is argued below that, in both cases, the answer may be no.

---

[177] Code, para. 4.44.   [178] *Ibid.*   [179] Code, para. 6.33.
[180] P. Bartlett, *Blackstone's Guide to the Mental Capacity Act 2005* (2nd edn) (Oxford University Press, 2008), p. 63.
[181] *Ibid.*
[182] *Bolam v. Friern Hospital Management Committee* [1957] 1 WLR 582, 586 *per* McNair J.
[183] MCA, s. 1(4) and s. 2(3).
[184] Code, para. 44.

Assessors' knowledge and skills

There have been relatively few empirical studies regarding how assessors operate and those that do exist tend to relate to medical professionals.[185] These studies have a range of different goals, they involve subjects with different kinds of incapacities and they adopt different methodological approaches. Further, because they do not relate to the MCA, it would be inappropriate to draw overly strong conclusions from them in respect of the MCA. Nonetheless, taken together, the studies do suggest that medical professionals encounter a number of difficulties when acting as capacity assessors. The studies also raise the question of how well equipped healthcare professionals are in carrying out their legal role in this regard.

The findings of several pre-MCA studies suggest that a significant number of healthcare professionals do not understand the role played by capacity under the law or the requirements of the legal test for capacity. Jackson and Warner's survey of 129 British medical professionals found that only 20 per cent of GPs, 34 per cent of consultant geriatricians and 15 per cent of medical students surveyed gave correct answers to basic legal questions relating to consent and capacity.[186] Psychiatrists were found to have a better understanding of the law but, even so, only 58 per cent gave correct answers to the questions. A similar picture emerges from these authors' study of emergency healthcare workers.[187] Suto *et al.* in a study

---

[185] The most relevant studies for the purposes of the discussion here are (in chronological order): D. Marson *et al.*, 'Consistency of Physicians' Judgments of Capacity to Consent in Mild Alzheimer's Disease' (1997) 45 *Journal of the American Geriatrics Society* 132; E. Jackson and J. W. Warner, 'How Much do Doctors Know About Consent and Capacity?' (2002) 95 *Journal of the Royal Society of Medicine* 601; W. Suto *et al.*, 'Substitute Financial Decision-making in England and Wales: A Study of the Court of Protection' (2002) 24 *Journal of Social Welfare and Family Law* 37; L. Ganzini *et al.*, 'Pitfalls in Assessment of Decision-Making Capacity' (2003) 44 *Psychosomatics* 237; A. Shah and S. Mukherjee, 'Ascertaining Capacity to Consent: A Survey of Approaches Used by Psychiatrists' (2003) 43 *Medicine, Science and the Law* 231; V. Raymont *et al.*, 'Prevalence of Mental Incapacity in Medical Inpatients and Associated Risk Factors: Cross-Sectional Study' (2004) 364 *Lancet* 1421; S. Ramsey, 'The Adults With Incapacity (Scotland) Act – Who Knows? Who Cares?' (2005) 45 *Scottish Medical Journal* 20; R. Cairns *et al.*, 'Reliability of Mental Capacity Assessments in Psychiatric In-Patients' (2005) 187 *British Journal of Psychiatry* 372; K. Evans *et al.*, 'How Much Do Emergency Healthcare Workers Know About Capacity and Consent?' (2007) 24 *Emergency Medicine Journal* 291; J. McCulloch, '(In)capacity Legislation in Practice' (2009) 33 *Psychiatric Bulletin* 20.

[186] Jackson and Warner, 'How Much do Doctors Know About Consent and Capacity', 603.

[187] Evans *et al.*, 'How Much Do Emergency Healthcare Workers Know About Capacity and Consent', 391–2. In the study of 86 emergency professionals (42 doctors, 21 nurses, 23 ambulance staff), 67 per cent of doctors, 10 per cent of nurses and no ambulance workers gave correct answers to legal questions about consent and capacity.

of assessors' evidence to the former Court of Protection in respect of the appointment of a receiver for a person lacking capacity[188] found that a startling 74 per cent of assessors relied on the fact that the person fitted within a specific clinical population (e.g. she had an intellectual disability) as the criterion for determining capacity to make financial decisions[189] and that only one-fifth of the assessors made specific reference to the skills needed for financial decision-making.[190]

While the legislative attention given to this issue by the MCA may have improved assessors' legal knowledge, the Scottish experience calls this proposition into question. One study across a range of Scottish healthcare professionals found that, two years after the introduction of the Adults with Incapacity (Scotland) Act 2000, 34 per cent of professionals had not heard of the Act.[191] A more recent Scottish study of consultant psychiatrists found that only 54 per cent of respondents felt confident in their use of the Act (although 74 per cent expressed confidence in their ability to assess capacity).[192]

Moving beyond knowledge of the technicalities of the legal position, the question arises regarding how the law is applied. Empirical data in this respect have tended to relate to inconsistencies in respect of findings of capacity, usually with reference to an expert view,[193] rather than to the detail of how the professionals actually performed their function.[194] Shah and Mukherjee's study of psychiatrists' assessment of capacity to consent to admission to a psychogeriatric ward found a 'weak concordance' between the assessments of psychiatrists on the ground and those of a psychiatrist with a specific expertise in capacity assessment.[195] Cairns *et al.*'s study of capacity in patients with mental disorders found a

---

[188] Under the Mental Health Act 1983, s. 99 (now replaced by the MCA), a receiver was appointed where a patient was found to be 'incapable, by reason of mental disorder, of managing and administering his property and affairs'.

[189] Suto *et al.*, 'Substitute Financial Decision-making in England and Wales', 48.

[190] *Ibid.*, 47.

[191] Ramsey, 'The Adults With Incapacity (Scotland) Act', 21. The study investigated 50 healthcare professionals (nurses, house officers and specialist registrars) working on acute and elective surgical and orthopaedic wards.

[192] McCulloch, '(In)capacity Legislation in Practice', 21.

[193] Most study methodologies involve steps to verify the conclusions of the experts.

[194] Note, however, the attempt to develop a pilot testing mechanism for assessors in S. Whyte *et al.*, 'Testing Doctors' Ability to Assess Patients' Competence' (2004) 27 *International Journal of Law and Psychiatry* 291.

[195] Shah and Mukherjee, 'Ascertaining Capacity to Consent', 233. The study was based on responses to two vignettes. The mean kappa score (i.e. the proportion of instances of agreement adjusted to take account of chance calculated on the basis that 'perfect' agreement is rated at 1) for agreement between the practising psychiatrists' assessment and that of the expert was 0.17 in respect of the first vignette and 0.12 in respect of the second.

'moderate level of agreement' between the expert interviewers who were part of the study team and the clinical teams responsible for the patients' care.[196] There is also evidence of inconsistency in Raymont *et al.*'s study of the prevalence of incapacity among medical inpatients. The researchers found a relatively high proportion of patients to lack the capacity to make healthcare decisions.[197] They also noted a significant discrepancy between their own conclusions regarding capacity and those reached by clinicians on the ground. In 76 per cent of cases where the researchers found the patient to lack decision-making capacity, the clinicians believed that the patient had capacity.[198] In the view of the researchers, 'in routine clinical practice, doctors most usually fail to identify that patients with significant cognitive impairment do not have capacity'.[199]

Evidence of inconsistency in conclusions about capacity is, of course, no surprise given the fluidity of the test. Nonetheless, the empirical evidence does raise concerns about how assessors actually operate.[200] These concerns are shared by some healthcare professionals working in the area. Whyte *et al.* summarise the position as follows: '[m]any, perhaps most, assessments of [capacity] by doctors and other health professionals in the UK are undocumented, highly informal, and unstructured'.[201] Shaun O'Keefe, an Irish geriatrician, concludes that '[w]hile one may have reasonably high confidence in, say, a liver specialist's judgement that a patient has cirrhosis, the same is not true for even an expert and conscientious judgement of a patient's capacity'.[202]

Assessment and the role of assessors' values

Although there is a shortage of specific studies on the role played by assessors' values in the capacity assessment process, some conclusions may

---

[196] Cairns *et al.*, 'Reliability of Mental Capacity Assessments, 374. The mean kappa score for agreement was 0.51.

[197] Raymont *et al.*, 'Prevalence of Mental Incapacity,' 1424. Out of the 159 patients assessed, 50 (31 per cent) were found to lack capacity.

[198] *Ibid.*

[199] *Ibid.*, 1425. Note also P. Guyer *et al*, 'The Mental Capacity Act 2005: Review of Mental Capacity Assessment in People with Proximal Femoral Fracture' (2010) 34 *The Psychiatrist* 284, which found only 2 percent of assessments (one out of fifty) had been done properly.

[200] See also the findings of a United States study on consistency (Marson, 'Consistency of Physicians' Judgments'). This found 'limited' agreement among senior doctors with an expertise in geriatrics in respect of whether a patient with mild Alzheimer's disease had the capacity to consent to medical treatment.

[201] Whyte *et al.*, 'Testing Doctors' Ability,' 291.

[202] S. O'Keefe, 'A Clinician's Perspective: Issues of Capacity in Care' (2008) 14 *Medico-Legal Journal of Ireland* 41, 44.

be drawn from related studies of healthcare professionals. These suggest that assessors' values may impact on the assessment in two ways. First, capacity assessors who are healthcare professionals may encounter a dissonance between their therapeutic role and their role as capacity assessor. Secondly, the relationship between the assessor and the assessed is personal (as well as, in many instances, professional) and this impacts on the way in which assessment is carried out.

(i) Sources of professional dissonance   There are a number of potential methodological and normative conflicts between the legal and the medical/healthcare professions in respect of capacity assessment.[203] In terms of methodology, because legal rights (and responsibilities) are predicated on an individual's capacity, the law requires a definite decision regarding whether or not a person has capacity. Thus, the law's focus is on ensuring clarity and certainty. From a healthcare professional's perspective, certainty is less important and less achievable. As O'Keefe points out, 'much of medical practice consists of dealing with uncertainty'.[204] Professional dissonance may also derive from the fact that legal capacity is 'a threshold concept, not a comparative one'.[205] A person either has or does not have capacity in respect of a particular decision; legally, there is no middle ground. As discussed in the previous chapter, from the perspective of a healthcare professional, this kind of binary division is difficult to defend.[206] In fact, as discussed in the next chapter, the law is moving away from a simplistic binary division between capacity and incapacity and working to facilitate the inclusion of the views of a person in the decision-making process notwithstanding that she has been found to lack capacity. However, for some healthcare professionals, the law's approach may still seem to be an artificial construct imposed on the situations in which they work.[207] Insofar

---

[203] On professional dissonance more generally, see G. Teubner, *Law as an Autopoietic System* (Florence: The European University Institute Press Series, 1993); N. Eastman and J. Peay, 'Law Without Enforcement: Theory and Practice' in N. Eastman and J. Peay (eds.) *Law Without Enforcement: Integrating Mental Health and Justice* (Oxford: Hart Publications, 1999), pp. 21–4.

[204] O'Keefe, 'A Clinician's Perspective', 47.

[205] Buchanan and Brock, *Deciding for Others*, p. 27.

[206] Note also the doubts raised about the law's approach in respect of people with mental disorders in E. Rutledge *et al.*, 'Functional Mental Capacity is not Independent of the Severity of Psychosis' (2008) 31 *International Journal of Law and Psychiatry* 9.

[207] See G. Richardson and D. Machin, 'Judicial Review and Tribunal Decision Making: A Study of the Mental Health Review Tribunal' [2000] *Public Law* 494, 508, who found that, in mental health tribunal hearings, 'the medical member cannot resist being a doctor and addressing the well/unwell debate, despite official guidance to the contrary'.

as they exist, the perceptions of artificiality and of imposed standards are unlikely to lead to serious engagement with the legal requirement.

The healthcare and legal professions also operate within different normative contexts. Writing from a legal perspective, Kirk and Bersoff characterise the normative differences between psychiatry and the law as arising from the fact that:

> Psychiatrists are trained and ethically bound to heal .... Lawyers and other law-trained persons are trained and ethically bound to defend individuals against foreseeable harm and governmental deprivation of constitutionally protected rights.[208]

Virginia Abernethy, an anthropologist, argues that capacity assessors who are healthcare professionals are put under pressure by other members of their profession to reach conclusions regarding capacity that facilitate the provision of treatment. She points out that assessors are the 'gate-keepers who can frustrate other specialists in their drive to treat'.[209]

Although there are no studies which directly address the impact of therapeutic motivations on how assessors carry out capacity assessments, there is evidence from related studies that therapeutic motivations play a role in respect of both positive and negative conclusions regarding a patient's capacity. In one study in the United States, 89 per cent of 395 medical professionals with an expertise in capacity assessment identified as a 'common' or 'very common' possibility that, among the doctors who referred patients for assessment to them, as long as the patient agrees with the doctor's recommendation, the doctor will not investigate whether the patient lacks capacity.[210] The position in the United Kingdom may be similar. Raymont et al. speculate that one reason for the substantial difference which they found between expert assessments of capacity and those of the medical clinicians on the ground was that 'a substantial proportion of patients with decisional difficulties place their trust in doctors, and passively acquiesce with treatment plans' and that these patients are unlikely to be regarded as lacking capacity.[211] Assessors' therapeutic motivations

---

[208] T. Kirk and D. Bersoff, 'How Many Procedural Safeguards Does it Take to Get a Psychiatrist to Leave the Lightbulb Unchanged? A Due Process Analysis of the MacArthur Treatment Competence Study' (1996) 2 *Psychology, Public Policy and Law* 45, 67.

[209] V. Abernethy, 'Judgments About Patient Competence: Cultural and Economic Antecedents' in M. Cutter and E. Shelp (eds.) *Competency: A Study of Informal Competency Determinations in Primary Care* (Dordrecht: Kluwer Academic Publishers, 1991), p. 218. See also, from a geriatrician's perspective, O'Keefe 'A Clinician's Perspective,' 44.

[210] See Ganzini, 'Pitfalls in Assessment,' 239.

[211] Raymont et al., 'Prevalence of Mental Incapacity,' 1425.

may also contribute to negative conclusions regarding capacity, especially where a patient disagrees with a proposed treatment. This possibility was recognised by the Law Commission,[212] the Expert Committee Review of the Mental Health Act 1983,[213] the Review of the Scottish Mental Health Act,[214] and the Mental Health Act Commission.[215] These assessments were reached following consultation with, among others, relevant healthcare professionals who, presumably, were presenting views based on their experience in practice.

While the negative consequences of inappropriate findings of incapacity are clear (within an autonomy-based paradigm at any rate), it might be argued that therapeutically motivated findings of capacity are less problematic. It might be asked whether it is really a difficulty if a person is spared the negative psychological consequences of being labelled as lacking capacity while the decision made (ostensibly by the person) is the same as the decision which would have been made in her best interests had she been found to lack capacity. For less serious decisions, this may well be true. If a person lacking capacity is happy to have a bath, it does not pose a particular problem that she was considered capable and consenting rather than lacking capacity and has been given the bath because it was in her best interests. However, especially in respect of serious decisions, it is important to remember that the application of the best interests standard requires more than simply the acquiescence of the person in respect of whom the decision is made. In respect of healthcare decisions in particular, it must also be recalled that a decision in respect of best interests must take account of more than medical factors.[216] Furthermore, as discussed in the next chapter, under the MCA an assessment of best interests requires that the decision-maker consult with a range of people and take account of past views of the person lacking capacity.[217] For these reasons, it cannot be concluded that a decision made by a professional and acquiesced in by the person concerned will be in the best interests of the person, as statutorily defined.

[212] Law Commission, *Report on Mental Incapacity*, pp. 39–40.
[213] Report of the Expert Committee *Review of the Mental Health Act 1983* (Department of Health, HMSO, 1999), para. 2.9.
[214] *Report of the Review of the Mental Health (Scotland) Act 1984: New Directions* (Chair: Rt Hon Bruce Millan) (Edinburgh: Scottish Executive, 2001), p. 55.
[215] Mental Health Act Commission, *Response to the Green Paper Proposals on the Reform of the Mental Health Act 1983* (MHAC, 2000), Appendix A, p. 34.
[216] See *Re A (Medical Treatment: Male Sterilisation)* [2000] 1 FCR 193, 201; *R (Burke)* v. *The General Medical Council and Others* [2004] EWHC 1879 (Admin), [76].
[217] MCA, s. 4(7).

(ii) Assessment: a personal encounter Regardless of who carries out an assessment of capacity, at a fundamental level the interaction is a personal encounter between two people: the assessor and the person being assessed. The outcome of the assessment will be determined, in part at least, by the effectiveness of the communication between these two people. As Neil Manson and Onora O'Neill argue, effective communication requires that the parties share a common language as well as sharing background knowledge about the world and about the social conventions that govern their behaviour[218] and that they believe in each other's essential honesty and good will, in respect of this interaction at any rate.[219] When viewed in this way, it is clear that there can be significant barriers to effective communication in the context of capacity assessment. Haavi Morreim sets out some of these impediments in the context of assessment by a healthcare professional:

> A patient may deliberately avoid reporting his thoughts fully and faithfully. He may wish to test his physician's motives; to manipulate the health care team; to elicit sympathy from friends and family; to enjoy the gamesmanship of leading others on; or to secure any of a variety of other hidden agendas. A patient may not have the language or the cultural sophistication to express his beliefs and values explicitly and coherently. He may not feel like discussing certain things with the health care team, or may be embarrassed to reveal his real beliefs and goals.[220]

Ineffective communication for any of these reasons means that the assessor does not have access to the necessary information upon which to make a judgement about capacity.

Communication difficulties may be accentuated where the assessor and the person assessed do not share a common background. Thus, race, gender, class, educational, cultural and other differences may have an impact on the assessment process. As discussed in the previous chapter, a number of studies conducted in the United Kingdom have investigated links between levels of incapacity and various socio-demographic variables. However, there is no empirical data regarding whether demographic variables have an impact on assessors' ability to perform accurate capacity assessments.[221] There is evidence, however, that demographic factors have

---

[218] N. Manson and O. O'Neill, *Rethinking Informed Consent in Bioethics* (Cambridge University Press, 2007), p. 56.

[219] *Ibid.*, pp. 60–1.

[220] H. Morreim, 'Competence: At the Intersection of Law, Medicine, and Philosophy' in Cutter and Shelp (eds.) *A Study of Informal Competency Determinations*, pp. 106–7.

[221] See J. Moye and D. Marson, 'Assessment of Decision-Making Capacity in Older Adults: An Emerging Area of Practice and Research' (2007) 62B *Journal of Gerontology B Psychological Sciences and Social Sciences* 3, 7.

an impact on the way in which the health system (and especially the mental health system) deals with patients in other respects. A leading examination of the role played by race in mental health care in England found that, in respect of patients with severe mental illnesses, 'patients from all minority groups are more likely than white majority patients to be misunderstood and misdiagnosed'.[222] It would seem reasonable to assume that the cultural factors that operate in the broader mental health context play at least some role in the context of capacity assessment.

Similar arguments may be made in respect of gender. Feminist work on mental health has long drawn attention to the role played by gender stereotyping in dictating the way women are perceived within mental health systems.[223] In the specific context of capacity, feminist commentators have argued that gender stereotyping of 'feminine' behaviour may lead to a greater likelihood of women's capacity being questioned and found lacking.[224] Women who are not sufficiently 'feminine' may also encounter difficulties. Eileen Fegan and Phil Fennell argue that this may explain the high number of women who have been found to lack the capacity to refuse caesarean sections. They suggest that, while the law allows a woman with capacity to place fetal life in danger by refusing medically indicated treatment, the courts' vision of normality is so challenged by any woman who actually avails herself of her right in this regard that her decision will automatically lead to her capacity being called into question.[225]

Ultimately, and inevitably, all capacity assessors come to the task clothed with their professional and personal values, motivations and beliefs. These factors impact on how assessors engage with the people whose capacity they assess and may determine the conclusions they reach.

---

[222] S. P. Sashidharan, *Inside Out: Improving Mental Health Services for Black and Minority Ethnic Communities in England* (London: National Institute of Mental Health, 2003), p. 13.

[223] See I. Broverman *et al.*, 'Sex Role Stereotypes and Clinical Judgements of Mental Health' (1970) 34 *Journal of Consulting and Clinical Psychology* 1; P. Chesler, *Women and Madness* (New York: Doubleday, 1972); E. Showalter, *The Female Malady: Women, Madness and English Culture: 1830–1985* (New York: Pantheon, 1985).

[224] See S. Stefan, 'Silencing the Different Voice: Competence, Feminist Theory and Law' (1993) 47 *University of Miami Law Review* 763, 772; S. Sherwin, *No Longer Patient: Feminist Ethics and Health Care* (Philadelphia: Temple University Press, 1992), pp. 93–4; B. Secker 'Labelling Patient (In)Competence: A Feminist Analysis of Medico-Legal Discourse' (1999) 30 *Journal of Social Philosophy* 295, 302.

[225] E. Fegan and P. Fennell, 'Feminist Perspectives on Mental Health Law' in S. Sheldon and M. Thompson eds. *Feminist Perspectives on Healthcare Law* (London: Cavendish Publishing, 1998), p. 89.

Yet, for the most part, the law operates as if these factors did not exist. In Susan Stefan's words:

> Although competence is a matter of a dynamic or dialogue between doctor and patient ..., legal doctrine sets up this dialogue so that the powerful half of the conversation remains entirely invisible'.[226]

Dealing with assessors' limitations

To its credit, the MCA shows a degree of awareness of the challenges faced by assessors. The statutory statement that a person is not to be treated as unable to make a decision merely because she makes an unwise decision[227] seeks to avoid therapeutic biases and the statement that lack of capacity cannot be established merely by reference to a person's age, appearance or to any condition or aspect of behaviour[228] seeks to avoid conclusions based on stereotyping. In this, the MCA is more sophisticated than many other legislative measures.[229] However, as will be seen, the MCA is limited in what it can deliver.

The Limitations of the MCA approach

A first limitation of the MCA approach relates to the wording of the statutory provisions mentioned above. Peter Bartlett notes the 'unfortunate' use of the term 'merely' in both provisions.[230] He argues that this 'suggests that these factors can be included in an assessment of capacity, even if they would lead to "unjustified" assumptions, so long as there is additional evidence corroborating incapacity'.[231] The risk is that once any of the factors mentioned in the MCA is present, a finding of incapacity may then be reached on the basis of very limited evidence corroborating incapacity.

A second limitation relates to the lack of enforcement mechanisms to ensure that assessors on the ground are persuaded (or compelled) to comply with the statutory provisions. The MCA framework includes no mechanisms to monitor the performance of assessors.[232] Thus, monitoring

---

[226] Stefan, 'Silencing the Difference Voice,' 783.
[227] MCA, s. 1(4).   [228] MCA, s. 2(3).
[229] Compare, for example, the Mental Health Act 1983, ss. 57, 58 and 58A and the Adults With Incapacity (Scotland) Act 2000, s. 1(6).
[230] Bartlett, *Blackstone's Guide*, p. 50.   [231] *Ibid.*
[232] There is, however, a degree of general monitoring in respect of deprivations of liberty: see the Mental Capacity Act 2005 (Deprivation of Liberty: Monitoring and Reporting) Regulations 2009, SI 827/2009.

is essentially a private matter, dependent on people either challenging the results of assessments in the Court of Protection or taking tort actions. In the latter respect, an action could be taken in battery, if the treatment or care involved physical contact, if the requirements for the operation of the statutory defence set out in section 5 of the MCA cannot be met.[233] Presumably also, although this has not occurred to date, an action in negligence could be taken against an assessor if she failed to exercise a reasonable standard of care in carrying out an assessment. There should be no difficulty in asserting that an assessor owes a duty of care to a person whose capacity she assesses. However, the question of harm could be more problematic. Difficulties could arise where the negligent assessment that a person lacked capacity led to treatment being given on the basis that this was in the person's best interests and this had the effect of saving the person's life or was clearly beneficial to her health. Even if damages were awarded in this context, the amount is unlikely to be very high.[234]

There are two problems with reliance on this kind of private monitoring to improve capacity assessments. First, it requires the person herself, or someone acting on her behalf, to initiate the legal process. For a person of borderline capacity, this may represent a considerable burden.[235] Secondly, legal actions of this kind are less effective at changing underlying patterns of behaviour than at developing ways to prove compliance with strict legal norms. Thus, while the MCA is to be commended for recognising the challenges faced by capacity assessors, the legislation is unlikely to have a deep practical impact on the process. If this is the case, the question which then arises is whether there are other ways in which the quality of capacity assessors can be improved.

Improving the quality of assessments

Because, under the MCA, capacity can be assessed by a wide range of people, including non-professionals, there is a risk that capacity assessment will be regarded as a task that anyone can perform. It is striking

---

[233] In addition to the requirement to take reasonable steps to establish that the person lacks capacity, the person providing care and treatment must be able to show that she reasonably believed that it was in the person's best interests that the act be done.

[234] Although note the preparedness of the Court of Appeal in *St George's Healthcare NHS Trust v. S* [1998] 3 WLR 936 to award substantial damages in the tort of trespass for wrongful interference with a woman's right to refuse a caesarean section even though the intervention had probably saved the woman's life and that of the fetus.

[235] See Bartlett and Sandland, *Mental Health Law*, p. 573.

that the Mental Capacity (Deprivation of Liberty) Regulations 2008[236] requires persons performing a 'mental health assessment' and 'best interests assessors' to obtain training but imposes no similar requirement in respect of capacity assessors.[237] In respect of capacity assessment, even relative specialists in the field, such as psychiatrists and gerontologists, are not exclusively concerned with assessing capacity while, at the general practitioner level, capacity assessment is just one of a myriad of functions. Thus, capacity assessment is an additional aspect of the functions of many professionals. This makes it all the more essential that steps be taken to emphasise the professional nature of the assessor's function (in cases where professional assessors are involved). The quality of capacity assessment will only improve if professional assessors are made aware of their professional duties and more effectively held to account for the way in which they perform these.

While the issues arising are not susceptible to neat or all-encompassing solutions, the quality of assessment could be improved through a vigorous approach to evidence on the part of the Court of Protection as well as through the use of more rigorous capacity testing mechanisms (although, as will be seen below, some caution is needed here), more focused research on the realities of capacity assessments, and increased efforts to educate assessors.

(i) **Capacity testing mechanisms** As described above, the earliest capacity testing mechanisms were general in nature and exclusively focused on cognitive abilities. With the growing demand for assessment of legal capacity, more specific testing mechanisms have been developed. Among these, the best known is the MacCAT-T, which originated in the United States[238] and tests for four abilities. These abilities were chosen by the test's devisors based on their view of the standards applied by the courts in the United States and the appropriate standards based on ethical commentaries.[239] These are the abilities to express a choice, to understand relevant information, to appreciate the situation and its consequences, and to manipulate information rationally. The test uses three separate measures (some of which have been discussed above) to test for

---

[236] Mental Capacity (Deprivation of Liberty: Standard Authorisations, Assessments and Ordinary Residence) Regulations 2008, SI 1858/2008.

[237] Compare Reg. 4 (mental health assessments) and Reg. 5 (best interests assessments) with Reg. 6 (capacity assessments).

[238] As described in Grisso and Appelbaum, *Assessing Competence*.

[239] *Ibid.*, p. 32.

these abilities.[240] Each measure is scored separately and there is no overall score.[241] Furthermore, there is no set level at which capacity is achieved. Grisso and Appelbaum point out that '[t]here are no test scores, ratings, or hard-and-fast rules to which clinicians can turn for definitive conclusions about patients' competence'.[242] This reflects their view that, while conclusions about capacity are assisted by empirical observations, they are ultimately normative.[243] A notable feature of the MacCAT-T is that the test programmes in the educative role of the assessor. For example, the requirement in the UDT part of the test that the patient must give an explanation of information provided in her own words offers an opportunity to enhance the patient's knowledge and address any misunderstandings she might have. Thus, the test is aimed not just at assessing capacity but also at enhancing it.

Capacity testing mechanisms, along the lines of the MacCAT-T, have a contribution to make to improving the quality of capacity assessment, since they can provide helpful guidance for assessors. The use of such measures also increases consistency in assessment.[244] If widely used, capacity testing mechanisms could also enhance the quality of expert evidence and allow courts to engage in closer scrutiny of the evidence. Furthermore, testing mechanisms which include measures to develop the capacity of the person assessed could help to ensure that the educative aspect of the process is not ignored. For these reasons, a testing mechanism which accurately reflects the underlying law could go some way towards addressing assessors' lack of knowledge and skills. This would, of course, be predicated on assessors actually using the testing mechanism in practice. In this respect, it is noteworthy that the MacCAT-T does not appear to have been widely adopted for use on the ground in the United States.[245]

Notwithstanding these advantages, capacity testing mechanisms should be approached with caution, especially if they emanate solely

---

[240] *Ibid.*, pp. 187–8.

[241] For details of the scoring procedure see *ibid.*, pp. 183–90.

[242] *Ibid.*, p. 129.

[243] T. Grisso and P. Appelbaum, 'Values and Limits of the MacArthur Treatment Competence Study' (1996) 2 *Psychology, Public Policy and Law* 167, 169.

[244] Cairns *et al.*, 'Reliability of Mental Capacity Assessments,' 374, found that, when clinicians and expert assessors both used the MacCAT-T, the level of agreement between them changed from moderate to 'near-perfect'.

[245] See the reasons put forward by Grisso, *Evaluating Competencies*, pp. 481–2 as to why this has been the case.

from the medical profession. First, as described above, the legal standard for capacity is, by necessity, vague. Its full meaning can only be appreciated in the light of the body of case law which explores what the statutory standard actually means. Because of this complexity, a testing mechanism could effectively set the standard for capacity rather than applying the standard which has been set by the law. This would be inappropriate because the adoption of a legal standard for capacity is not just a technical matter but, rather, represents a balance between the competing values of protecting individual freedom, on the one hand, and protecting the welfare of (possibly) vulnerable people, on the other. This is a policy matter, not a medical one. Secondly, a capacity testing mechanism runs the risk of becoming what one set of commentators described as a 'capacimeter',[246] with assessors and courts regarding test results as conclusive. Given the law's need for certain answers, Grisso and Appelbaum's contention that the MacCAT-T is not intended to provide hard and fast answers would be unlikely to survive for long in a formal legal setting. Thus, the test could create a false impression of objectivity, which would in fact further obscure the personal nature of the interaction between assessor and assessed and the issues to which this gives rise.

Therefore, while recognising the possible contribution of a legally sensitive capacity testing mechanism, it must also be remembered that such a mechanism can only be effective as part of a larger effort to address the difficulties to which capacity assessment gives rise.

(ii) Further empirical research A better understanding of how capacity assessors operate is essential if the quality of the process is to be improved. As Jennifer Moye and Daniel Marson argue, '[a] solid empirical research base will be necessary to ensure the quality and accuracy of capacity determinations'.[247] While the body of empirical work that has been carried out to date has been valuable in developing understanding of the assessment process, most of it has not related to the position under the MCA. Further, most current research has emanated from the medical and psychiatric professions and has paid little attention to assessors from other professional backgrounds (or to non-professional assessors). Nor have the existing studies addressed the issues that arise from the personal nature of the encounter between the assessor and the person assessed.

---

[246] M. Kapp and D. Mossman, 'Measuring Decisional Capacity: Cautions on the Construction of a "Capacimeter"' (1996) 2 *Psychology, Public Policy and Law* 73.

[247] Moye and Marson, 'Assessment of Decision-Making Capacity in Older Adults,' 9.

Some aspects of the assessment process are undoubtedly easier to research than others. It should be a relatively straightforward matter to establish how much professional assessors know about the law and how they apply the legal test in practice. An appropriate tool to investigate the impact of therapeutic motivations on assessors or to explore the more personal aspects of the process would be more difficult to formulate. However, this does not diminish the need for research on this aspect of capacity assessment. In this respect, it would be instructive to see how assessors from different professional backgrounds respond to capacity assessment (e.g. do psychiatrists conduct assessments differently from gerontologists?) and to consider what benefits, if any, a multi-disciplinary approach brings to the process.

(iii) Engaging with assessors   Advocating education as a way of dealing with difficulties in applying legal standards is so obvious as to be almost a cliché. Nonetheless, the quality of assessment could be improved by increasing assessors' awareness of the law and the nature of the legal tests.[248] It would, of course, be inaccurate to suggest that assessors are left wholly without education in respect of the MCA. The Code of Practice is expressed in language that is largely user-friendly for non-lawyers, although at times it has had to sacrifice complexity for accessibility.[249] The Office of the Public Guardian has also produced helpful booklets for both professional and non-professional assessors and the welcome new edition of the joint publication of the British Medical Association and the Law Society on assessment of capacity has been updated to take account of the MCA.[250] Widely read medical journals have also provided synopses of the MCA.[251] The commencement of the MCA also led to the provision of training by many local authorities in respect of a range of aspects of the Act although the extent to which training has been availed of by medical professionals is unclear.

---

[248]   In both studies of the operation of the Adults With Incapacity (Scotland) Act 2000 discussed above, the professionals indicated a need for further training on the Act. Note improvement to assessment under the MCA guidance and training: see P. Guyer *et al* 'The Mental Capacity Act 2005'.

[249]   Note for example, the very limited guidance in the Code, paras. 4.21–4.22 regarding what the ability to 'use and weigh' information requires.

[250]   See *Assessment of Mental Capacity: Guidance for Doctors and Lawyers* (3rd edn) (London: BMA, Law Society, 2009).

[251]   See, for example, A. Alonzi and M. Pringle, 'The Mental Capacity Act 2005' (2007) 335 *British Medical Journal* 898; T. Nicholson *et al.*, 'Assessing Mental Capacity: The Mental Capacity Act' (2008) 336 *British Medical Journal* 322.

The need for education extends beyond legal instruction. More significant, perhaps, is that all assessors become more aware of the possible impact of their own values on the assessment. As Michael Gunn notes 'any person assessing the competence of another individual must be aware of their own values so that assumptions and decisions are not made which are unjustifiable'.[252] He reminds us that, while values cannot be removed from the assessment process, 'assessors of capacity can be educated to be aware of their own values'.[253]

However, while education offers opportunities, the practical challenges of delivering meaningful education on capacity assessment should not be underestimated. For many busy professional assessors, the attractions of education in the detail of the law are not wholly obvious. In this respect, the persuasive impact of a vigorous Court of Protection could play a significant role in convincing professionals that it is worth engaging with the law. If this does not yield results, it may become necessary to revisit the way in which the MCA deals with professional assessors and to introduce formal mechanisms to monitor professional assessors' compliance with the statutory standards.

Conclusion

This chapter has shown the essentially porous nature of the boundary between capacity and incapacity when viewed through the lens of real-life assessments of capacity. The abilities tested for and both the formal and the informal assessment processes all indicate the epistemological fallibility of determinations regarding capacity and incapacity. Furthermore, as matters stand, and despite some efforts in the MCA, current approaches to the assessment process do not take sufficient account of the relational nature of capacity and of the obligations, created by the MCA and arising under the CRPD, to develop the capacity of the individuals assessed. Some of these difficulties can be addressed through closer judicial engagement with the test for capacity, better oversight by the Court of Protection and ongoing research and education in respect of the assessment process. However, these moves would diminish rather than remove the essential artificiality of dividing people's decisions according to a standard based on capacity. Thus, it becomes essential to engage critically with the law's treatment of people who are found to lack decision-making capacity. The next chapter will look at the questions to which decision-making in this context gives rise.

[252] Gunn, 'The Meaning of Incapacity,' 21.   [253] *Ibid.*

5

Autonomy, rights and decision-making for patients lacking capacity

A consequence of the legal and ethical fixation on autonomy has been a lack of conceptual engagement with the position of people who cannot make autonomous decisions.[1] Thus, while one can neatly trace the philosophical lineage of the right of the capable patient to refuse treatment, it is much more difficult to identify a solid philosophical basis for healthcare decision-making for people who do not have capacity. In the absence of an independent theoretical model, the law traditionally dealt with decision-making for people lacking capacity using one of two unsatisfactory approaches. On the one hand, courts in England and Wales viewed a finding of incapacity as justifying a return to full-scale paternalism, where treatment decisions could be made on the basis of the patient's best interests with few safeguards and little analysis. The second approach, preferred by courts in the United States, has been to attempt to extend the principle of autonomy, notwithstanding the patient's lack of capacity, through the application of a substituted judgment standard based on what the patient would have wished had she had capacity notwithstanding, in some cases, very limited evidence of the patient's likely views or preferences. In England and Wales, this unsatisfactory position has begun to change. The Mental Capacity Act 2005 (MCA) contains provisions that allow people to make advance healthcare decisions and which require efforts to be made to facilitate participation by the person lacking capacity in the decision-making process. The legislation reflects a shift towards a more rights-based approach to decision-making in respect of people lacking capacity. In this respect, the European Convention on Human Rights (ECHR) and the United Nations Convention on the Rights of Persons with Disabilities (CRPD) have made an important contribution.

---

[1] See A. Buchanan and D. Brock, *Deciding for Others: The Ethics of Surrogate Decision Making* (Cambridge University Press, 1989), p. 3.

This chapter examines healthcare decision-making for people lacking capacity.[2] It begins by exposing the limits of the traditional approaches, identifying the deficiencies in both the best interests and the substituted judgment standards. It then looks at attempts to preserve and protect the autonomy of people lacking capacity and evaluates the MCA's efforts in this regard. It argues that the MCA makes an important contribution but that it also encounters significant challenges in delivering on its promise. Accordingly, the MCA cannot provide a complete framework in respect of decision-making for people lacking capacity. The final part of the chapter considers the role of rights beyond the right of autonomy, looking in particular at the right to dignity. While recognising difficulties in developing the law in this regard, it argues that European Court of Human Rights (ECtHR) jurisprudence can make a valuable contribution to the ongoing development of an appropriate conceptual framework for decision-making.

The traditional models and their limits

In order to appreciate the progress made (and the issues that remain), it is helpful to look first at the traditional models for decision-making and their limits, beginning by exploring the historical context in which the law developed.

Decision-making for people lacking capacity: historical antecedents

Although concern with the way in which healthcare decisions for people lacking capacity are made is a relatively recent phenomenon, the law has been concerned with the task of making property and financial decisions in this context for many hundreds of years.[3] Traditionally, these decisions were made under the prerogative authority arising under the *parens patriae* jurisdiction, exercised by the Lord Chancellor and, subsequently, by the Courts

---

[2] The discussion in this chapter draws on M. Donnelly, 'Best Interests, Patient Participation and the Mental Capacity Act 2005' (2009) 17 *Medical Law Review* 1.

[3] See B. Hoggett, 'The Royal Prerogative in Relation to the Mentally Disordered: Resurrection, Resuscitation, or Rejection?' in M. Freeman (ed.) *Medicine, Ethics and the Law: Current Legal Problems* (London: Stevens, 1988); C. Unsworth, 'Mental Disorder and Tutelary Relationship: From Pre- to Post-carceral Legal Order' (1991) 18 *Journal of Law and Society* 254; J. Seymour, '*Parens Patriae* and Wardship Powers: Their Nature and Origins' (1994) 14 *Oxford Journal of Legal Studies* 159.

of Chancery.[4] In one 1827 case, Lord Eldon described the jurisdiction as 'founded on the obvious necessity that the law should place somewhere the care of individuals who cannot take care of themselves, particularly in cases where it is clear that some care should be thrown around them'.[5] As initially operated, the *parens patriae* jurisdiction required all decisions to be made for the 'benefit' of the person lacking capacity.[6] In a number of decisions, beginning with *Ex Parte Whitbread*, this was held to involve an investigation of what the person would have wished had she had capacity.[7] Thus, the early operation of the *parens patriae* jurisdiction provides the foundations for both the best interests and the substituted judgment standards.

The prerogative authority was given a statutory basis in the nineteenth century with the establishment of the Court of Protection (although the underlying *parens patriae* jurisdiction continued to apply alongside the operative statutes).[8] In England and Wales, the *parens patriae* jurisdiction in respect of adults was abolished in 1959. To replace it, the Mental Health Act 1959 gave the Court of Protection jurisdiction over 'the property and affairs' of adults lacking capacity while personal decisions, including healthcare decisions, were removed from the ambit of the legislation. This reflected the contemporary view that adult guardianship was a restriction on civil rights.[9] In other jurisdictions, including Australia,[10] Canada,[11] Ireland[12] and the United States,[13] the *parens patriae* jurisdiction continued to apply alongside the relevant statutory provisions.

---

[4] The first formal statement of the jurisdiction dates back to the fourteenth century: see *de Prærogativa Regis* 17 Edward II, c. 9 and c.10. However, it would seem that the jurisdiction pre-dates this and can be traced to the reign of Edward I (1275–1306), when it would appear that the King took responsibility for the 'custody of the persons and inheritances *idiotarum et stultorum*': see L. Shelford, *Practical Treatise on the Law Concerning Lunatics, Idiots, and Persons of Unsound Mind* (Philadelphia: J. S. Littell, 1833), p. 6.

[5] *Wellesley* v. *Duke of Beaufort* (1827) 4 ER 1078, 1081.

[6] Shelford, *Practical Treatise*, pp. 129–30, cites a number of cases based on benefit: see *In re Bird*, March 9 1827; *In re Baker*, June 20 1827; and *In re Harris*, August 9 1827.

[7] (1816) 35 Eng Rep 878, 879. Lord Eldon justified making provision for an incapable man's niece out of his estate 'because the Court will not refuse to do, for the benefit of the Lunatic, that which it is probable the Lunatic himself would have done'. See L. Harmon, 'Falling Off the Vine: Legal Fictions and the Doctrine of Substituted Judgment' (1990) 100 *Yale Law Journal* 1, 19–26.

[8] See Unsworth, 'Mental Disorder and Tutelary Relationship,' 260.

[9] See P. Bartlett and R. Sandland, *Mental Health Law: Policy and Practice* (3rd edn) (Oxford University Press, 2007), p. 504.

[10] See A. Graham, 'Parens Patriae: Past, Present and Future' (1994) 32 *Family Court Review* 184.

[11] See *Re Eve* [1986] 2 SCR 388.

[12] See *In re A Ward of Court* [1996] 2 IR 79, 103–7; *In re Wards of Court and In re Francis Dolan* [2007] IESC 26.

[13] See *Mormon Church* v. *United States* (1890) 136 US 1.

An unforeseen consequence of the abolition of the *parens patriae* jurisdiction in England and Wales was that there was no legal mechanism whereby personal decisions could be made for an adult lacking capacity. This gap in the law was identified and addressed by the House of Lords in *Re F (Mental Patient: Sterilisation)*.[14] The House of Lords held that the common law doctrine of necessity permitted the medical treatment of adults who were unable to give personal consent.[15] For the doctrine to apply, the relevant medical professional had to consider that the intervention was in the best interests of the adult lacking capacity. The House of Lords noted that a formal application could be made to the Family Division of the High Court for a declaration that a procedure was in a patient's best interests. While the House of Lords did not consider a court declaration to be necessary,[16] the declaratory jurisdiction came to be widely used. Subsequent Practice Directions required that the declaratory jurisdiction be utilised in a range of cases, including applications in respect of non-consensual sterilisation, the withdrawal of treatment from patients in a persistent vegetative state (PSV) and certain terminations of pregnancy, as well as serious treatment decisions in which there were doubts in respect of best interests.[17] Because the declaratory jurisdiction was exercised in open court (although patients' names were anonymised), an extensive body of pre-MCA case law developed.

The best interests standard

In the foundational decision in *Re F (Mental Patient: Sterilisation)*,[18] although the House of Lords was careful to clarify the formal legal basis for decision-making, it dedicated little attention to the values underlying the law. This may have been because it had been accepted at first instance and by the Court of Appeal that the proposed sterilisation was in the best interests of the woman and there was no appeal against this finding.[19]

---

[14] [1990] 2 AC 1, 74–7.

[15] See *ibid.*, 55–6 *per* Lord Brandon; 74 *per* Lord Goff.

[16] See Lord Brandon [1990] 2 AC 1, 56–7. However, his Lordship (57) regarded court involvement in a case such as *Re F*, which involved non-consensual sterilisation, as 'highly desirable'.

[17] See *Practice Note: (Official Solicitor: Declaratory Proceedings: Medical and Welfare Decisions for Adults Who Lack Capacity)* [2006] 2 FLR 373, [5].

[18] [1990] 2 AC 1. See M. Donnelly, 'Decision Making for Mentally Incompetent People: The Empty Formula of Best Interests' (2001) 20 *Medicine and Law* 405.

[19] The Court of Appeal considered briefly how to assess best interests. Neill LJ [1990] 2 AC 1, 32 noted the need to consider 'the alternatives to an operation and the dangers or disadvantages to which the patient may be exposed if no action is taken'.

However, it is also likely that the omission reflected an attitude that this kind of question did not fall comfortably within the judicial remit and was best left to the medical professionals. The House of Lords confirmed the applicability of the best interests standard in determining if the treatment should be given but, other than identifying the relevance of medical best interests,[20] it did not specify in any detail how the standard should be applied.[21] Nor, in a pre-Human Rights Act (HRA)-era, did the House of Lords raise the issue of the rights of the person lacking capacity.[22] The House of Lords also stated that the Bolam test for medical negligence applied to determinations of best interests.[23] This meant that the task of determining best interests was effectively delegated to the medical profession.[24]

Clarifying the jurisdiction

Notwithstanding this unpromising beginning, the growing declaratory jurisdiction facilitated the development of a more sophisticated conception of best interests. In *Re A (Medical Treatment: Male Sterilisation)*,[25] in the context of the proposed sterilisation of a 28-year-old man with Down's syndrome, Dame Butler-Sloss P reiterated that the best interests standard 'encompasses medical, emotional and all other welfare issues'.[26] She also distanced the assessment of best interests from the Bolam test, rejecting the suggestion that the duty to act in the patient's best interests could be conflated with the professional duty of care.[27] With the incorporation of the ECHR imminent, Dame Butler-Sloss P also noted the relevance of respect for human rights in the application of the best interests

---

[20] [1990] 2 AC 1, 55 *per* Lord Brandon.
[21] In *Airedale NHS Trust* v. *Bland* [1993] AC 789 the House of Lords held that the best interests standard adopted in *Re F* was also applicable to treatment withdrawal. In relation to a patient in a persistent vegetative state, the appropriate question was (808 *per* Lord Goff) whether it was in the patient's best interests to continue to receive life-sustaining treatment.
[22] This accords with the approach taken in the earlier case of *Re B (A Minor) (Wardship: Sterilisation)* [1988] 1 AC 199, 204 *per* Lord Hailsham.
[23] *Re F (Mental Patient: Sterilisation)* [1990] 2 AC 1, 52 *per* Lord Bridge; 68 *per* Lord Brandon; 69 *per* Lord Griffiths; 78 *per* Lord Goff.
[24] I. Kennedy, 'Patients, Doctors and Human Rights' in R. Blackburn and J. Taylor (eds.) *Human Rights for the 1990s* (London: Mansell, 1991), pp. 89–90.
[25] [2000] 1 FCR 193.
[26] *Ibid.*, 200. This view had already been established in *Re Y (Mental Patient: Bone Marrow Donation)* [1997] Fam 110; *Re MB (An Adult: Medical Treatment)* [1997] 2 FCR 541.
[27] [2000] 1 FCR 193, 200–1. This position was affirmed in *Re SL (Adult Patient: Medical Treatment)* [2000] 2 FCR 452 and *NHS Trust* v. *A and Another* [2005] EWCA Civ 1145.

standard,[28] although she did not discuss in any detail how the ECHR would apply.

Re A also saw the Court of Appeal move towards a more systematic approach to the assessment of best interests. Drawing on the checklist approach advocated by the Law Commission in its *Report on Mental Incapacity*,[29] Thorpe LJ utilised a balance sheet, setting out the actual benefits to be gained from the medical procedure and any 'counterbalancing dis-benefits'.[30] He also noted that, in making entries on either side, the judge should include a realistic assessment of the possibility that the loss or gain would occur. It is only if the account is in 'relatively significant' credit that the procedure can be considered to be in the best interests of the individual.[31] The balance sheet approach is formalised in the *Practice Note (Declaratory Proceedings: Medical and Welfare Decisions for Adults Who Lack Capacity)*, which states that, if advantages and disadvantages are being relied upon, the court will wish to assess in percentage terms the likelihood of these occurring.[32]

Best interests and the patient's views

Notwithstanding the Law Commission's inclusion of the patient's views in its best interests checklist, this factor is notably absent from Thorpe LJ's balance sheet in *Re A*. This was in spite of the fact that A had clearly indicated that he did not want the proposed sterilisation.[33] Reference to the views of the person lacking capacity is also absent from the list of relevant considerations set out in the *Practice Note*. It is unsurprising, therefore, that the views of the person lacking capacity played a limited role in subsequent pre-MCA case law.[34] Insofar as these views were acknowledged

---

[28] *Ibid.*, 201.

[29] Law Commission, Report No. 231 *Report on Mental Incapacity* (London: HMSO, 1995), para. 3.28.

[30] [2000] 1 FCR 193, 206.

[31] *Ibid.* For examples of balancing in operation, see *A National Health Trust* v. C unreported, High Court (Family Division), 8 February 2000 (in the context of non-consensual sterilisation); *Simms* v. *Simms and Another; A* v. *A and Another* [2002] EWHC 2734 (Fam), [60] – [64] (in the context of experimental treatment for variant Creutzfeldt–Jakob disease (vCJD); *A Hospital NHS Trust* v. *S* [2003] EWHC 365 (Fam), [47] (in the context of receipt of a kidney transplant).

[32] [2006] 2 FLR 373, [18].

[33] The man's refusal was mentioned by Dame Butler-Sloss P [2000] 1 FCR 193, 196, although she continued by noting the consultant psychiatrist's view that this was not an informed refusal because the patient 'could not understand the reason for the operation'.

[34] Although note the approach of Hale LJ in *R (Wilkinson)* v. *Broadmoor Special Hospital Authority* [2002] 1 WLR 419, 446.

at all, it was generally as a prelude to overriding them. In *Re X (Adult Sterilisation)*,[35] Holman J had cause to 'hesitate' before granting a declaration to permit the sterilisation of a woman who had significant intellectual disabilities due to Down's syndrome because the woman had said that she would like a baby. Nonetheless, he went on to authorise the sterilisation, stating that:

> X is quite unable to make any sensible, informed decision for herself, so other people have to make it for her. Even though subjectively she feels she would like to have a baby, it remains objectively completely contrary to *her* (I emphasise the word 'her') best interests to do so.[36]

Given the weight of expert evidence in favour of the sterilisation, Holman J's decision to override the woman's wishes is not especially surprising. In contrast, in *Re SS (Medical Treatment: Late Termination)*,[37] the expert evidence was described as 'very finely balanced'.[38] This case concerned an application regarding the late termination of the pregnancy of a woman with a serious mental disorder. Wall J included the patient's 'repeated and powerful insistence' on the termination of her pregnancy in the best interests 'balance sheet'.[39] He was also critical of the health authority's approach, which had led to the case coming to court at a very advanced stage in the pregnancy rather than when the woman had originally requested the termination. Nonetheless, he declined to make an order permitting the termination, holding that the procedure was not in the woman's best interests.

While the contemporaneous views of the person lacking capacity played little role in judicial determinations of best interests prior to the MCA, courts tended to be more facilitative in respect of views expressed prior to incapacity. Thus, there is a body of authority confirming the enforceability of advance decisions to refuse treatment.[40] Courts have also recognised the relevance of prior beliefs, notwithstanding the absence of formal instructions. In *Ahsan* v. *University Hospitals Leicester NHS Trust*, Hegarty QC (sitting as a Deputy Judge of the High Court) found that a profoundly brain-damaged Muslim woman (who had not

---

[35] [1998] 2 FLR 1124.

[36] *Ibid.*, 1128. See also *NHS Trust* v. *T* [2004] EWHC 1279 (Fam), [66].

[37] [2002] 1 FLR 445.   [38] *Ibid.*, 452.   [39] *Ibid.*, 451–2.

[40] See *Re T (Adult: Refusal of Medical Treatment)* [1992] 3 WLR 782, 787; *Re C (Adult: Refusal of Medical Treatment)* [1994] 1 WLR 290; *Airedale NHS* v. *Bland* [1993] A. 789, 864; *St George's Healthcare NHS Trust* v. *S* [1998] 3 WLR 936, 969; *Re AK (Medical Treatment: Consent)* [2001] 1 FLR 129, 134; *HE* v. *A Hospital NHS Trust* [2003] EWHC 1017.

left any instructions regarding her preferences) should be cared for at home in a Muslim environment where the family could pray together in her presence and could ensure the observances of Muslim traditions and practices.[41] He considered that:

> [T]he wishes and beliefs of Mrs Ahsan's family and, so far as they can properly be attributed to her, those which she herself would have held ... are factors which can and should be taken into account ... even though no tangible benefits, whether physical or emotional, are likely to flow from a recognition of those wishes and beliefs'.[42]

Conceptual grounding

Although judges became better at breaking down the factual bases for decisions made, they remained reluctant to explore the conceptual or normative grounding for the application of the best interests standard.[43] One exception in this respect was Munby J who, in *R (Burke)* v. *the General Medical Council and Others*, noted that, while best interests may be the legal test, 'it is on its own a poor signpost to sound decision-making in an area as grave and difficult as this'.[44] Munby J grounded his discussion of the circumstances in which artificial nutrition and hydration (ANH) could be withdrawn from a sentient incapable patient in the ECHR rights to autonomy and dignity and in the principle of the sanctity of life.[45] This led him to conclude that there was a 'very strong presumption in favour of taking steps which will prolong life'.[46] He considered that:

> In the context of life-prolonging treatment the touchstone of best interests is intolerability. So if life-prolonging treatment is providing *some* benefit it should be provided unless the patient's life, if thus prolonged, would from the patient's point of view be intolerable.[47]

On appeal, the Court of Appeal rejected the 'intolerability' standard, stating instead that 'the test of whether it is in the best interests of the patient to provide or continue ANH must depend on the particular circumstances'.[48] In respect of the question of what the best interests test involved, the Court considered that 'it is best to confine the use of the phrase "best interests" to an objective test, which is of most use when

---

[41] [2006] EWHC 2624 (QB), [56].   [42] *Ibid.*

[43] See similar arguments in the context of non-therapeutic research in P. Lewis, 'Procedures That are Against the Medical Interests of Incompetent Adults' (2002) 22 *Oxford Journal of Legal Studies* 575.

[44] [2004] EWHC 1879 (Admin), [115].   [45] *Ibid.*, [116].   [46] *Ibid.*

[47] *Ibid.*, original emphasis.   [48] [2005] EWCA Civ 1003, [62].

considering the duty owed to a patient who is not competent and is easiest to apply when confined to a situation where the relevant interests are medical'.[49] Although the Court did not expressly distance itself from Munby J's identification of a strong presumption in favour of life, such a presumption is not mentioned in the Court of Appeal's subsequent decision in *An NHS Trust* v. *A and Another*.[50] In approving the withdrawal of medical treatment from an elderly patient, the Court noted the trial judge's description of the treatment as 'painful, uncomfortable and undignified',[51] but it did not ask whether the degree of discomfort involved in the treatment would outweigh a presumption in favour of life.

The Court of Appeal's decision in *Burke* is notable for the vigour with which it rejected Munby J's efforts to ground the discussion of best interests in human rights and his attempt to develop a more precise test for the application of the standard in end-of-life contexts.[52] In this, it reaffirms a judicial reluctance to engage with the conceptual underpinnings of the law in respect of people lacking capacity and a preference to leave this matter to the 'good faith and self-regulation of the medical profession'.[53] Jonathan Montgomery argues that this reluctance is best understood as part of a broader culture of judicial deference to doctors.[54] Montgomery argues that this deference derives from 'a belief that [medical] practice enshrines moral values and the aspiration to construct a legal relationship between patients and health professionals that enables that morality to flourish'.[55] Regardless of the broader cultural context for the Court of Appeal's attitude, since the MCA has come into force, it is difficult to see how the Court's description of best interests as an 'objective test' can be justified. As will be seen below, the MCA involves a fundamental shift towards a more subjective assessment of best interests. Before considering the impact of the MCA, however, it will be helpful to examine the other 'traditional' approach to decision-making for people lacking capacity. Unlike the best interests standard, substituted judgment does have a clear conceptual grounding which may be located in respect for the right of autonomy. However, as will be seen, the operation of this standard is far from satisfactory.

---

[49] *Ibid.*, [29].   [50] [2005] EWCA Civ 1145.   [51] *Ibid.*, [89].
[52] See D. Gurnham, 'Losing the Wood for the Trees: Burke and the Court of Appeal' (2006) 14 *Medical Law Review* 253, 257.
[53] *Ibid.*, 263.
[54] J. Montgomery, 'Law and the Demoralisation of Medicine' (2006) 26 *Legal Studies* 185.
[55] *Ibid.*, 206.

The substituted judgment standard

Decision-making on the basis of substituted judgment involves asking what the patient would have decided if she had capacity. As noted above, like the best interests standard, this too has its antecedents in the *parens patriae* jurisdiction where it was used in respect of property and affairs. The first reference to the standard in a medical context seems to have been by the Kentucky Court of Appeals in *Strunk* v. *Strunk*.[56] The case concerned a proposal to remove a kidney from a man with a significant degree of intellectual disability, for transplant purposes in order to save the life of his brother. The Court considered that '[t]he right to act for the incompetent in all cases has been recognized in this country as the doctrine of substituted judgment and is broad enough to cover not only property but also matters touching on the well-being of the ward'.[57] On the facts of the case, however, the decision was based more on an assessment of the intellectually disabled man's best interests. The Court regarded the procedure as involving 'minimal danger'[58] and noted the close relationship between the brothers and the (emotional) cost to the man if his brother was to die.[59]

The standard applied

The first significant application of the substituted judgment standard is found in the decision of the Supreme Court of New Jersey in *Re Quinlan*.[60] In response to an application to remove ventilation from a young woman in a PVS, the Court held that the woman's constitutional right of privacy could only be protected by permitting her guardian and family 'to render their best judgment ... as to whether she would exercise it in these circumstances'.[61] Holding that she would choose to exercise her right to refuse the ventilation, the Court authorised the cessation of ventilation (although, in fact, the young woman continued to breathe without ventilation and lived for a number of years subsequently). Following *Quinlan*, the substituted judgment standard was quickly adopted in most jurisdictions across the United States, where it was used primarily in the context of treatment refusal in end-of-life situations.[62] The widespread adoption of the standard may have reflected the fact that the standard offered courts

---

[56] (1969) 445 SW 2d 145.   [57] *Ibid.*, 148.   [58] *Ibid.*   [59] *Ibid.*   [60] (1976) 70 NJ 10.
[61] *Ibid.*, 41–2.
[62] For cross-jurisdictional surveys of case law, see J. J. Delaney, 'Specific Intent: Substituted Judgment and Best Interests: A Nationwide Analysis of an Individual's Right to Die' (1991) 11 *Pace Law Review* 565; Harmon, 'Falling Off the Vine,' 40–55.

several advantages over a best interests standard, especially in end-of-life contexts. First, it could be placed within a clear and neat conceptual framework based on respect for individual autonomy, which accorded well with the dominant contemporary discourse. Secondly, it spared judges having to make decisions regarding the relationship between best interests and sanctity of life in treatment withdrawal cases.[63] It also allowed the avoidance of difficult issues regarding resource provision.[64] Costly treatments could be ordered to be withdrawn from patients, not to save money but in order to respect the patient's wishes.

Their enthusiasm for the standard led courts to use substituted judgment in circumstances in which there was no possibility of discerning what the person would have wanted had she had legal capacity. Thus, the standard was applied in decisions regarding the non-consensual sterilisation of,[65] and the refusal and withdrawal of treatment from, patients with life-long intellectual disabilities[66] who had never had legal capacity and had never given any indication of how they would wish a situation like this to be resolved. Substituted judgment began to look more and more like a legal fiction whereby judges made decisions which they considered appropriate under the guise that this was what the patient would have wanted.

The fictional element of substituted judgment became increasingly difficult to justify as courts began to question the legitimacy of their application of the standard, recognising perhaps that, as Louise Harmon notes, '[s]omething hidden, something potentially dangerous or brutal, can go on beneath the surface of a legal fiction'.[67] Courts in a number of states responded by imposing a heavy evidential standard (usually requiring 'clear and convincing' evidence of intention[68]) in order to establish the

---

[63] Some flavour of the contentious nature of the discussion thereby avoided may be found in R. Destro, 'Quality-of-Life Ethics and Constitutional Jurisprudence: The Demise of Natural Rights and Equal Protection for the Disabled and Incompetent' (1986) 2 *Journal of Contemporary Health Law and Policy* 71; K. Quinn, 'The Best Interests of Incompetent Patients: The Capacity for Interpersonal Relationships as a Standard for Decisionmaking' (1988) 76 *California Law Review* 897.

[64] The troubling nature of this question is explored in D. Callahan, 'Terminating Life-Sustaining Treatment of the Demented' (1995) 25 *Hastings Center Report* 25.

[65] See *In re Grady* (1979) 170 NJ Super 98; *In re Moe* (1982) 385 Mass 555.

[66] See *Superintendent of Belchertown v. Saikewicz* (1977) 370 NE 2d 417; (1977) 373 Mass 723, 752–3.

[67] Harmon, 'Falling Off the Vine,' 70.

[68] This is the most demanding standard used in civil cases in the United States: see *Cruzan v. Director, Missouri Health Department* (1990) 497 US 261, 282.

prior wishes of the person lacking capacity.[69] This standard was most frequently (although not exclusively)[70] satisfied where patients, while capable, had executed a formal advance directive setting out their wish to refuse the treatment in question. In the absence of the required evidence, courts had to rely on the *parens patriae* jurisdiction which, in some instances, resulted in an absolute refusal to permit a withdrawal of treatment[71] and, in others, led to a best interests type balancing with a heavy evidential burden on the party seeking to have treatment withdrawn.[72] The freedom of each state to set its own standard of proof in cases of this kind was upheld by the United States Supreme Court in *Cruzan* v. *Director, Missouri Department of Health*.[73] Noting that 'the choice between life and death is a deeply personal decision of obvious and overwhelming finality', Rehnquist CJ, for the majority, held that individual states 'may legitimately seek to safeguard the personal elements of this choice through the imposition of heightened evidentiary requirements'.[74]

Substituted judgment post-Cruzan: a private affair

In the fragmented legal environment following *Cruzan*, the question of how to deal with the situation of patients who failed to meet the higher

[69] See the decisions of the New York Court of Appeals in *In re Storar* (1981) 52 NY 2d 363 and *In re Eichner* (1981) 52 NY 2d 363 (the two cases were decided together) and of the Supreme Court of Missouri in *Cruzan* v. *Harmon* (1988) 760 SW 2d 408.

[70] See, for example, *In re Eichner* (1981) 52 NY 2d 363 where the required standard was met on the basis of evidence that, during serious community discussion of Catholic moral principles, the patient (an 83-year-old priest) had indicated that he would not wish to have his life sustained in the circumstances which subsequently arose.

[71] In *In re Storar* (1981) 52 NY 2d 363, 375 the New York Court of Appeals held that the exercise of the *parens patriae* jurisdiction was equivalent to the exercise of parental powers in respect of a minor. The Court held that just as parents do not have the right to refuse life-saving treatment for a child, the State was prohibited from exercising its jurisdiction in a way which involved the refusal of life-saving treatment.

[72] See the decision of the Supreme Court of New Jersey in *Re Conroy* (1985) 98 NJ 321. Here, the Court outlined two best interests tests that would apply depending on the circumstances: the first, the 'limited objective test' arises where there is some trustworthy evidence that the person would have refused the treatment, while the second, the 'pure objective test', arises where there is no evidence to this effect. In the first instance, treatment might be withdrawn where the burden of life with treatment outweighed the benefits; in the second, *ibid.*, 366, treatment might be withdrawn where the net burdens of life with the treatment clearly outweigh the benefits of the treatment and the 'recurring, unavoidable and severe pain of the patient's life with the treatment' would be such that administering the treatment would be 'inhumane'. For a critique of the Court's reasoning, see G. Annas, 'When Procedures Limit Rights: From Quinlan to Conroy' (1985) 15 *Hastings Center Report* 24.

[73] (1990) 497 US 261.   [74] *Ibid.*, 281.

evidentiary standard continued to create difficulties. At a federal level, the Patient Self-Determination Act 1990 was introduced, requiring hospitals and other facilities for persons covered by Medicare and Medicaid to draw patients' attention to their right to make an advance directive. However, this left the underlying difficulty unresolved. The Uniform Health-Care Decisions Act 1994 provided a model framework which was subsequently widely adopted. The Act contains model provisions relating to advance directives and the conferring of a durable power of attorney. In the absence of advance planning of this kind, the Act provides for surrogate decision-making as the fall-back position.[75]

The 1994 Act sets out the automatic order in which surrogates are appointed, provided that they are 'reasonably available', beginning with the patient's spouse; an adult child; a parent; an adult brother or sister.[76] In the absence of these people, any adult 'who has exhibited special care and concern for the patient, who is familiar with the patient's personal values, and who is readily available' may act as surrogate.[77] The surrogate is required to make decisions 'in accordance with the patient's individual instructions, if any, to the extent known to the surrogate'.[78] Otherwise, the surrogate is required to make the decision 'in accordance with the surrogate's determination of the patient's best interest'.[79] In determining the patient's best interest, the surrogate is required to consider the patient's 'personal values to the extent known to the surrogate'.[80] Thus, surrogate decision-making stays within a conceptual framework centred on respect for autonomy.

The effect of the surrogate decision-making provisions has been to privatise the decision-making process, shifting responsibility away from the courts and onto family members or others. Although surrogates are told how they must make decisions, there is no formal mechanism to record the factors that actually motivate surrogates in reaching decisions.

Other than circumstances, such as those which arose in *Schindler Schiavo v. Schiavo*,[81] where there is family disagreement, the decision-making process takes place privately, without review or oversight.[82]

---

[75] Uniform Health-Care Decisions Act 1994, s. 5(a).

[76] Uniform Health-Care Decisions Act 1994, s. 5(b).

[77] Uniform Health-Care Decisions Act 1994, s. 5(c).

[78] Uniform Health-Care Decisions Act 1994, s. 5(f).   [79] *Ibid.*   [80] *Ibid.*

[81] (2005) 544 US 915.

[82] For other, less widely discussed, instances of family disagreements, see *In re Martin* (1995) 538 NW 2d 399 and *Conservatorship of Wendland v. Wendland* (2001) 28 P 3d 151.

Difficulties revealed: Schiavo and the limits of surrogate decision-making

Surrogate decision-making recognises that people without capacity are, for the most part, situated within families or other social networks. In doing this, it has the undoubted advantage of minimising families' trauma in what may be difficult circumstances. Most of the time, this approach probably operates reasonably well in practice. Carl Schneider notes that, in an end-of-life context, '[d]ecisions ordinarily seem to be made as a consensus grows among the physicians and the family that further treatment is bootless'.[83] However, 'hard' cases, such as *Schindler Schiavo v. Schiavo*, serve as a reminder that difficult issues of principle do not go away simply because they are decided in the private rather than the public sphere.[84] In a case which received a great deal of publicity, a dispute arose between the patient's husband and surrogate decision-maker and the patient's parents.[85] Mr Schiavo sought to have life-sustaining treatment (including ANH) removed from his wife who was in a persistent vegetative state following an accident. His wife's parents strongly opposed the removal of treatment. As was required under Florida law, both parties grounded their arguments in what Ms Schiavo would have wanted, although Ms Schiavo had not made an advance directive and had given no express indication of her views regarding how such a situation might be dealt with.

[83] C. Schneider, 'Hard Cases and the Politics of Righteousness' (2005) 35 *Hastings Center Report* 24, 27.

[84] See R. Dresser, '*Schiavo*: A Hard Case Makes Questionable Law' (2004) 34 *Hastings Center Report* 8.

[85] The case had a long, complex and in some ways bizarre history. Prior to the final set of decisions, which took place between 2003 and 2005, the issue had already been litigated in 1998, 2000 and 2001. The final phase of the litigation began with the decision of the Florida District Court of Appeal (2003) 851 So 2d 182 to grant Mr Schiavo's application as legal surrogate to permit the removal of ANH. When final appeals were rejected, the then Governor of Florida, Jeb Bush, introduced emergency legislation (H.B. 35E. Authority for the Governor to Issue a One-Day Stay to Prevent the Withholding of Hydration and Nutrition from a Patient) permitting ongoing ANH. On appeal by Mr Schiavo, (*Schiavo* v. *Bush*, Baird J, Florida Circuit Court, May 5 2004), this legislation was found to be unconstitutional, a finding upheld by the Second District Court of Appeals (*Bush* v. *Schiavo* (2004) 871 So 2d 1012) and ultimately by the Florida Supreme Court (*Bush* v. *Schiavo* (2004) 885 So 2d 321). At this point, the focus shifted to Washington and legislation was approved by both the Senate and the House of Representatives and signed into law by President Bush (who returned from holidays to do this) to transfer jurisdiction of the case to the federal courts. There then began a series of petitions and appeals, until finally the United States Supreme Court denied certiorari in *Schindler Schiavo* v. *Schiavo* (2005) 544 US 915 and the decision of the Florida Court of Appeal was allowed to stand.

The discussion in *Schiavo* took place in a highly politicised environment which had a detrimental impact on the quality of the debate surrounding the case.[86] Nonetheless, the case is a reminder of the potential for conflicts of interests that are hidden by the privatising of the decision-making process.[87] Jay Wolfson, the Special Guardian *ad litem* in the case, notes his belief that both sets of parties were 'honestly motivated by what they believed was right and in [the patient's] interests'.[88] However, he points out the patient's parents' conviction that her husband was motivated by financial interests (following a substantial award of damages in an action for medical negligence) in seeking the removal of ANH. Although this claim was rejected by Wolfson and was not upheld by the courts,[89] it is not beyond imagining that, in some situations, factors other than the protection of the person lacking capacity might motivate decision-making. Wolfson also points out that the parents themselves, who had strong Catholic religious beliefs, conceded that just having their daughter alive produced 'joy' for them and that they would, if necessary to save her life, be prepared to approve the amputation of all of her limbs and subject her to further surgery thereafter.[90] Thus, if Mr Schiavo had declined to act as surrogate (or had predeceased his wife), an entirely different scenario would have played itself out in this case. In either set of circumstances, it is easy to see how the patient herself could disappear from the discussion and the surrogate's views become determinative.

Schiavo also shows, yet again, the lack of a principled basis in autonomy where there is no indication of what the person would have wanted. This problem is not restricted to high-profile, politically changed contexts but may be an issue in many exercises of surrogate decision-making. Research suggests that a significant number of surrogates cannot accurately predict what patients would have chosen. A study by Sulmasy *et al.* found that surrogates made inaccurate predictions in approximately a third of cases in respect of treatment choices for patients who had illnesses which were categorised as 'probably terminal'.[91] This would seem to be the case even in

---

[86] As noted by Schneider, 'Hard Cases', 24–5, the positions of both 'left' and 'right' became entrenched with both 'right-to-life' organisations and their liberal critics finding it difficult to see merit in any position other than their own.

[87] See M. Wicclair, *Ethics and the Elderly* (New York: Oxford University Press, 1993), p. 56.

[88] J. Wolfson, 'Erring on the Side of Theresa Schiavo: Reflections of the Special Guardian Ad Litem' (2005) 35 *Hastings Center Report* 16, 19.

[89] *Ibid.*, 18–19. Mr Schiavo had been prepared to concede any entitlement to monies in his wife's trust fund if she died before the fund was exhausted.

[90] *Ibid.*, 19.

[91] Sulmasy *et al.*, 'The Accuracy of Substituted Judgments in Patients With Terminal Diagnosis' (1998) 128 *Annals of Internal Medicine* 621. The study matched the preferences

marriages of long duration.[92] Difficulties in this regard are accentuated by the fact that many people do not discuss their treatment preferences with surrogates. Mark Wicclair notes that many elderly people (a group likely to be highly represented within the category of patients for whom surrogates make treatment decisions) do not discuss their preferences with family members and that, when elderly people do talk with their families about future care, comments may be vague, off-hand, and ambiguous. Statements such as 'I would rather die than be dependent' may reflect a desire for reassurance, or may be a result of temporary depression and not represent considered views on future medical care.[93] This is, of course, not just an issue with elderly people. Views formulated and expressed, perhaps with force and conviction, about life with a disability while young and healthy may not necessarily be fully thought through or indeed represent what the person would wish when such circumstances arise.[94] In such circumstances of uncertainty, the protection of the individual's right of autonomy afforded by surrogate decision-making judgment is 'at best indirect,'[95] at worst, non-existent. In such circumstances, as Rebecca Dresser notes, there is no option but to return to a best interests standard for decision-making.[96] Yet in the

of patients with capacity with the views of the people who would be likely to act as their surrogate if they lost capacity. Interestingly, the study found (627), that surrogates who had a strong religious belief and high rates of church attendance tended to reach the most inaccurate conclusions. Factors linked with accurate predictions were levels of education in both the patient and the surrogate (627). See also studies cited in L. Francis, 'Decision Making at the End of Life: Patients With Alzheimer's or Other Dementias' (2001) *Georgia Law Review* 539, 569–70.

[92] See S. Moorman and D. Carr, 'Spouses' Effectiveness as End-of-Life Health Care Surrogates: Accuracy, Uncertainty and Errors of Overtreatment and Undertreatment' (2008) 48 *Gerontologist* 811 (spousal surrogates made errors in 12–22 per cent of cases and expressed uncertainty in 11–16 per cent of cases); see also studies cited by Wicclair, *Ethics and the Elderly*, p. 56.

[93] Wicclair, *Ethics and the Elderly*, p. 55

[94] See *In re Martin* (1995) 538 NW 2d 399, where the patient's wife sought to have tube feeding of her husband (who was seriously brain-damaged following a car accident) withdrawn on the basis that, while capable, her husband had spoken disparagingly about people with severe disabilities and had expressed a desire not to have his life sustained in these circumstances. Other members of the patient's family contended that, even if he had had these views prior to his accident, Mr Martin had now had a change of heart and was contented and cooperative with his carers. The case was ultimately decided in favour of the continuance of feeding because of a lack of the necessary clear and convincing evidence of Mr Martin's prior desires (Mrs Martin's evidence was the sole basis for her claim). See commentary in T. Marzen and D. Avila, 'Will the Real Michael Martin Please Speak Up! Medical Decisionmaking for Questionably Competent People' (1995) 72 *University of Detroit Mercy Law Review* 833.

[95] Francis, 'Decision Making at the End of Life', 563.

[96] R. Dresser, 'Schiavo's Legacy: The Need for an Objective Standard' (2005) 35 *Hastings Center Report* 20, 21.

private decision-making environment created post-*Cruzan*, this standard remains underdeveloped in United States jurisprudence.[97]

The limits of the traditional approaches

Neither of the traditional approaches discussed above provides an appropriate conceptual basis for healthcare decision-making in respect of people lacking capacity. In their own ways, both the best interests standard and the substituted judgment standard leave too little scope for the inclusion of the views of the person lacking capacity. The views of others, whether in respect of what is in her best interests or in respect of what she would have wanted can serve to obscure the real person to whom the decision relates. As will be explored in the next section, it is possible, to a degree, to move beyond the limits of these traditional approaches and to deliver more meaningful protection for autonomy, notwithstanding incapacity.

Protecting autonomy in incapacity: frameworks for decision-making

There are clear conceptual attractions in an approach to healthcare decision-making that attempts to provide meaningful protection for autonomy notwithstanding incapacity. Such an approach attempts to address the limitations of a binary division based on capacity which, for the reasons discussed in the previous chapters, lacks credibility. It recognises, as summarised by the Law Commission, that 'even where a person does not have capacity to make an effective decision, he or she may have an important contribution to make to any decision-making process'.[98] In addition, this approach accords with international human rights standards. The protection of autonomy and the prevention of discrimination on the grounds of disability is a core principle of the CRPD.[99] More specifically, Article 12 (3) of the CRPD requires States Parties to provide appropriate measures to provide access by persons with disabilities to the support they may require in exercising their legal capacity.[100] The inclusion of the person lacking capacity in the decision-making process is also a requirement

---

[97] See *ibid.*   [98] Law Commission, *Report on Mental Incapacity*, p. 46.
[99] CRPD, Art. 3.
[100] See P. Weller, 'Supported Decision-Making and the Achievement of Non-Discrimination: The Promise and Paradox of the Disabilities Convention' (2008) 26 *Law in Context* 85.

under the Council of Europe *Recommendation on the Legal Protection of Incapable Adults*.[101]

Broadly speaking, there are two ways to protect the autonomy of a person lacking capacity. The first involves the preservation of the autonomy of the once capable person (sometimes described as precedent autonomy), either through formal advance decision-making mechanisms or by the less formal means of taking account of past views, preferences and opinions in the decision-making process. The second involves supporting people lacking capacity so as to enable them to participate to the maximum degree possible in decision-making. The first of these is most consistent with the traditional liberal approach to decision-making for people lacking capacity while the second is more in line with the approach favoured by the CRPD. The MCA allows for both of these ways of protecting autonomy and an analysis of the MCA provisions reveals some of the practical and normative issues to which these legal mechanisms give rise.

Protecting precedent autonomy: advance decision-making

Legislative provision for advance directives, or 'living wills', and enduring powers of attorney has been a feature of the law in the United States since early 1990s and in some Australian jurisdictions[102] and New Zealand[103] since the late 1990s. More recently, the MCA gave legislative effect to existing practice by providing a framework for advance decision-making in England and Wales.[104]

Formal mechanisms for advance decision-making

The MCA 2005 provides a person with capacity with two mechanisms to make provision for healthcare decision-making in the event of future incapacity. The first is by making an advance refusal of treatment; the second by granting a lasting power of attorney (LPA). Section 24 of the MCA allows a person with capacity aged over the age of 18 to make an

---

[101] *Recommendation No. R (99) 4 of the Committee of Members to Member States on Principles Concerning the Legal Protection of Incapable Adults* (adopted February 23 1999), Principle 9.

[102] See Medical Treatment Act 1998 (Victoria); Powers of Attorney Act 1998 (Queensland).

[103] See Right 7(5) of Code of Health and Disabilities Services Consumers' Rights, which became law on 1 July 1996.

[104] There is no equivalent legislation in Scotland or Ireland. The Adults With Incapacity (Scotland) Act 2000 makes no reference to advance directives. In Ireland, a Law Reform Commission Report has recommended the introduction of legislation on advance directives: see *Bioethics: Advance Care Directives* LRC 94–2009 (Dublin: LRC, 2009).

advance decision to refuse specified treatment(s) in specified circumstances to apply if she subsequently loses capacity. The decision may be
expressed in 'layman's terms'[105] and, unless the refusal relates to life-sustaining treatment, there is no requirement that it must be in writing.[106]

Before the advance decision will be given effect, it must be 'valid' and
'applicable to the treatment'.[107] A decision is not valid if the person has
withdrawn it when she had capacity to do so,[108] if a later LPA has conferred
authority on a donee to consent to or refuse the designated treatment,[109] or
if the person 'has done anything else clearly inconsistent with the advance
decision remaining his fixed decision'.[110] In the last situation, there is no
express requirement that the person must have capacity when she performs the inconsistent action in question.[111] An advance decision is not
applicable if the person has capacity at the time the question of treatment
refusal arises,[112] if the treatment in question is not covered by the advance
decision,[113] if any circumstances specified in the advance decision are
absent,[114] or if there are 'reasonable grounds' for believing that circumstances exist which the person did not anticipate at the time of making
the advance decision and which would have affected the decision had she
anticipated them.[115] Issues relating to the existence of an advance decision
and its validity or applicability may be the subject of a court declaration[116]
and nothing in an advance decision stops a person from providing life-
sustaining treatment to a patient or preventing a serious deterioration in a
patient's condition while a decision is being sought from the court.[117]

The second way in which a person may provide for her future incapacity is through the creation of an LPA. An LPA may be granted by any
person who is aged over 18 years and who has legal capacity.[118] The LPA
may relate to welfare and/or property and affairs and includes authority
to make decisions in these respects in circumstances where the donor no

---

[105] MCA, s. 24(2).
[106] An advance refusal does not apply to 'life-sustaining treatment' unless verified by a
written statement to the effect that it is to apply even if life is at risk (MCA, s. 25(5)).
[107] MCA, s. 25(1).
[108] MCA, s. 25(2)(a). Section 24 (3) states that a person may withdraw or alter an advance
decision while she has the capacity to do so. This need not be done in writing (MCA, s.
24(4)).
[109] MCA, s. 25(2)(b).   [110] MCA, s. 25(2)(c).
[111] See A. Maclean, 'Advance Directives and the Rocky Waters of Anticipatory Decision-
Making' (2008) 16 *Medical Law Review* 1, 20.
[112] MCA, s. 25(3).   [113] MCA, s. 25(4)(a).   [114] MCA, s. 25(4)(b).   [115] MCA, s. 25(4)(c).
[116] MCA, s. 26(4).   [117] MCA, s. 26(5).
[118] MCA, s. 9(2)(c). For details on the appointment of donees, see MCA, s. 10. The LPA must
comply with procedural requirements set out in Part II of the Lasting Powers of Attorney,

longer has capacity.[119] A welfare LPA extends to 'giving or refusing consent to the carrying out or continuation of a treatment by a person providing healthcare' to the person lacking capacity.[120] The treatment covered may include life-sustaining treatment;[121] in such circumstances, however, the creating instrument must contain a specific provision to this effect and the donee's power is subject to any conditions or restrictions in the instrument.[122]

Like all decision-makers under the MCA, the donee of an LPA must act in the best interests of the person lacking capacity.[123] Although as discussed further below, best interests in this context includes the 'past and present wishes and feeling' of the person lacking capacity,[124] this means that the framework for decision-making within which an LPA must operate is substantially different from that applicable to surrogate decision-making under a substituted judgment standard.

Assessing the contribution of the frameworks for advance decision-making

Formal advance decision-making mechanisms allow individuals, while capable, to make treatment decisions for their incapable selves or to give authority to do so to someone of their choosing. Their contribution within a liberal framework for healthcare decision-making based on autonomy is therefore indisputable. However, for a number of reasons they provide less protection for autonomy than might be supposed. First, advance decision-making is an option open only to people who have capacity. Secondly, the available evidence suggests that advance decision-making, whether through advance directives or the creation of LPAs, is unlikely to be used to any significant degree in practice.[125] Dresser notes that, in the

Enduring Powers of Attorney and Public Guardian Regulations 2007, SI 1253/2007 (as amended by the Lasting Powers of Attorney, Enduring Powers of Attorney and Public Guardian (Amendment) Regulations 2009, SI 1884/2009).

[119] MCA, s. 9(1).   [120] MCA, s. 11(7)(c).

[121] MCA, s. 11(8). Contrast the approach in Part 2 of the Adults With Incapacity (Scotland) Act 2000 where no mention is made of donees' powers in this regard.

[122] MCA, s. 11(8).   [123] MCA, s. 1(5).   [124] MCA, s. 4(6).

[125] See studies cited in A. Fagerlin et al., 'The Use of Advance Directives in End-of-Life Decision Making: Problems and Possibilities' (2002) 46 American Behavioral Scientist 268, 271–2; Francis, 'Decision Making at the End of Life,' 561. There would seem to be ethnic differences in this respect with non-white groups having less knowledge of the possibility of advance decision-making: see J. Kwak and W. Haley, 'Current Research Findings on End-of- Life Decision Making Among Racially or Ethnically Diverse Groups (2005) 45 Gerontologist 634.

United States, 'living wills' have been promoted since the 1970s with an 'especially big push' in the 1990s but that they 'have yet to become a major factor in decisions at the bedside'.[126] There is no reason to believe that matters will be different in other jurisdictions not least because advance decision-making requires people to contemplate the frightening prospect of their physical and mental decline and ultimate demise.

Thirdly, as commentators have pointed out, the MCA approach to advance decision-making militates against measures of this kind being able to override the best interests of the patient, especially in contentious contexts. Jo Samantha argues that the value of LPAs is limited because donees are constrained by the requirement to act in the best interests of the individual,[127] and that the MCA 'offers a "taster" for prospective self-determination, but little more than that'.[128] Alasdair Maclean advances a similar argument in respect of advance treatment refusals. He argues that the requirements for validity and applicability are likely to leave advance decisions 'vulnerable to challenge and thus undermines their value as protection for precedent autonomy'.[129] Certainly, there is nothing in the MCA to change the demanding evidentiary approach to advance treatment refusals taken by Munby J in *HE* v. *A Hospital NHS Trust*.[130] Indeed, the circumstances in this case might comfortably be brought within the ambit of a 'clearly inconsistent' action, which would render the advance refusal of treatment invalid.[131] Judicial views regarding what constitute 'reasonable grounds' for believing that circumstances exist which the person did not anticipate at the time of making the advance decision[132] will also be crucial in determining the extent to which advance decisions are upheld. If this provision is interpreted to include the situation of a patient who made an advance decision to refuse treatment if a particular set of circumstances arose but who is apparently contented in her current (incapable) state, it would undoubtedly undercut the scope of advance decision-making.

---

[126] Dresser, 'Schiavo's Legacy,' 20.

[127] J. Samantha, 'Lasting Powers of Attorney for Healthcare Under the Mental Capacity Act 2005: Enhanced Prospective Self-Determination for Future Incapacity or a Simulacrum?' (2009) 17 *Medical Law Review* 377, 379.

[128] *Ibid.*, 409.

[129] A. Maclean, 'Advance Directives and the Rocky Waters', 16. See also S. Michalowski, 'Advance Refusals of Life-Sustaining Medical Treatment: The Relativity of the Absolute Right' (2005) 68 *Modern Law Review* 958, 982.

[130] [2003] EWHC 1017 (Fam).

[131] Evidence was introduced (*ibid.*, [13]) that the patient had ceased to practise as a Jehovah's Witness and had agreed to convert to Islam upon her forthcoming marriage.

[132] MCA, s. 25(4)(c).

Although, in the absence of judicial elucidation, the question remains open, Samantha and Maclean are likely to be correct in their assessment of the MCA. It is doubtful that a person can confidently presume that, regardless of the circumstances which subsequently arise, the MCA absolutely requires that her advance refusal of treatment will be upheld. However, the cautious approach taken by the MCA is not necessarily inappropriate (or indeed unusual).[133] With advance refusals, the difficult normative question which arises is whether, and how, a legal framework in respect of advance decision-making should take account of the fact that, in Dresser's words, '[p]eople experiencing various life events, including set-backs in their physical and mental functioning, may revise their goals, values and definitions of personal wellbeing'.[134] The section below will ask whether the fate of the person lacking capacity should be determined by the views of her capable self while the succeeding section will evaluate the normative decision to retain a best interests focus in the context of LPAs.

Advance decisions: the normative question explored

On the normative question, traditional liberal theorists are clear. The liberal position, argued perhaps most famously by Ronald Dworkin,[135] is that that an individual's past (capable) preferences must be respected even if these conflict with the individual's current best interests or her current (incapable) wishes or desires. Dworkin illustrates his argument with a scenario involving Margo, a 54-year-old woman with Alzheimer's disease who lives a contented and happy life.[136] He develops the example by imagining that Margo, prior to her incapacity, would have been appalled by her current condition and had made an advance directive to the effect that, in the event of a terminal illness, she wished to refuse life-saving treatment (even if this was pain-free and highly likely to prolong her

---

[133] According to Marzen and Avila, 'Will the Real Michael Martin Please Stand up!' 852, in almost 30 states in the United States, legislation governing advance directives includes a provision whereby an advance treatment refusal may be withdrawn by a patient, even if she lacks capacity, if she shows a desire for the treatment.

[134] R. Dresser, 'Life, Death, and Incompetent Patients: Conceptual Infirmities and Hidden Values in the Law' (1986) 28 *Arizona Law Review* 373, 379.

[135] R. Dworkin, *Life's Dominion: An Argument About Abortion, Euthanasia, and Individual Freedom* (New York: Alfred A Knopf, 1993). For broadly similar arguments, see N. Rhoden, 'Litigating Life and Death' (1988) 102 *Harvard Law Review* 375; N. Cantor, 'Prospective Autonomy: On the Limits of Shaping One's Postcompetence Medical Fate' (1992) 13 *Journal of Contemporary Health Law and Policy* 13; Michalowski, 'Advance Refusals of Life-Sustaining Medical Treatment'.

[136] *Ibid.*, p. 220. Margo was a real woman, whose situation was described in A. Firlik, 'Margo's Logo' (1991) 265 *Journal of the American Medical Association* 201.

life). Justifying his argument that Margo's advance directive should be respected, Dworkin contrasts two kinds of interests which people have in their lives. Experiential interests are concerned with quality of life issues, such as pleasure, contentment or lack of pain. Critical interests are concerned with making value judgements and reaching autonomous decisions on this basis.[137] The right of autonomy protects critical interests which, within liberal theory, are fundamental. Accordingly, for Dworkin, the capable individual's critical evaluation of her own life and how she wishes to live it must be prioritised ahead of her experiential interests after she loses capacity.

However, there are reasons to question Dworkin's elevation of critical over experiential interests in all instances. A closer look at the context for advance decision-making supports Allen Buchanan's contention that there are 'several morally significant asymmetries between the contemporaneous choice of a competent individual and the issuance of an advance directive to cover future decisions'.[138] First, advance directives are made in a context which is epistemologically inferior. Important information (for example, information as to the kind of treatments available for the condition in question) may be absent at the time that the patient makes the advance directive.[139] While this is not always the case, the likelihood of this happening is accentuated where there is a significant time-lag (and consequent medical and technological developments) between the time at which the advance directive was made and the time at which it comes to be relied on. Furthermore, unlike contemporaneous healthcare decisions, which are made in the context of contact with others, including healthcare professionals, a person may make an advance refusal without any advice or even contact with another person.

In addition, the assumption that a capable person is the best judge of her own (critical) interests is weakened (although by no means wholly eliminated) because she inevitably lacks awareness of future contingencies, including how she will respond to a particular set of circumstances.[140]

---

[137] *Ibid.*, pp. 201–2.

[138] A. Buchanan, 'Advance Directives and the Personal Identity Problem' (1988) 17 *Philosophy and Public Affairs* 277, 278.

[139] See *ibid.*, 278–9. See also R. Dresser, 'Missing Persons: Legal Perceptions of Incompetent Patients' (1994) 46 *Rutgers Law Review* 609, 624–30; Buchanan and Brock, *Deciding for Others*, pp. 101–8.

[140] See Buchanan, 'Advance Directives' 279; J. Herring, 'Losing It, Losing What?: The Law on Dementia' (2009) 21 *Child and Family Law Quarterly* 3, 20. Note the impact of changing health states on views of what constitutes a state 'worse than death': D. Patrick *et al.*, 'Validation of Preferences for Life-Sustaining Treatment: Implications for Advance Care

Søren Holm argues that critical interests cannot be evaluated without understanding the context in which these were formulated (and whether this context still exists).[141] He gives the example of a person who makes an advance directive because she considers that life has meaning only if one can read and understand Joyce and Proust. If, having developed dementia, she is now happy watching 'Wheel of Fortune', it is, he argues, difficult to see why her previous interest, despite its critical importance at the time, should now guide decisions.[142]

Secondly, the issue of changing identity following a lack of capacity arises.[143] Here, Derek Parfit's work on psychological continuity and its role in the creation of identity has been especially influential.[144] Parfit disputes the idea of an essential human identity, arguing instead that our identity is based on the fact of psychological continuity which in turn is dependent on various factors, including the retention of memories. If psychological continuity is broken, for example, through a loss of memory, the person becomes a different person from the one she was before this loss took place. Applied to the context of advance directives, this would mean that a directive made prior to incapacity has no more moral force for the person lacking capacity than a directive by a stranger.[145]

There are difficulties with the argument based on the lack of psychological continuity as presented in this absolute way. As Buchanan notes, the notion of psychological continuity is 'inherently vague, since the continuity between mental states (including memories, affective states and dispositions admits of degrees'.[146] Even as someone loses her memory, other aspects of her 'prior' self will remain. Thus, Eric Matthews describes an elderly woman of his acquaintance who recalls little of her past life and

Planning' (1997) 127 *Annals of Internal Medicine* 509, 513, found that nursing home residents were less likely than any other category of patients (younger healthy adults, older healthy adults, adults with AIDS) to categorise hypothetical health states (dementia, severe stroke, severe pain, and coma) as worse than death.

[141] S. Holm, 'Autonomy, Authenticity or Best Interest: Everyday Decisionmaking and Persons With Dementia' (2001) 4 *Medicine, Healthcare and Philosophy* 153, 157.

[142] *Ibid.*

[143] See Buchanan, 'Advance Directives', 280–3; Dresser, 'Life, Death and Incompetent Patients', 380–1. See also the essays in J. Hughes *et al.* (eds.) *Dementia: Mind, Meaning and the Person* (Oxford University Press, 2006).

[144] See D. Parfit, *Reasons and Persons* (Oxford: Clarendon, 1984), p. 216 *et seq.* Parfit in turn draws on John Locke, *An Essay Concerning Human Understanding* (1690) in A. Campbell Fraser (ed.) (New York: Dover Publishing, 1959).

[145] See A. Maclean, 'Advance Directives, Future Selves and Decision-Making' (2006) 14 *Medical Law Review* 291, 299.

[146] Buchanan, 'Advance Directives,' 280.

has limited awareness of where she is yet who retains 'an ingrained sense of politeness' which for those who knew her is 'a surviving fragment of a once much richer identity'.[147] Additionally, many of our societal norms assume an ongoing identity throughout a person's life. Many people continue to visit unconscious family members and relatives with dementia even when their relatives do not recognise them or even know of their presence because this person remains their parent or sibling notwithstanding their current state.[148]

Notwithstanding the difficulties with an absolute psychological continuity argument, it must also be recognised that there are important differences between a person with advanced dementia or Alzheimer's disease and her pre-incapacity self.[149] Even if she is not a wholly different person, her post-incapacity self cannot simply be equated with her pre-incapacity self as if her post-incapacity self does not exist. As Buchanan points out, this philosophical difficulty arises only when some form of a personality is still extant and where the post-incapacity person still has some degree of ability to form preferences.[150] A person in a PVS, for example, does not have a personality in this sense in that she no longer has any capacity for views or preferences. Therefore, there is no possibility of conflict between her pre- and post-incapacity selves. However, many patients, notwithstanding their lack of capacity, may still be sentient and capable of pain and physical pleasure. Furthermore, as Holm points out, except in the very late stages of dementia, people still have wishes and desires with a 'complex cognitive nature' (i.e. not only desires to avoid pain, thirst, hungriness etc)'.[151] In such circumstances, it is difficult to see why the views and preferences of the person as she currently is should be wholly devalued and priority accorded to the views of the person she used to be.

Most commentators who recognise changing identity as an issue in respect of advance directives do not argue that changing identity completely deprives advance directives of moral authority.[152] Rather, the argument is

---

[147] E. Matthews, 'Dementia and the Identity of the Person' in Hughes *et al.* (eds) *Dementia: Mind, Meaning and the Person* (Oxford University Press, 2006), p. 175.

[148] See Holm, 'Autonomy, Authenticity or Best Interest,' 157.

[149] See J. McMillan, 'Identity, Self, and Dementia' in Hughes *et al.* (eds) *Dementia: Mind, Meaning and the Person*, p. 175.

[150] Buchanan, 'Advance Directives,' 281.

[151] Holm, 'Autonomy, Authenticity or Best Interest,' 153.

[152] See P. Lewis, 'Medical Treatment of Dementia Patients at the End of Life: Can the Law Accommodate the Personal Identity and Welfare Problems?' (2006) 13 *European Journal of Health Law* 219, 230–4, on the difficulties of introducing a legal limit on the effectiveness of advance directives on the basis of changing identity.

that it denies advance directives an absolute status. Buchanan argues that, so long as the degree of psychological continuity which we regard as necessary for personal identity is present, the directive retains full moral authority.[153] However, as we move downwards from this threshold, the moral authority of the directive diminishes accordingly. The weaker the degree of psychological continuity, the more readily the directive may be overridden on the basis of competing moral considerations, including concern for the wellbeing of the person lacking capacity. He suggests that even when the diminution of psychological continuity is sufficient to suggest that the person is not the same as her former capable self, there may still be enough continuity to allow some degree of recognition of the wishes of her capable self in reaching a decision.[154] Alasdair Maclean reaches a broadly similar conclusion, albeit by a different route, arguing that the relationship between pre- and post-incapacity selves might be analogised to the relationship between a parent and child.[155] Maclean argues that just as it is recognised that in most instances parents can make healthcare decisions for their children but that, in exceptional circumstances, parental views may be overridden, so too, it should be recognised that, in some exceptional circumstances, the prior decisions of a capable self in respect of her later incapable self should not be determinative.[156]

Some of the 'morally significant asymmetries' outlined above can be addressed by an approach to autonomy based on empowerment rather than as simple non-interference. Thus, for example, concerns about a lack of knowledge on the part of the person making an advance decision might be addressed by having mechanisms in place which facilitate people in engaging critically with their choices and in revisiting these choices in the event of deteriorating health or other major life changes. Furthermore, the asymmetries identified do not diminish the degree of respect which should be accorded to advance refusals in most situations. In this context, it must not be forgotten that relatively few people will make advance

---

[153] Although Buchanan argues that 'full' moral authority in respect of an advance directives is still less than in respect of a contemporaneous decision ('Advance Directives,' 297).

[154] *Ibid.*, 297–8. See the similar argument in Buchanan and Brock, *Deciding for Others*, pp. 182–3; see also R. Dresser, 'Dworkin on Dementia: Elegant Theory, Questionable Policy' (1995) 25 *Hastings Center Report* 32.

[155] Maclean, 'Advance Directives, Future Selves and Decision-Making,' (2006) 14 *Medical Law Review* 291, 315–16. Maclean defends this position on the basis that, even if they might be regarded as psychologically discontinuous, connections and relationships remain between pre- and post-incapacity selves.

[156] *Ibid.*

decisions to refuse treatment and that, while there is no mechanism to ensure they do so, many people who make advance decisions are likely to have thought carefully about the consequences of their decision. The existence of these asymmetries does, however, suggest that caution and care is not an inappropriate response to advance refusals of treatment, at either legislative or judicial levels, in situations where there is a conflict between a person's current (incapable) preferences and interests and her past (capable) wishes as set out in an advance directive. For this reason, the normative choices made by the MCA would seem to be appropriate, notwithstanding that the legislative framework undoubtedly limits the potential for advance decision-making.

A place for past views within a best interests framework

Outside of advance decisions, the decision-making standard under the MCA remains focused on the best interests of the person lacking capacity. As described above, this is the case even where an LPA has been appointed. However, the best interests standard set out in the MCA is defined in way which has crucial differences to the traditional standard.[157] As noted by the Law Commission, the standard contains 'a strong element' of the substituted judgment standard.[158] Of particular relevance is section 4(6), which requires a person making a determination of best interests to consider, 'so far as is reasonably ascertainable':

(a) the person's past and present wishes and feelings (and, in particular, any relevant written statement made by him when he had capacity),
(b) the beliefs and values that would be likely to influence his decision if he had capacity, and
(c) the other factors that he would be likely to consider if he were able to do so.

Furthermore, the decision-maker must take account 'if it is practicable and appropriate to consult them' of the views of 'anyone named by the

---

[157] Although note the pre-MCA recognition accorded to past preferences (in terms of religious beliefs) in *Ahsan* v. *University Hospitals Leicester NHS Trust* [2006] EWHC 2624 (QB), [51].

[158] Law Commission, *Report on Incapacity*, para. 3.25. Although the substituted judgment standard was rejected by the House of Lords in *Airedale NHS Trust* v. *Bland* [1993] AC 789, 872 *per* Lord Goff; 895 *per* Lord Mustill, some English courts incorporated aspects of the standard into their best interests assessment at common law by asking what the patient would have wanted as part of this assessment (see the approach of the Court of Appeal in *Bland ibid.*; *Re J (A Minor) (Wardship: Medical Treatment)* [1991] Fam. 33, 55; *Portsmouth NHS Trust* v. *Wyatt and Another* [2004] EWHC 2247 (Fam), [30]).

person as someone to be consulted on the matter in question or on matters of that kind', anyone engaged in caring for the person or interested in the person's welfare, any donee of an LPA (covering another kind of decision), and any deputy appointed by the court. This consultation must relate to what is in the person's best interests and what her wishes would have been.[159]

By recognising past wishes and beliefs and by imposing consultation requirements in order to ascertain these, the MCA attempts to mitigate the consequences of a loss of capacity while staying within a best interests framework. This approach is not without difficulties. First, by retaining the best interests focus, the MCA does not leave room for decision-makers to assume wholly altruistic or benevolent motives on the part of the person lacking capacity if these would lead to decisions which are not in her best interests. In respect of most decision-makers, there are good reasons for this. As described above in the context of substituted judgment, even close friends or family members cannot always know the preferences or the relevant beliefs and values of the person lacking capacity. Furthermore, the possibility of a conflict of interest must be acknowledged, especially in respect of altruistic decisions. However, the normative choice is more difficult to defend where an LPA has been created.[160] In this situation, a person while capable is more likely to have communicated preferences (which may include preferences which are wholly altruistic) to the donee of the LPA and has made a decision to place trust in the donee. The reasons for overriding the donee's choice are therefore diminished. However, because altruistic or benevolent motives must be taken into account in accessing best interests under section 4(6), the circumstances of a direct conflict between prior wishes and current best interests should be limited. Furthermore, a person does have the possibility of making an advance decision if concerned that a best interests assessment may not give sufficient weight to her altruistic motives.[161] On balance, therefore, it may be that the cautious approach taken by MCA is defensible, even in the case of LPAs.

Secondly, in treatment refusal situations, section 4(6) must be considered alongside other provisions in the MCA, in particular, section 4(5) and the provisions on advance refusals. Section 4(5) states that, in situations

---

[159] MCA, s. 4(7).

[160] See criticism of the MCA on this basis in Samantha 'Lasting Powers of Attorney,' 402–4.

[161] This, of course, presumes that people are aware of the detail of the law in this regard. Greater efforts to ensure patients' awareness of the legal position may well be needed.

where a decision relates to life-sustaining treatment, the decision-maker must not be motivated by a desire to bring about the death of the person lacking capacity. John Coggon describes this sub-section as a 'sorry compromise' with sanctity of life doctrine.[162] He argues that 'best interests and the climate in which they must be assessed render the application of section 4(5) wholly unworkable'.[163] The difficulty is that the section seeks to limit permissible motives for decision-makers but does not limit what decision-makers may actually decide. When section 4(5) is considered alongside section 4(6), the question which arises is whether a decision-maker may be said to be motivated by a desire to bring about the death of the person lacking capacity where she decides that it is in the best interests of a person to remove life-sustaining treatment because this accords with the person's past wishes. The Code of Practice to the MCA suggests that this would not be the case.[164] The Code requires that 'all reasonable steps' to preserve life must be taken but recognises that 'in a limited number of cases', an assessment of best interests may lead to the conclusion that treatment should be withdrawn or withheld even if this results in the patient's death.[165] Significantly, the Code states that, in making a decision in this respect, '[a]ll factors in the best interests checklist should be considered, and in particular, the decision-maker should consider any statements that the person had previously made about their wishes and feelings about life-sustaining treatment'.[166] Presumably, in such circumstances, the decision-maker's 'motivation' would not be regarded as the desire to bring about the person's death but rather as the desire to give effect to her wishes.

Thirdly, questions arise regarding the role played in the assessment of best interests under section 4(6) by advance decisions which have failed to meet the statutory requirements regarding validity or applicability. Does the fact of the advance decision remain relevant to the section 4(6) determination or is it to be completely disregarded? Presumably, the answer will lie in the basis on which the advance decision was found to lack validity or applicability. For example, if the basis for concluding that an

[162] J. Coggon, 'Ignoring the Moral and Intellectual Shape of the Law after *Bland*: The Unintended Side-Effect of a Sorry Compromise' (2007) 27 *Legal Studies* 110, 125.

[163] *Ibid.*, 119.

[164] See also the finding of the ECHR in *Widmer* v. *Switzerland* Application 20527/92, unreported Commission decision, 10 February 1992 that the protection of life under Art. 2 of the ECHR did not require the criminalisation of the removal of life-sustaining treatment (provided that any decision in this respect was made in the best interests of the person). See also *NHS Trust A* v. *M; NHS B* v. *H* [2001] 2 WLR 942, 953.

[165] Code, para. 5.31.   [166] Code, para. 5.32.

advance decision is not applicable is because the treatment in question is not covered or the circumstances referred to in the advance decision do not arise,[167] the advance decision should still provide a basis for ascertaining past views within the best interests framework set out in section 4(6) in respect of broadly analogous treatment or in broadly equivalent circumstances. However, it is more difficult to see a role within the section 4(6) framework for a decision which has been found inapplicable because of 'reasonable grounds' for believing that circumstances exist which the person did not anticipate at the time of making the decision[168] or which has been found invalid because the person 'has done anything else clearly inconsistent with the advance decision remaining his fixed decision'.[169]

Recognising current views: participative decision-making

A second way of dealing with decision-making incapacity is by supporting people who lack capacity in making decisions for themselves, where this is possible, and, if it is not possible, by providing mechanisms to maximise the participation of the person in the decision-making process. As well as complying with human rights norms outlined earlier in the chapter, facilitating participation in this way has practical advantages. It recognises that the inclusion of the subject of a decision in the decision-making process improves the quality of the decision reached.[170] This approach reflects best practice in terms of approaches to decision-making in general,[171] not least because, in Jonathan Herring's words, it pays 'attention to the lived experiences' of people lacking capacity.[172] Participation may also have therapeutic benefits in terms of enhancing individual well-being and self-esteem[173] and, in a healthcare context, may lead to better possibilities of compliance with recommended treatments.[174] Participation in

---

[167] MCA, s. 25(4)(a), (b).   [168] MCA, s. 25(4)(c).   [169] MCA, s. 25(2)(c).

[170] D. Galligan, *Due Process and Fair Procedures: A Study of Administrative Procedures* (Oxford: Clarendon, 1996), pp. 131–2.

[171] See, in the specific context of learning disabilities, K. Keywood *et al.*, *Best Practice?: Healthcare Decision-Making by, with and for Adults With Learning Disabilities* (Manchester: National Development Team, 1999).

[172] Herring, 'Losing it, Losing What?', 26.

[173] See B. Winick, 'The Right to Refuse Mental Health Treatment: A Therapeutic Jurisprudence Analysis' (1994) 17 *International Journal of Law and Psychiatry* 99, 100.

[174] See, for example, B. Schulman, 'Active Patient Orientation and Outcomes in Hypertensive Treatment' (1979) 17 *Medical Care* 267; L. Fallowfield *et al.*, 'Psychological Outcomes of Different Treatment Policies in Women With Early Breast Cancer Outside a Clinical Trial' (1990) 301 *British Medical Journal* 575. Although this research relates to adults with capacity, there seems to be no reason why the therapeutic benefit of participation,

the decision-making process also reduces the possibilities of conflict be-tween the person lacking capacity and healthcare professionals. As Hale LJ (as she then was) noted in *R (Wilkinson)* v. *Broadmoor Special Hospital Authority*, 'most people are able to appreciate that they are being forced to do something against their will even if they are not able to make the deci-sion that it should or should not be done'.[175] While participation does not prevent conflict from ever arising, a participative framework does serve to minimise the frequency of such occurrences.

Participation by the person lacking capacity in the assessment of her best interests is a key component of the definition of best interests in sec-tion 4 of the MCA. Section 4(4) states that the decision-maker must 'so far as reasonably practicable, permit and encourage the person to participate, or to improve his ability to participate, as fully as possible in any act done for him and any decision affecting him', while, as described above, sec-tion 4(6) requires that account be taken of the present (as well as the past) wishes and feelings of the person lacking capacity. In order to enhance the participative aspect of the MCA, section 35 provides for the establish-ment of an Independent Mental Capacity Advocate Service. This section provides that the 'appropriate authority' must make arrangements to en-able advocates to be available to provide support to the person lacking legal capacity so that she may 'participate as fully as possible in any rele-vant decision'.[176] The circumstances in which this service is activated in-clude the provision of 'serious medical treatment' by the National Health Service.[177] The appointment of an advocate occurs only where the relevant body 'is satisfied that there is no person, other than one engaged in pro-viding care or treatment for [the person lacking capacity] in a professional capacity or for remuneration, whom it would be appropriate to consult in determining what would be in [her] best interests'.[178]

The practical application of the participation requirement is addressed further in the MCA Code of Practice, which reflects ongoing research into developing better methods of communicating with people lack-ing capacity.[179] Chapter 3 of the Code outlines a series of suggestions to

---

including a feeling of ownership of the treatment process, would not apply in relation to at least some adults without legal capacity.

[175] [2002] 1 WLR 419, 446.   [176] MCA, s. 36.   [177] MCA, s. 37.   [178] MCA, s. 37(1)(b).

[179] Much of this work has been in the context of people with learning disabilities: see C. Kearney and T. McKnight, 'Preference, Choice, and Persons With Disabilities: A Synopsis of Assessments, Interventions, and Future Directions' (1997) 17 *Clinical Psychology Review* 217; L. Cameron and J. Murphy, 'Enabling Young People With a Learning Disability to Make Choices at a Time of Transition' (2002) 30 *British Journal of Learning Disabilities* 105; C. Regnard *et al.*, 'Understanding Distress in People With

facilitate participation. These include using simple language, speaking at the appropriate volume and speed, using appropriate words and sentence structure, breaking down information into smaller points, and using illustrations and/or photographs to help the person understand the decision to be made. Chapter 3 also suggests asking the person about the decision at a time and location where the person feels most relaxed and at ease and, if necessary, using specialist interpreters or signers to communicate with the person. In relation to a person with specific communication or cognitive problems, the Code suggests that decision-makers find out how the person is used to communicating, e.g. by means of picture boards, Makaton,[180] signing, or technological aids, and that they use the preferred method of communication. In this context, the Code also notes that, for some people who are restricted to non-verbal methods of communication, their behaviour and, in particular, changes in their behaviour may provide indications of their feelings.

By recognising that people lacking capacity have views and engaging with the substantive ways in which they might be facilitated in formulating and expressing these, the Code helps to create a climate for participation and adds detail to the minimal provisions in the MCA. However, as will be seen below, participative models for decision-making give rise to challenges which must be engaged with in a more conceptual way.

Challenges for participative decision-making

The primary challenge for developing a meaningful framework for patient participation lies in the difficulties that may arise in interpreting the views and feelings of the person lacking capacity. While some people lacking capacity can unambiguously communicate their views, in other cases there may be elements of uncertainty and ambiguity or the need for an interpretation of words or signals. The issues become more acute where observers have to rely on behavioural signals. Rebecca Dresser notes the inherent difficulties in understanding the perspective of someone who may 'often respond to the world in ways that mystify and perplex the "normal" persons observing them'.[181] Even something as apparently

Severe Communication Difficulties: Developing and Assessing the Disability Distress Assessment Tool (DisDAT)' (2006) 51 *Journal of Intellectual Disability Research* 277; A. Young and R. Chesson, 'Obtaining Views on Health Care from People With Learning Disabilities and Severe Mental Health Problems' (2006) 34 *British Journal of Learning Disabilities* 11.

[180] Makaton is a communication system based on visual representation through gestures and signs.

[181] Dresser, 'Missing Persons,' 666-7.

straightforward as ascertaining that a person is distressed or in pain can be difficult if the person does not have words to share the experience.[182]

Researchers into communication with people with profound learning disabilities have identified a number of difficulties in interpreting responses, which are also likely to arise in relation to people who lack capacity for other reasons.[183] The person lacking capacity may have idiosyncratic responses that have a specific meaning which may only be ascertained after repeated efforts. Furthermore, the person trying to interpret the response may lack the skills, patience or time to establish effective communication; she may assume that she knows the answer already and may interpret the responses accordingly, or she may have decided on the most appropriate course of action and may communicate this, either verbally or non-verbally, to the person lacking capacity, leaving the person little option but to acquiesce in a pre-ordained plan.[184]

It is in order to combat some of these difficulties that section 4(7) of the MCA obliges the decision-maker to consult with other people who, the Code notes, may be able to help the person lacking capacity to express wishes or aspirations or indicate a preference between different options.[185] The range of possible consultees is extensive,[186] recognising that different people may have quite different approaches to, and understandings of, the person lacking capacity. A carer who is a family member may have a nuanced and complex understanding of the person which a professional may lack. On the other hand, a family carer may have a degree of emotional involvement in the situation, which makes it difficult to make the kind of objective assessment of the person's own wishes that is envisaged by the MCA. Because the people consulted inevitably have different perspectives, conflicts may arise among them as to the wishes of the person lacking capacity.[187] The Code offers little insight regarding how a

---

[182] See the efforts of Regnard et al., 'Understanding Distress' to develop ways to understand distress signals in people with severe communication difficulties.

[183] See J. Porter et al., 'Interpreting the Communication of People With Profound and Multiple Learning Difficulties' (2001) 29 *British Journal of Learning Disabilities* 12; J. Ware, 'Ascertaining the Views of People With Profound and Multiple Learning Disabilities' (2004) 32 *British Journal of Learning Disabilities* 175.

[184] Some commentators have argued that the risk of acquiescence is heightened in the context of people with learning disabilities: see C. Sigelman et al., 'When in Doubt, Say Yes: Acquiescence in Interviews With Mentally Retarded Persons' (1981) 19 *Mental Retardation* 53; L. Heal and C. Sigelman, 'Response Biases in Interviews of Individuals With Limited Mental Ability' (1995) 39 *Journal of Intellectual Disability Research* 331.

[185] Code, para.. 5.24.   [186] See list in text to note 158 above.

[187] This is usefully exhibited in a case study described by Porter 'Interpreting the Communication,' 16. Peter, a young man with profound learning disabilities, tapped

divergence in opinion should be resolved, noting simply that, no matter who makes the decision, they should try to 'work out' what is in the best interests of the person lacking capacity.[188]

The challenges in establishing communication create two kinds of difficulties for meaningful operation of participative decision-making. The first is that the requirement for patient participation might end up as delivering little more than an acknowledgement of the views of the person lacking capacity before going on to make the decision regarding best interests that would have been made in any case. Thus, the approach to assessment of best interests after the MCA might turn out to be little different from the pre-MCA approach which was discussed in the early part of this chapter. This kind of tokenistic approach to participation would fail to deliver on the potential of the MCA. The second risk is that decision-makers will invent or interpret patients' wishes in a way which accords with the decision-makers' own views. Dresser argues that, when confronted with patients with high degrees of disability who proffer ambiguous signals, courts (and others) construct 'a mythical, generalized competent person to inhabit the body that lies before them'.[189] When interpreting signals from a person whose views and feelings are essentially alien to them, decision-makers may fall back on what they believe to be a 'normal' response to the situation. In so doing, the wishes identified may not be those of the person lacking capacity but those which the decision-maker believes she would have if she were in that person's situation.[190]

Delivering on the participative model

The inclusion of the wishes and feelings of the person lacking capacity in the assessment of best interests presents a challenge for a legal system which, to date, has taken an 'all or nothing' approach in dealing with preferences, depending on whether or not a person has capacity. By adding the preference of the person involved into the best interests 'balance sheet', the MCA introduces a subjective element into the best interests standard, thereby fundamentally challenging the objective nature of the standard. While the policy basis for the MCA approach is undeniable, the coherence of the resulting standard is questionable. For this reason, it is

at a helium balloon when it came near him. The staff at his school believed him to be playing with the balloon, his family believed that he was trying to push the balloon away and the researchers for the case study noted that Peter had difficulty controlling his arm movements.

[188] Code, para. 5.12.   [189] Dresser, 'Missing Persons', 612.

[190] For an example of this approach in practice, see G. Annas, 'The Case of Mary Hier: When Substituted Judgment Becomes Sleight of Hand' (1984) 14 *Hastings Center Report* 23.

essential to think in terms of practical ways in which the MCA standard
might be given effect and to develop a sustainable framework around the
concept of participative best interests.

At a practical level, the participation requirement should necessitate
the active seeking out and acknowledgement of the views of the person
lacking capacity and require the presentation of evidence to this effect
in all formal assessments of best interests. If the preference of the person
lacking capacity is contrary to the professional evidence in respect of her
best interests, this fact should lead to a rigorous scrutiny of the professional evidence presented and an effort to find a compromise position if
this is possible. As Herring argues, 'the wishes of the incompetent person should be followed unless there is a good reason for not doing so'.[191]
Certain factors should alert decision-makers to the need to be especially
careful before overriding the preference of the patient lacking capacity.
First, where the evidence is 'finely balanced,'[192] there should be a strong
presumption in favour of upholding the patient's preference. Secondly,
where the patient's level of capacity falls towards the higher end of the
capacity continuum, her views should be accorded greater weight. Thirdly,
decision-makers must take account of the extent of unwillingness shown
by the person lacking capacity. The more strongly felt is a person's objec-
tion, the less justification there is for intervention. As discussed below,
this aspect of participative decision-making has a basis in the ECHR, in
addition to its basis in the MCA.

In a broader sense, the participative model requires decision-makers to
strive, imaginatively if necessary, to ensure that the patient's views are not
lost in the midst of the professional evidence adduced. The attitude of the
Court of Protection is crucial in setting the standard in this respect. Unlike
the operation of the declaratory jurisdiction in the pre-MCA era, the Court
of Protection Rules state that, in general, the Court will operate in private[193]
(although the Court may authorise full publication or publication of a summary of a judgment).[194] While a limited number of judgments and summaries
are available, it is difficult to develop a clear picture of how the Court is operating. However, the decision of Sir Nicolas Wall P in *DH NHS Foundation
Trust* v. *PS* does not suggest much in the way of imaginative engagement. In
a brief judgment, the Court approved the performance of surgery in order to
treat the patient's cancer as well as the use of sedation and such force as was

---

[191] Herring, 'Losing it, Losing What?', 16.
[192] As was the case in *Re SS (Medical Treatment: Late Termination)* [2002] 1 FLR 445, 452.
[193] Court of Protection Rules, SI 1744/2007, r. 90. On this matter, see *Independent News
        Media* v. *A* [2009] EWHC 2858 (Fam); [2010] EWCA Civ 343.
[194] r. 91.

necessary to convey her to hospital. The Court did not call the learning disability community sister who had provided evidence regarding the patient's state of mind and no judicial attempt seems to have been made to require the facilitation of compromise. While the ultimate finding may (or may not) be appropriate, as a rare published example of the kind of reasoning employed, the case does not establish an appropriately rigorous precedent.

While participative decision-making offers the potential for new ways of thinking about autonomy and moving beyond the narrowness of binary divisions based on capacity, even if delivered to the maximum extent possible, it can never provide a complete conceptual framework for decision-making for people lacking capacity. Best interests, even in the modified form set out in the MCA, cannot provide all the answers. Rather, it is necessary to engage broader human rights frameworks as part of the conceptual grounding for decision-making in this context. The final part of this chapter will identify the potential and the limitations of looking to rights beyond autonomy.

A rights framework beyond autonomy

The human rights basis for the law's treatment of people lacking capacity is set out in international and European human rights instruments. While, as argued above, respect for autonomy is central, especially in the CRPD, the scope of human rights instruments is broader than this. The stated purpose of the CRPD is to 'promote, protect and ensure the full and equal enjoyment of all human rights and fundamental freedoms by all persons with disabilities, and to promote respect for their inherent dignity'.[195] The principle of 'respect for the dignity of each person as a human being' also underlies the Council of Europe *Recommendation on the Legal Protection of Incapable Adults*[196] as well as the United Nations *Principles for the Protection of Persons with Mental Illness and for the Improvement of Mental Health Care*.[197]

Notwithstanding widespread endorsement in human instruments, the courts in England and Wales have, as described above, shown little enthusiasm for establishing a conceptual grounding in human rights, such as dignity or bodily integrity, for decision-making for people lacking

---

[195] CRPD, Art. 1. This is given effect in the substantive articles: see Art. 15 (freedom from torture and inhuman and degrading treatment); Art. 17 (respect for physical and mental integrity); Art. 22 (respect for privacy).

[196] *Recommendation No. R (99)4 of the Committee of Members to Member States on Principles Concerning the Legal Protection of Incapable Adults*, adopted 23 February 1999.

[197] General Assembly Resolution 119, UN Document A/46/49 (1991), discussed further in Chapter 6.

capacity.[198] While there may be many reasons for this, one reason for judicial reluctance may be the inherently vague nature of the rights in question. When compared with the straightforwardness of an autonomy-based legal framework, references to rights such as dignity or bodily integrity seem to lack a clear focus and scope.[199] There are undoubtedly challenges in defining the scope of rights such as dignity or bodily integrity in respect of healthcare decision-making for people lacking capacity. What does a right to dignity mean in the context of physical restraint of a resistant patient in order to administer medical treatment which may save her life? What does a right to physical integrity mean for a patient who lacks even a basic understanding of the proposed treatment and what it is intended to achieve? In the light of the difficulties, it is perhaps understandable that courts prefer to avoid these questions, leaving the matter, as much as possible, to be determined by medical professionals and to the fluidity of the best interests standard. However, as will be seen below, there is a basis in ECtHR jurisprudence for the development of a more rigorous conceptual framework around dignity and other rights.

Understanding dignity

The meaning of a right to dignity is, as David Feldman notes, especially difficult to 'pin down'.[200] Feldman presents two conceptions of dignity, both of which are helpful in the current discussion. The first conception is subjective; it is concerned with one's sense of self-worth and is reflected in 'a readiness to confront the realities of one's circumstances ... and readiness to accept responsibility for the consequences of one's own actions and decisions'.[201] The second is objective; it is 'concerned with the State's and other people's attitudes to an individual or group'.[202] People who lack

---

[198] This is in some contrast with European jurisprudence where a right to dignity plays a much more significant role: see E. Grant, 'Dignity and Equality' (2007) 7 *Human Rights Law Review* 299, 306–11; C. Dupré, 'Unlocking Human Dignity: Towards a Theory for the 21st Century' (2009) *European Human Rights Law Review* 190, 200–2.

[199] This is evident in the decision of the Supreme Court of Ireland in *In Re A Ward of Court* [1996] 2 IR 79 where the Court permitted the withdrawal of hydration and nutrition from a woman in a 'near PVS' on the basis of her constitutional rights to autonomy, privacy, bodily integrity, dignity, life and equality, with little analysis of what the rights meant or how they interacted with each other. For a critique of the decision, see J. Keown, 'Life and Death in Dublin' (1996) 55 *Cambridge Law Journal* 6; G. Hogan and G. Whyte, *JM Kelly: The Irish Constitution* (4th edn) (Dublin: Lexis Nexis Butterworths, 2003), pp. 1397–401.

[200] D. Feldman, 'Human Dignity as a Legal Value: Part I' [1999] *Public Law* 682, 682.

[201] *Ibid.*, 685.   [202] *Ibid.*, 686.

the capacity for dignity in the subjective sense may still enjoy dignity in the objective sense. In Feldman's words, '[m]any people would agree that there are certain things that cannot be done even to unconscious or dependent people without violating their dignity and denying them the respect that is due to them as fellow-creatures inhabiting a common moral universe'.[203] Neither of these conceptions of dignity is capacity-dependent.[204] A person does not have to have decision-making capacity in order to have a sense of self-worth or a subjective sense of dignity while, clearly, dignity in an objective sense is not derived from the possession of the abilities necessary for legal capacity.

Feldman argues that dignity in either sense is not an 'end in itself'. Rather it is an 'expression of an attitude to life which we as humans should value'.[205] Accordingly, it generally makes little sense to talk of a right to dignity. The law can 'at best provide a circumscribing circle of rights which, in some of their effects, help to preserve the field for a dignified life'.[206] While, Feldman argues, there is arguably no human right which is unconnected to dignity, some rights have a 'particularly prominent role in upholding human dignity'.[207] Of relevance to the discussion here are the right to be free from inhuman and degrading treatment and the right to private life. By grounding the 'right' to dignity in these more defined rights, it is possible to begin the process of developing a human rights framework beyond autonomy. Emerging ECtHR jurisprudence in respect of healthcare decision-making for people lacking capacity is helpful in providing an indication of the scope of these rights and what they might require in practice.

Protecting dignity: the contribution of the ECHR

While the prohibition on inhuman and degrading treatment in Article 3 of the ECHR is perhaps the most obvious protection for dignity afforded by the ECHR, as will be seen below, the high threshold for the application

---

[203] *Ibid.*, 687.

[204] See an alternative conception of dignity 'as empowerment' put forward in D. Beyleveld and R. Brownsword, *Human Dignity in Bioethics and Biolaw* (Oxford University Press, 2001), pp. 21–7, which regards dignity as dependent on agents having the capacity for autonomy. Although Beyleveld and Brownsword argue (p. 128) that precautionary reasoning means that all persons should be assumed to be agents, and hence to have a right of dignity, this conception of dignity remains focused on autonomy and accordingly is unhelpful in the current context.

[205] Feldman, 'Human Dignity as a Legal Value', 687.   [206] *Ibid.*   [207] *Ibid.*, 690.

of the protection and the approach taken to medical treatment in ECtHR jurisprudence has limited the application of this Article. For this reason, to date, the more helpful jurisprudence has derived from the Article 8 protection for private and family life.

Protection from inhuman and degrading treatment

Article 3 sets out an absolute prohibition on torture, inhuman or degrading treatment. In *Pretty* v. *United Kingdom*, the ECtHR described treatment as inhuman or degrading where it 'humiliates or debases an individual showing a lack of respect for, or diminishing, his or her human dignity or arouses feelings of fear, anguish or inferiority capable of breaking a person's moral and physical resistance'.[208] The treatment must involve 'actual bodily injury or intense physical or mental suffering'.[209] It is not necessary that the aim of the treatment must be to humiliate or degrade the person if the effect is humiliating or degrading for the person involved.[210] Furthermore, it is clear that an individual does not have to be legally capable in order to feel degraded or humiliated.[211]

It is less clear whether degradation has an objective element and whether a person can be degraded if she is incapable of feeling degraded. This question has not been considered by the ECtHR, although there is English jurisprudence on the question. In *NHS Trust A* v. *Mrs M; NHS Trust B* v. *Mrs H*, Dame Butler-Sloss P held that Article 3 could not apply to patients in a PVS because the Article 'requires the victim to be aware of the inhuman and degrading treatment or at least to be in a state of physical or mental suffering'.[212] However, Hale LJ's comment in *R (Wilkinson)* v. *Broadmoor Special Hospital Authority* that 'the degradation of an incapacitated person shames us all even if that person is unable to appreciate it' suggests that the test for degradation has an objective, as well as a subjective, dimension.[213] This understanding of degradation would also seem

---

[208] (2002) 35 EHRR 1, para. 52.   [209] *Ibid.*

[210] See *Raninen* v. *Finland* (1997) 26 EHRR 563. Contrast the decision of the Irish High Court (in respect of the protection afforded under the Constitution of Ireland) in *The State (C)* v. *Frawley* [1976] IR 365, 374. The intention behind the treatment is, however, a factor in the Court's assessment: see *Price* v. *United Kingdom* (2002) 34 EHRR 1285, para. 24; *D* v. *United Kingdom* (1997) 24 EHRR 423.

[211] See *Herczegfalvy* v. *Austria* (1992) 15 EHRR 437.

[212] [2001] 2 WLR 942, 956. For a critique of Dame Butler-Sloss P's reasoning in this regard, see A. Maclean, 'Crossing the Rubicon on the Human Rights Ferry' (2001) 64 *Modern Law Review* 775, 790–1.

[213] [2002] 1 WLR 419, 446. This was also the view of Munby J in *R (Burke)* v. *the General Medical Council and Others* [2004] EWHC 1879 (Admin), [58].

to be more in line with the objective conception of dignity which was recognised by the Court of Appeal in *Airedale NHS Trust* v. *Bland* where Hoffman LJ described respect for dignity as based in 'our belief that quite irrespective of what the person concerned may think about it, it is wrong for someone to be humiliated or treated without respect for his value as a person'.[214]

The applicability of Article 3 to medical treatment was first recognised in *X* v. *Denmark*, where it was held that the Article could extend to 'medical treatment of an experimental character and without the consent of the person involved'.[215] The framework for the application of Article 3 to medical treatment was established by the ECtHR in *Herczegfalvy* v. *Austria*.[216] The case concerned treatment for a mental disorder, which had been forcibly imposed contrary to the wishes of an involuntarily detained patient who lacked capacity.[217] The ECtHR held two factors to be relevant in establishing Article 3 protection in relation to medical treatment. First, as with any application of the Article, the treatment must reach a minimum level of severity in terms of degradation and humiliation.[218] In the case in question, the ECtHR did not question the proposition that the treatment, which included forced feeding, isolation and the forcible injection of sedatives involving the applicant being handcuffed and tied to a security bed (which led to broken ribs), reached the standard. In individual cases, the question of whether treatment will reach this threshold will depend on the circumstances. Case law indicates that relevant factors include the nature of the treatment,[219] the physical effects of the

---

[214] [1993] AC 789, 826. The issue of dignity was not central to the House of Lords' discussion in *Bland*.

[215] (1983) 32 DR 282, 283. Cf *Simms* v. *Simms and Another* [2002] EWHC 2734 (Fam), where Dame Butler-Sloss P permitted an experimental treatment to be carried out on two patients at an advanced stage of vCJD on the basis that this treatment was in the patients' best interests. Dame Butler-Sloss P did not refer to Art. 3 of the ECHR in reaching this conclusion although she did refer to Arts. 2 and 8 [61].

[216] (1992) 15 EHRR 437.

[217] Although this applicant was involuntarily detained, the application of Article 3 is not restricted to people who are in state custody. See *D* v. *United Kingdom* (1997) 24 EHRR 423, para. 49. Note also *A* v. *United Kingdom* (1998) 27 EHRR 611, para. 22, where the ECtHR accepted that Art. 3 requires States to take steps 'to ensure that individuals within their jurisdiction are not subjected to torture or inhuman or degrading treatment or punishment, including such ill-treatment administered by private individuals'.

[218] See *Ireland* v. *United Kingdom* [1978] ECHR 5310/71; *Keenan* v. *United Kingdom* (2001) 33 EHRR 913.

[219] See *Jalloh* v. *Germany* (2006) 44 EHRR 667, para 67. In *R (on the application of PS)* v. *Responsible Medical Officer and Another* [2003] EWHC 2335 (Admin), [107], Silber J described the relevant factors to be taken into account as: 'all the circumstances, including the positive and adverse mental and physical consequences of the treatment, the

treatment,[220] the way in which the treatment is administered and whether physical restraint is used[221] and the level of resistance to the treatment on the patient's part.[222]

The second factor to be taken into account in deciding if Article 3 applies is whether the treatment is therapeutically necessary. In *Herczegfalvy*, the ECtHR held that the imposed treatment was permissible because it was a medical or therapeutic[223] necessity. The Court held that, 'as a general rule, a measure which is a therapeutic necessity cannot be regarded as inhuman or degrading'.[224] In essence, the decision introduced a justification for interference with the 'absolute' right.[225] While the extent of the therapeutic necessity justification is unclear, it seems clear that a therapeutic necessity requirement differs from the broader best interests standard, which extends beyond medical best interests only. In other words, treatment could be found to be in a patient's best interests yet not be therapeutically necessary (and vice versa). In *R (on the application of N) v. Doctor M and Others*, Dyson LJ accepted that, provided the minimum severity threshold is reached, in order for treatment without the patient's consent to be permissible, it must be both in the patient's best interests and therapeutically necessary.[226] In this way, it would seem that Article 3 adds a new element to the decision-making process (in cases where the minimum severity threshold is reached).

A further aspect of the therapeutic necessity exception relates to the steps that have to be taken to establish therapeutic necessity. In *Herczegfalvy*, the ECtHR held that the court must 'satisfy itself that the medical necessity has been convincingly shown to exist'.[227] The ECtHR did not elaborate on what

---

nature and context of the treatment, the manner and method of its execution, its duration, and if relevant, the sex, age and health of the patient'.

[220] In *Grare v. France* (1991) 15 EHRR CD 100, the European Commission of Human Rights accepted that imposed anti-psychotic medication had distressing side-effects for the patient; however, these were not considered sufficiently distressing for the treatment to reach the level of minimum severity required under Art. 3.

[221] See *Herczegfalvy v. Austria* (1992) 15 EHRR 437; *Nevmerzhitsky v. Ukraine* (2006) 43 EHRR 32.

[222] In *R (Wilkinson) v. Broadmoor Special Hospital Authority* [2002] 1 WLR 419, the Court of Appeal appeared to accept that Article 3 was implicated by the forcible administration, under restraint, of anti-psychotic medication to a vigorously resisting patient.

[223] The Court used the terms 'medical' and 'therapeutic' interchangeably in its judgment.

[224] (1992) 15 EHRR 437, para. 82.

[225] For a critique, see O. Lewis, 'Protecting the Rights of People With Mental Disabilities: the European Convention on Human Rights' (2002) 9 *European Journal of Healthcare Law* 293, 305–6.

[226] [2002] EWCA Civ 1789, [16].   [227] (1992) 15 EHRR 437, para. 82.

was necessary in order to do this. In the circumstances of the case itself, the Court accepted the argument of the Austrian government that the treatment was necessary according to the psychiatric principles generally accepted at the time of the treatment.[228] This suggests that a fairly minimal level of proof would establish the therapeutic necessity of treatment. However, in *Nevmerzhitsky* v. *Ukraine*,[229] the ECtHR was significantly more demanding in respect of this aspect of the therapeutic necessity test. Here, the ECtHR held that the applicant's Article 3 rights had been violated through force-feeding when he was on hunger strike while a prisoner. Although it reiterated the proposition that 'a measure which is of therapeutic necessity from the point of view of established principles of medicine cannot in principle be regarded as inhuman or degrading,'[230] the ECtHR held that sufficient steps had not been taken to establish the need for force-feeding at the point at which it took place and accordingly that the defendant State could not establish that force-feeding was in the best interests of the applicant.[231]

While *Herczgafalvey* established a foundation for ECHR-based engagement with treatment decisions, including decisions in respect of people lacking capacity, the ECtHR was clearly reluctant to allow Article 3 to interfere to any substantial degree with the therapeutic endeavour. This reluctance, combined with the difficulty in meeting the minimum severity requirement, has meant that there has been relatively limited scope for the development of Article 3 rights in respect of medical treatment of people lacking capacity. However, a number of decisions, which are not immediately related to medical treatment, may presage further scope for development. First, in respect of the minimum severity requirement, in *Selmouni* v. *France*,[232] the ECtHR noted the changing nature of acceptable behaviour and considered that 'the increasingly high standard being required in the area of the protection of human rights and fundamental liberties correspondingly and inevitably requires greater firmness in assessing breaches of the fundamental values of democratic societies'.[233] This changing attitude may be seen in *Jalloh* v. *Germany*, where the administration of an emetic through the nose, in order to force the regurgitation of a small plastic bag of cocaine, was held to be a violation of Article 3.[234] The

---

[228] *Ibid.*, para. 83.   [229] (2006) 43 EHRR 32.   [230] *Ibid.*, para. 94.
[231] *Ibid.*, para. 96. See also *Ciorap* v. *Moldova* [2007] ECHR, 12066/02, para. 83. Compare the early decision in *X* v. *Germany* (1984) 7 EHRR 152 that the forced feeding of a capable prisoner on hunger strike did not constitute a violation of Art. 3 because the State was justified in its intervention in order to fulfil its obligations under the Art. 2 protection of the right to life.
[232] (2000) 29 EHRR 403.   [233] *Ibid.*, para. 101.   [234] (2006) 44 EHRR 667, para. 83.

ECtHR found that, although Article 3 (and Article 8) of the ECHR did not prohibit recourse to a medical procedure against the will of a suspect in respect of a criminal offence, 'any recourse to a forcible medical intervention must be convincingly justified on the facts of a particular case'.[235] In this case, the plastic bag could have been retrieved by less intrusive means and the failure to use such means was found to be in violation of Article 3. Similarly, in *Wiktorko* v. *Poland*, the ECtHR found that the applicant's right to dignity had been breached by her being required to undress in front of male staff, and being manhandled by staff when she resisted while she was held at a sobering-up centre.[236] The ECtHR also expressed its concern regarding the fact that the woman was physically restrained by belts for a period of ten hours.[237]

Secondly, Article 3 has also provided the basis for a positive right to a basic level of protection in respect of the broader aspects of the right to dignity.[238] In *Keenan* v. *United Kingdom*, the ECtHR found a violation of Article 3 in circumstances where a mentally disordered prisoner was segregated in a punishment cell where he was held without proper medical monitoring and where he eventually committed suicide.[239] The ECtHR held that 'treatment of a mentally ill person may be incompatible with the standards imposed by Article 3 in the protection of fundamental human dignity, even though that person may not be able, or capable of, pointing to any specific ill-effects'.[240] The State's failure to provide 'effective monitoring' of the deceased's condition and 'informed psychiatric input into his assessment and treatment' was held to constitute a breach of his rights under Article 3.[241] This approach to Article 3 was extended in *Dybeku* v. *Albania* where the ECtHR itself raised the question of Article 3 in the context of the conditions in which the applicant, a mentally disordered prisoner, had been held.[242] The Court considered that 'the very nature of the applicant's psychological condition made him more vulnerable than the average detainee'.[243] In these circumstances, it was not enough that the applicant was held in conditions similar to other prisoners. Rather, his condition required specific psychiatric care and this

---

[235] *Ibid.*, para. 71.   [236] [2009] ECHR 14612/02, para. 54.   [237] *Ibid.*, para. 55.

[238] See A. Lawson, 'Disability, Degradation and Dignity: The Role of Article 3 of the European Convention on Human Rights' (2006) 56 *Northern Ireland Legal Quarterly* 462, 467–72.

[239] (2001) 33 EHRR 913, para. 116.   [240] *Ibid.*, para. 113

[241] *Ibid.*, para. 116. See also *Kucheruk* v. *Ukraine* [2007] ECHR, 2570/04, para. 147–152; *Musial* v. *Poland* [2009] ECHR, 28300/06, para. 97.

[242] [2007] ECHR 41153/06, para. 24.   [243] *Ibid.*, para. 48.

should have been provided. The argument that the dignity of certain categories of vulnerable people requires special protection could reasonably
be presumed to include people who lack capacity for reasons other than
a mental disorder. If accepted in this broader context, this imposition of
positive obligations could play a role in the future development of Article
3 jurisprudence, including in respect of medical treatment and the manner in which it is provided.

The right to private and family life

Article 8 states that 'everyone has a right to respect for his private and
family life, his home and his correspondence'. Unlike Article 3, possible
interference with a right protected by Article 8 does not have to reach
a minimum severity threshold and therefore Article 8 may apply in circumstances in which Article 3 does not.[244] However, Article 8 is subject to limitations, which permit interference with the rights protected
provided the interference is 'in accordance with the law' on a number of
bases, including 'for the protection of health'.[245] Although, as discussed
in Chapter 2, the protection of private and family life incorporates protection for the right of autonomy of patients with capacity, the application of Article 8 is not restricted to such patients.[246] In *Glass* v. *United
Kingdom*, the ECtHR found that the right to private life encompassed a
right to physical integrity and that the decision of healthcare professionals to treat a child with severe mental and physical disabilities contrary to
the wishes of his mother was a violation of the child's right.[247] The ECtHR

---

[244] See *Bensaid* v. *United Kingdom* (2001) 33 EHRR 205, para 46; *B* v. *Dr SS, Dr G and the
Secretary of State for the Department of Health* [2005] EWHC 1936 (Admin), [47] ; *R (B)*
v. *Dr SS, Second Opinion Appointed Doctor and Secretary of State for the Department of
Health* [2006] EWCA Civ 28, [49].

[245] See Article 8(2). The other bases for interference are: the interests of national security, public safety or the economic well-being of the country, the prevention of disorder
or crime, the protection of morals, and the protection of the rights and freedoms of
others.

[246] Although an attempt could be made to argue that the right of autonomy should be
extended to people lacking capacity on the basis of the Article 14 prohibition on discrimination, this is unlikely to be successful. Article 14 permits differential treatment
if there is an objective and reasonable justification for the treatment and in *Pretty* v.
United Kingdom (2002) 35 EHRR 1, para. 88 (in the context of possible discrimination
between people with physical disabilities and those without arising from the prohibition
on assisted suicide), the ECtHR set out rather generous parameters for the establishment
of an 'objective or reasonable justification' for differential treatment.

[247] (2004) 29 EHRR 341, para. 70. The treatment in question involved placing a do-not-
resuscitate (DNR) order on the child's file without his mother's knowledge or consent and the administration of diamorphine which, in addition to its pain-relieving

found that the child's mother's views should not have been overridden in the absence of authorisation by a court.[248] Although recognising a greater role for parental involvement (and presumably, by extension, the involvement of other family members or close associates),[249] the ECtHR was still quite clear regarding its reluctance to interfere with the medical decisions made. In fact, the ECtHR stressed that it was 'not its function to question the doctors' clinical judgment as regards the seriousness of the first applicant's condition or the appropriateness of the treatment they proposed'.[250] Nonetheless, the case was significant in establishing the individual's right to a more inclusive decision-making process.[251]

The decision in *Storck* v. *Germany* is, arguably, a more significant extension of the protections afforded to people lacking capacity in respect of medical treatment.[252] In this case, the ECtHR held that Article 8 had been breached by the administration of medication to the applicant against her will while she was being detained, also against her will, at a private psychiatric clinic. The ECtHR found that 'even a minor interference with the physical integrity of an individual must be regarded as an interference with the right to respect for private life under Article 8, if it is carried out against the individual's will'.[253] The Court noted that the applicant had constantly resisted the imposition of the treatment and that medication had at all times been administered by force.[254] The Court was not concerned with whether or not the applicant had capacity at the time the treatment was administered[255] and the clear message from the decision is that treatment cannot be imposed against a person's will simply because she lacks capacity. Thus, *Storck* provides the basis for an approach

---

qualities, is known to speed up death. The focus of the ECtHR was entirely on the second aspect, although Casadavell J in a separate opinion annexed to the judgment examined the question of the DNR, which he considered should have been discussed by the majority.

[248] *Ibid.*, para. 83.

[249] The question of how far the ECtHR's findings extend beyond parental involvement is, of course, open: note Casadevall J's reference to 'maternal instinct' (separate opinion, *ibid.*, para. 1).

[250] *Ibid.*, para. 87. For a critique of this aspect of the case, see R. Huxtable and K. Forbes, 'Case Commentary: *Glass* v. *United Kingdom*: Maternal Instinct v Medical Opinion' (2004)16 *Child and Family Law Quarterly* 339, 351.

[251] Although Mrs Glass also brought proceedings in respect of her own right under Article 8, the ECtHR did not address this matter, considering *ibid.*, para. 72 that it was required only to consider the matter from the first applicant's standpoint.

[252] (2005) 43 EHRR 96.   [253] *Ibid.*, para. 143.   [254] *Ibid.*, para. 144.

[255] Although capacity was not central, the ECtHR, *ibid.*, para. 76, stated that it was proceeding on the basis of a presumption that the applicant had been capable of refusing consent to admission at the time she was admitted against her will although it also acknowledged the possibility that, having been medicated, she may subsequently have lost capacity.

to decision-making that looks beyond questions of capacity or incapacity and addresses issues of willingness, restraint and force. The decision makes it clear that the absence of capacity does not justify a treatment 'free-for-all'. In addition, the ECtHR recognised the positive obligations which Article 8 imposes 'to take reasonable and appropriate measures to secure and protect individuals' right to respect for their private life'.[256] The ECtHR found that the State's failure to establish and maintain effective 'supervision and control' over the private psychiatric facility in which the applicant was held failed to meet the State's obligation to protect individuals against infringements of their physical integrity.[257]

Practical application of ECHR rights

While relatively limited, ECtHR jurisprudence to date has been important in shifting the debate on medical treatment for people lacking capacity away from the simplicity of an autonomy-based model and focusing additionally on the rights of patients who lack capacity. Furthermore, the recognition of positive obligations on the State to protect the dignity and privacy of individuals requires greater engagement with broader issues in respect of the appropriateness of treatment provided and the manner in which it is given.[258]

Rights and restraint

For practical purposes, the most obvious contribution of ECHR-derived jurisprudence is likely to be in respect of treatment of unwilling patients and in particular in respect of the use of restraint. In light of the decision in *Storck*, any imposition of treatment on an unwilling patient must be in accordance with the justifications for interference with Article 8 as set out in Article 8(2). Thus, restraint, if used, must be 'in accordance with law' and 'necessary in democratic society' in pursuance of one of the aims recognised as legitimate by the Article. In respect of the use of restraint, the law in England and Wales has come some distance from the approach of the Court of Appeal in *Re MB (An Adult: Medical Treatment)*, where the Court was happy to delegate to the medical professionals involved the determination of the level of force to be used in providing treatment to a patient found to lack capacity.[259] Some of these changes preceded

---

[256] *Ibid.*, para. 149.   [257] *Ibid.*, para. 150.

[258] See D. Feldman, 'Human Dignity as a Legal Value: Part 2' [2000] *Public Law* 61, 70–1.

[259] [1997] 2 FCR 541, 556. Although, note DH NHS Foundation Trust v. PS (By her litigation friend, the official solicitor) [2010] EWHC 1217 (Fam) which adopts a largely similar attitude to restraint.

the commencement of the MCA. In *Re JT (Adult: Refusal of Medical Treatment)*, Wall J stated that the use of restraint to administer kidney dialysis (required on an ongoing basis) to a woman without her consent would be 'inappropriate and, indeed, wholly unethical'.[260] However, he did not explore why this would be the case, finding instead that the woman had legal capacity to refuse the treatment in question. In *Trust A and Trust B* v. *H (An Adult Patient)*, Sir Mark Potter P described it as lawful to provide treatment and 'even to overcome non-co-operation of a resisting patient by sedation and a moderate and reasonable use of restraint'.[261] However, he noted that the extent to which restraint may be needed 'has to be carefully considered when assessing the balance of benefit and disadvantage in the giving of the proposed medical treatment and where the best interest of the patient truly lies'.[262] Thus, while not prepared to interfere with therapeutic decisions, the President was clear that the fact that restraint would have to be used must be included in the best interests 'balance sheet'.

This approach is largely reflected in the approach to restraint taken by the MCA. An underlying principle of the MCA is that, before any act is done or decision made in respect of a person lacking capacity, 'regard must be had to whether the purpose for which it is needed can be as effectively achieved in a way that is less restrictive of the person's rights and freedom of action'.[263] More specifically, section 6 of the MCA states that, before a 'restraining act' in respect of a person lacking capacity is permissible, the person who performs the act must first, 'reasonably believe that it is necessary to do the act in order to prevent harm', and, secondly, the act must be a 'a proportionate response' to the likelihood of harm occurring and to the seriousness of that harm.[264] A person restrains another, for the purposes of section 6, where she 'uses, or threatens to use, force to secure the doing of an act' which the other person resists or where she restricts the other person's movement, whether or not the person resists.[265] However, a person does more than merely restrain if she deprives the person lacking capacity of her liberty within the meaning of Article 5 of the ECHR.[266]

---

[260] [1998] 2 FCR 662, 665. Note also the finding of Ward J in *Re E (A Minor)* [1993] 1 FLR 386 that, unlike the situation in the Canadian case of *Re LDK* (1985) 48 Rep Fam L 2d (Ont) 164 to which he was referred, there was no evidence that the young man in question would suffer emotional trauma from the imposition of the transfusion.

[261] [2006] EWHC 1230 (Fam), [27].   [262] *Ibid.*   [263] MCA, s. 1(6).   [264] MCA, s. 6(3).

[265] MCA, s. 6(4).

[266] MCA, s. 6(5). A deprivation of liberty is defined in the relevant subsection in accordance with the jurisprudence in respect of Article 5 of the ECHR: see generally N. Allen,

The extent to which section 6 will have an impact on the use of restraint in respect of unwilling patients will depend on the interpretation of the concepts of necessity and harm. The Code to the MCA makes it clear that a carer or professional may not use restraint simply to enable themselves to do something more easily and that any restraint used must involve the minimum amount of force for the shortest time possible.[267] The Code also suggests that healthcare staff should consult with other people involved in the person's care to see if they can avoid or minimise the need for restraint.[268] It remains to be seen whether or not this degree of protection is sufficient in light of the rights protections afforded by the ECHR. In particular, issues may arise in respect of the lack of robustness of the mechanisms in the MCA to monitor the use of restraint and to ensure compliance with the MCA. Like other aspects of the MCA, the provision in respect of restraint relies on private monitoring. Thus, enforcement of section 6 is dependent on someone (most likely the patient or her family members) making a complaint in respect of the use of restraint. For the reasons explored in Chapter 4, reliance on private monitoring of this kind is not a particularly effective way of protecting rights.

Rights and review

A second way in which ECHR-derived jurisprudence may make a practical contribution to the development of the law relates to mechanisms for review of treatment decisions. This issue will be discussed in more detail in Chapter 6. In brief, there is an argument that there are insufficient review mechanisms provided by the MCA in respect of some treatment decisions. Although under the current *Practice Note*, some treatment decisions, including non-consensual sterilisation, withdrawal of treatment from PVS patients and some terminations of pregnancy, are automatically judicially reviewed[269] while others are judicially reviewed where there is doubt or dispute in respect of best interests,[270] most decisions are not subject to any form of review. Thus, even decisions that have a significant long-term impact on the health and well-being of a person lacking capacity (for example, a decision to prescribe anti-psychotic medication to a

---

'Restricting Movement or Depriving Liberty?' (2009) 18 *Journal of Mental Health Law* 19. In circumstances involving a deprivation of liberty, the elaborate admission procedure set out in Schedule A1 to the MCA (inserted by the Mental Health Act 2007, s. 50) applies: see generally P. Bartlett, *Blackstone's Guide to the Mental Capacity Act 2005* (2nd edn) (Oxford University Press, 2008), Chapter 4.

[267] Code, para. 6.44.   [268] Code, para. 6.48.   [269] [2006] 2 FLR 373, [5].
[270] Code, para. 8.18.

patient with dementia) take place without any form of external review. It will be argued in Chapter 6 that the lack of any systematic mechanism for review of these treatment decisions may fail to provide adequate protection for rights arising under the ECHR.

Conclusion

Patients lacking capacity have long been fitted into legal frameworks developed for patients with capacity. Whether through a wholesale return to paternalism or through largely unconvincing attempts to maintain a façade of respect for autonomy through substituted judgment, the law has traditionally failed to serve people in this situation. In many ways, there have been significant improvements in recent years. The MCA is an important legislative attempt to protect and develop autonomy in a way that focuses on the person lacking capacity on the basis of who she is, rather than on the basis of what she lacks. However, the success of the participative model adopted by the MCA is by no means assured. The requirements to take account of past and present wishes may well turn out to be no more than a rhetorical nicety. In this context, the support of a conceptual framework provided by the ECHR may become increasingly important.

There are undoubted difficulties with reliance on ECHR rights in developing a conceptual framework for healthcare decision-making for people lacking capacity. First, the ongoing development of jurisprudence requires action by people lacking capacity. For many people in this situation, the obstacles to be confronted in order to establish their legal rights (consulting a solicitor, initiating a legal action) may be insurmountable. Thus, the protection of rights becomes a matter of happenstance. Secondly, the ECHR may be better at changing procedures than it is at changing mindsets.[271] Yet, for all that, emerging jurisprudence in respect of rights beyond autonomy does help to give form to nebulous rights such as dignity and, in this way, it can make a contribution to a better framework for healthcare decision-making for people lacking capacity. As Chapter 6 will show, this is especially needed in respect of decisions relating to treatment for a mental disorder.

---

[271] See (in the context of mental health law): B. Hale, 'The Human Rights Act and Mental Health Law: Has it Helped?' (2007) 13 *Journal of Mental Health Law* 7; B. Hale, 'Justice and Equality in Mental Health Law: The European Experience' (2007) 30 *International Journal of Law and Psychiatry* 18; G. Richardson, 'The European Convention and Mental Health Law in England and Wales: Moving Beyond Process' (2005) 28 *International Journal of Law and Psychiatry* 127.

6

Treatment for a mental disorder: a case apart?

For many years, the law relating to treatment for a mental disorder has constituted an anomaly within legal systems which purport to privilege and protect the individual's right of autonomy. In many jurisdictions, including England and Wales, Australia, Ireland and New Zealand, mental health legislation limits the right of patients to make decisions in respect of treatment for their mental disorder, regardless of their capacity. Unsurprisingly, this differential treatment of people with mental disorders has attracted criticism from a range of perspectives. Indeed, as discussed in Chapter 1, critiques emanating from the 'anti-psychiatry movement' were part of the impetus for the move to an autonomy-based approach to healthcare decision-making more generally. As with the position in respect of people lacking capacity which was discussed in Chapter 5, there has been a significant shift towards more rights-based legal discourse in respect of people with a mental disorder. People with mental disorders come within the ambit of the European Convention on Human Rights (ECHR)[1] and the United Nations Convention on the Rights of Persons with Disabilities (CRPD). Additionally, non-binding instruments setting out specific protections for the rights of patients with mental disorders have been adopted at United Nations[2] and European levels.[3] However, as will be seen below, it is unlikely that any of these human rights instruments will require a substantive reversal of the differential approach taken to the right of autonomy.

---

[1] In addition, treatment for a mental disorder may implicate the *European Convention for the Prevention of Torture and Inhuman or Degrading Treatment or Punishment 1987*.

[2] See United Nations *Principles for the Protection of Persons With Mental Illness and the Improvement of Mental Health Care* General Assembly Resolution 119, adopted 17 December 1991, UN Document A/46/49 (1991).

[3] See Council of Europe *Recommendation No R(83)2 of the Committee of Ministers to Member States Concerning the Legal Protection of Persons Suffering from Mental Disorders Placed as Involuntary Patients; Recommendation 2004(10) of the Committee of Ministers to Member States Concerning the Protection of the Human Rights and Dignity of Persons With Mental Disorder*.

This chapter explores the legal and normative framework within which decisions about treatment for a mental disorder are made. Core to this discussion is the question of whether respect for patient autonomy should provide the basis for the law in this context in the same way as it does in respect of treatment for a physical disorder. The chapter begins by outlining the law in respect of treatment for a mental disorder in England and Wales. This is an interesting example of a legal model which has moved to include greater protections for patient rights while, at the same time, continuing to permit treatment to be administered notwithstanding the refusal of a capable patient.[4] Having established the legal framework, the chapter looks at the normative issues arising. These are made all the more difficult because of the stigma attached to mental disorder,[5] the long history of abusive treatment practices[6] and the invasive nature of some of the treatments involved.[7] The chapter examines the relationship between mental health law and liberal theory and assesses the classic autonomy-based treatment model adopted in the United States and some Canadian provinces. From this, it concludes that there is reason for scepticism about what an approach based on respect for autonomy as non-interference can deliver. It shows why it is important to look beyond forced treatment to broader issues of autonomy enhancement, empowerment and power redistribution and to engage with the position of people lacking capacity (whether or not they are involuntary patients), and with the development of positive rights in respect of access to treatment and treatment reviews.

Treatment for a mental disorder: the law in England and Wales

The Mental Health Act 1983 (MHA) establishes a complex legal framework to regulate the detention and treatment of patients with a mental disorder. For the most part, the legislation applies only to involuntary patients, whether they have been formally admitted to a psychiatric

---

[4] For broadly similar models, see the Mental Health Act 1986 (Victoria); the Mental Health (Compulsory Assessment and Treatment) Act 1992 (New Zealand); the Mental Health Act 2001 (Ireland); the Mental Health Act 2007 (New South Wales, Australia).

[5] The scale of the impact of stigmatisation is explored in G. Thornicroft, *Shunned: Discrimination Against People With Mental Illness* (Oxford University Press, 2007).

[6] See P. Fennell, *Treatment Without Consent: Law, Psychiatry and the Treatment of Mentally Disordered People Since 1845* (London: Routledge, 1995), Chapters 3, 5, 9 and 10.

[7] On modern treatments, see P. Bartlett and R. Sandland, *Mental Health Law: Policy and Practice* (3rd edn) (Oxford University Press, 2007), pp. 278–8.

facility or made subject to 'supervised community treatment' (SCT). For all other patients, and for treatment of involuntary patients for a physical disorder, the common law rules apply. The decision to admit a patient under the MHA is based on her need for treatment or on the protection of others and on the availability of appropriate treatment.[8] The patient's capacity is not a relevant factor.[9] Although extending only to a relatively small proportion of people with mental disorders, the effect of the MHA is felt beyond the immediate category of involuntary patients.[10] The involuntary admission provisions may be invoked where a voluntary patient in a psychiatric facility refuses to comply with treatment, leading the patient's status to be changed from voluntary to involuntary.[11] Furthermore, for both hospitalised and community patients, the threat that treatment will be compulsorily imposed, if not voluntarily acceded to, can lead patients to consent to treatment in order to avoid the stigma of compulsion.[12]

The legislative framework: Part 4 of the MHA

Bartlett and Sandland describe Part 4 of the MHA as 'double-edged'.[13] On the one hand, this Part of the MHA gives extensive powers to impose treatment on patients; on the other hand, it restricts the imposition of treatment in some situations. Section 63 sets out the basic power to treat. This section states that, other than for certain specified treatments, the consent of a patient is not required for any medical treatment given for the mental disorder from which the patient is suffering, provided that the treatment is 'given by or under the direction of' the patient's approved

[8] A person may be formally admitted for assessment, under the MHA, s. 2, or for treatment, under MHA, s. 3. For details, see Bartlett and Sandland, *Mental Health Law*, pp. 122–33; on the 'appropriate treatment' requirement, see P. Fennell, *Mental Health: The New Law* (Bristol: Jordans, 2007), pp. 67–9.

[9] A small study by J. Bellhouse *et al.*, 'Capacity-Based Mental Health Legislation and its Impact on Clinical Practice: 2) Treatment in Hospital' [2003] *Journal of Mental Health Law* 24 found that 2 out of 10 involuntary patients evaluated had legal capacity to consent to treatment for their mental disorder.

[10] The numbers are still relatively substantial. In England alone, approximately 45,000 people are admitted under the MHA every year: see Mental Health Act Commission, Thirteenth Biennial Report 2007–2009, *Coercion and Consent* (London: The Stationery Office, 2009), p. 24.

[11] Bartlett and Sandland, *Mental Health Law*, p. 133, note that the applicable provision in such circumstances (MHA, s. 5) is 'notably lax in its requirements'.

[12] See A. Zigmond and A. Holland, 'Unethical Mental Health Law: History Repeats Itself' (2000) 3 *Journal of Mental Health Law* 49, 53.

[13] Bartlett and Sandland, *Mental Health Law*, p. 275.

clinician (AC) (formerly the responsible medical officer (RMO)).[14] There is no statutory indication of how the AC should determine whether to provide treatment and section 63 does not make any distinction between patients on the basis of capacity.

The power to treat in section 63 is restricted by sections 57, 58 and 58A.[15] Section 57 applies only to the rare instances of psychosurgery[16] and the surgical implantation of sexual suppressants.[17] This section (which applies to voluntary as well as involuntary patients)[18] requires that the patient must be certified as having capacity and must give consent to the procedure.[19] Section 58A applies to electro-convulsive therapy (ECT).[20] This section, which was inserted by the MHA 2007,[21] provides that, other than in emergency situations, ECT may only be administered to patients with capacity provided that they consent to the treatment.[22] For patients without capacity, ECT may be administered only if an independently appointed registered medical practitioner other than the patient's AC (usually known as a second-opinion appointed doctor or SOAD) certifies in writing that the patient lacks capacity, that it is appropriate for the treatment to be given and that giving the treatment does not conflict

---

[14] Treatment is broadly defined in MHA, s. 145(4) as 'medical treatment the purpose of which is to alleviate, or prevent a worsening of, the disorder or one or more of its symptoms or manifestations'. Treatment for a mental disorder has been held to include forced feeding: see *B v. Croydon Health Authority* [1995] 2 WLR 294 and the performance of caesarean sections: see *Tameside and Glossop Acute Services Trust v. CH* [1996] 1 FCR 753. Fennell, *The New Law*, p. 292, notes that this is contrary to the original intention that s. 63 was to apply to less controversial treatments.

[15] This is unless the treatment in question comes within the emergency treatment exception set out in s. 62. See Bartlett and Sandland, *Mental Health Law*, pp. 333–5.

[16] The Mental Health Act Commission Thirteenth Biennial Report, p. 167, states that in the reporting period covered, two such procedures were authorised (and no other applications were made). Both patients reported very positive outcomes.

[17] The s. 57 protection was extended to the surgical implantation of sexual suppressants by the Mental Health (Hospital, Guardianship and Consent to Treatment) Regulations 1983, SI 893/1983, Reg. 16. However, sexual suppressants are usually administered by depoinjections rather than surgically implanted (see Fennell, *Treatment Without Consent*, pp. 187–8) and therefore do not come within the section.

[18] MHA, s. 56(2).   [19] MHA, s. 57(2)(a).

[20] The United Kingdom ECT Review Group, *Systematic Review of the Efficacy and Safety of Electroconvulsive Therapy* (London: Department of Health, 2003), p. 57, found that ECT appears to be an effective short-term treatment for patients with depression although the group found no evidence demonstrating its effectiveness for other conditions.

[21] MHA, s. 27. Other treatments may be included by regulation within the protections afforded by s. 58A (s. 58A(1)(b)).

[22] MHA, s. 58A(3).

with a valid and applicable advance decision or a decision made by a donee of a lasting power of attorney or by a deputy or by the Court of Protection.[23]

Section 58 applies to the administration of medication for more than three months. It states that medication may continue to be administered only with the consent of a capable patient or if approved by a SOAD. The SOAD must certify in writing that the patient does not have capacity or that she has not consented to the treatment but that 'it is appropriate for the treatment to be given'.[24] The MHA states that treatment is 'appropriate' for a patient 'if the treatment is appropriate in his case, taking into account the nature and degree of the mental disorder from which he is suffering and all other circumstances of his case'.[25] The issue of capacity is not emphasised in the MHA Code of Practice[26] or in the Guidance to SOADs provided by the Care Quality Commission (CQC) (formerly the Mental Health Act Commission (MHAC)).[27] Instead, the Code sets out a series of principles which must be considered in making decisions about a course of action under the MHA. These principles include a requirement to maximise the safety and well-being of patients; a requirement to minimise any restrictions on liberty imposed; a requirement to respect the diverse needs, values and circumstances of each patient and to consider the patient's views, wishes and feelings so far as they are reasonably ascertainable and to follow those wishes wherever practicable; a requirement to allow patients the opportunity to participate as far as practicable in planning, developing and reviewing their own treatment and care and to encourage the involvement of carers, family members and other people with an interest in the patients' welfare; and a requirement for effective, efficient and equitable use of resources.[28] The CQC Guidance emphasises the principles of participation and the need to recognise the views and wishes of the person with a mental disorder regardless of capacity.[29] As will be seen below, ECHR-based jurisprudence has been significant in developing standards in this area.

---

[23] MHA, s. 58A(5). Advance decisions in this respect are covered by the provisions in respect of advance decisions under the MCA (s. 58A(9)).

[24] MHA, s. 58(2)(b) (as amended by MHA 2007, s. 6(2)(b)).

[25] MHA, s. 64(3) (as inserted by MHA 2007, s. 6(3)).

[26] Revised in 2008 (London: The Stationery Office, 2008).

[27] See *Guidance for SOADs: Consent to Treatment and the SOAD Role under the Revised Mental Health Act* (London: Care Quality Commission, 2008).

[28] See Code, paras. 1.2–1.6.   [29] *Guidance for SOADs*, Annex A.

Defining capacity in Part 4 of the MHA

Sections 57, 58 and 58A adopt the same definition of capacity, which requires that the patient be capable of understanding the 'nature, purpose, and likely effects' of the treatment. Strikingly, the definition makes no mention of the ability to use and weigh information which, as was discussed in Chapters 3 and 4, is a core aspect of the MCA definition of capacity. Thus, on the face of the statute, the MHA standard for capacity requires less in terms of abilities than that of the MCA and would not cover a situation where, for example, because of a compulsive disorder, a person was unable to use and weigh information relevant to the decision. It is difficult to find any justification for this and in *R (Wilkinson)* v. *Broadmoor Special Hospital Authority*, Hale LJ suggested that the common law test (now set out in the MCA) 'would be equally suitable for assessing capacity for the purpose of section 58(3)(b) of the Mental Health Act 1983'.[30] It was not clear whether Hale LJ meant 'would be' as an indicator of the possible direction of future law reform or whether she intended that the common law test should be applied notwithstanding the wording of the statute. In *B* v. *Dr SS, Dr G and Secretary of State for the Department of Health*, Charles J seems to have taken the latter view, finding the patient to lack capacity under section 58 because of his inability to use and weigh information.[31] In considering the case on appeal, the Court of Appeal was conscious of the conflict between the wording of the statute and the common law test, recognising that it was arguable that the statutory test did not 'go far enough to define capacity'.[32] The Court interpreted Hale LJ's comment to mean that she believed that the common law test should apply to assessment under the MHA but it did not indicate its approval of this position.[33] Instead, the Court stated that '[w]hatever the precise test of the capacity to consent to treatment, we think that it is plain that a patient will lack that capacity if he is not able to appreciate the likely effects of having or not having the treatment'.[34] While the question remains open, it is unlikely that the wording of the statutory test will be found to limit the application of the MHA. The more likely response will be to extend the interpretation of the understanding requirement to incorporate aspects of the requirement to use and weigh.

---

[30] [2002] 1 WLR 419, 443.

[31] [2005] EWHC (Admin) 1936, [190]. See also *R (on the application of B)* v. *Haddock and Others* [2005] EWHC 921.

[32] *R (on the application of B)* v. *Dr SS and Dr AC* [2006] EWCA Civ 28, [33].

[33] *Ibid.*   [34] *Ibid*, [34].

The move to supervised community treatment

The MHA 2007 introduced for the first time in England and Wales, provision for 'supervised community treatment' (SCT).[35] Under the legislation, a person may be made subject to a community treatment order (CTO), which obliges her to receive treatment (and may oblige her to comply with other designated conditions).[36] Although relatively novel in Europe,[37] this kind of measure has been widely used in Australia and New Zealand since the mid-1980s[38] and is also increasingly common in the United States[39] and Canada.[40] While there are significant differences in the models employed in different jurisdictions (especially in respect of the criteria for granting an order),[41] in essence, the idea of compulsory treatment without detention has now been widely adopted across the common law world.[42] As well as dealing with treatment, in most jurisdictions CTOs may also extend to other aspects of a person's life-style, for example requiring her to attend at monitoring meetings, or to live within a particular area or restricting certain behaviours such as alcohol or drug consumption.[43] The model of compulsory care in the community has enthusiastic advocates

---

[35] MHA 2007, s. 32 inserted ss. 17A-17G and 20A-20B into the MHA: see generally Fennell, *The New Law*, pp. 210–19. The relevant provisions came into effect in November 2008.

[36] MHA, s. 17B.

[37] Although see the Mental Health (Care and Treatment) (Scotland) Act 2003, which contains a similar measure. In respect of other European approaches, according to S. Lawton-Smith, *A Question of Numbers: The Potential Impact of Community Based Treatment Orders in England and Wales* (King's Fund, London, 2005), p. 21, four European countries (Belgium, Luxembourg, Spain and Portugal) are reported as having a form of compulsory community treatment.

[38] Provision for compulsory community treatment was introduced in Victoria by the Mental Health Act 1986; in New South Wales by the Mental Health Act 1990; and in New Zealand by the Mental Health (Compulsory Assessment and Treatment) Act 1992.

[39] 'Assisted Outpatient Treatment' (as termed in the United States) is now statutorily provided for in 44 states, including California and New York: see the Treatment Advocacy Center (www.psychlaws.org) (which advocates in favour of changes in the law in this regard).

[40] See, for example, Mental Health Services Act 1995 (Saskatchewan); Mental Health Act 2000 (Ontario): see generally J. Gray and R. O'Reilly, 'Canadian Compulsory Community Treatment Laws: Recent Reforms' (2005) 28 *International Journal of Law and Psychiatry* 13.

[41] The differences in models, impact greatly on the extent to which compulsory community treatment is used in practice: see Lawton-Smith, *A Question of Numbers*, p. 22.

[42] There is, however, currently no formal provision for compulsory community treatment in Ireland.

[43] In practice, sometimes arbitrary restrictions may be imposed: see A. Gibbs *et al.*, 'Community Treatment Orders for People With Serious Mental Illness: A New Zealand Study' (2006) 36 *British Journal of Social Work* 1085, 1093.

but it has also been subject to criticism.[44] Advocates argue that compulsion can reduce incidences of hospitalisation, homelessness, arrest and incarceration[45] and lead to greater health, stability and quality of life for people with mental disorders and a better quality of life for their families.[46] Others, however, question the effectiveness of compulsion in delivering better health outcomes.[47] A systematic review of 72 studies found 'very little evidence of positive effects of compulsion in the areas where they might have been anticipated'.[48]

The path leading to the introduction of SCT in England and Wales was tortuous, commencing with an Expert Committee review in 1999,[49] which was followed by a Government White Paper (which ignored most of the Expert Committee's recommendations),[50] and two draft bills introduced in 2002[51] and 2004,[52] which were abandoned.[53] Particular concerns were raised about the potentially open-ended nature of the compulsion, perhaps best summarised by Professor Genevra Richardson's description, in her evidence to the Joint Committee on the Draft Mental Health Bill 2004, of the proposed model as 'a sort of lobster pot; it is easy to get in, but it is very difficult to get out'.[54] The third effort at introducing legislation was much more limited in scope and the model for supervised community treatment contained in the MHA 2007 is considerably more

---

[44] See generally M. Donnelly, 'Community-Based Care and Compulsion: What Role for Human Rights?' (2008) 15 *Journal of Law and Medicine* 783, 785–6.

[45] See *Kendra's Law: Final Report on the Status of Assisted Outpatient Treatment* (New York, New York State Office of Mental Health, 2005), pp. 17–18; E. F. Torrey and M. T. Zdanowicz, 'Outpatient Commitment: What, Why and for Whom?' (2001) 52 *Psychiatric Services* 337; K. Kress, 'An Argument for Assisted Outpatient Treatment for Persons With Serious Mental Illness Illustrated With Reference to a Proposed Statute for Iowa' (2000) 85 *Iowa Law Review* 1269.

[46] See Gibbs *et al.*, 'Community Treatment Orders,' 1094–5.

[47] See R. J. Calsyn *et al.*, 'Do Consumers Who Have a Choice Have Better Outcomes?' (2000) 36 *Community Mental Health Journal* 149.

[48] See R. Churchill *et al.*, *International Experiences of Using Community Treatment Orders* (London: Department of Health, Institute of Psychiatry, 2007), p. 14. The review was also critical of the methodological basis on which much of the evidence in respect of the evaluation of CTOs was collected.

[49] Report of the *Expert Committee Review of the Mental Health Act 1983* (Department of Health, HMSO, 1999).

[50] *Reforming the Mental Health Act: The New Legal Framework* (Cm 5015-I, 2000) (London: Department of Health, 2001).

[51] Draft Mental Health Bill 2002, Cm 5538-I (London: HMSO, 2002).

[52] Draft Mental Health Bill 2004, Cm 6305-I (London: HMSO, 2004).

[53] For summary of background to the legislation, see Fennell, *The New Law*, pp. 7–12.

[54] See *Report of the Joint Committee on the Draft Mental Health Bill 2004*, HL Paper 79–1; HC 95–1 (London: The Stationery Office, 2005), [193].

restrictive than that in any of the preceding Draft Bills. Most crucially, a person may be subject to a CTO only following a period of detention in hospital, thus restricting the 'lobster pot' effect.[55] However, the recommendation of the Joint Committee that a CTO should only be made in respect of a person with significantly impaired decision-making[56] was rejected by the government.[57]

Treatment under SCT: Part 4A of the MHA

Part 4A of the MHA sets out the circumstances in which treatment may be administered to a patient while she continues to live in the community.[58] In brief, except in an emergency situation,[59] the effect of Part 4A is that treatment in the community may be given to a patient with capacity only if she consents to the treatment.[60] For patients lacking capacity, treatment may be given only if consent to the treatment on the patient's behalf is given by a donee of a lasting power of attorney, or a deputy appointed by the Court or Protection or by the Court of Protection itself[61] or the requirements set out in section 64D are met.[62] This section requires the AC should take reasonable steps to establish that the person lacks capacity to consent to the treatment in question,[63] that the AC must reasonably believe that the patient lacks capacity,[64] and either that the AC has no reason to believe that the patient objects to the treatment or that she has reason to believe that the patient does object but that it is not necessary to use force against the patient in order to give the treatment.[65] The AC must also be satisfied that the giving of the treatment does not conflict with a valid and applicable advance decision or with a decision made by a donee of a lasting power of attorney or a deputy or the Court of Protection.[66] In addition, regardless of whether or not the patient has capacity and of whether or not she consents to the treatment, there is a procedural requirement

[55] MHA, s. 17A(1). See additional criteria which must be met: s. 17A(5).

[56] The *Report of the Joint Committee*, [156] recommended that, before a patient could be subject to compulsory powers of any sort, her ability to make decisions about her medical treatment must be 'significantly impaired' (as is the position under the Mental Health (Care and Treatment) (Scotland) Act 2003).

[57] *Government Response to the Report of the Joint Committee on the Draft Mental Health Bill 2004* Cm 6624 (Stationery Office, London, 2005), p. 16.

[58] Inserted by MHA 2007, s. 35: see generally Fennell, *The New Law*, pp. 294–9.

[59] Emergency treatment in the community is covered by MHA, s. 64G; if the criteria set out in the section are met, force may be used, if necessary, in the administration of treatment.

[60] MHA, s. 64C(2)(a).   [61] MHA, s. 64C(2)(b).   [62] MHA, s. 64C(2)(c).

[63] MHA, s. 64D(2).   [64] MHA, s. 64D(3).   [65] MHA, s. 64D(4).   [66] MHA, s. 64D(5).

that a SOAD must certify that it is appropriate for the treatment to be given subject to such conditions, if any, specified in the certificate.[67] If these requirements cannot be met, either because a patient with capacity objects to treatment or because force would be necessary to administer treatment to a patient without capacity, the only way in which treatment may be administered is by either recalling the patient to hospital or revoking the CTO.[68]

The protracted law reform process leading to the MHA 2007, and the legislative model ultimately adopted, shows the increased role for human rights in developing mental health policy. Whether or not one agrees with all aspects of the final legislation,[69] there is little doubt that the human rights scrutiny required under the Human Rights Act (HRA) and the human rights norms derived from the ECHR substantially changed the legislation which had initially been proposed in 2002. As will be seen below, the ECHR has also had an impact in respect of other aspects of treatment provision, although the extent of this is open to debate.

The impact of the ECHR on Part 4 of the MHA

Following the incorporation of the ECHR into UK domestic law, a relatively substantial body of case law in respect of the provision of treatment to people with a mental disorder has developed.[70] As a result, a number of principles have now been established. These suggest that the ECHR does not require that the consent of a capable involuntary patient must be obtained for treatment covered by the MHA. However, ECHR rights have limited the circumstances in which treatment may be imposed on patients with and without capacity and have required procedural protections beyond those afforded on the face of the MHA.

---

[67] MHA, s. 64C(4).
[68] If recalled to hospital, the provision of treatment is covered by MHA, s. 62A; in such circumstances, the patient is treated as if she remained liable to be detained since the time the CTO was made and may be given treatment which would otherwise require approval under MHA, s. 58 and 58A on the basis of a certificate by a SOAD under Part 4A which must state that it is appropriate that the treatment be given on recall; if the CTO is revoked, the patient is once again treated as detained in hospital and treatment is provided on this basis: see Fennell, *The New Law*, pp. 289–90.
[69] See criticism of the Act in A. Boyle, 'The Law and Incapacity Determinations: A Conflict of Governance' (2008) 71 *Modern Law Review* 433.
[70] This level of activity is in striking contrast to the position in Ireland where, notwithstanding an extant bill of rights (the Constitution of Ireland 1937) and the incorporation of the ECHR into domestic law by the European Convention on Human Rights Act 2003, there has been no case law in respect of treatment on foot of the Mental Health Act 2001.

The first domestic decision to consider the impact of ECHR rights on Part 4 of the MHA also represents, perhaps, the zenith of judicial activism in this respect. *R (Wilkinson)* v. *Broadmoor Special Hospital Authority*[71] concerned an applicant who had been formally detained at Broadmoor Special Hospital for 34 years, having been diagnosed with a psychopathic disorder following a violent attack. In July 1999, he came under the care of a new RMO, who concluded that the applicant additionally suffered from a psychotic disorder which could be treated with anti-psychotic medication. The RMO believed that, if successful, this could ultimately lead to the applicant's release. The applicant strenuously resisted any attempt at administration of this medication. As the medication was required for a period of more than three months, the RMO obtained the necessary SOAD's certificate, which certified that the applicant lacked the capacity to consent. The applicant continued to resist and treatment was imposed by force, resulting in the applicant, who had a heart condition, having an angina attack. The applicant sought judicial review of the decision to impose treatment on him and sought a full hearing, with the introduction of oral evidence from an independent psychiatrist hired by his legal team and the cross-examination of the prescribing doctor and of the SOAD who had authorised the treatment.[72]

The substantive issue: a capacity-based right to refuse?

Although the issue before the Court of Appeal was the procedural one of whether the applicant was entitled to a formal hearing before treatment could be imposed, two members of the Court offered views regarding whether the ECHR required that an involuntary patient with capacity should be allowed to refuse treatment for a mental disorder. Simon Brown and Hale LJ found that Articles 3 and 8 of the ECHR were implicated by the imposition of treatment on a patient in the applicant's situation.[73] However, in the light of the decision of the European Court of Human Rights (ECtHR) in *Herczegfalvy* v. *Austria*,[74] the imposition of treatment

---

[71] [2002] 1 WLR 419.

[72] A notable feature of *Wilkinson* is the extent to which the reports prepared by the RMO and the SOAD differed from the report of the psychiatrist employed by the patient's legal team, including on the question of capacity. See the evidence outlined by Simon Brown LJ [2002] 1 WLR 419, 424–5.

[73] *Ibid.*, 432–33 *per* Simon Brown LJ; 445–6 *per* Hale LJ. In addition, Simon Brown LJ considered that the right to life, protected under Art. 2, was implicated given the real risk to the patient's life posed by a possible future angina attack brought on by the forcible administration of the medication.

[74] (1992) 15 EHRR 437.

was permissible, provided it was convincingly shown to be therapeutic-ally necessary. Both judges discussed the relevance of the patient's cap-acity in determining whether treatment was therapeutically necessary.

Hale LJ held that the law had not yet reached the point where it was an accepted norm that a patient with capacity 'can only be treated against their will for the protection of others or for their own safety'.[75] This did not mean, however, that treatment could be imposed without having regard to the rights and the wishes of the patient.[76] Rather, it had to be asked if the treatment was so likely to benefit the patient as to justify its forcible imposition. Hale LJ went on to note that '[g]iven that under the Convention forcible treatment which is not a "medical necessity" may well be inhuman and degrading, substantial benefit from it would be required for it to be justified'.[77] In this regard, Hale LJ focused on the question of willingness, noting that 'most people are able to appreciate that they are being forced to do something against their will even if they are not able to make the decision that it should or should not be done'.[78]

On a first reading of his judgment, Simon Brown LJ appears to have accorded greater significance to the matter of capacity than Hale LJ. Noting that '[t]he precise equivalence under section 58(3)(b) between in-competent patients and competent but non-consenting patients seems to me increasingly difficult to justify',[79] he considered that '[i]f in truth this claimant has the competence to refuse consent to the treatment proposed here, it is difficult to suppose that he should nevertheless be forcibly sub-jected to it'.[80] While this could be interpreted to support a capacity-based right to refuse treatment,[81] it is probable that his Lordship intended his comments to be restricted to the situation of the applicant before him.[82] This is the view taken in subsequent cases which have agreed with Hale LJ's assessment that an involuntary patient with capacity does not have an ECHR-based right to refuse treatment covered by the MHA.[83] Support for Hale LJ's position may be derived also from the subsequent decision of the ECtHR in *Storck* v. *Germany*,[84] which was discussed in Chapter 5.

---

[75] [2002] 1 WLR 419, 446.   [76] *Ibid.*   [77] *Ibid.*, 447.   [78] *Ibid.*, 446.   [79] *Ibid.*, 433.

[80] *Ibid.*

[81] See D. Hewitt, 'An End to Compulsory Treatment?' (2002) 152 *New Law Journal* 194.

[82] His Lordship referred to 'this claimant' rather than 'a claimant'. The level of resistance to the treatment in *Wilkinson* was extreme (and rare) (see evidence given by the RMO [2002] 1 WLR 419, 424) and gave rise to additional health risks because of the claimant's heart condition.

[83] See *R (on the application of PS)* v. *Responsible Medical Officer and Another* [2003] EWHC 2335, [116]; *R (on the application of B)* v. *Dr SS and Dr AC* [2005] EWHC 86 (Admin); [2006] EWCA Civ 28, [50].

[84] (2005) 43 EHRR 96.

Although the case does not support a capacity-based right to refuse treatment, as a result of *Wilkinson* it is clear that treatment which implicates ECHR rights must be shown to comply with the ECHR. Thus, if Article 3 is engaged (i.e. if the minimum severity level is reached), the treatment must be shown to be therapeutically necessary[85] and, if Article 8 is engaged, the treatment must be 'in accordance with law'.[86] In respect of both Articles, it has been judicially accepted that, in addition, it must be established that the treatment is in the best interests of the person.[87] Thus, the ECHR has required the addition of a new dimension to the statutory decision-making process. This is now reflected in the guidance provided to clinicians[88] (although whether this actually impacts on individual treatment decisions in practice is less clear).

Procedural entitlements

On the specific procedural question raised in *Wilkinson*, all three members of the Court of Appeal held that a case, such as the one in question, which involved interference with an individual's human rights, required a higher level of judicial review than the 'heightened scrutiny' provided for under the 'super-*Wednesbury* test'.[89] On the facts of *Wilkinson*, the applicant was entitled to a full review hearing, with oral expert evidence, including that of his own medical witness, and the possibility of cross-examination, as to whether the statutory standard for the imposition of treatment had been met.[90] Hale LJ was clear that this did not mean that doctors always had to go to court to obtain authorisation to treat.[91] However, she found that, 'once a situation exists in which the treatment can be scrutinised, whether before or after the event, then that scrutiny should take place'.[92]

The Court in *Wilkinson* also set down parameters for the operation of the treatment review function performed by the SOAD. The Court

---

[85] *Herczegfalvy* v. *Austria* (1992) 15 EHRR 437.

[86] Article 8(2). See *B* v. *Dr SS, Dr G and the Secretary of State for the Department of Health* [2005] EWHC 1936 (Admin), [91] *per* Charles J.

[87] See *R (on the application of N)* v. *Doctor M and Others* [2002] EWCA Civ 1789, [16] *per* Dyson LJ (in respect of Art. 3); *R (on the application of B)* v. *Dr SS and Dr AC* [2006] EWCA Civ, 28, [62] *per* Phillips CJ (in respect of Art. 8).

[88] See Code, para. 24.58; *Guidance for SOADs* (Care Quality Commission, 2008), p. 9.

[89] [2002] 1 WLR 419, 432–33 *per* Simon Brown LJ; 439 *per* Brooke LJ; 447 *per* Hale LJ. Under this test, in cases involving human rights, the courts were obliged to conduct a 'heightened scrutiny' of the decision or policy in question. In *Smith and Grady* v. *United Kingdom* (1999) 29 EHRR 493, the ECtHR held that the test provided insufficient protection for individual rights arising under the ECHR.

[90] [2002] 1 WLR 419, 432–3 *per* Simon Brown LJ; 439 *per* Brooke LJ; 447 *per* Hale LJ.

[91] *Ibid.*, 447.   [92] *Ibid.*

rejected the view that the SOAD must simply determine whether the RMO's decision is reasonable.[93] Rather, the SOAD must form her own independent judgement as to whether or not the treatment should be given.[94] The SOAD's obligations in this respect were further extended in *R (on the application of Wooder)* v. *Feggetter and the Mental Health Act Commission* where the Court of Appeal held that a SOAD must give reasons for her decision 'on the RMO's proposal to override [the patient's] will'.[95] Although 'the law does not require a SOAD to dot every "i" and cross every "t" when giving reasons for his opinion', the Court held that it is necessary that 'he gives his reasons clearly on what he reasonably regards as the substantive points on which he formed his clinical judgment'.[96] Again, this requirement is now reflected in the guidance for clinicians.[97]

The decision in *Wilkinson* left open a number of questions regarding the circumstances in which a hearing would be required before treatment could be imposed under the MHA and as regards the nature of such a hearing. Notwithstanding several attempts by the Court of Appeal to stem a possible flood of applications for review,[98] in *R (on the application of B)* v. *Haddock and Others*, the Court seemed to accept that patients who requested judicial review of a treatment decision were, in most cases, going to succeed in establishing a right to a hearing.[99] The Court seems also to have accepted that the effect of the ruling in *Wilkinson* was that the hearing would have to be a 'full merits' review as to whether the proposed treatment infringed the patient's human rights. Accordingly, a patient will be entitled to require the attendance of witnesses and to the cross-examination of those witnesses.[100]

Assessing the contribution of the ECHR

Although it has given rise to a relatively extensive body of jurisprudence, the actual contribution of the ECHR in respect of treatment decisions

---

[93] *Ibid.*, 434 *per* Simon Brown LJ. This was the tenor of the guidance to SOADs given by the Mental Health Act Commission (MHAC) at this time.

[94] *Ibid.*   [95] [2002] EWCA Civ 554, [49] *per* Sedley LJ.

[96] *Ibid.*, [29] *per* Brooke LJ.

[97] See *Guidance for SOADs: Giving Reasons when Certifying Appropriate Treatment* (Care Quality Commission, 2008).

[98] See the *R (on the application of N)* v. *Doctor M and Others* [2002] EWCA Civ 1789, [39] *per* Dyson LJ; *R (on the application of B)* v. *Dr SS and Dr AC* [2006] EWCA Civ 28, [68] *per* Phillips CJ.

[99] [2006] EWCA Civ 961, [65]. See P. Bartlett, 'A Matter of Necessity: Enforced Treatment under the Mental Health Act' (2007) 15 *Medical Law Review* 86, 90.

[100] [2006] EWCA Civ 961, [64].

might be seen as relatively limited. Patients have a right to a review of treatment decisions but they do not have a right to refuse unwanted treatment. Patients have a right to treatment which is in their best interests but the decision as to what is in their best interests is made by others. In a rather bleak assessment of the position, Baroness Hale, writing extra-judicially, asked whether the incorporation of the ECHR had helped mental health law in the United Kingdom and concluded that '[t]he short and gloomy answer must be – not very much'.[101] Certainly, notwithstanding the increased procedural protections afforded to patients in respect of treatment decisions, the courts have not indicated any willingness to interfere with decisions made by medical professionals. Bartlett and Sandland point out that, '[t]o date, High Court judges have felt themselves able to reject *all* medical opinion proffered in support of the patient in *all* cases subsequent to *Wilkinson*, in each case being "convinced" that the treatment should be given'.[102] This attitude of deference is perhaps best encapsulated in Auld LJ's statement in *R (on the application of B)* v. *Haddock and Others* that 'the safeguards provided by the ECHR should not be deployed so as to "cut across the grain of medical good practice"'.[103]

However, it must also be recognised that, even where individuals' cases have been unsuccessful, the litigation has meant that the need to protect human rights in making decisions about treatment for a mental disorder has, to a degree at least, become concretised. Both the Code and the guidance for mental health professionals make it clear that the requirement to respect human rights has a practical impact on decisions made by individual clinicians. Furthermore, the possibility of future developments at an ECtHR level remains open and, indeed, probable. In this respect, while it is possible that the ECtHR will focus on capacity, it is more likely that the ECtHR will build on its decision in *Storck* by developing protections for unwilling patients, regardless of capacity, and by requiring that a clear case for compulsory treatment must be made.[104] It is likely that developing ECtHR jurisprudence will be influenced by international human rights law and in particular by the CRPD. Thus, the question of the impact of the

---

[101] B. Hale, 'The Human Rights Act and Mental Health Law: Has it Helped?' (2007) 13 *Journal of Mental Health Law* 7, 7.

[102] Bartlett and Sandland, *Mental Health Law*, p. 312, original emphasis.

[103] [2006] EWCA Civ 961, [33]. See also *R (Wilkinson)* v. *Broadmoor Special Hospital Authority* [2002] 1 WLR 419, 447 *per* Simon Brown LJ.

[104] In this respect, it is notable that the European Committee for the Prevention of Torture (CPT), which is increasingly influential on the ECtHR (see *Dybeku* v. *Albania* [2007] ECHR 41153/06, paras. 19–20), stops short of recommending an outright ban on compulsory treatment of people with capacity: see the *8th General Report on the Committee*

CRPD on compulsory treatment is significant, both in respect of ratifying States' compliance with CRPD obligations and in respect of the ongoing development of domestic and ECtHR jurisprudence.

The CRPD: a ban on compulsion?

Based on the principles of dignity, autonomy, non-discrimination, participation, inclusion, and respect for difference, the CRPD combines both positive and negative rights to provide a conceptual framework against which to evaluate mental health legislation.[105] The possible influence of the CRPD on broader questions in respect of treatment will be discussed further below. For the present, the question is whether the CRPD requires that patients with capacity should have a right to refuse treatment for their mental disorder.[106]

The issue of involuntary treatment is not addressed directly in the CRPD. Article 17 states that '[e]very person with disabilities has a right to respect for his or her physical and mental integrity on an equal basis with others'. Bernadette McSherry outlines the drafting history of this provision and demonstrates how the negotiations may be seen as a conflict between a pragmatic position, as advocated by Australia, which accepted that some degree of compulsory treatment was inevitable and that the conditions in which it might be used needed to be circumscribed, and a more idealistic position put forward by the International Disability Caucus that any statement which permitted involuntary treatment could be used 'to legitimate abuse through involuntary treatment and represented a lower standard for persons with disabilities with regard to free and informed consent'.[107] As McSherry points out, the scope of very brief final article is far from clear.[108]

It has been argued that Article 17 requires 'the immediate cessation of forced psychiatric interventions'.[109] However, as McSherry demonstrates,

---

for the Prevention of Torture's Activities Covering the Period 1 January to 31 December 1997 (CPT/Inf (98) 12) (1998)), para. 41.

[105] See A. Kämpf, 'The Disabilities Convention and its Consequences for Mental Health Laws in Australia' (2008) 26 Law in Context 10, 29–32.

[106] Note that the United Nations Principles for the Protection of Persons With Mental Illness and the Improvement of Mental Health Care do not prohibit compulsory treatment (see Principle 11(6)(b)).

[107] B. McSherry, 'Protecting the Integrity of the Person: Developing Limitations on Involuntary Treatment' (2008) 26 Law in Context 111, 114.

[108] Ibid., 115.

[109] T. Minkowitz, 'The United Nations Convention on the Rights of Persons With Disabilities and the Right to be Free from Nonconsensual Psychiatric Interventions' (2006–7) 34 Syracuse Journal of International Law and Commerce 405, 405.

this interpretation of Article 17 does not accord with 'the (albeit limited) caselaw' in respect of similar rights under regional charters of rights.[110] Nor does this interpretation represent that taken by at least some of the States Parties. On ratifying the CRPD, Australia issued a declaration of its understanding that the CPRD allows for compulsory 'assistance or treatment of persons, including measures taken for the treatment of mental disability, where such treatment is necessary, as a last resort and subject to safeguards'.[111] Interestingly, although on ratifying the CRPD, the United Kingdom made a number of reservations and declarations, there is no mention of this issue.[112] It is highly probable that this is not because of a plan to abolish compulsory treatment but because the possibility of such an interpretation was not considered sufficiently likely to merit the inclusion of a reservation or declaration. The more plausible interpretation is that, as McSherry argues, Article 17 requires the limitation of 'unbeneficial and overly intrusive treatment'.[113] Thus, the CRPD is likely to lend further support to the need for a more rigorous overview of all treatment decisions, regardless of the capacity of the person.

On the basis of the preceding discussion, some degree of compulsion in respect of patients with capacity is likely to remain a feature of the law for the foreseeable future.[114] This, of course, does not make such a position appropriate. As will be seen in the next section, the role of autonomy in respect of treatment for a mental disorder raises difficult questions. It will be shown that these are not appropriately resolved by the simple application of a right of autonomy as non-interference in the context of treatment for a mental disorder.

A differential approach to autonomy: the normative questions

On its face, any legal provision that limits the right of a capable patient to refuse treatment is directly in conflict with the liberal underpinnings of

---

[110]   McSherry, 'Protecting the Integrity of the Person,' 121.

[111]   The full text of all Declaration and Reservations may be accessed at www.un.org/disabilities.

[112]   The UK included reservations in respect of Arts. 12 (4), 24, 27 and a declaration in respect of Art. 24. None of these measures is relevant to the current discussion.

[113]   McSherry, 'Protecting the Integrity of the Person,' 122.

[114]   Although note that the Northern Ireland Minister for Health has confirmed plans for the introduction of a single piece of legislation in Northern Ireland dealing with mental health and mental capacity, which has its basis in respect for the principle of autonomy (as was recommended by the *Bamforth Review of Mental Health and Mental Disability* (Belfast: The Stationery Office, 2007)). The legislation is not expected to be ready before

healthcare law. In addition, given that the limitation applies to patients with a mental disorder only, it would appear to discriminate against this category of patients.[115] Before reaching conclusions in this respect, however, it is necessary to look first at the possible case for differential treatment within a traditional liberal view and in particular at the role played by the rights of others in limiting individual autonomy within such an approach.[116]

Differential treatment and the rights of others

As discussed in Chapter 1, it is entirely consistent with liberal theory that an individual's right of autonomy may be limited in some circumstances in order to prevent harm to others. In order to consider whether this might justify the differential approach to the right of autonomy of people with a mental disorder, it is necessary to separate two kinds of possible 'harm' to others which might be addressed by the imposition of treatment. The first is harm in the traditional sense of a threat or danger, usually physical, to a person's life or health. The second is a broader conception of harm, which encompasses social, emotional and family harm.

Applicability of 'traditional' conceptions of harm

In respect of 'traditional' conceptions of harm, Ronald Dworkin suggests that, before interference with individual rights is permissible on the basis of harm to others, the danger presented to others must be 'vivid'.[117] Although Dworkin does not expand on what constitutes a 'vivid' danger, Bottoms and Brownsword suggest that the relevant factors are the seriousness, the immediacy and the certainty of the possible harm.[118] This would seem to provide a reasonable summation of the relevant factors to be considered

---

2011: see *Legislative Framework for Mental Capacity and Mental Health Legislation in Northern Ireland: A Policy Consultation Document* (Belfast: Department of Health, 2009).

[115] See T. Campbell and C. Heginbotham, *Mental Illness: Prejudice, Discrimination and the Law* (Aldershot: Dartmouth, 1991), pp. 24–6. See also M. Perlin, ('"Half-Wracked Prejudice Leaped Forth": Sanism, Pretextuality, and Why and How Mental Disability Law Developed as it Did' (1999) 10 *Journal of Contemporary Legal Issues* 3; '"Where the Winds Hit Heavy on the Borderline": Mental Disability Law, Theory and Practice, "Us" and "Them"' (1998) 31 *Loyola of Los Angeles Law Review* 775.

[116] This discussion draws on M. Donnelly, 'From Autonomy to Dignity: Treatment for Mental Disorders and the Focus for Patient Rights' (2008) 26 *Law in Context* 37, 41–4.

[117] R. Dworkin, *Taking Rights Seriously* (London: Duckworth, 1977), p. 11.

[118] A. Bottoms and R. Brownsword, 'Dangerousness and Rights' in J. Hinton (ed.) *Dangerousness: Problems of Assessment and Prediction* (London: Allen and Unwin, 1983), p. 9.

in assessing whether there is a harm-based justification for a differential approach to treatment for a mental disorder. In this assessment, two questions must be asked; these are first, whether, as a category, involuntary patients pose a sufficient threat of harm to others to justify a separate legal framework to govern their treatment and, secondly, whether specifically identifiable involuntary patients pose a sufficient threat of harm to justify differential legal treatment in these individuals' cases. In considering the level of threat posed, a distinction must be made between a threat posed by a patient in the community and the threat posed by the patient if left untreated after having been detained. The threat to others, and therefore the argument that rights may be limited, is likely to be stronger where a patient remains in the community than it is where she has already been detained in a psychiatric facility. However, a detained patient could still pose a threat to fellow patients and staff.[119]

Although violence by people with mental disorders receives a good deal of publicity when it occurs,[120] the evidence suggests that the level of threat posed by people with mental disorders, as a category, is not especially high. Using the available epidemiological data, Walsh and Fahy concluded that less than 10 per cent of serious violence, including homicide, is attributable to psychosis.[121] When compared with other factors such as age, gender, socio-economic status, drug or alcohol usage and family breakdowns, the risk posed by people with mental disorders appears to be relatively low.[122] Thus, it would seem to be difficult to provide a coherent justification for intervention in respect of this category of patient without, for example, introducing similar measures in respect of drug and alcohol addiction.

[119] See J. Crichton, 'Psychiatric Inpatient Violence' in Walker (ed.) *Dangerous People*.

[120] Acts of violence committed by people with mental disorders have provided an impetus for legislative action in many jurisdictions. In the United Kingdom, the killings of Jonathan Zito and of Lyn and Megan Russell led, eventually, to the MHA 2007 (see Fennell, *The New Law*, p. 7); in North American, laws introduced in this context have tended to carry the name of a person killed allegedly due to the gap in the law which the reform is intended to address: see, for example, 'Brian's Law' (Ontario); 'Kendra's Law' (New York); 'Laura's Law' (California); 'Kevin's Law' (Michigan).

[121] E. Walsh and T. Fahy, 'Violence in Society' (2002) 325 *British Medical Journal* 507. This finding is replicated in many other surveys: see P. Bowden, 'Violence and Mental Disorder' in Walker (ed.) *Dangerous People*, pp. 19–22; P. Taylor and J. Gunn, 'Homicides by People With Mental Illness: Myth and Reality' (1999) 174 *British Journal of Psychiatry* 9; H. Anckarsäter *et al.*, 'Mental Disorder is a Cause of Crime: The Cornerstone of Forensic Psychiatry' (2009) 32 *International Journal of Law and Psychiatry* 342, 343–4.

[122] Note, however, the increased risk when a person with a mental disorder is also a drug user: see J. W. Swanson *et al.*, 'Violence and Psychiatric Disorder in the Community: Evidence from the Epidemiologic Catchment Area Surveys' (1990) 41 *Hospital and Community Psychiatry* 761.

In respect of a particular individual with a mental disorder, there would seem to be a better chance of identifying a threat to others. Sophisticated risk predication mechanisms are being developed which allow for more accurate assessment of risk.[123] However, there is still no foolproof means of predicting the level of future threats.[124] Even using a sophisticated risk-assessment test, 37 per cent of patients placed by the test in the two most violent categories (out of five categories in total) were not actually violent within one year of the prediction.[125] Nonetheless, if one takes a fairly lax interpretation of the certainty requirement, the threat to others may justify overriding a patient's right of autonomy in some circumstances. However, this would only be convincing in limited circumstances based on an individualised risk assessment and it is difficult to see how it could justify differential treatment of the right of autonomy of all involuntary patients.

A broader conception of harm?

In the light of the difficulties in establishing the necessary level of threat to others, the question arises of whether a broader conception of harm should be employed in this context. As discussed in Chapter 1, the traditional liberal conception of individuals as independent isolated entities is unsustainable. All people, including people with mental disorders, are socially embedded and operate in a relational context. From this perspective, it is clear that our actions can harm others in ways that are emotional and social and which may be as far-reaching as the physical threats with which traditional liberal theory has been concerned. In its exploration of the policy basis for differential treatment of patients with a mental disorder, the Expert Committee identified a belief among respondents that 'the consequences of untreated mental disorder may impact more directly and significantly on carers and relatives than do the consequences of untreated physical disorder'.[126] Empirical studies indicate that family members and carers of some people with mental disorders experience significant burdens and pressures[127] as well as, in some instances,

---

[123] See for example the MacArthur Study of Mental Disorder and Violence: J. Monahan, et al., *Rethinking Risk: The MacArthur Study of Mental Disorder and Violence* (New York: Oxford University Press, 2001).

[124] See evidence of the Royal College of Psychiatrists in the *Report of the Joint Committee on the Draft Mental Health Bill 2004*, para. 125.

[125] Bartlett and Sandland, *Mental Health Law*, p. 147.

[126] *Expert Committee Review of the Mental Health Act 1983*, para. 2.9.

[127] See D. Marsh and D. Johnson, 'The Family Experience of Mental Illness: Implications for Intervention' in R. Marinelli and A. del Orto (eds.) *The Psychological and Social Impact*

stigmatisation.[128] On this basis, it might be argued that family members may be harmed by the refusal of treatment by a person with a mental disorder.

It was argued in Chapter 1 that there is a case to be made for the recognition of responsibilities, at least at a moral level, in respect of healthcare decision-making. It was also acknowledged that there are real difficulties in translating a moral duty of this kind into a legal one, not least because a vulnerable person can become 'lost' within a web of connections, which have the effect of prioritising other people. Even accepting the view that patients owe responsibilities, however, it is very difficult to sustain an argument that only people with mental disorders should have this legal burden of responsibility imposed on them. Why should a parent of young children be permitted to refuse a life-saving blood transfusion while a person with a mental disorder is not permitted to refuse treatment for her disorder? Even if it is the case that people who suffer from mental disorders are more likely to refuse treatment in 'unreasonable' circumstances,[129] it is difficult to see why a different approach to responsibility should be employed here. Furthermore, it is by no means clear that compulsory treatment of people with capacity delivers a better protection from harm (in this broader sense) for family members or carers than better access to treatment or other support measures. For example, a study by G. Faden et al. found that family members were concerned about lack of information, support, and advice from professionals.[130] Thus, relying on a relational argument to justify compulsory treatment may in fact mask inadequate treatment of the person with the mental disorder and inadequate supports for her family and carers.

On the basis of these arguments, it would seem that, while some differential treatment of some people with mental disorders may be justified, a treatment model that permits wholesale overriding of the right of autonomy of people with a mental disorder is difficult to defend, within a liberal conception of the law at any rate.

Yet, as will be seen below, resolving this situation is not a straightforward matter of introducing a capacity-based model for treatment for a

of Disability (New York: Springer, 1999), pp. 340–6; N. Sartorius et al. (eds.) Families and Mental Disorder: From Burden to Empowerment (Chichester: John Wiley & Sons, 2005).

[128] See P. Corrigan and F. Miller, 'Shame, Blame, and Contamination' (2004) 13 Journal of Mental Health 537.

[129] Because the law limits the right to refuse treatment, it is difficult to assess whether or not this is the case.

[130] G. Faden et al., 'The Burden of Care: The Impact of Functional Psychiatric Illness on the Patient's Family' (1989) 150 British Journal of Psychiatry 285.

mental disorder. In order to explore why this is the case, it is helpful to begin by looking at the experience in practice of such models as they have operated in the United States and Canada.

Autonomy in action: a capacity-based approach to treatment

The right of a capable involuntary patient to refuse treatment for her mental disorder has been recognised at state-level in the United States since the 1979 decision of *Rogers* v. *Okin*.[131] In this case, Tauro J found that it was 'an unreasonable invasion of privacy, and an affront to basic concepts of human dignity, to permit forced injection of a mind-altering drug into the buttocks of a competent patient unwilling to give informed consent'.[132] Courts across the United States began to recognise that the right of individual autonomy extends 'equally to mentally ill persons who are not to be treated as persons of lesser status or dignity because of their illness'.[133] However, this approach has neither been confirmed nor rejected at Supreme Court level.[134]

In addition to these judicial initiatives, many states introduced legislation enshrining the right of capable involuntary patients to refuse treatment for a mental disorder. There is some variation among states regarding how the right is given effect.[135] In some states, patients are entitled to a judicial determination of capacity;[136] in others, the determination of capacity is an administrative or tribunal decision[137] or a decision

---

[131] (1979) 478 F Supp 1342. The case involved a class action taken by residents in the Boston State Hospital against the forcible administration of anti-psychotic medication. For factual background to the case (including a description of the appalling living conditions for patients in the hospital at this time), see P. Appelbaum, *Almost a Revolution: Mental Health Law and the Limits of Change* (New York: Oxford University Press, 1994), pp. 114–16.

[132] *Ibid.*, 1371.

[133] *Rivers* v. *Katz* (1986) 67 NY 2d 485, 493. See also *Rennie* v. *Klein* (1978) 462 F Supp 1131; *Bee* v. *Greaves* (1984) 744 F 2d 1387; *Nelson* v. *Heyne* (1974) 491 F 2d 352; *Scott* v. *Plante* (1976) 532 F 2d 939; *Riese* v. *St Mary's Hospital and Medical Centre* (1987) 243 Cal Rptr 241.

[134] The Supreme Court has recognised a limited right of remand prisoners to refuse treatment for a mental disorder although this has primarily been linked to a right to a fair trial rather than autonomy: see *Washington* v. *Harper* (1990) 494 US 210; *Riggins* v. *Nevada* (1992) 504 US 127; *Sell* v. *United States* (2003) 539 US 166. See Anon 'Developments in the Law: The Law of Mental Illness' (2008) 121 Harvard Law Rev 1114, 1121–1132.

[135] See B. Winick, *The Right to Refuse Mental Health Treatment* (Washington DC: American Psychological Association, 1997), Chapter 19.

[136] See Massachusetts: *Rogers* v. *Commissioner, Department of Mental Health* (1983) 458 NE 2d 308); New York: *Rivers* v. *Katz* (1986) 67 NY 2d 485.

[137] See the Californian Welfare and Institutions Code (AB 1421), which states that a patient is entitled to a hearing in front of a 'law-trained decision maker' (an attorney appointed from a panel).

made by the treatment team.[138] Where patients are found to lack capacity, most states assign the power to make treatment decisions to a court using a best interests standard. This is in interesting contrast to the substituted judgment standard which is favoured in respect of decision-making for people lacking capacity in other contexts.[139]

Like many jurisdictions, there have been recent moves in the United States to introduce legislation providing for community-based treatment, with most states now having introduced legislation allowing for 'Assisted Outpatient Treatment' (AOT). Section 9.60 of the New York Mental Hygiene Law is typical of legislation in this regard.[140] Under the section, a patient aged more than 18 years with a mental illness may be ordered to obtain AOT in defined circumstances.[141] Crucially, a patient with capacity may be made subject to an AOT order without her consent. If the patient fails to comply with the AOT order, she may be admitted to hospital, provided that the requirements for involuntary detention are met (i.e. that she is a danger to herself or others)[142] although, if she has capacity, treatment may not be administered without her consent during her detention. Notwithstanding the recognised right of a capable involuntary patient to refuse treatment for a mental disorder, AOT legislation has withstood constitutional challenge. In *In the Matter of KL*, the New York Court of Appeals upheld section 9.60 on the basis that a patient could still exercise her right to refuse treatment, albeit that this may have to occur within the confines of a psychiatric facility.[143] The Court also held that, even if the patient's right to refuse were interfered with, the patient's rights were outweighed by 'the state's compelling interests in both its police and *parens*

---

[138] See New Jersey: *Rennie* v. *Klein* (1981) 653 F 2d 836.

[139] Although see *Rogers* v. *Commissioner, Department of Mental Health* (1983) 458 NE 2d 308, where the substituted judgment standard was adopted.

[140] See J. Gutterman, 'Waging a War on Drugs: Administering a Lethal Dose to Kendra's Law' (2000) 68 *Fordham Law Review* 2401; M. Perlin, 'Therapeutic Jurisprudence and Outpatient Commitment Law: Kendra's Law as Case Study' (2003) 9 *Psychology, Public Policy & Law* 183.

[141] These include that a court finds that the patient is unlikely to survive safely in the community without supervision; that she has a history of non-compliance with the treatment previously prescribed for her mental illness and is unlikely voluntarily to participate in the treatment programme; that she needs an assisted treatment programme in order to prevent a relapse or deterioration that would be likely to result in serious harm to herself or others, that it is likely that she will benefit from assisted treatment and that the treatment is the least restrictive alternative.

[142] However, a patient may be held in hospital for up to 72 hours while it is determined if the requirements for detention are met.

[143] (2004) 1 NY 3d 362, 373.

patraie powers'.[144] The state's interests in this regard were considered to be greater than in a case where the patient was already detained because a patient who was not in detention posed a greater risk to the community.[145]

Legal protection for autonomy: the practical consequences

Paul Appelbaum describes psychiatrists' initial response to *Rogers* v. *Okin* as 'vitriolic'.[146] Psychiatrists feared that the recognition of the right to refuse treatment would lead to wide-scale refusals by patients, that psychiatric hospitals would effectively become detention centres and that resources would have to be relocated into the legal process and away from providing patient care. In Appelbaum's words, '[t]he image of an untreated patient – huddling in the corner of a ward, ignored by everyone else, bearing in solitude the burden of a personal psychosis – pervaded the clinical imagination'.[147] In a frequently quoted comment, Appelbaum and Gutheil argued that '[t]he way is paved for patients to "rot with their rights on"'.[148]

Some flavour of the actual consequences of the legal protection for autonomy may be obtained from Appelbaum's 1994 collation of a range of empirical studies relating to the impact of the right to refuse on the practice of mental health care at that time.[149] In interpreting the data, it is important to remember that involuntary admission to a psychiatric facility is on the basis of dangerousness (to self or others)[150] rather than because of a need for treatment (as is the case in England and Wales and many other jurisdictions). The first notable point is that the widespread refusals initially feared by psychiatrists did not take place. Studies quoted suggested that refusal rates in civil psychiatric hospitals ranged from 0.4 per cent to 15.6 per cent with more than half the studies reporting rates at below 5 per cent and very few recording refusal rates of more than 10 per cent.[151] Rates were higher for patients held at criminal psychiatric facilities, ranging

---

[144] *Ibid.*, 371.

[145] *Ibid.*, 373. A similar conclusion was reached in *In the Matter of Leonel Urcuyo* (2000) 714 NYS 2d 862.

[146] Appelbaum, *Almost a Revolution*, p. 124.   [147] *Ibid.*, p. 127.

[148] P. Appelbaum and T. Gutheil, 'Rotting With Their Rights On: Constitutional Theory and Clinical Reality in Drug Refusal by Psychiatric Patients' (1979) 7 *Bulletin of the American Academy of Psychiatry and the Law* 306.

[149] Appelbaum, *Almost a Revolution*, Chapter 4. Appelbaum himself is not supportive of an autonomy-based approach.

[150] This standard, which was first established in the Wisconsin case of *Lessard* v. *Schmidt* (1972) 349 F Supp 1078, has been accepted across the United States: see Appelbaum, *ibid.*, pp. 27–9.

[151] *Ibid.*, p. 133.

from a low of 11 per cent to a high of 45 per cent.[152] A second point is that, when patients did wish to refuse treatment, the review system, whether judicial or otherwise, did not generally permit them to do so. Appelbaum cites a number of studies which indicated a finding of patient incapacity in well over 90 per cent of treatment refusal cases that went to a formal hearing.[153] He suggests that reviews at administrative level or by the treatment team led to fewer findings of incapacity than was the case with judicial reviews. However, these reviews also resulted in a high proportion of patients being found to lack capacity.[154] Thus, refusing patients were rarely left untreated, if their psychiatrists chose to pursue the matter. This view is confirmed by other commentators,[155] leading Michael Perlin to describe the right to refuse treatment under United States law as a 'right without a remedy', creating 'the illusion of a right without any legitimate expectation that the right will be honored'.[156]

The studies outlined above suggest that a capacity-based right to refuse treatment for a mental disorder had a relatively limited impact in practice. In this respect, however, it should be noted that, while patients may rarely win where capacity is disputed, it is probable that only the stronger cases for imposed treatment actually reached the hearing stage.[157] Thus, for example, a study by Hoge *et al.*, found that the cases of only 18 per cent of patients who refused treatment actually reached formal judicial review (although, in each case that did reach judicial review, treatment was ordered).[158] This may be contrasted with the findings of Kasper *et al.*'s study of treatment refusal in Virginia, which does not allow a capacity-based right to refuse treatment.[159] Here, all patients who refused treatment

[152] *Ibid.*, p. 134.
[153] *Ibid.*, pp. 143–4. See also the studies cited by L. Roth, 'The Right to Refuse Psychiatric Treatment: Law and Medicine at the Interface' (1986) 35 *Emory Law Journal* 139, 156.
[154] *Ibid.*, p. 144. According to the studies cited, reviews by medical directors resulted in treatment being approved in the range of 70–80 per cent of cases.
[155] See T. Kirk and D. Bersoff, 'How Many Procedural Safeguards Does it Take to Get a Psychiatrist to Leave the Lightbulb Unchanged? A Due Process Analysis of the MacArthur Treatment Competence Study' (1996) 2 *Psychology Public Policy and Law* 45, 57.
[156] M. Perlin, 'Is it More Than "Dodging Lions and Wastin' Time"'? Adequacy of Counsel, Questions of Competence, and the Judicial Process in Individual Right to Refuse Treatment Cases' (1996) 2 *Psychology, Public Policy and Law* 114, 119.
[157] See Appelbaum, *Almost a Revolution*, p. 144.
[158] Hoge *et al.*, 'A Prospective, Multi-Centre Study of Patients' Refusal of Antipsychotic Medication' (1990) 47 *Archives of General Psychiatry* 949, 956.
[159] Kasper *et al.*, 'Prospective Study of Patients' Refusal of Antipsychotic Medication Under a Physician Discretion Review Procedure' (1997) 154 *American Journal of Psychiatry* 483, 488.

were treated within an average of 2.8 days of the refusal. As yet, there would seem to be little empirical data on the impact of AOT on rates of treatment refusal or as regards the numbers of patients who choose to exercise their right to refuse AOT and what the consequences of this were for them. A review of the New York legislation does include the views of recipients of AOT, which generally favour the treatment programmes and say that they have been assisted by them.[160] However, the overall tenor of the review is to explain the desirability of AOT rather than to provide information on what might be termed civil liberties issues.

The decision of the Supreme Court of Canada in *Starson* v. *Swayze*[161] and its subsequent outcomes show a different set of practical consequences arising from the capacity-based right to refuse treatment for a mental disorder. Under the Ontario Health Care Consent Act 1996, a capable adult has the right to refuse treatment, including treatment for a mental disorder even if she has been involuntarily admitted under the Ontario Mental Health Act 1990. The applicable test for capacity is based on the ability 'to understand the information relevant to the decision' and 'to appreciate the reasonably foreseeable consequences of a decision or lack of decision'.[162] The case concerned the refusal of treatment by Professor Starson, who was described by the Court as an 'exceptionally intelligent man who in earlier years did remarkable work in physics'.[163] However, he also suffered from bipolar disorder and, as a result of his illness, he had been admitted periodically to mental hospitals in the United States and Canada since 1985. Because of his illness, he had received anti-psychotic medication, which had eased his symptoms but which he also felt 'dulled his mind and diminished his creativity'.[164] Although he had never actually hurt either himself or others, Professor Starson was compulsorily admitted in 1998, having been tried and found not criminally responsible due to his illness for having made death threats.[165] He refused treatment for his disorder and his application in this respect came before the Supreme Court.

A majority of the Supreme Court held that Starson had the necessary capacity, notwithstanding that he did not acknowledge that he had a mental disorder, and that, accordingly, he had a right to refuse treatment.

---

[160] *Kendra's Law* (New York State Office of Mental Health, 2005), pp. 20–1.

[161] [2003] SCC 32.

[162] Health Care Consent Act 1996, s. 4(1). On the capacity aspects of the case, see R. Sklar, 'Starson v. Swayze: The Supreme Court Speaks Out (Not all that Clearly) on the Question of "Capacity"' (2007) 52 *Canadian Journal of Psychiatry* 390.

[163] [2003] SCC 32, [2].   [164] *Ibid.*, [3].   [165] *Ibid,* [66].

In the view of the majority, a patient 'is not required to describe his mental condition as an "illness," or to otherwise characterize the condition in negative terms'.[166] The majority also found that, in reaching its conclusions in respect of capacity, the Ontario Consent and Capacity Board[167] had been 'overly influenced by its conviction that medication was in Professor Starson's best interest'.[168]

John Gray and Richard O'Reilly draw on reports from the Ontario Review Board (ORB)[169] to follow Professor Starson's progress following the Supreme Court's decision.[170] They show that although, at the time of the Supreme Court decision, Professor Starson had believed that he would shortly be released, he continued to be held in detention while he refused treatment. During this time his general health and his mental state deteriorated to the point where his condition was described as being close to catatonic.[171] Eventually, he reached the point where he was found to lack capacity and, beginning in 2005, anti-psychotic medication was administered against his will. The ORB report suggests that, following this, his concentration levels improved, he was able to leave bed, his weight increased and he lost a good deal of his paranoid thinking.[172] Professor Starson was eventually released in 2007, having been detained for nine years and having refused treatment for the first seven of those years.

It is unlikely that many patients will fall into the same category as Professor Starson. Thus, the case is perhaps best viewed as an example of what could be a practical consequence of a capacity-based right to refuse treatment rather than one which commonly applies. Furthermore, it would be much more difficult for a patient who refuses to accept that she has a mental 'illness' to come within the 'use and weigh' test set out in the Mental Capacity Act 2005 (MCA) or within the broader definition of 'understanding' in the statutory standard in the MHA adopted by the Court of Appeal in *R (on the application of B)* v. *Dr SS and Dr AC*.[173] Nonetheless, the possible consequences which the case reveals do raise normative questions, which are considered below.

---

[166] *Ibid.*, [79].
[167] The Board is charged with oversight of operation of the Health Care Consent Act 1996 and sits with one, three or five members.
[168] [2003] SCC 32, [91].
[169] The ORB annually reviews the status of any person found not criminally responsible or unfit to stand trial because of a mental disorder.
[170] J. Gray and R. O'Reilly, 'Supreme Court of Canada's 'Beautiful Mind' Case' (2009) 32 *International Journal of Law and Psychiatry* 315, 318–19.
[171] *Ibid.*, 318.   [172] As reported in Gray and O'Reilly, *ibid.*
[173] [2006] EWCA Civ 28, [34].

Assessing the autonomy-based model

The preceding discussion suggests that the traditional autonomy-based approach to treatment for a mental disorder has had some impact on treatment decisions in practice. Writing about the position in Ontario, Peter Bartlett notes anecdotal evidence which suggests that there are few outright refusals and that while some patients may consent to treatment which their psychiatrists do not consider to be optimal, in practice, both parties seem to negotiate a solution with which they are content.[174] This would seem to be borne out by the evidence from the United States that only stronger cases proceed to formal hearings. It is not clear how other conflicts between psychiatrists and patients are resolved but presumably in some circumstances at least, a negotiated agreement is reached. The value of a consensual approach is widely recognised from a therapeutic (as well as a rights-centred) perspective.[175] Thus, insofar as the traditional approach to autonomy as non-interference delivers a consensual approach to decisions about health care, it makes a valuable contribution.

However, the autonomy-based approach does not seem to have succeeded in transforming 'the relations between expertise and those subject to it'.[176] It would seem that patients who wish to refuse treatment either have treatment imposed on the basis of a lack of capacity if their psychiatrists pursue the matter or they are permitted to exercise their right to refuse treatment at a (probable) cost to their liberty. Nor does the approach taken in the United States seem to have greatly reduced the stigma attached to mental illness or alleviated broader experiences of discrimination in that jurisdiction.[177] There are a number of reasons why this is the case. First, there are the inherent limitations of the binary division of patients' decisions based on a finding of capacity or incapacity. As was argued in Chapter 4, capacity is an inherently malleable concept

---

[174] P. Bartlett, 'The Test of Compulsion in Mental Health Law: Capacity, Therapeutic Benefit and Dangerousness as Possible Criteria' (2003) 11 *Medical Law Review* 326, 333–4.

[175] See B. Winick, 'The Right to Refuse Mental Health Treatment: A Therapeutic Jurisprudence Analysis' (1994) 17 *International Journal of Law and Psychiatry* 99, 104–5; B. Winick, *Civil Commitment: A Therapeutic Jurisprudence Model* (Durham, NC: Carolina Academic Press, 2005); M. Perlin 'A Law of Healing' (2000) 68 *University of Cincinnati Law Review* 407. For a similar argument from a psychiatrist's perspective, see L. Roth, 'The Right to Refuse Psychiatric Treatment' 150.

[176] N. Rose, 'Unreasonable Rights: Mental Illness and the Limits of the Law' (1985) 12 *Journal of Law and Society* 199, 206.

[177] See S. Hinshaw, *The Mark of Shame: Stigma of Mental Illness and An Agenda for Change* (New York: Oxford University Press, 2007).

and capacity assessors can and do, perhaps unwittingly, manipulate the assessment process. Furthermore, as discussed in Chapter 3, some mental disorders give rise to particular difficulties in assessing capacity. The discussion in Chapter 3 noted the difficulties created by situations of fluctuating capacity and by situations where a mental disorder has an impact on a core component of a person's identity. In such contexts, it can be very difficult for capacity to act as a meaningful sorting mechanism for decisions. This is likely to undermine assessors' belief in the process and to lead assessors to fall back on factors such as the nature of the decision the person proposes to make.

Secondly, a focus on the right of autonomy serves to obscure the exercise of power and its implications in respect of patients both with and without capacity. For patients found to lack capacity, a focus on autonomy fails to recognise the right to dignity and bodily integrity which, it was argued in the previous chapter, are implicated whenever treatment is provided against the will of a person, regardless of her capacity. The possible trauma of, for example, compulsory feeding for a person with anorexia nervosa is likely to be experienced in no less a way because she has been deemed to lack the capacity to consent to the procedure.[178] Indeed, with an egosyntonic disorder such as anorexia nervosa, the deeper the impact of the illness on a person's self-perception and identity, the more likely it is that she will be found to lack capacity and the more traumatic the effect of imposed treatment. The point here is not that compulsory treatment of a person with anorexia nervosa can never be justified but that the fact that a person lacks capacity does not of itself provide a justification for compulsory treatment.

For patients with capacity, as the decision in *Starson* shows, the exercise of a capacity-based right to refuse treatment may come at the cost of an ongoing loss of liberty unless one accepts a particular treatment. The AOT model under US law confirms this in more prosaic, and more prevalent, contexts. Thus, the recognition of a right of autonomy does not stop the exercise of power nor does it prevent a person being subject to control. Rather, it simply changes the site of impact. In this respect, the profound nature of the loss of liberty faced by detained patients must be recalled.[179]

[178] This point is confirmed in a study of the attitudes to compulsory treatment among patients with anorexia nervosa: see J. Tan *et al.*, 'Attitudes of Patients With Anorexia Nervosa to Compulsory Treatment and Coercion' (2010) 33 *International Journal of Law and Psychiatry* 13, 16.

[179] See E. Goffman, *Asylums: Essays on the Social Situation of Mental Patients and Other Inmates* (Doubleday, New York, 1961), p. 24, who depicts psychiatric hospitals as 'total institutions' within which the self is 'systematically, if often unintentionally, mortified'.

Incarceration may challenge the individual's conception of herself in a way which over a longer period of time may, as happened in *Starson*, lead to the loss of the autonomy which the capacity-based right to refuse treatment sought to protect.

Thirdly, for the reasons discussed in Chapter 1, the thin 'take-it-or-leave it' conception of autonomy from which the right to refuse treatment is derived does little to deliver choice or appropriate treatment[180] or to contribute to the achievement of 'the highest attainable standard of health' for patients with a mental disorder.[181] Indeed, a focus on this form of autonomy may serve to prevent the delivery of needed services.[182] In this respect, as Bernadette McSherry argues, people with mental disorders are discriminated against in terms of access to treatment.[183] Because of social stigma, many patients with mental disorders do not seek medical help and accordingly may not have access to treatment until their situations become critical (at which point compulsion may be utilised). Nor, it would seem does this conception of autonomy meet patients' needs in other respects. A study by Tan *et al.* into the experiences of young women with anorexia nervosa reached the conclusion that 'what mattered most to participants was not whether they were compelled to have treatment but the nature of their relationships with parents and mental health professionals'.[184] Many participants 'described decisions made on the basis of trust and good relationships rather than on the basis of the elements highlighted by most theoretical, clinical and legal descriptions of capacity'.[185] The view of autonomy as non-interference does little to facilitate the development of trust and good relationships.

A more profound difficulty with the traditional view of autonomy as non-interference arises from the possibility that, in some cases, the

---

[180] See C. Unsworth, *The Politics of Mental Health Legislation* (Oxford: Clarendon, 1987), p. 336.

[181] As required under Art. 25 of the CRPD and more generally by Art. 12 of the *International Covenant on Economic, Social and Cultural Rights 1966*, General Assembly Resolution 2200A (XXI).

[182] As argued forcibly in P. Sedgwick, *Psychopolitics* (London: Pluto Press, 1982); see also T. Carney, 'The Mental Health Service Crisis of Neoliberalism: An Antipodean Perspective' (2008) 31 *International Journal of Law and Psychiatry* 101, 103–4.

[183] McSherry 'The Right of Access to Mental Health Care: Voluntary Treatment and the Role of Law' in B. McSherry and P. Weller (eds.) *Rethinking Rights Based Mental Health Law* (Oxford: Hart Publishing, 2010).

[184] J. Tan *et al.*, 'Attitudes of Patients', 18. The study was based on interviews with 29 young women (aged between 15 and 26 years) who either were suffering from or had suffered from anorexia nervosa.

[185] *Ibid.*, 16.

highest attainable standard of mental health can only be achieved with some degree of compulsion. As Nikolas Rose points out, sometimes mental disorder impacts on the autonomy of the individual who suffers from the disorder and the restoration of autonomy requires intervention to which the person does not agree.[186] In such circumstances, he argues that '[l]ibertarian arguments are ill-equipped to weigh up the choice between a short period of "coercion" leading to a long period of "autonomy", and radical non-intervention leading to a life permanently at the mercy of the fates'.[187] Thus, both compulsion and non-compulsion may impede individual autonomy, albeit in different ways and within different temporal frames. On the view of autonomy as empowerment outlined in Chapter 1, it is possible to envisage a very limited set of circumstances in which compulsory treatment might be justified as part of the goal of restoring autonomy, provided that such treatment could be directly linked to the enhancement of autonomy and that it could be shown to be a last resort. This could only be justified, however, within a broader framework for empowerment, the details of which are discussed below.

Beyond traditional liberalism: a framework for decision-making

The preceding section has argued that the traditional liberal view of autonomy is ill-equipped to deal with decision-making in respect of mental disorders. Accordingly, although as Zigmond and Holland note, capacity became the 'holy grail for "enlightened" professionals and campaigning groups,'[188] simple recourse to a capacity-based model, even if it were politically feasible, fails to recognise the complexities involved in decision-making by and for some people with a mental disorder. This final section of the chapter looks beyond traditional liberalism and asks what factors might contribute to a better framework for what Terry Carney describes as 'mental health law in postmodern society'.[189] It argues that discussion of autonomy in mental health law must move away from the view of autonomy as non-interference and instead seek to incorporate the view of autonomy as achievement or empowerment which was elaborated upon in Chapter 1. This requires the imposition of positive obligations, including in respect of choice and communication. In order to do this in a

---

[186] Rose, 'Unreasonable Rights', 214.   [187] *Ibid.*
[188] Zigmond and Holland, 'Unethical Mental Health Law', 54.
[189] T. Carney, 'Mental Health Law in Postmodern Society? Time for New Paradigms?' (2003) 10 *Psychiatry, Psychology and Law* 12.

meaningful way, it is necessary to ground any proposals in the practical realities of decision-making in respect of treatment for a mental disorder. Accordingly, the discussion begins with a brief look at the picture that emerges from the informative biennial reports of the MHAC regarding the position in England and Wales.

The realities of decision-making: the extent of formal compulsion

The MHAC Thirteenth Biennial Report, which covers the period from 2007 to 2009, provides important insights into the current climate in respect of healthcare decision-making under the MHA. The report shows the extent to which compulsion is an everyday reality of the application of the MHA. In 2008–09, out of a total of 9,102 cases in which a request for a SOAD review was sought, approximately 37 per cent of patients were recorded as refusing treatment.[190] Against this background, it is hardly surprising that mechanisms to facilitate participation by patients seem to be lacking. The report notes that over half of all patients' treatment plans sampled did not even record the patient's views.[191]

Given that SCT only became operational from November 2008, it is too soon to assess the impact of this aspect of the law on compulsion. Because SCT can only arise following a period of detention in circumstances in which it is possible for the treatment to be given in the community,[192] presumably patients for whom SCT is proposed have been 'consenting' to treatment before a CTO will be made[193] (insofar as a decision to accept treatment in order to avoid ongoing detention might be described as consensual).[194] The available data for the first six months of operation of the legislation indicates that, out of 2,100 CTOs, there were 206 recalls to hospital and 142 revocations of the order and reversion to ongoing

---

[190] Thirteenth Biennial Report, Figure 46, p. 151. This figure is fairly representative of the position over the previous five years: see Figure 46.

[191] *Ibid.*, para. 1.102. To be fair, the Thirteenth Biennial Report relates in part to the time before the Principles set out in the revised Code of Practice became operational, and it may be the case that the more participative approach set out in the Code has led to improvements on this rather dismal statistic.

[192] MHA, s. 17A.

[193] The Code of Practice, para. 28.6 states that a factor in determining whether a patient should be covered by SCT is that 'the patient appears prepared to consent or comply with the treatment they need'.

[194] Thirteenth Biennial Report, Figure 61, p. 170, shows that, on the statistics available in January 2009, over half of SCT patients had capacity to consent.

detention.[195] Presumably, the decisions to recall and revoke were based on the patients' non-compliance with treatment. At 16.5 per cent of the total orders granted, this would seem relatively high (given the criteria for granting a CTO) but it is too soon to reach any meaningful conclusions. Furthermore, a close qualitative consideration of the circumstances of recall and revocation (as well as of the supports provided to patients who are subject to CTOs) will be essential in order to assess the workings of the legislation in this regard.

Autonomy as 'achievement' in mental health law

The view of autonomy as achievement explored in Chapter 1 drew on the work of Joseph Raz and of relational theorists to argue that respect for autonomy requires more than non-interference. Instead, a legal framework for autonomy must be concerned with issues such as the adequacy of choice and with the development of autonomy-building measures aimed at enhancing individual agency and affecting a shift in decision-making power to the individual. This would also seem to be the view of autonomy underlying the CRPD. Under this view of autonomy, capacity and incapacity are less important than under the traditional liberal view. The aim is to empower individuals and to support them in making decisions for themselves regardless of capacity. As was acknowledged in Chapter 1, this richer conception of autonomy is an ideal that is difficult to 'technicalise' within a legal framework. It would seem to be clear, however, from the discussion in Chapter 2 that better information and communication and better choice of options are key aspects of the process which the law can, to a degree at least, help deliver.

Information and communication

Although, as was acknowledged in Chapter 2, adequate information and communication would seem to be in short supply for all patients, these attributes of a positive right of autonomy would seem to be especially lacking in the context of patients with a mental disorder. Bartlett and Sandland survey a range of English studies on information and communication and conclude that 'there seems to be a good deal of patient dissatisfaction with the information that is provided about the purpose and potential effects of treatment, particularly drug

---

[195] See *Inpatients Formally Detained in Hospital under the Mental Health Act 1983 and Patients Subject to Supervised Community Treatment: 1998–99 to 2008–09* (London: Health and Social Care Information Centre, 2009), para. 2.6.

treatments'.[196] This view is confirmed in the Thirteenth Biennial Report,[197] which also notes that some clinical teams deliberately withheld information from patients on the basis of an assumption that '"too much" information about drugs would undermine treatment compliance'.[198] This was, notwithstanding that, as the report also notes, there is no evidence to support such assumptions.[199]

The kind of attitude described in the biennial report is in some ways a consequence of the possibility of compulsion. Treatment discussions which take place in the shadow of compulsion, with the final outcome assured, will inevitably differ in quality from discussions where a case for treatment must be made and a person convinced. Thus, as the Biennial Report notes, a willingness to discuss issues of the patient experience, such as weight gain or diminished sexual functioning 'are often pushed aside when the powers of the Mental Health Act have been used to address acute mental disorder'.[200] In such circumstances, the need for a positive requirement to develop communication is all the more apparent. Yet, strikingly, unlike the position under the MCA, there is no statutory requirement that patients must be provided with information in an accessible form,[201] although the need for this is acknowledged in guidance to professionals[202] and in the Code of Practice.[203] The need for statutory backing for this position would seem obvious.

With any measure requiring better communication (whether statutorily based or not), the primary difficulty is one of enforcement. The limited enforcement possibilities offered by the duty to disclose in the law of tort are even less effective in the context of treatment for a mental disorder than they are in respect of other kinds of treatment decisions. As Peter Bartlett points out, negligence actions of any sort against mental health professionals are rare and there have been no successful actions in England and Wales based on failure to disclose in this context.[204] Indeed, in a compulsion situation, it is difficult to see how a causation requirement might be met. Given that the patient is already deprived of her choice to

---

[196] Bartlett and Sandland, *Mental Health Law*, p. 292.

[197] Thirteenth Biennial Report, para. 3.16. This is also the experience of Irish service users: see E. Dunne, *The Views of Adult Users of the Public Sector Mental Health Service* (Dublin: Mental Health Commission, 2006), p. 29 (available at www.mhcirl.ie).

[198] Thirteenth Biennial Report, para 3.16.   [199] *Ibid.*   [200] *Ibid.*   [201] See MCA, s. 3(2).

[202] See *Guidance for Clinicians and SOADs: The Imposition of Treatment in the Absence of Consent* (London: Care Quality Commission, 2008), para. 7.

[203] Code, para. 23.33–23.36.

[204] P. Bartlett, 'Psychiatric Treatment: In the Absence of Law?' (2006) 14 *Medical Law Review* 124, 128–9.

refuse the treatment by the legislation, it is difficult to see how a causal link might be established between any harm suffered and the failure to disclose information about risks in the treatment.[205] This inherent weakness in mental health law must therefore be addressed in a more formal way. The MHA efforts in this respect will be assessed below. Prior to that however, the question of adequate choice arises.

Adequate choice

It was argued in Chapter 1 that a second aspect of autonomy as achievement is that the individual has a choice between adequate or meaningful options. Given that, within current legal frameworks, involuntary patients have no choice at all, the ideal of a meaningful choice may seem an unrealistic aspiration. Yet, as the Expert Committee argued in putting forward a principle of reciprocity, if society is prepared to compel a person to comply with treatment, it would seem reasonable that there would be a reciprocal obligation to ensure that appropriate services are available.[206] This must include the provision of options and the delivery of choice. For example, the Thirteenth Biennial Report noted the wish of many patients to access psychological treatments and the cost reasons which prohibit this.[207] As with information and communication, the ideal of involving the patient and of providing access to psychological treatments is set out in the Code to the MHA.[208] However, once again, the issue of enforcement is core to delivering on this ideal.

Delivering on autonomy as achievement in mental health law

It was argued above that the recognition of an obligation to empower patients should be a core part of the conceptual foundation for the future development of mental health law. However, this obligation is made meaningful only if accompanied by mechanisms to deliver on it. As will be seen below, both advocacy and treatment reviews have the potential to empower patients although, in both respects, a great deal depends on how the systems are operated.

---

[205] This difficulty would not be addressed even by the broader understanding of causation in *Chester* v. *Afshar* [2004] UKHL 41.

[206] *Expert Committee Review of the Mental Health Act* 1983, p. 23. See also N. Eastman, 'Mental Health Law: Civil Liberties and the Principle of Reciprocity' (1994) 308 *British Medical Journal* 43.

[207] Thirteenth Biennial Report, para. 3.23.   [208] See Code, para. 1. 5; paras. 23.45–23.47.

The contribution of advocacy

Since April 2009, the Independent Mental Capacity Advocacy Service introduced under the MCA has been extended to patients covered by the MHA.[209] Among the statutory functions of the Independent Advocate are the requirement to help the patient to obtain information about the medical treatment which is given to her or that which is proposed or discussed; to help her to understand why the treatment is given or proposed; and to help her obtain information about and understand the authority under which the treatment is given and the legislative requirements which apply.[210] The Independent Advocate also has the function of helping patients to understand the rights under the legislation that may be exercised by or in relation to them as well as helping them in the exercise of their rights.[211]

While the extension of the advocacy scheme to mental health undoubtedly makes a positive contribution to patient empowerment in this area, the effectiveness of the advocacy model in practice must be monitored.[212] Clearly, adequate funding is essential if the scheme is to work effectively as is the establishment of patient trust in the scheme.[213] While it is too early to assess the effectiveness of the scheme in practice, it is subject to some statutory limits which may limit its effectiveness. First, although there is a statutory requirement to inform patients of the existence of the scheme,[214] nothing in the Act 'prevents the patient from declining to be provided with help'.[215] While, on one level, the idea of forcing advocacy on an unwilling patient is counter-intuitive, the effect of this provision is that some patients, possibly including very ill patients who may need the help of an advocate most, may reject the possibility of advocacy either because they do not understand the scheme or because they see the advocate as yet another 'establishment' figure. It is possible that strategies may be developed to minimise this difficulty in practice. It is, however, essential to closely monitor the circumstances of uptake on the advocacy scheme to ensure that people who need advocacy as a mechanism for empowerment are not denied the opportunity.

---

[209] See MHA, s. 130A-130D as inserted by MHA 2007, s. 30. Details of the Scheme are set out in the Mental Health Act 1983 (Independent Mental Health Advocates) England Regulations 2008, SI 3166/2008.

[210] MHA, s. 130B(1).   [211] MHA, s. 130B(2).

[212] For an empirical study of the role of advocacy (usually involving legal professionals) in Australian mental health tribunal hearings, see T. Carney *et al.*, 'Advocacy and Participation in Mental Health Cases: Realisable Rights or Pipe-Dreams?' (2008) 26 *Law in Context* 125.

[213] See Fennell, *The New Law*, p. 118.   [214] MHA, s. 130D.   [215] MHA, s. 130B(6).

Secondly, the advocate's legislative functions are focused more on assisting the patient in understanding decisions made about her and the reasons for the decisions rather than on assisting the patient in directing these decisions. This is perhaps unsurprising given that the possibility of compulsion means that, even with an advocate's assistance, an involuntary patient can only direct treatment decisions up to a certain point. However, even within a compulsory treatment model, negotiated treatment decisions should remain the ideal with compulsion used only as a final resort and mechanisms need to be put in place to ensure this. Again, it is possible that, in practice, the advocacy model can operate in a way that facilitates a negotiated solution. However, there is a risk that the statutory parameters will prove too narrow to deliver any degree of meaningful empowerment for involuntary patients.

The contribution of treatment reviews to empowerment

As discussed above, ECHR-derived case law has established a right of judicial review of treatment decisions and it is likely that a hearing will be granted in most situations in which it is formally sought. While the possibility of judicial review looks like a mechanism to empower patients, in reality it is not so clear that involuntary patients are actually empowered by the right. First, as noted above, judicial reviews have not tended to result in any requirement for a change to treatment plans. Secondly, judges have tended to be dismissive of patients' own evidence, in one case even rejecting the applicant's application to provide his own evidence on the basis that this could not 'conceivably assist' in reaching the decision.[216] As Bartlett notes, it was as if the patient was 'somehow peripheral to the decision at issue'.[217] Thirdly, for most patients, especially patients who are very ill, organising legal representation and mounting a judicial review in respect of treatment is very difficult to achieve. Thus, while it is not denied that there are benefits to judicial review, the possibility of such review would not seem to contribute substantially to the empowerment of patients or to the enhancement of their autonomy.[218]

The statutory review mechanism under the MHA is centred on a SOAD review. This operates in a less public context than judicial review

---

[216] *R (on the application of B)* v. *Haddock and Others* [2005] EWHC 921 (Admin), [14] *per* Collins J.

[217] Bartlett, 'A Matter of Necessity?,' 91.

[218] See M. Donnelly, 'Treatment Reviews: Legalism, Process and Rights Protection' in B. McShery and P. Weller (eds.) Rethinking Rights-Based Mental Health Law, p. 283.

and accordingly, it is more difficult to assess the extent to which SOAD reviews facilitate the empowerment of patients. From an empowerment perspective, the SOAD model has a number of positive aspects. Because this review happens automatically, it is available to all patients, not just those who have the resources to initiate actions.[219] Furthermore, because reviews take place on site with minimal disruption, even very ill patients have access to the review process. As discussed further below, there is also evidence that, unlike judicial reviews, SOAD reviews do result in changes in treatment plans.[220] It would seem reasonable to assume that patient views must play a role in at least some of these changes.[221] If this is the case, SOAD reviews offer at least the possibility of empowerment for some patients.

While the SOAD review offers patients the opportunity to explain concerns about treatment to an independent professional, a 2005 review of the SOAD service conducted by the MHAC suggests that the empowerment potential of the SOAD review is not being maximised.[222] Few patients interviewed recalled having been told about the review in advance of the SOAD visit and very few reported having received a clear explanation of the SOAD's role from the SOAD herself.[223] Clearly, any empowerment potential is restricted if patients are unaware of what the review offers. Jill Peay's investigation of SOAD responses to a hypothetical scenario involving the administration of ECT (prior to the changes introduced by the MHA 2007) suggests that SOADs' own attitudes might constitute a barrier to the empowerment potential of the SOAD review.[224] Peay found that SOADs were more likely than treating clinicians to advocate the provision of ECT, notwithstanding the hypothetical patient's probable capacity and deeply felt opposition to the treatment.[225] Peay also found SOADs to be more confident in their decision to treat notwithstanding

---

[219] On the advantages of this, see G. Richardson, 'Autonomy, Guardianship and Mental Disorder: One Problem, Two Solutions' (2002) 65 *Modern Law Review* 702, 710–11.

[220] See text to n 239 below.

[221] Fennell's study from the early 1990s found that, in some cases, the 'lucidly expressed opposition of the patients' did impact on SOADs' decisions: see Fennell, *Treatment Without Consent*, pp. 208–9.

[222] Mental Health Act Commission *Review of the Second Opinion Appointed Doctor Service* (2006) summarised in Mental Health Act Commission Twelfth Biennial Report 2005–2007 *Risk, Rights, Recovery* (London: The Stationery Office, 2008), paras 6.10–6.11.

[223] *Ibid.*, para. 6.11.

[224] J. Peay, *Decisions and Dilemmas: Working With Mental Health Law* (Oxford: Hart Publishing, 2003), p. 100.

[225] *Ibid.* As the study pre-dated the changes introduced in the MHA 2007, the issue of capacity was not central in respect of this treatment.

the patient's opposition.[226] Insofar as this attitude currently exists among SOADs, it would seem to present a significant barrier to the SOAD review as a source of patient empowerment.

Beyond autonomy: review and accountability

While a legal framework which recognises the significance of empowerment can improve the way in which decisions in respect of treatment for a mental disorder are made, it is clear that, even if developed to the maximum extent possible, this framework cannot take account of the situations of all patients with mental disorder. For some patients, the nature of their illness will make empowerment difficult, at least in the short term. In these situations, the law must provide mechanisms to protect patients both from possible infringements of their rights and from possibly abusive treatment practices.

In the latter context, there is now a substantial body of research suggesting over-prescription of high dosage medication and anti-psychotic medication as well as the over-use of polypharmacy for people with mental disorders.[227] An independent study of medication practices in respect of people with dementia found that approximately 180,000 people with dementia (up to a quarter of all such people) are being treated with anti-psychotic medication.[228] This is in spite of evidence that anti-psychotic drugs 'show minimal efficiency' in treatment for behavioural and psychological symptoms in dementia (BPSD) such as agitation, aggression, wandering, shouting, depression, sleep disturbance and psychosis.[229] Although the Royal College of Psychiatrists has issued guidance in respect of high dosage medication and polypharmacy,[230] the MHAC Thirteenth Biennial Report suggests that this has not (yet) been effective in changing treatment practices.[231] This is perhaps unsurprising given the lack of enforcement mechanisms.

---

[226] *Ibid.*

[227] See the studies cited in Twelfth Biennial Report, *Risk, Rights, Recovery*, pp. 203–4; see also P. Fennell, *Treatment Without Consent*, pp. 202–3 (on polypharmacy) and p. 215 (on high dosage medication). In Ireland, see Mental Health Commission *Annual Report 2008* (Dublin: Mental Health Commission, 2009), p. 85–88.

[228] S. Banerjee *The Use of Antipsychotic Medication for People With Dementia: Time for Action* (London: Department of Health, 2009), p. 20.

[229] *Ibid.*, p. 25.

[230] See *Revised Consensus Statement on High-Dosage Antipsychotic Medication and Polypharmacy* (London: Royal College of Psychiatrists, 2006).

[231] *Coercion and Consent*, para. 3.37.

The common law is clearly ill-equipped to protect patients with a mental disorder from abusive treatment practices. For many patients, judicial reviews of treatments or actions in negligence are out of reach because of the practical difficulties involved in mounting the action. Even if patients do succeed in bringing an action in negligence, they are likely to encounter difficulties in establishing a breach of the duty of care. As Bartlett notes, '[i]f diagnosis is neither easy nor clear cut, the margin of judgement allowed to psychiatrists must be correspondingly large'.[232] For most involuntary patients, therefore, the SOAD review is the only protective mechanism available both in respect of their rights and in respect of abusive or inappropriate treatment practices.

SOAD reviews as a protective mechanism: involuntary patients

In terms of providing protections for patient rights, the obvious limitation of the SOAD system is that SOADs are not legally trained. In *R (on the application of B)* v. *Haddock and Others*,[233] Auld LJ described the SOAD's task as 'a medical one, to be undertaken on the *Bolam* principle'.[234] He was clear that it does not, and could not, properly include a conclusion by the SOAD 'as to whether his decision is a Convention compliant application' of the MHA.[235] As Bartlett notes, Auld LJ's reference to the *Bolam* test for medical negligence is concerning because '[i]t would significantly reduce the value of the SOAD as a safeguard if his or her role were merely to ensure that a patient was not treated negligently'.[236] Auld LJ's approach would also seem to run contrary to the approach to the SOAD function taken in *R (Wilkinson)* v. *Broadmoor Special Hospital Authority*, where the Court of Appeal rejected the view that the SOAD must simply determine whether the RMO's decision is reasonable.[237] However, Auld LJ does, perhaps unwittingly, identify the core problem with SOAD reviews. Even if it is recognised that the review should meet a higher standard than Auld LJ indicated, the fact remains that SOADs are ill-equipped to engage with questions of human rights.

In terms of protection against abusive or inappropriate treatment practices, Phil Fennell's study of the SOAD system as it operated in the early 1990s suggested that the protective potential of the SOAD review was very limited. Fennell found that there was 96 per cent agreement between SOADs and prescribing doctors[238] and that the review system was not even

---

[232] Bartlett, 'Psychiatric Treatment,' 129.   [233] [2006] EWCA Civ 961.   [234] *Ibid.*, [34].
[235] *Ibid.*   [236] Bartlett, 'A Matter of Necessity?', 92.   [237] [2002] 1 WLR 419, 434.
[238] Fennell, *Treatment Without Consent*, p. 208.

effective in 'inhibiting plans which require megadoses of drugs'.[239] There are, however, some indications of a change in the intervening period. MHAC data suggest that, from 2003 to 2007, SOAD reviews required changes in patients' treatment plans in approximately 15 per cent of cases, with approximately 2 per cent requiring substantial changes. In 2008, the number of reviews requiring changes increased considerably, with over 25 per cent of reviews requiring some changes and over 4 per cent requiring substantial changes.[240] Whether or not this increase is an indication of a substantial shift in pattern is, as yet, unclear. While a closer analysis of the basis for SOAD decisions (along the lines of Fennell's study) is the only way to be sure if meaningful protection is being delivered, it would nonetheless seem to be the case that the SOAD review is becoming more effective.

Treatment without review: 'voluntary,' 'consenting' and short-term patients

While the SOAD review might be criticised, it nonetheless provides an automatic review which, if operated properly, may have the potential to help empower patients and to protect them from abusive or inappropriate treatment practices. For most patients with a mental disorder, however, a SOAD review is not an option. First, the review operates only in respect of involuntary patients. Yet, it is likely that many patients agree to be voluntarily admitted in order to avoid the stigma of involuntary admission. For these patients, the experience of treatment may be no less coercive than is the case for involuntary patients.[241] Yet there is no mechanism either to protect or to empower them.[242] Patients lacking capacity who are admitted under the admission procedures for a deprivation of liberty as set out in the MCA 2005[243] also have no automatic right of review. Although patients admitted on this basis must have a representative who must maintain contact with, represent and support them,[244] this still falls far short of an automatic review of treatment.

Secondly, treatment reviews are available only for detained patients lacking capacity or for patients who refuse treatment. Consenting detained patients have no right to a SOAD review (although consenting patients under SCT are entitled to such a review).[245] On a traditional view

---

[239] *Ibid.*, p. 217.   [240] Thirteenth Biennial Report, Figure 50, p. 154.
[241] This is confirmed in Tan *et al.*, 'Attitudes of Patients', 15.
[242] See McSherry, 'The Right of Access to Mental Health Care'.
[243] See MCA, ss. 4A, 4B and 16A and Schedules A1 and 1A.
[244] Schedule A1 to the MCA, s. 140.
[245] The oddness of this is noted in the Thirteenth Biennial Report, para. 3.66.

of autonomy, the absence of review for consenting patients does not pose a difficulty on the basis that there is no reason for a capable patient to need protection. However, this view does not recognise the inherently coercive context in which detained people 'consent' to treatment. Accordingly, it provides no mechanism to protect or empower them. The extent to which detained people are inappropriately categorised as 'consenting' to treatment is unclear. However, the MHAC suggests that this may be a relatively common phenomenon. The Thirteenth Biennial Report notes:

> We have no doubt that there are many patients who, throughout their detention are erroneously described as giving consent to their treatment, mainly because they have been asked to agree to treatment without it being explained sufficiently to allow for informed consent, but also because of unrecognised mental incapacity or refusal of consent.[246]

Thirdly, because the SOAD review comes into effect only after three months (other than in respect of ECT), many involuntary patients may be released (or 'consent' to treatment) without ever having had their treatment reviewed. The MHAC Twelfth Biennial Report found that only 27.6 per cent of detained patients in hospitals on the designated census day in 2006 were entitled to a SOAD review.[247]

The lack of any form of review leaves most patients with a mental disorder without effective protection from inappropriate treatment practices. In its biennial reports, the MHAC provided a forum for the ventilation of some of the issues which arise for patients who do not have access to review. While clearly less effective that an individualised review, the MHAC did at least maintain a generalised oversight of how the treatment process operated. However, the MHAC was abolished in 2009.

In *Savage* v. *South Essex Partnership NHS Foundation Trust*, in exploring the extent of the positive duties imposed by the protection of the right to life under Article 2 of the ECHR, Baroness Hale noted the differing legal status of patients in psychiatric facilities and the difficulties in distinguishing 'between different classes of people deprived of their liberty by the state'.[248] She asked '[i]s it, then, possible to draw any distinction between the State's protective duties towards all mental patients,

---

[246] *Ibid.*, para. 3.2.

[247] Mental Health Act Commission, Twelfth Biennial Report 2005–2007. *Risk, Rights, Recovery*: (London: The Stationery Office, 2008), para. 3.61. On these census figures, had the review period been two months rather than three, 30.5 per cent of patients would have received a SOAD review and, had it been one month, 34 per cent would have had a SOAD review.

[248] [2008] UKHL 74, [101].

whether *de iure, de facto* or potentially deprived of their liberty?'.[249] While Baroness Hale did not attempt to resolve this question, her recognition that formal legal status should not be the sole basis for determining the extent of rights protection suggests the possibility of future human rights scrutiny in respect of the categories of patients discussed in this section.

It is unclear whether the failure to provide any form of review in the context discussed would withstand such scrutiny. Phil Fennell notes the 'scope of the positive obligations'[250] arising under Article 8, which the ECtHR had recognised in *Storck v. Germany.*[251] It is entirely conceivable that the requirement 'to take reasonable and appropriate measures to secure and protect individuals' right to respect for their private life'[252] requires a more significant effort to protect the rights of all patients with a mental disorder who, whatever their legal status, are receiving treatment in a psychiatric facility. Fennell also argues that, in some circumstances, the provision of certain treatments may implicate the protection against unlawful deprivations of liberty under Article 5 of the ECHR.[253] Fennell argues that, where a decision-maker assumes complete control over a patient's treatment 'to the extent that they are making decisions about the administration of strong psychotropic medication or even ECT to a patient',[254] this could be 'a factor tipping the balance firmly towards there being a deprivation of liberty'.[255] If this were to be the case, the absence of review mechanisms is unlikely to meet the standard of being in accordance with a procedure prescribed by law as required under Article 5.

There is also an argument that three months is a very long time for a patient who has been formally deprived of liberty to receive treatment, possibly against her will, without any form of review.[256] In *Storck*, the ECtHR noted that 'retrospective measures alone are not sufficient to provide appropriate protection of the physical integrity of individuals in such a vulnerable position as the applicant'.[257] Although in this instance, the ECtHR was referring to the respondent state's argument that German law provided for retrospective criminal sanctions for assault and the possibility

---

[249] *Ibid.*   [250] Fennell, *The New Law*, p. 301.   [251] (2005) 43 EHRR 96.

[252] *Ibid.*, para. 149.

[253] P. Fennell, 'The Mental Capacity Act 2005, the Mental Health Act 1983, and the Common Law' (2005) 12 *Journal of Mental Health Law* 163; Fennell, *The New Law*, pp. 300–1.

[254] *Ibid.*, 167.   [255] *Ibid.*

[256] Compare the position in Victoria, where all involuntary patients have a right to an automatic review of their 'treatment plans' before a tribunal within eight weeks of admission: see Mental Health Act 1986 s. 22(1)(b), inserted by the Mental Health (Amendment) Act 2003.

[257] (2005) 43 EHRR 96, para. 150.

of damages in tort, it would seem clear from the tenor of the ECtHR's comments that measures provided after an event has taken place do not provide adequate protection for patient rights.

Conclusion

The development of an appropriate framework for decision-making in respect of treatment for a mental disorder is especially challenging. The differential legal model adopted in England and Wales, and in many other jurisdictions, offers a lesser degree of protection to the right of autonomy of people with a mental disorder. In this respect, it may fairly be described as discriminatory. In this, the legal framework may also contribute to the stigma experienced by many people with a mental disorder. However, it was argued in this chapter that the matter of treatment for a mental disorder cannot be addressed by the adoption of a simple non-discriminatory approach to autonomy. The experience in the United States shows that traditional liberalism does not provide answers to the legal and ethical conundrums posed by treatment for a mental disorder. Rather, it is necessary to move beyond a view of autonomy as a right of non-interference and instead to engage critically with mechanisms to deliver on autonomy as empowerment. Such mechanisms must be evaluated not simply on the basis of what they promise but on how effectively they deliver on this promise in practice. However, even if this model of autonomy were to be delivered upon, protective measures would still continue to be necessary. This chapter has argued that the inherently coercive environment in which decisions in respect of treatment for a mental disorder are made should be recognised and that a greater degree of protection is required in respect of decisions about treatment made by 'voluntary' and 'consenting' patients. Respect for autonomy alone cannot deliver an appropriate framework for decision-making in this context.

~

Conclusion

This book has explored the difficult legal and normative questions to which healthcare decision-making gives rise. It has shown that, while the legal status of the autonomy principle appears to be well established and stable, in reality the position is doctrinally less clear and normatively more problematic than classic legal dicta might suggest. This concluding chapter revisits the arguments made in earlier chapters and identifies some of the implications of these arguments for the future development of the law in respect of healthcare decision-making. In doing this, it identifies some of the major themes which have emerged from the discussion throughout the book. Five such themes are explored. These are first, the view of autonomy as achievement or empowerment; secondly, the limitations of capacity as a gatekeeper for the right of autonomy; thirdly, the appropriate role for law in healthcare decision-making; fourthly, the possibilities and limitations of a human rights focus in healthcare decision-making; and, finally, the need for closer empirical interrogation of the law in practice.

Autonomy as empowerment

A recurrent theme throughout this book has been the limitations of the conception of autonomy as non-interference. This account of autonomy, which derives from Mill's liberal view of the individual operating within a sphere of freedom protected from state interference, has been highly influential in the development of healthcare law and ethics. However, this view of autonomy is flawed in a number of respects. As explored in Chapter 1, it ignores questions of agency and does not recognise the impact of social context on the ways in which real people make decisions. It is individualistic in focus, failing to recognise values such as responsibility or trust. Furthermore, in practical terms, this account offers patients little beyond a right to be left alone.

The failure to address questions of agency is especially problematic in respect of patients who are vulnerable because of social, cultural or economic disadvantage. For people in these situations, the liberal presumption of free and autonomous decision-making may not represent their reality. Furthermore, as was discussed in Chapter 6, for patients in psychiatric facilities, the pressures on agency may be particularly acute. Patients may 'voluntarily' consent to treatment in order to avoid the stigma of having treatment imposed on them through the legal mechanisms for compulsion. However, even patients who do not suffer from any other obvious disadvantage may encounter difficulties in circumstances of serious physical illness and the stresses which this imposes on the mind. To borrow from Virginia Woolf (who was referring to the view of illness in literature rather than law), this traditional view 'does its best to maintain that its concern is with the mind; that the body is a sheet of plain glass through which the soul looks straight and clear'.[1]

While the case for recognising the agency issues which are obscured within the traditional view of autonomy would seem straightforward, the way in which this should be done is much less so. It is immediately evident that concerns about agency could lead quickly back to paternalistic models for decision-making where 'the patient's duty was to be patient'.[2] While the unattractiveness of such an option may seem so obvious as not to require discussion, it is perhaps worth recalling that respect for the traditional view of autonomy has contributed hugely to the way in which we approach healthcare decision-making. Patients today have more religious and personal freedom, more access to information and more control over their decisions because of the legal and ethical recognition of the importance of autonomy. We may argue about what autonomy should mean and about how the principle of autonomy should interact with other principles, but few would contend that respect for autonomy is irrelevant or would seek to reverse the decision-making freedoms which traditional liberalism has delivered in the context of health care.

The view of autonomy as empowerment which was set out in Chapter 1 of this book draws on the work of Joseph Raz and of some feminist theorists, and argues that autonomy is better seen as 'a kind of achievement'.[3] While such a view encompasses the view of autonomy as non-interference to a large extent, it differs from the traditional liberal view in a number of ways. First, its concern is primarily with positive obligations to build and

---

[1] V. Woolf, 'On Being Ill' in D. Bradshaw (ed.) *Virginia Woolf: Selected Essays* (Oxford University Press, 2008), p. 101.

[2] M. Brazier, 'Do No Harm – Do Patients Have Responsibilities Too?' (2006) 65 *Cambridge Law Journal* 397, 401.

[3] J. Raz, *The Morality of Freedom* (Oxford: Clarendon Press, 1986), p. 204.

develop agency and to deliver adequate choice. It is perfectionist in a way which traditional liberalism is not, in that it contends that the State (and the law) has a role in developing individual autonomy and in facilitating individual empowerment. In a legal context, this involves the development of a jurisprudence of positive rights, the early stages of which may be seen in some decisions of the ECtHR. This view also differs from the traditional liberal view in that it recognises a justification for interference with individual autonomy in some, albeit very limited, circumstances in which the traditional liberal view does not. Thus, this view requires an investigation of the consequences of decisions about treatment for the individual involved and of whether decisions made will impact on her broader rights to autonomy and liberty. This is because it is concerned with the exercise of power over the individual in a broader sense rather than simply in the context of treatment provision. It does not regard the choice between treatment refusal and ongoing detention (in, for example, the context of mental health or public health legislation) as a meaningful choice and it does not regard a model that allows treatment refusal at a cost of ongoing deprivation of liberty as respectful of autonomy.

A focus on empowerment is not restricted to patients with capacity. Rather, a theme throughout the book has been the need for empowerment in respect of all aspects of the law's approach to healthcare decision-making. The ideal of supported decision-making, which is so central to the CRPD, draws on notions of empowerment. This ideal, which is given practical effect in England and Wales in the MCA, requires that positive steps be taken to facilitate a person in reaching the standard for capacity where possible. If this is not possible, it requires workable mechanisms to ensure that a person without capacity can participate to the maximum extent possible in decisions which concern her. This ideal is equally important in respect of patients with a mental disorder where, as explored in Chapter 6, the impediments to empowerment are especially significant. In this context, further engagement with positive rights, including the establishment of a statutory right to information and to consensual treatment to the greatest extent possible (regardless of capacity) are necessary if the law is to begin to address the discrimination and stigmatisation experienced by many people with a mental disorder within (and outside) the healthcare system.

While a view of autonomy as empowerment is advocated throughout this book, the limitations of such a view must also be borne in mind. First, the law is not an especially effective instrument of empowerment. As was clear from the discussion of positive legal rights and obligations in Chapter 2, the jurisprudence to date suggests, at best, an incremental rather than a substantial enhancement of patient autonomy. Secondly, it is all too easy to develop the rhetoric of empowerment without actually changing the way in which power is exercised. The challenges faced in attempting to deliver on the ideal of participation emerged from the analysis of the MCA in Chapter 5. Thus, it was argued that there is an ongoing need for empirical investigation and legal oversight of the ways in which legislative attempts at empowerment operate. Thirdly, as also emerged from the discussion in Chapter 5, the choice of mechanisms of empowerment for people lacking capacity requires normative choices to be made. On the one hand, the law can attempt to empower people by allowing them, while they have legal capacity, to make decisions about their future incapacity; on the other, the law can focus on facilitating the participation by people lacking capacity in the healthcare decision-making process. While conflicts between these two mechanisms are by no means inevitable, they are not inconceivable. The cautious approach taken by the MCA was defended in Chapter 5 because of the recognition it affords to the current preferences of people lacking capacity. However, there is little doubt that this limits the effectiveness of advance decision-making mechanisms. Fourthly, a focus on empowerment cannot take account of all situations in respect of people lacking capacity. Even if empowerment could be delivered to the maximum extent possible, there will be situations where people cannot participate in decision-making in a meaningful way and where pretending otherwise would give rise to a new form of 'legal fiction', with all the dangers to which such fictions give rise. Accordingly, it was recognised that protective measures will continue to be needed. Thus, empowerment provides, at best, part of an appropriate framework for healthcare decision-making.

Capacity: a flawed gatekeeper

Within classic liberal accounts of autonomy, the requirement for capacity plays the central gatekeeper role, determining whose right of autonomy should be respected (and whose should not). Throughout this book, it has been argued that capacity is a less effective gatekeeper than liberal accounts presume. Capacity, as a concept, is fluid and, to a degree at least, malleable. The issues arising in this respect are both conceptual and practical. At a conceptual level, it was argued in Chapter 3 that the view of capacity as an internal phenomenon unrelated to surrounding circumstances is unsustainable. Chapter 3 also identified conceptual difficulties with the functional test for capacity in situations of fluctuating capacity and in situations where particular mental disorders, such as anorexia nervosa, have a profound impact on the identity of the person who suffers from the disorder. The extent of the practical problems with capacity assessment is more difficult to assess because of the law's delegation of much of the capacity assessment function to the healthcare profession. Nonetheless, as was argued in Chapter 4, the available empirical evidence suggests that capacity assessors encounter difficulties in performing this function and this raises doubts about the reliability of capacity assessments.

While capacity is a flawed gatekeeper, it is nonetheless probably the best way of sorting decisions. Certainly, the analysis in Chapter 3 of standards based on vulnerability or 'significantly impaired decision-making' suggested that these standards are no less malleable than capacity and that they present less potential for legal oversight or conceptual development. Thus, it has been argued that the establishment of ways to work within the limitations of capacity represents the best option for future development of the law in respect of healthcare decision-making. In this respect, a number of suggestions were made in Chapter 4 as regards how the operation of the capacity assessment process might be improved. First, more work, both empirical and conceptual, is needed in order to develop our understanding of the concept of capacity and the way in which the capacity requirement is applied in practice. Secondly, there is a need for closer judicial involvement with the capacity assessment process and for better legal guidance for healthcare professionals. Thirdly, legally enforceable capacity enhancement mechanisms are needed. In this respect, while the MCA may deservedly be lauded for recognising the principle of capacity enhancement, the lack of enforceable mechanisms to deliver on this undermines the potential of the MCA.

As a consequence of the limitations of capacity as a gatekeeper for the right of autonomy, conclusions about capacity are, in some situations at least, epistemologically fallible. It was argued in Chapter 3 that this fallibility has consequences that are both normative and practical. At a practical level, it was argued that it makes it very difficult to remove recourse to outcome from the capacity assessment process. If in doubt, assessors are more likely to base their decision on factors which seem to them to be objectively verifiable, including the wisdom, or otherwise, of the course of action proposed by the person whose capacity is being assessed. At a normative level, the fallibility of conclusions about capacity adds further support to the need for a meaningful participative model for decision-making for patients found to lack capacity as was advocated in Chapter 5.

It was argued in Chapter 3 that the fallibility of conclusions also provides a normative justification for the adoption of a variable standard for capacity depending on the levels of risk involved in the decision. Although it was recognised in Chapter 3 that this standard is by no means unproblematic, it was argued that the balance to be struck between autonomy and the competing interests of beneficence and the sanctity of life is different in a context of uncertainty and that this is best reflected in the adoption of a variable standard.

The role of law

The arguments made throughout this book suggest the need, in some instances at least, for better legal oversight of the way in which healthcare professionals operate. Chapter 4 identified the need for closer legal monitoring of the way in which capacity assessment is carried out, while Chapter 5 argued in favour of a conceptually more defensible legal framework for decision-making in respect of people lacking capacity and criticised the 'privatisation' of the decision-making process in the United States. However, the possible negative consequences of greater legal involvement must also be recognised. As David Rothman wryly notes, 'that dying has become a legal process is not an unqualified sign of progress'.[4] Rothman points out the irony in the fact that the response to the power imbalance between doctors and patients was the creation of other authority figures, whether in the form of judges, lawyers, ethicists, advocates or others.[5] In Rothman's words, '[t]o make certain that the patient's voice would be heard and respected demanded the support of a chorus, and as sometimes happens, the chorus can overwhelm the soloist'.[6] Rothman identifies the levels of dissatisfaction and demoralisation among the medical profession (in the United States) because of the increased 'legalisation' of the context within which healthcare professionals operate. Quoting from an article in the *New England Journal of Medicine*, he notes that physicians see themselves 'cast as wrongdoers and incompetents who yearly require new laws, regulations, admonitions, court decisions and exposés in order to make them more honest, ethical, competent, corrigible, and contrite'.[7]

---

[4] D. Rothman, *Strangers at the Bedside: A History of How Law and Bioethics Transformed Medical Decision Making* (New York: Basic Books, 1991), p. 261.

[5] *Ibid.*   [6] *Ibid.*

[7] *Ibid.*, p. 260, quoting from S. Radovsky, 'US Medical Practice Before Medicare and Now: Differences and Consequences' (1990) 322 *New England Journal of Medicine* 263.

Jonathan Montgomery argues that closer legal involvement may contribute to the 'demoralisation' of medicine in a different sense.[8] Montgomery agues that the 'non-interventionist stance' formerly taken by the law to questions of medical ethics was based on 'a belief that [the medical profession's] practice enshrines moral values and the aspiration to construct a legal relationship between patients and health professionals that enables that morality to flourish'.[9] Montgomery contrasts this position with that taken by 'new model' judges, whom he considers to be exemplified by Munby J (as he then was).[10] This approach 'rejects deference to the health professionals, sees healthcare as equivalent to other (commercial) enterprises and, therefore, to be regulated from outside without any trust in industry values and without any special rules for healthcare'. Montgomery suggests that this approach 'constructs the position of the patient as consumer dictating what should happen, with little scope for moral independence of health professionals'.[11] Such a construction, he argues, is 'essentially value neutral' and serves to 'marginalise the moral content of medical law'.[12] Montgomery argues that as a consequence of this approach, the moral values underpinning the practice of medicine are 'supplanted by an amoral commitment to choice and consumerism'.[13] This concern is echoed by Margaret Brazier in her discussion of why the issue of patient responsibilities needs to be addressed by the law. Brazier argues that '[m]edical practitioners who find themselves subject to what they perceive as unethical demands will consider two options. Some may well embrace the consumer-orientated model of medicine rejoicing in the ensuing profit and freedom. Beneficence will fade away'. [14]

There are good reasons for concern regarding the impact of free-market consumerism on healthcare practices.[15] This is especially the case in respect of the many patients who do not comply with the free-market ideal of the consumer who is self-directed, informed, confident and wealthy. A legal framework which accentuates free-mark consumerism should be regarded with scepticism. However, it is not clear that closer legal engagement is necessarily a demoralising force (in Montgomery's sense). Indeed, it might well be argued that closer legal engagement may have the opposite effect. The involvement of the law may offer better scope for moral engagement, discussion and critique than was possible

[8] Montgomery, J. 'Law and the Demoralisation of Medicine' (2006) 26 *Legal Studies* 185.
[9] *Ibid.*, 206.   [10] *Ibid.*   [11] *Ibid.*   [12] *Ibid.*   [13] *Ibid.*, 186.
[14] Brazier, 'Do No Harm', 422.
[15] On the role of markets in healthcare provision, see J. Harrington, 'Visions of Utopia: Markets, Medicine and the National Health Service' (2009) 29 *Legal Studies* 379.

in 'the good old days that understood doctors to be good old boys who could work out moral problems among themselves in the locker room'.[16] This has the potential to be as valuable for healthcare professionals as for other participants in the system. The private 'dyad of the doctor and the patient alone in the examining room'[17] offered little support for health-care professionals facing difficult treatment decisions. Nor is it clear that a legal framework which does not take itself seriously can contribute to the development of moral structures to accommodate the new challenges facing health care. As matters stand, the law has delegated certain tasks to the healthcare profession. Yet the applicable legal framework provides little indication of what is expected and the law has shown relatively little interest in how the task is carried out. This failure is likely to contribute to healthcare professionals' disinterest in, and dismissal of, the 'legal' concern for protecting patients' rights. If the law is not concerned about maintaining legal standards, it is difficult to see why healthcare professionals should be expected to be.

Equally, however, it is clear that healthcare decision-making is not, and should not be, simply about the law. An awareness of the potential for negative (as well as positive) consequences arising from legal involvement in the process of healthcare decision-making is essential for the development of appropriate legal frameworks. If, as has been argued in this book, healthcare professionals must recognise their obligations in respect of the law, so too must law-makers listen more closely to the contribution of healthcare professionals as regards what constitute appropriate and effective legal mechanisms. Mechanisms that appear to protect rights when viewed from a legal perspective may seem to healthcare professionals to constitute little more than bureaucratic annoyances. In this respect, critical assessment of the law by healthcare professionals has an important contribution to make in the development of appropriate legal frameworks and the facilitation of such assessment must be a goal of policy. The most appropriate approach to law-making is not, as is currently the case, to develop legal frameworks and then leave the way they work to the discretion of the healthcare profession. Rather, it is necessary to monitor closely how the law operates from the perspective of all parties involved and to reassess critically the normative bases for the law in light of the day-to-day operation of the law in practice from this broad perspective.

[16] D. Callahan, 'Autonomy: A Moral Good, Not a Moral Obsession' (1984) 14 *The Hastings Centre Report* 40, 42.
[17] Rothman, *Strangers at the Bedside*, p. 9.

Human rights and patient rights

The arguments made throughout this book have drawn to a significant extent on human rights instruments, especially the European Convention on Human Rights (ECHR) and the United Nations Convention on the Rights of Persons with Disabilities (CRPD). Thus, it was argued in Chapter 2 that the legal formulation of positive obligations in respect of autonomy is most likely to find a basis in the jurisprudence of the European Court of Human Rights (ECtHR). ECtHR jurisprudence was also presented in Chapter 5 as providing a basis for better engagement with the right to dignity, a right of particular significance in respect of decision-making for people lacking capacity. It was also argued in Chapter 6 that the protection of rights arising under the ECHR requires restrictions on compulsory treatment for a mental disorder and the development of better oversight and review mechanisms in this context. A human rights framework also provides a mechanism within which to deal with questions of limitations on the right of autonomy. The contribution of the CRPD is likely to be most significant in providing human rights support for the development of legal obligations to empower patients, in the contexts of capacity assessment, decision-making on behalf of people lacking capacity and treatment for a mental disorder.

However, there are risks in an over-reliance on human rights standards, especially when these are derived from international or European human rights instruments rather than domestically initiated bills of rights. First, as discussed in earlier chapters, any framework for protection that requires litigation in order to assert rights is inevitably limited in the protections which it can afford, especially in respect of vulnerable patients who lack the resources to pursue claims. Secondly, as Baroness Hale has noted extra-judicially, the House of Lords (now the Supreme Court) and the lower courts are reluctant 'to imply obligations into the Convention ahead of the Strasbourg case-law'.[18] She argues that this caution derives from a belief that '[i]t is not for the courts to tell Parliament that it has got things wrong if Strasbourg would not do so'.[19] Insofar as this is the case, the development of domestic jurisprudence may, in fact, be impeded by the possibility of later ECtHR jurisprudence.

Thirdly, even when a supra-national instrument has been incorporated into a domestic legal framework, as is the case with the ECHR in the United

---

[18] B. Hale, 'The Human Rights Act and Mental Health Law: Has it Helped?' (2007) 13 *Journal of Mental Health Law* 7, 17.

[19] *Ibid.*, 17–18.

Kingdom, there is a risk that the rights implicated may be regarded as externally imposed rather than derived from principle. Merris Amos notes the 'fierce criticism' which has been levelled against the Human Rights Act 1998 (HRA) in its 'relatively short life'.[20] She notes the lack of respect for the HRA 'throughout elements of the media and amongst prominent political and public figures'.[21] In the words of the (then) Lord Chancellor, the HRA has not become 'an iconic statement of liberty'.[22] Although criticisms of the HRA have not tended to relate to the rights issues discussed in this book,[23] an attitude of scepticism on the part of stakeholders has the potential to undermine the credibility of human rights based argument in all contexts. Given that many of the human rights solutions discussed in this book require commitment on the part of healthcare professionals, the consequences of scepticism could be significant. This problem is accentuated by a lack of principled discussion in the domestic courts of the issues arising. Accordingly, the future development of the law in respect of healthcare decision-making requires rigorous engagement by domestic courts with questions of rights, rather than simple reliance on ECtHR jurisprudence.

Empirical evaluation and the law in practice

A final theme which has emerged in respect of all aspects of the discussion in this book has been the need to understand more about how healthcare decisions are made in practice. The real location of decision-making powers must be understood, regardless of whether or not the person concerned has decision-making capacity. This kind of understanding can only be achieved through close empirical study of the realities of healthcare decision-making. We need to know more about the way in which people make decisions about their health care, the heuristics they apply and the impact of information and communication on how decisions are made. As relational theorists have pointed out, we also need to appreciate the non-medical factors that impact on decisions about health care. The impact of economic and social circumstances, of religious adherence and

---

[20] M. Amos, 'Problems With the Human Rights Act 1998 and How to Remedy Them: Is a Bill of Rights the Answer?' (2009) 72 *Modern Law Review* 883, 883.

[21] *Ibid.*, 888.

[22] The Right Honourable Jack Straw MP, Lord Chancellor 'Towards a Bill of Rights and Responsibility,' 21 January 2008 (available at www.justice.gov.uk), quoted in Amos, *ibid.*

[23] Most criticisms have related to public safety and terrorist threats: see Amos, *ibid.*, 883–4.

of cultural factors must be understood in order to facilitate the development of the optimal context for healthcare decision-making and to deliver on the ideal of autonomy as empowerment as put forward in Chapter 1.

It is also essential to understand the role played by judges and non-judicial decision-makers within decision-making processes. Thus, it was argued in Chapter 4 that it is necessary to study the way in which assessors make decisions about capacity; how well they understand the test they apply; and whether they are actually performing their legislatively required function of facilitating the development of patients' capacity. It is also important to investigate the factors which influence assessors in reaching conclusions about capacity and the impact of race, gender, cultural, religious and other factors on the assessment process. The role of healthcare professionals, advocates and other representatives who act for and in respect of people covered by the MCA or the MHA must also be investigated. In particular, it is necessary to monitor the extent to which legislative rhetoric that suggests a shift towards greater empowerment is matched by action on the ground. The accumulation of these kinds of data is essential for the evaluation of current legal strategies as well as for the future development of the law.

The need for empirically justifiable policies is recognised by the CRPD, which requires States Parties to 'collect appropriate information, including statistical and research data, to enable them to formulate and implement policies to give effect' to the CRPD[24] and to disaggregate this information in order 'to help assess the implementation of States Parties' obligations'.[25] In meeting the need for data, it is essential that the people affected by state policies are involved in the determination of the research agenda and not just as research subjects. This is especially important in respect of the collection of data regarding people lacking capacity and people with mental disorders.[26] There is also a need for more legal involvement in the empirical work conducted. This book has reviewed a fair number of empirical studies, all of which have contributed to a better understanding of how different aspects of the healthcare decision-making process work. With some notable exceptions, most of these have not included a legal input. This constitutes a significant gap in the literature. A realistic assessment of legal policy requires the involvement of lawyers as well as of the other professionals who are charged with giving effect to the law in practice.

---

[24] CRPD, Art. 31(1).   [25] CRPD, Art. 31(20).

[26] This point is also recognised in the CRPD, Art. 33(3) which requires that persons with disabilities and their representative organisations must be involved in and participate fully in the monitoring of the CRPD.

Final observations

As is clear from the discussion throughout this book, the issues which arise are not easy to resolve. This is unsurprising. It is much easier to develop legal frameworks around the ideal of autonomous self-reliance than it is to accommodate the much less straightforward needs of real, connected, embodied people. What is important, however, is that we think about what we want from the law in respect of healthcare decision-making and that we rigorously interrogate the law's offerings not just for what they promise but for what they can deliver.

BIBLIOGRAPHY

Abernethy, Virginia, 'Compassion, Control and Decisions About Competency' (1984) 141 *American Journal of Psychiatry* 53

Allen, Neil, 'Restricting Movement or Depriving Liberty?' (2009) 18 *Journal of Mental Health Law* 19

Alonzi, Andrew and Pringle, Mike, 'The Mental Capacity Act 2005' (2007) 335 *British Medical Journal* 898

Amos, Merris, 'Problems With the Human Rights Act 1998 and How to Remedy Them: Is a Bill of Rights the Answer?' (2009) 72 *Modern Law Review* 883

Anckarsäter, H., Radovic, S., Svennerlind, C., Höglund, P. and Radovic, F., 'Mental Disorder is a Cause of Crime: The Cornerstone of Forensic Psychiatry' (2009) 32 *International Journal of Law and Psychiatry* 342

Annas, George, 'The Case of Mary Hier: When Substituted Judgment Becomes Sleight of Hand' (1984) 14 (4) *Hastings Center Report* 23

'When Procedures Limit Rights: From Quinlan to Conroy' (1985) 15 (2) *Hastings Center Report* 24

Some Choice: Law, Medicine and the Market (New York: Oxford University Press, 1998)

Annas, George and Densberger, Joan, 'Competence to Refuse Medical Treatment: Autonomy and Paternalism' (1984) 15 *Toledo Law Review* 561

Anon, 'Medical Technology and the Law' (1990) 103 *Harvard Law Review* 1643

'Developments in the Law: The Law of Mental Illness' (2008) 121 *Harvard Law Review* 1114

Appelbaum, Paul, *Almost a Revolution: Mental Health Law and the Limits of Change* (New York: Oxford University Press, 1994)

'Ought We to Require Emotional Capacity as a Part of Decisional Competence?' (1999) 8 *Kennedy Institute of Ethics Journal* 377

'Assessment of Patients' Competence to Consent to Treatment' (2007) 357 *New England Journal of Medicine* 1834.

Appelbaum, Paul and Grisso, Thomas, 'Assessing Patients' Capacities to Consent to Treatment' (1988) 319 *New England Journal of Medicine* 1635

Appelbaum, Paul and Roth, Loren H., 'Competency to Consent to Research: A Psychiatric Overview' (1982) 39 *Archives of General Psychiatry* 951

Appelbaum, Paul and Grisso, Thomas, 'The MacArthur Treatment Competence Study I: Mental Illness and Competence to Consent to Treatment' (1995) 19, *Law and Human Behavior*, 105

'Patients who Refuse Treatment in Medical Hospitals' (1983) 250 *Journal of the American Medical Association* 1296

Assessment of Mental Capacity: Guidance for Doctors and Lawyers (3rd edn) (London: BMA, Law Society, 2009)

Atkins, Kim, 'Autonomy and the Subjective Character of Experience' (2000) 17 *Journal of Applied Philosophy* 7

Baier, Annette, *Postures of the Mind: Essays on Mind and Morals* (Minneapolis: University of Minnesota Press, 1985)

Bailey-Harris, Rebecca, 'Pregnancy, Autonomy and the Refusal of Treatment' (1998) 114 *Law Quarterly Review* 550

Bamforth Review of Mental Health and Learning Disability (Belfast: The Stationery Office, 2007)

Banerjee, Sube, *The Use of Antipsychotic Medication for People With Dementia: Time for Action* (London: Department of Health, 2009)

Bartlett, Peter, 'Doctors as Fiduciaries: Equitable Regulation of the Doctor–Patient Relationship' (1997) 5 *Medical Law Review* 193

'Adults, Mental Illness and Incapacity: Convergence and Overlap in Legal Regulation' (2003) 25 *Journal of Social Welfare and Family Law* 341

'The Test of Compulsion in Mental Health Law: Capacity, Therapeutic Benefit and Dangerousness as Possible Criteria' (2003) 11 *Medical Law Review* 326

'Psychiatric Treatment: In the Absence of Law?' (2006) 14 *Medical Law Review* 124

'A Matter of Necessity: Enforced Treatment under the Mental Health Act' (2007) 15 *Medical Law Review* 86

Blackstone's Guide to the Mental Capacity Act 2005 (2nd edn) (Oxford University Press, 2008)

Bartlett, Peter and Sandland, Ralph, *Mental Health Law: Policy and Practice* (3rd edn) (Oxford University Press, 2007)

Bartlett, Peter, Lewis, Oliver and Thorold, Oliver *Mental Disability and the European Convention on Human Rights* (Leiden: Martinus Nijhoff, 2007)

Bauby, Jean-Dominique, *The Diving Bell and the Butterfly* (Paris: A. Knopf, 1997)

Beauchamp, Tom L. and Childress, James F., *Principles of Biomedical Ethics* (1st edn) (New York: Oxford University Press, 1979); (4th edn) (New York: Oxford University Press, 1994); (5th edn) (New York: Oxford University Press, 2001); (6th edn) (New York: Oxford University Press, 2008)

Beecher, Henry, 'Ethics and Clinical Research' (1966) 274 *New England Journal of Medicine* 1354

Behnke, Steven H. and Saks, Elyn R., 'Therapeutic Jurisprudence: Informed Consent as a Clinical Indication for the Chronically Suicidal Patient With Borderline Personality Disorder' (1998) 31 *Loyola of Los Angeles Law Review* 945

Bellhouse, John, Holland, Anthony, Clare, Isobel and Gunn, Michael, 'Capacity-Based Mental Health Legislation and its Impact on Clinical Practice: 2) Treatment in Hospital' (2003) *Journal of Mental Health Law* 24

Benaroyo, Lazare and Widdershoven, Guy, 'Competence in Mental Health Care: A Hermeneutic Perspective' (2004) 12 *Health Care Analysis* 295

Bergler, Jane, Pennington, Cleo and Metcalfe, Madeline, 'Informed Consent: How Much Does the Patient Understand?" (1980) 27 *Clinical Pharmacology and Therapeutics* 435

Bersoff, Donald, 'Judicial Deference to Nonlegal Decisionmakers: Imposing Simplistic Solutions on Problems of Cognitive Complexity in Mental Disability Law' (1992) 46 *Southern Methodist University Law Review* 329

Beyleveld, Deryck and Brownsword, Roger, *Human Dignity in Bioethics and Biolaw* (Oxford University Press, 2002)

Blackhall, Leslie, Murphy, Sheila, Frank, Gelya, Michel, Vicky and Azen, Stanley, 'Ethnicity and Attitudes Towards Patient Autonomy' (1995) 274 *Journal of American Medical Association* 820

Bopp, James Jr and Avila, Daniel, 'The Sirens' Lure of Invented Consent: A Critique of Autonomy-Based Surrogate Decision Making for Legally-Incapacitated Older Persons' (1991) 42 *Hastings Law Journal* 779

Boyle, Aisling, 'The Law and Incapacity Determinations: A Conflict of Governance' (2008) 71 *Modern Law Review* 433

Bradshaw, David (ed.) *Virginia Woolf: Selected Essays* (Oxford University Press, 2008)

Brazier, Margaret, 'Patient Autonomy and Consent to Treatment: The Role of the Law?' (1987) 7 *Legal Studies* 169

'Hard Cases Make Bad Law' (1997) 23 *Journal of Medical Ethics* 341

'Do No Harm – Do Patients Have Responsibilities Too?' (2006) 65 *Cambridge Law Journal* 397

Brazier, Margaret and Bridge, Caroline, 'Coercion or Caring: Analysing Adolescent Autonomy' (1996) 16 *Legal Studies* 84

Brazier, Margaret and Cave, Emma, *Medicine, Patients and the Law* (4th edn) (London: Penguin, 2007)

Brazier, Margaret and Harris, John, 'Public Health and Private Lives' (1996) 4 *Medical Law Review* 171

Brazier, Margaret and Miola, José, 'Bye-Bye Bolam: A Medical Litigation Revolution?' (2000) 8 *Medical Law Review* 85

Breden, Torsten and Vollmann, Jochen, 'The Cognitive-Based Approach of Capacity Assessment in Psychiatry: A Philosophical Critique of the MacCAT-T' (2004) 12 *Health Care Analysis* 273

Bridgeman, Jo, *Parental Responsibility, Young Children and Healthcare Law* (Cambridge University Press, 2007)

Brock, Dan, 'Decisionmaking Competence and Risk' (1991) 5 *Bioethics* 107

Brody, Baruch A., *Life and Death Decision Making* (New York: Oxford University Press, 1988)

Broverman, I, Broverman, D, Clarkson, F, Rosenkrantz, P and Vogel, S., 'Sex Role Stereotypes and Clinical Judgements of Mental Health' (1970) 34 *Journal of Consulting and Clinical Psychology* 1

Brownsword, Roger, 'The Cult of Consent: Fixation and Fallacy' (2004) 15 *King's College Law Journal* 223

Buchanan, Allen, 'Advance Directives and the Personal Identity Problem' (1988) 17 *Philosophy and Public Affairs* 277

Buchanan, Allen and Brock, Dan, *Deciding for Others: The Ethics of Surrogate Decision Making* (Cambridge University Press, 1989)

Buller, Tom, 'Competence and Risk-Relativity' (2001) 15 *Bioethics* 93

Byrne, D. J., Napier, A. and Cuschieri, A., 'How Informed is Signed Consent?' (1988) 296 *British Medical Journal* 839

Cairns, R., Maddock, C., Buchanan, A., David, A., Hayward, P., Richardson, G. and Szmukler, G., 'Prevalence and Predictors of Mental Incapacity in Psychiatric In-Patients' (2005) 187 *British Journal of Psychiatry* 379

Cale, Gita, 'Risk-Related Standards of Competence: Continuing the Debate Over Risk-Related Standards of Competence' (1999) 13 *Bioethics* 132

Callahan, Daniel, 'Autonomy: A Moral Good, Not a Moral Obsession' (1984) 14 *Hastings Center Report* 40

   'Terminating Life-Sustaining Treatment of the Demented' (1995) 25 *Hastings Center Report* 25

   'Can the Moral Commons Survive Autonomy?' (1996) 26 *Hastings Center Report* 41

   'Individual Good and Common Good: A Communitarian Approach to Bioethics' (2003) 46 *Perspectives in Biology and Medicine* 496

Calsyn, R. J., Winter, J. P. and Morse, G. A., 'Do Consumers Who Have a Choice Have Better Outcomes?' (2000) 36 *Community Mental Health Journal* 149

Cameron, L. and Murphy, J., 'Enabling Young People With a Learning Disability to Make Choices at a Time of Transition' (2002) 30 *British Journal of Learning Disabilities* 105

Campbell, Tom and Heginbotham, Christopher, *Mental Illness: Prejudice, Discrimination and the Law* (Aldershot: Dartmouth, 1991)

Cantor, Norman, 'Prospective Autonomy: On the Limits of Shaping One's Postcompetence Medical Fate' (1992) 13 *Journal of Contemporary Health Law and Policy* 13

   'Discarding Substituted Judgment and Best Interests: Toward a Constructive Preference Standard for Dying Previously Competent Patients Without Advance Instructions' (1996) 48 *Rutgers Law Review* 1193

Carney, Terry, 'Mental Health Law in Postmodern Society? Time for New Paradigms?' (2003) 10 *Psychiatry, Psychology and Law* 12

   'The Mental Health Service Crisis of Neoliberalism: An Antipodean Perspective' (2008) 31 *International Journal of Law and Psychiatry* 101

Carney, Terry and Tait, David, *The Adult Guardianship Experiment* (Annandale, NSW: Federation Press, 1997)

'Sterilization: Tribunal Experiments in Popular Justice?' (1999) 22 *International Journal of Law and Psychiatry* 177

Carney, Terry, Beaupert, Fleur, Perry, Julia and Tait, David, 'Advocacy and Participation in Mental Health Cases: Realisable Rights or Pipe-dreams?' (2008) 26 *Law in Context* 125

Carson, David, 'Disabling Progress: The Law Commission's Proposals on Mentally Incapacitated Adults' Decision-Making' (1993) 15 *Journal of Social Welfare and Family Law* 304

Cassell, Eric, 'Unanswered Questions: Bioethics and Human Relationships' (2007) 37 *Hastings Center Report* 20

Cassell, Eric, Leon, Andrew, and Kaufman, Stacey, 'Preliminary Evidence of Impaired Thinking in Sick Patients' (2001) 134 *Annals of Internal Medicine* 1120

Cassileth, B. R., Zupkis, R. V., Sutton-Smith, K. and March, V., (1980) 302 *New England Journal of Medicine* 896

Chadwick, J. and Mann, W. N., trans. *Hippocratic Writings* (London: Penguin Books, 1950)

Charland, Louis, 'Is Mr Spock Mentally Competent?: Competence to Consent and Emotion' (1998) 5 *Philosophy, Psychiatry and Psychology* 67

'Appreciation and Emotion: Theoretical Reflections on the MacArthur Treatment Competence Study' (1999) 8 *Kennedy Institute of Ethics Journal* 359

Charlesworth, Max, *Bioethics in a Liberal Society* (Cambridge University Press, 1993)

Chesler, Phyllis *Women and Madness* (New York: Doubleday, 1972)

Childress, James, Meslin, Eric and Shapiro, Harold *Belmont Revisited: Ethical Principles for Research With Human Subjects* (Washington: Georgetown University Press, 2005)

Christman, John, 'Constructing the Inner Citadel: Recent Work on the Concept of Autonomy' (1988) 99 *Ethics* 109

'Relational Autonomy, Liberal Individualism, and the Social Construction of Selves' (2004) 117 *Philosophical Studies* 143

Christman, John (ed.) *The Inner Citadel: Essays on Individual Autonomy* (New York: Oxford University Press, 1989)

Churchill, R., Owen, G., Singh, S. and Hotopf, M., *International Experiences of Using Community Treatment Orders* (London: Department of Health, Institute of Psychiatry, 2007)

Churchland, Patricia, *Neurophilosophy: Towards a Unified Science of the Mind-Brain* (Cambridge, MA: MIT Press, 1986)

Churchland, Paul, *Neurophilosophy at Work* (New York: Cambridge University Press, 2007)

Ciccone, J. R., Tokoli, J. F., Clements, C. D. and Gift, T. E., 'Right to Refuse Treatment: Impact of *Rivers* v *Katz*' (1990) 18 *Bulletin of the American Academy of Psychiatry and Law* 203

Clegg, Jennifer, 'Practice in Focus: A Hermeneutic Approach to Research Ethics' (2004) 32 *British Journal of Learning Disabilities* 186

Clouser, K. Danner and Gert, Bernard, 'A Critique of Principalism' (1996) 15 *Journal of Medical Philosophy* 219.

Code of Medical Ethics (Chicago: American Medical Association, 2008–9)

Code of Practice to the Mental Health Act 1983, Revd 2008 (London: The Stationery Office, 2008)

Coggan, John, 'Ignoring the Moral and Intellectual Shape of the Law After *Bland*: the Unintended Side-Effect of a Sorry Compromise' (2007) 27 *Legal Studies* 110

Consent: Patients and Doctors Making Decisions Together (London: General Medical Council, 2008)

Consultation Paper on the Code of Practice to the Mental Capacity Act 2005 (CP 05/06) March 2006

Corrigan, P. and Miller, F., 'Shame, Blame, and Contamination' (2004) 13 *Journal of Mental Health* 537

Cox White, Becky, *Competence to Consent* (Washington DC: Georgetown University Press, 1994)

Crenshaw, Kimberle, 'Demarginalizing the Intersection of Race and Sex: A Black Feminist Critique of Antidiscrimination Doctrine, Feminist Theory and Antiracist Politics' [1989] *University of Chicago Legal Forum* 139

Culver, Charles M. and Gert, Bernard., 'The Inadequacy of Incompetence' (1990) 68 *Milbank Quarterly* 619

Cutter, Mary Ann Gardell and Shelp, Earl E. (eds.) *Competency: A Study of Informal Competency Determinations in Primary Care* (Dordrecht: Kluwer, 1991)

Damasio, Antonio R., *Descartes' Error: Emotion, Reason and the Human Brain* (New York: Grosset/Putnam, 1994)

Dan-Cohen, Meir, *Harmful Thoughts: Essays on Law, Self and Morality* (Princeton University Press, 2002)

Davies, Mark, *Medical Self-Regulation: Crises and Change* (Aldershot: Ashgate, 2007)

de Beauvoir, Simone, *The Second Sex* (1949) Parshley, H. M., trans. (London: Penguin, 1972)

de Vries, Raymond and Subedi, Janardan (eds.) *Bioethics and Society: Constructing the Ethical Enterprise* (Upper Saddle River, NJ: Prentice Hall, 1998)

Deci, Edward, *Intrinsic Motivation* (New York; Plenum Press, 1975)

Delaney, Jeffrey J., 'Specific Intent: Substituted Judgment and Best Interests: A Nationwide Analysis of an Individual's Right to Die' (1991) 11 *Pace Law Review* 565

deMarco, Joseph, 'Competence and Paternalism' (2002) 16 *Bioethics* 231

Dennett, Daniel *Elbow Room: The Varieties of Free Will Worth Wanting* (Cambridge, MA: MIT Press, 1984)

Dennis, Deborah and Monahan, John (eds.) *Coercion and Aggressive Community Treatment: A New Frontier in Mental Health Law* (New York: Plenum Press, 1996)

Destro, Robert 'Quality-of-Life Ethics and Constitutional Jurisprudence: The Demise of Natural Rights and Equal Protection for the Disabled and Incompetent' (1986) 2 *Journal of Contemporary Health Law and Policy* 71

Devaney, Sarah, 'Autonomy Rules OK' (2005) 13 *Medical Law Review* 102

Dhanda, Amita, 'Legal Capacity in the Disability Rights Convention: Stranglehold of the Past or Lodestar for the Future?' (2006–2007) 34 *Syracuse Journal of International Law and Commerce* 429

Diesfeld, Kate and Freckelton, Ian (eds.) *Involuntary Detention and Therapeutic Jurisprudence: International Perspectives on Civil Commitment* (Aldershot: Ashgate, 2003)

Donnelly, Mary, 'Decision Making for Mentally Incompetent People: The Empty Formula of Best Interests' (2001) 20 *Medicine and Law* 405

   Consent: Bridging the Gap Between Doctor and Patient (Cork University Press, 2002)

   'Assessing Legal Capacity: Process and the Operation of the Functional Test' [2007] 2 *Judicial Studies Institute Journal* 141

   'From Autonomy to Dignity: Treatment for Mental Disorders and the Focus for Patient Rights' (2008) 26 *Law in Context* 37

   'Community-Based Care and Compulsion: What Role for Human Rights?' (2008) 15 *Journal of Law and Medicine* 783

   'The Right of Autonomy in Irish Law' (2008) 14 *Medico-Legal Journal of Ireland* 34

   'Assessing Capacity under the Mental Capacity Act 2005: Delivering on the Functional Approach?' (2009) 29 *Legal Studies* 464

   'Best Interests, Patient Participation and the Mental Capacity Act 2005' (2009) 17 *Medical Law Review* 1

   'Public Health and Patient Rights: S v HSE' (2009) 15 *Medico-Legal Journal of Ireland* 66

Douglas, Gillian, 'The Retreat From *Gillick*' (1992) 55 *Modern Law Review* 569

Drane, James, 'The Many Faces of Competency' (1985) 15 *Hastings Center Report* 17

Dresser, Rebecca, 'Life, Death, and Incompetent Patients: Conceptual Infirmities and Hidden Values in the Law' (1986) 28 *Arizona Law Review* 373

   'Relitigating Life and Death' (1990) 50 *Ohio State Law Journal* 425

   'Missing Persons: Legal Perceptions of Incompetent Patients' (1994) 46 *Rutgers Law Review* 609

'Dworkin on Dementia: Elegant Theory, Questionable Policy' (1995) 25 *Hastings Center Report* 32

'*Schiavo*: A Hard Case Makes Questionable Law' (2004) 34 *Hastings Center Report* 8

'Schiavo's Legacy: The Need for an Objective Standard' (2005) 35 *Hastings Center Report* 20

du Bois, Ellen, Dunlop, Mary, Gilligan, Carol, MacKinnon, Catherine, Menkel-Meadow, Cassie, 'Feminist Discourse, Moral Values and the Law: A Conversation' (1985) 34 Buffalo Law Review

Dunn, Laura, Nowrangi, Milap, Palmer, Barton, Jeste, Dilip and Saks, Elyn, 'Assessing Decisional Capacity for Clinical Research or Treatment: A Review of Instruments' (2006) 163 *American Journal of Psychiatry* 1323

Dunn, Michael, Clare, Isabel and Holland, Anthony, 'To Empower or to Protect? Constructing the "Vulnerable Adult" in English Law and Public Policy' (2008) 28 *Legal Studies* 234

Dunne, Elizabeth, *The Views of Adult Users of the Public Sector Mental Health Service* (Dublin: Mental Health Commission, 2006)

Dupré, Catherine, 'Unlocking Human Dignity: Towards a Theory for the 21st Century' (2009) *European Human Rights Law Review* 190

Dworkin, Gerald, *The Theory and Practice of Autonomy* (New York: Cambridge University Press, 1988)

Dworkin, Ronald, *Taking Rights Seriously* (London: Duckworth, 1977)

A Matter of Principle (Oxford University Press, 1985)

Sovereign Virtue: The Theory and Practice of Equality (Cambridge, MA: Harvard University Press, 2000)

Life's Dominion: An Argument About Abortion, Euthanasia, and Individual Freedom (New York: Alfred A. Knopf, 1993)

Eastman, Nigel, 'Mental Health Law: Civil Liberties and the Principle of Reciprocity' (1994) 308 *British Medical Journal* 43

Eastman, Nigel and Dhar, Rajeev, 'The Role and Assessment of Mental Incapacity: A Review' (2000) 13 *Current Opinion in Psychiatry* 557

Eastman, Nigel and Peay, Jill (eds.) *Law Without Enforcement: Integrating Mental Health and Justice* (Oxford: Hart Publishing, 1999)

ECT Review Group, *Systematic Review of the Efficacy and Safety of Electroconvulsive Therapy* (London: Department of Health, 2003)

Elliot, Carl, *Bioethics, Culture and Identity: A Philosophical Disease* (New York: Routledge, 1999)

Elliott, Tracey, 'Body Dysmorphic Disorder, Radical Surgery and the Limits of Consent' (2009) 17 *Medical Law Review* 149

Emanuel, L. L., Emanuel, E. J., Stoeckle, J. D., Hummel, L. R. and Barry, M. J., 'Advance Directives: Stability of Patients' Treatment Choices' (1994) 154 *Archives of Internal Medicine* 209

Engelhardt, Tristram, *The Foundations of Bioethics* (New York: Oxford University Press, 1986)

Enright, Mairéad, 'Choice, Culture and the Politics of Belonging: The Emerging Law of Forced and Arranged Marriage' (2009) 72 *Modern Law Review* 331

Estroff, Sue, Lachicotte, William, Illingworth, Linda and Johnston, Anna, 'Everybody's Got a Little Mental Illness: Accounts of Illness and Self Among People With Severe Persistent Mental Illness' (1991) 5 *Medical Anthropology Quarterly* 331

European Committee for the Prevention of Torture, *8th General Report on the CPT's Activities Covering the Period 1 January to 31 December 1997* (CPT/Inf (98) 12) (1998))

Evans, K., Warner, J. and Jackson, E., 'How Much do Emergency Healthcare Workers Know about Capacity and Consent?' (2007) 24 *Emergency Medicine Journal* 291

Expert Committee Review of the Mental Health Act 1983 (London: Department of Health, HMSO, 1999)

Faden, G., Bebbington, P. and Kuipers, L., 'The Burden of Care: The Impact of Functional Psychiatric Illness on the Patient's Family, (1989) 150 *British Journal of Psychiatry* 285

Faden, Ruth and Beauchamp, Tom, *A History and Theory of Informed Consent* (New York: Oxford University Press, 1986)

Fagerlin, A., Ditto, P., Ayers Hawkins, N., Schneider, C. and Smucker, W., 'The Use of Advance Directives in End-of-Life Decision Making: Problems and Possibilities' (2002) 46 *American Behavioral Scientist* 268

Fallowfield, LJ, Hall A., Maguire GP., Baum M., 'Psychological Outcomes of Different Treatment Policies in Women With Early Breast Cancer Outside a Clinical Trial' (1990) 301 *British Medical Journal* 575

Feinberg, Joel, 'Legal Paternalism' (1977) 1 *Canadian Journal of Philosophy* 106
The Moral Limits of the Criminal Law: Vol III: Harm to Self (New York: Oxford University Press, 1986)

Feldman, David, 'Human Dignity as a Legal Value: Part I' [1999] *Public Law* 682
'Human Dignity as a Legal Value: Part 2' [2000] *Public Law* 61
Civil Liberties and Human Rights in England and Wales (2nd edn) (Oxford University Press, 2002)

Fennell, Phil, 'Inscribing Paternalism in the Law: Consent to Treatment and Mental Disorder' (1990) 17 *Journal of Law and Society* 29
'Informal Compulsion: The Psychiatric Treatment of Juveniles under Common Law' (1992) 14 *Journal of Social Welfare and Family Law* 311
'Balancing Care and Control: Guardianship, Community Treatment Orders and Patient Safeguards' (1992) *International Journal of Law and Psychiatry* 205

'Statutory Authority to Treat, Relatives and Treatment Proxies' (1994) 2 *Medical Law Review* 30

Treatment Without Consent: Law, Psychiatry and the Treatment of Mentally Disordered People Since 1845 (London: Routledge, 1995)

'The Mental Capacity Act 2005, the Mental Health Act 1983, and the Common Law' [2005] *Journal of Mental Health Law* 163

Mental Health: The New Law (Bristol: Jordans, 2007)

Fineman, Martha, *The Autonomy Myth: A Theory of Dependency* (New York: New Press, 2003)

Firlik, Andrew, 'Margo's Logo' (1991) 265 *Journal of the American Medical Association* 201

First Report of the Joint Committee on the Draft Mental Health Bill HL Paper 79–1; HC 95–1 (London: The Stationary Office, 2005)

Fletcher, Ruth, Fox, Marie and McCandless, Julie, 'Legal Embodiment: Analysing the Body of Healthcare Law' (2008) 16 *Medical Law Review* 321

Folstein, M. F., Folstein, S. E. and McHugh, P. R., 'Mini Mental State – A Practical Method for Grading the Cognitive State of Patients for the Clinician' (1975) 12 *Journal of Psychiatric Research* 189

Fortin, J., 'Children's Rights: Are the Courts Now Taking Them More Seriously?' (2004) 15 *King's College Law Journal* 253

Foster, Charles, *Choosing Life, Choosing Death: The Tyranny of Autonomy in Medical Ethics and Law* (Oxford: Hart Publishing, 2009)

Fox, R., 'The Evolution of American Bioethics: A Sociological Perspective' in G. Weisz (ed.) *Social Science Perspectives on Medical Ethics* (Philadelphia: University of Philadelphia Press, 1990)

Francis, Leslie, 'Decision Making at the End of Life: Patients With Alzheimer's or Other Dementias' (2001) 35 *Georgia Law Review* 539

Frankfurt, Harry, 'Freedom of the Will and the Concept of a Person' (1971) 68 *Journal of Philosophy* 5

Frazer, Elizabeth and Lacey, Nicola, *The Politics of Community: A Feminist Critique of the Liberal-Communitarian Debate* (London: Harvester Wheatsheaf, 1993)

Freckelton, Ian, 'Mental Health Review Tribunal Decision-Making: A Therapeutic Jurisprudence Lens' (2003) 10 *Psychiatry, Psychology and Law* 44

Freeman, Michael (ed.) *Medicine, Ethics and the Law: Current Legal Problems* (London: Stevens, 1988)

Freud, Sigmund, *On Narcissism : An Introduction* (1914) reproduced in Freud, S., Sandler, J., Person, E., Fonagy, P., *Freud: On Narcissism: An Introduction* (New Haven, CT: Yale University Press, 1991)

Galligan, D. J., *Due Process and Fair Procedures: A Study of Administrative Procedures* (Oxford: Clarendon, 1996)

Ganzini, L., Volicer, L., Nelson, W., Derse A., 'Pitfalls in Assessment of Decision-Making Capacity' (2003) 44 *Psychosomatics* 237

Gaylin, Williard, *How Psychotherapy Really Works* (New York: McGraw Hill, 2001)

Gaylin, Willard and Jennings, Bruce *The Perversion of Autonomy: Coercion and Constraints in a Liberal Society* (Washington: Georgetown University Press, 2003)

George, Katrina, 'A Woman's Choice?: The Gendered Risks of Voluntary Euthanasia and Physician-Assisted Suicide' (2007) 15 *Medical Law Review* 1

Gibbs, A., Dawson, J. and Mullen, R., 'Community Treatment Orders for People With Serious Mental Illness: A New Zealand Study' (2006) 36 *British Journal of Social Work* 1085

Gilligan, Carol, *In a Different Voice: Psychological Theory and Women's Development* (Cambridge, MA: Harvard University Press, 1982)

Gillon, Ranaan, *Philosophical Medical Ethics* (Chichester: John Wiley, 1985)
'Ethics Needs Principles – Four can Encompass the Rest – and Respect for Autonomy should be "First Among Equals"' (2003) 29 *Journal of Medical Ethics* 307

Gillon, Ranaan (ed.) *Principles of Healthcare Ethics* (London: John Wiley & Sons, 1995)

Glass, Kathleen, 'Refining Definitions and Devising Instruments: Two Decades of Assessing Mental Competence' (1997) 20 *International Journal of Law and Psychiatry* 5

Glendon, Mary Ann, *Rights Talk: The Impoverishment of Political Discourse* (New York: Free Press, 1991)

Goffman, Erving, *The Presentation of Self in Everyday Life* (New York: Doubleday, Anchor, 1959)
Asylums: Essays on the Social Situation of Mental Patients and Other Inmates (New York: Anchor Books, 1961)

Good Medical Practice (London: General Medical Council, 1995)

Good Medical Practice (London: General Medical Council, 2006)

Government Response to the Report of the Joint Committee on the Draft Mental Health Bill 2004 Cm 6624 (London: HMSO, 2005)

Graham, Anthony, 'Parens Patriae: Past, Present and Future' (1994) 32 *Family Court Review* 184

Grant, Evadné, 'Dignity and Equality' (2007) 7 *Human Rights Law Review* 299

Gray, John and O'Reilly, Richard, 'Canadian Compulsory Community Treatment Laws: Recent Reforms' (2005) 28 *International Journal of Law and Psychiatry* 13
'Supreme Court of Canada's "Beautiful Mind" Case' (2009) 32 *International Journal of Law and Psychiatry* 315

Green, Leslie, 'Un-American Liberalism: Raz's "Morality of Freedom"' (1988) 38 *University of Toronto Law Journal* 317

Green, Milton, 'Fraud, Undue Influence and Mental Incompetency: A Study in Related Concepts' (1943) 43 *Columbia Law Review* 176

'Proof of Mental Incompetency and the Unexpressed Major Premise' (1944) 53
    Yale Law Journal 271
Grisso, Thomas, *Evaluating Competencies: Forensic Assessments and Instruments*
    (2nd edn) (Dordrecht: Kluwer Academic, 2002)
    'The MacArthur Treatment Competence Study III: Abilities of Patients to
    Consent to Psychiatric and Medical Treatments' (1995) 19 *Law and Human
    Behavior* 149
    'Values and Limits of the MacArthur Treatment Competence Study' (1996) 2
    Psychology, Public Policy and Law 167
    *Assessing Competence to Consent to Treatment: A Guide for Physicians and Other
    Health Professionals* (New York: Oxford University Press, 1998)
Grisso, Thomas, Appelbaum, Paul, Mulvey, Edward P. and Fletcher, Kenneth,
    'The MacArthur Treatment Competence Study II: Measures of Abilities
    Related to Competence to Consent to Treatment' (1995) 19 *Law and Human
    Behaviour* 127
Grubb, Andrew, 'The Emergence and Rise of Medical Law and Ethics' (1987) 50
    Modern Law Review 241
    'The Doctor as Fiduciary' (1994) 47 *Current Legal Problems* 311
    Kennedy and Grubb Medical Law (3rd edn) (London: Butterworths, 2000)
Grubb, Andrew (ed.) *Decision-Making and Problems of Incompetence*
    (Chichester: John Wiley and Sons, 1994)
    *Guidance for Clinicians and SOADS: The Imposition of Medical Treatment in the
    Absence of Consent* (London: Care Quality Commission, 2008)
    *Guidance for SOADs: Consent to Treatment and the SOAD Role under the Revised
    Mental Health Act* (London: Care Quality Commission, 2008)
    Guidance for SOADs: Giving Reasons when Certifying Appropriate Treatment
    (Care Quality Commission, 2008
Gunderson, Martin, 'Being a Burden: Reflections on Refusing Medical Care' (2004)
    34 *Hastings Center Report* 37
Gunn, M. J., Wong, J. G., Clare, I. C. H. and Holland, A. J., 'Decision Making
    Capacity' (1999) 7 *Medical Law Review* 269
Gunn, Michael, 'The Meaning of Incapacity' (1994) 2 *Medical Law Review* 8
Gurnham, David, 'Losing the Wood for the Trees: Burke and the Court of Appeal'
    (2006) 14 *Medical Law Review* 253
Gutheil, Thomas and Bursztajn, Harold, 'Clinicians' Guidelines for Assessing and
    Presenting Subtle Forms of Patient Incompetence in Legal Settings' (1986)
    143 *American Journal of Psychiatry* 1020
Gutterman, Jennifer, 'Waging a War on Drugs: Administering a Lethal Dose to
    Kendra's Law' (2000) 68 *Fordham Law Review* 2401
Guyer, P., Hindle, P., Harrison, J., Jain, N., Brinsden, M., 'The Mental Capacity
    Act 2005: Review of Mental Capacity Assessment in People with Proximal
    Femoral Fracture' (2010) 34 *The Psychiatrist* 284

Hale, Brenda, 'Justice and Equality in Mental Health Law: The European Experience' (2007) 30 *International Journal of Law and Psychiatry* 18

'The Human Rights Act and Mental Health Law: Has it Helped?' (2007) 13 *Journal of Mental Health Law* 7

Hall, Mark, Camacho, Fabian, Dugan, Elizabeth, Balkrishnan, Rajesh, 'Trust in the Medical Profession: Conceptual and Management Issues' (2002) 37 *Health Services Research* 1419

Hardwig, John, 'What About the Family?' (1990) 20 *Hastings Center Report* 5

'Is there a Duty to Die?' (1997) 27 *Hastings Center Report* 34

Hardwig, John with Hentoff, N., Callahan, D., Churchill, L., Cohn, F. and Lynn J., *Is There a Duty to Die? And Other Essays in Medical Ethics* (New York: Routledge, 2000)

Harmon, Louise, 'Falling Off the Vine: Legal Fictions and the Doctrine of Substituted Judgment' (1990) 100 *Yale Law Journal* 1

Haroun, Ansar M. and Morris, Grant H., 'Weaving a Tangled Web: The Deceptions of Psychiatrists' (1999) 10 *Journal of Contemporary Legal Issues* 227

Harrington, John, 'Privileging the Medical Norm: Liberalism, Self-Determination and Refusal of Treatment' (1996) 16 *Legal Studies* 348

'Visions of Utopia: Markets, Medicine and the National Health Service' (2009) 29 *Legal Studies* 379

Harris, John, *The Value of Life* (London: Routledge and Keegan Paul, 1985)

Heal, L. and Sigelman, C. 'Response Biases in Interviews of Individuals With Limited Mental Ability' (1995) 39 *Journal of Intellectual Disability Research* 331

Held, Virginia, *Feminist Morality: Transforming Culture, Society and Politics* (Chicago: University of Chicago Press, 1993)

Hendricks, Aart, 'UN Convention on the Rights of Persons With Disabilities' (2007) 14 *European Journal of Health Law* 272

Herring, Jonathan, 'Losing It? Losing What? The Law on Dementia' (2009) 21 *Child and Family Law Quarterly* 3

'Protecting Vulnerable Adults: A Critical Review of Recent Case Law' (2009) 21 *Child and Family Law Quarterly* 498

'*R* v. *C*: Sex and Mental Disorder' (2010) 126 *Law Quarterly Review* 36

Hewitt, David, 'An End to Compulsory Treatment?' (2002) 152 *New Law Journal* 194

Heywood, Rob, 'Medical Disclosure of Alternative Treatments' (2009) 68 *Cambridge Law Journal* 30

Hill, Thomas, *Autonomy and Self-Respect* (Cambridge University Press, 1991)

Hinshaw, Stephen, *The Mark of Shame: Stigma of Mental Illness and An Agenda for Change* (New York: Oxford University Press, 2007).

Hinton, John W (ed.) *Dangerousness: Problems of Assessment and Prediction* (London: Allen and Unwin, 1983)

Hogan, Gerard and Whyte, Gerry, *JM Kelly: The Irish Constitution* (4th edn) (Dublin: Lexis Nexis Butterworths, 2003)

Hoge, S. K., Appelbaum P. S., Lawlor T., Beck J. C., Litman R., Greer, A., 'A Prospective, Multi-Centre Study of Patients' Refusal of Antipsychotic Medication' (1990) 47 *Archives of General Psychiatry* 949

Hohfeld, Wesley Newcomb, 'Some Fundamental Legal Conceptions as Applied in Judicial Reasoning' (1913) 23 *Yale Law Journal* 16

Holm, Søren, 'Not Just Autonomy – the Principles of American Biomedical Ethics' (1995) 21 *Journal of Medical Ethics* 332

'Autonomy, Authenticity or Best Interest: Everyday Decisionmaking and Persons With Dementia' (2001) 4 *Medicine, Healthcare and Philosophy* 153

Honderich, Ted, *How Free are You? The Determinism Problem* (2nd edn) (Oxford University Press, 2002)

House of Lords House of Commons Joint Committee on Human Rights, Seventh Report of Session 2003–04 *The Meaning of Public Authority under the Human Rights Act* (London: HMSO: HL Paper 39; HC 382)

Høyer, Georg, Kjellin, Lars, Engberg, Marianne, Kaltiala-Heino, Tiittakerttu, Nilstun, Tore, Sigurjónsdóttir and Aslak Syse, 'Paternalism and Autonomy: A Presentation of a Nordic Study on the Use of Coercion in the Mental Health Care System' (2002) 25 *International Journal of Law and Psychiatry* 93

Hughes, J., Louw, S. and Sabat, S. (eds.) *Dementia: Mind, Meaning and the Person* (Oxford University Press, 2006)

Huxtable, Richard., 'A Right to Die Or Is it Right to Die?' (2002) 14 *Child and Family Law Quarterly* 341

Huxtable, Richard and Forbes, Karen, '*Glass* v *United Kingdom*: Maternal Instinct v Medical Opinion' (2004) 16 *Child and Family Law Quarterly* 339

Inpatients Formally Detained in Hospital under the Mental Health Act 1983 and Patients Subject to Supervised Community Treatment: 1998–99 to 2008–09 (London: Health and Social Care Information Centre, 2009)

Jackson, Elizabeth and Warner, James W., 'How Much do Doctors Know About Consent and Capacity?' (2002) 95 *Journal of the Royal Society of Medicine* 601

Jaggar, Alison, *Feminist Politics and Human Nature* (Totowa, NJ: Rowman & Littlefield, 1983)

Janofsky, J. S., McCarthy, R. J. and Folstein, M. F., 'The Hopkins Competency Assessment Test: A Brief Method for Evaluating Patients' Capacity to Give Informed Consent' (1992) 43 *Hospital and Community Psychiatry* 132

Jones, James, *Bad Blood: The Tuskagee Syphilis Experiment* (New York: Free Press, 1981)

Jones, Michael, 'Informed Consent and Other Fairy Stories' (1999) 7 *Medical Law Review* 103

Jones, Michael and Keywood, Kirsty, 'Assessing the Patient's Competence to Consent to Medical Treatment' (1996) 2 *Medical Law International* 107

Jones, Richard, *Mental Capacity Act Manual* (3rd edn) (London: Sweet and Maxwell, 2009)

Kämpf, Annegret, 'The Disabilities Convention and its Consequences for Mental Health Laws in Australia' (2008) 26 (2) *Law in Context* 10

Kane, Robert, *The Significance of Free Will* (New York: Oxford University Press, 1996)

Kant, Immanuel, *Groundwork of the Metaphysics of Morals* (1785) (from Gregor, Mary J. (ed.) *Kant: Groundwork of the Metaphysics of Morals (Cambridge Texts in the History of Philosophy)* (Cambridge University Press, 1997)
  Critique of Practical Reason (1785) in M. Gregor (ed.) *Kant, Practical Philosophy* (Cambridge University Press, 1996)

Kaplan, Robert, 'Health-Related Quality of Life in Patient Decision Making' (1991) 47 *Journal of Social Issues* 69

Kapp, Marshall and Mossman, Douglas, 'Measuring Decisional Capacity: Cautions on the Construction of a "Capacimeter"' (1996) 2 *Psychology, Public Policy and Law* 73

Kara, Mahmut, 'Applicability of the Principle of Respect for Autonomy: The Perspective of Turkey' (2007) 33 *Journal of Medical Ethics* 627

Kasper, J. A., Hoge, K., Feucht-Haviar, T., Cortina, J. and Cohen, B., 'Prospective Study of Patients' Refusal of Antipsychotic Medication Under a Physician Discretion Review Procedure' (1997) 154 *American Journal of Psychiatry* 483

Kayess, Rosemary and French, Philip, 'Out of Darkness into Light? Introducing the Convention on the Rights of Persons With Disabilities' (2008) 8 *Human Rights Law Review* 1

Kearney, C. and McKnight, T., 'Preference, Choice, and Persons With Disabilities: A Synopsis of Assessments, Interventions, and Future Directions' (1997) 17 *Clinical Psychology Review* 217

Kemp, Peter, Rendtorff, Jacob and Mattsson, Niels (eds.) *Bioethics and Biolaw: Vol II: Four Ethical Principles* (Copenhagen: Rhodos International Science and Art Publishers and Centre for Ethics and Law, 2000)

Kendra's Law: Final Report on the Status of Assisted Outpatient Treatment (New York, New York State Office of Mental Health, 2005)

Keown, John, 'Life and Death in Dublin' (1996) 55 *Cambridge Law Journal* 6
  'Restoring Moral and Intellectual Shape to the Law after *Bland*' (1997) 113 *Law Quarterly Review* 481
  'A Futile Defence of *Bland*: A Reply to Andrew McGee' (2005) 13 *Medical Law Review* 393

Kesey, Ken, *One Flew Over the Cuckoo's Nest* (New York: Viking Press, 1962)

Keys, Mary, 'Legal Capacity Law Reform in Europe: An Urgent Challenge' in Quinn, Gerard and Waddington, Lisa (eds.) *European Yearbook of Disability Law* (Oxford, Hart Publishing, 2009)

Keyserlingk, Edward, *Sanctity of Life or Quality of Life in the Context of Ethics, Medicine and Law* (Ottawa: Law Reform Commission of Canada, 1979)

Keywood, Kirsty, Fovargue, Sara and Flynn, Margaret, *Best Practice: Healthcare Decision-Making by, With and for Adults With Learning Disabilities* (Manchester: National Development Team, 1999)

Kirk, Trudi and Bersoff, Donald, 'How Many Procedural Safeguards Does it Take to Get a Psychiatrist to Leave the Lightbulb Unchanged? A Due Process Analysis of the MacArthur Treatment Competence Study' (1996) 2 *Psychology, Public Policy and Law* 45

Kitamura, Toshinori, Fusako, Kitamura, Mitsuhashi, Takayuki, Ito, Atsushi, Okazaki, Yukko, Okuda, Nana and Katoh, Hisao, 'Image of Psychiatric Patients' Competency to Give Informed Consent to Treatment in Japan' (1999) 22 *International Journal of Law and Psychiatry* 45

Kmietovicz, Zosia, 'R.E.S.P.E.C.T – Why Doctors are Still Getting Enough of it' (2002) 324 *British Medical Journal* 11

Koehler, Derek and Harvey, Nigel (eds.) *Blackwell Handbook of Judgment and Decision Making* (Chichester: Wiley Blackwell, 2004)

Kopelman, L., 'On the Evaluative Nature of Competency and Capacity Judgments' (1990) 13 *International Journal of Law and Psychiatry* 309

Krasik, Margaret, 'The Lights of Science and Experience: Historical Perspectives on Legal Attitudes Toward the Role of Medical Expertise in Guardianship of the Elderly' (1989) 33 *The American Journal of Legal History* 201

Kress, Kenneth, 'An Argument for Assisted Outpatient Treatment for Persons With Serious Mental Illness Illustrated With Reference to a Proposed Statute for Iowa' (2000) 85 *Iowa Law Review* 1269

Kwak, J and Haley, W, 'Current Research Findings on End-of-Life Decision Making Among Racially or Ethnically Diverse Groups' (2005) 45 (5) *Gerontologist* 634

Law Commission, Consultation Paper No. 128. *Mentally Incapacitated Adults and Decision-Making: A New Jurisdiction* (London: HMSO, 1993)

Consultation Paper No. 129. *Mentally Incapacitated Adults and Decision-Making: Medical Treatment and Research* (London: HMSO, 1993)

Report No. 231. *Report on Mental Incapacity* (London: HMSO, 1995)

Law Reform Commission *Vulnerable Adults and the Law: Capacity* (LRC CP 37–2005) (Dublin: LRC, 2005)

Bioethics: Advance Care Directives LRC 94–2009 (Dublin: LRC, 2009)

Lawrence, R. E. and Curlin, F. A., 'Autonomy, Religion, and Clinical Decisions: Findings From a National Physician Survey' (2009) 35 *Journal of Medical Ethics* 214

Lawson, Anna, 'Disability, Degradation and Dignity: The Role of Article 3 of the European Convention on Human Rights' (2006) 56 *Northern Ireland Legal Quarterly* 462

'The United Nations Convention on the Rights of Persons With Disabilities: New Era or False Dawn?' (2006–2007) 34 *Syracuse Journal of International Law and Commerce* 563

Lawton-Smith, S.A., *Question of Numbers: The Potential Impact of Community Based Treatment Orders in England and Wales* (King's Fund, London, 2005)

Learning From Bristol: The Report of the Public Inquiry Into Children's Heart Surgery at the Bristol Royal Infirmary 1984–1995 (Cm 5297(1), 2001)

Legal Services Commission, *Guidance on Mental Capacity Cases* (October 2007), available at www.legalservices.gov.uk

Legislative Framework for Mental Capacity and Mental Health Legislation in Northern Ireland: A Policy Consultation Document (Belfast: Department of Health, 2009)

Lewis, Oliver, 'Protecting the Rights of People With Mental Disabilities: the European Convention on Human Rights' (2002) 9 *European Journal of Healthcare Law* 293

Lewis, Penney, 'Feeding Anorexic Patients who Refuse Food' (1999) 7 *Medical Law Review* 21

'Procedures That are Against the Medical Interests of Incompetent Adults' (2002) 22 *Oxford Journal of Legal Studies* 575

'Medical Treatment of Dementia Patients at the End of Life: Can the Law Accommodate the Personal Identity and Welfare Problems?' (2006) 13 *European Journal of Health Law* 219

Assisted Dying and Legal Change (Oxford University Press, 2007)

Lidz, Charles W. and Arnold, Robert, 'Institutional Constraints on Autonomy' (1990) 14 *Generations* 65

'Rethinking Autonomy in Long Term Care' (1993) 47 *University of Miami Law Review* 603

Lidz, Charles W., Fischer, Lynn and Arnold, Robert, *The Erosion of Autonomy in Long-Term Care* (New York: Oxford University Press, 1992)

Lloyd, Genevieve, *The Man of Reason: 'Male' and 'Female' in Western Philosophy* (London: Metheun Publishing, 1984)

Luker, Kristen, *Taking Chances: Abortion and the Decision not to Contracept* (Berkeley: University of California Press, 1975)

Lundin, Roger, Thiselton, Anthony and Walhout, Clarence *The Promise of Hermeneutics* (Cambridge: Paternoster Press, 1999)

MacIntyre, Alasdair, *After Virtue: A Study in Moral Theory* (London: Duckworth, 1981)

MacKay, Don, 'The United Nations Convention on the Rights of Persons With Disabilities' (2006–2007) 34 *Syracuse Journal of International Law and Commerce* 323

Mackenzie, Catriona, 'Abortion and Embodiment' (1992) 70 *Australian Journal of Philosophy* 136.

Mackenzie, Catriona and Stoljar, Natalie (eds.) *Relational Autonomy: Feminist Perspectives on Autonomy, Agency, and the Social Self* (New York: Oxford University Press, 2000)

Feminism Unmodified: Discourses on Life and Law (Cambridge, MA: Harvard University Press, 1987)

Maclean, Alasdair, 'Crossing the Rubicon on the Human Rights Ferry' (2001) 64 *Modern Law Review* 775

'The Doctrine of Informed Consent: Does it Exist and Has it Crossed the Atlantic?' (2004) 24 *Legal Studies* 386

'Advance Directives, Future Selves and Decision-Making' (2006) 14 *Medical Law Review* 291

'Advance Directives and the Rocky Waters of Anticipatory Decision-Making' (2008) 16 *Medical Law Review* 1

Autonomy, Informed Consent and Medical Law: A Relational Challenge (Cambridge University Press, 2009)

Maeckelberghe, Els, 'Feminist Ethic of Care: A Third Alternative Approach' (2004) 12 *Health Care Analysis* 317

Making Decisions: The Government's Proposals for Making Decisions on Behalf of Mentally Incapacitated Adults (Cm 4465) (London: HMSO, 1999)

Manson, Neil and O'Neill, Onora, *Rethinking Informed Consent in Bioethics* (Cambridge University Press, 2007)

Marinelli, Robert and del Orto, Arthur (eds.) *The Psychological and Social Impact of Disability* (New York: Springer, 1999)

Marson, D. C., Ingram, K. K. and Cody, H. A., 'Assessing the Competency of Patients With Alzheimer's Disease Under Different Legal Standards: A Prototype Instrument' (1995) 52 *Archives of Neurology* 949

Marson, D. C., McInturff, B., Hawkins, L., Harrell L., 'Consistency of Physicians' Judgments of Capacity to Consent in Mild Alzheimer's Disease' (1997) 45 *Journal of the American Geriatrics Society* 132

Marzen, Thomas J. and Avila, Daniel, 'Will the Real Michael Martin Please Speak Up! Medical Decisionmaking for Questionably Competent People' (1995) 72 *University of Detroit Mercy Law Review* 833

Mason, Kenyon, 'Master of the Balancers; Non-Voluntary Therapy Under the Mantle of Lord Donaldson' (1993) 2 *Juridical Review* 115

Mason, Kenyon and Brodie, Douglas, 'Bolam, Bolam – Wherefore art thou *Bolam*?' (2005) 9 *Edinburgh Law Review* 398

Mason, Kenyon and Laurie, Graeme *Mason and McCall Smith's Law and Medical Ethics* (7th edn) (Oxford University Press, 2006)

Matthews, Eric, 'Autonomy and the Psychiatric Patient' (2000) 17 *Journal of Applied Philosophy* 59

McCall Smith, Alexander, 'Beyond Autonomy' (1997) 14 *Journal of Contemporary Health Law and Policy* 23

McCoid, Allan, 'A Reappraisal of Liability for Unauthorised Medical Treatment' (1957) 41 *Minnesota Law Rev* 381

McCulloch, Justine, '(In)capacity Legislation in Practice' (2009) 33 *Psychiatric Bulletin* 20

McGee, Andrew, 'Finding a Way Through the Ethical and Legal Maze: Withdrawal of Medical Treatment and Euthanasia' (2005) 13 *Medical Law Review* 357

McSherry, Bernadette, 'Protecting the Integrity of the Person: Developing Limitations on Involuntary Treatment' (2008) 26(2) *Law in Context* 111

McSherry, Bernadette and Weller, Penny (eds.) *Rethinking Rights-Based Mental Health Law* (Oxford: Hart Publishing, 2010)

Mental Capacity Act 2005: Code of Practice (London: The Stationery Office, 2007)

Mental Capacity: Deprivation of Liberty Safeguards Code of Practice (London: The Stationery Office, 2008)

Mental Health (Care and Treatment) (Scotland) Act 2003 Consultation Report on Draft Code of Practice and Regulations Policy Proposals (Edinburgh: Scottish Executive Social Research, 2005)

Mental Health (Care and Treatment) (Scotland) Act Code of Practice, Vol II, Civil Compulsory Powers (Edinburgh: Scottish Executive, 2005)

Mental Health Act Commission, *Response to the Green Paper Proposals on the Reform of the Mental Health Act 1983* (Nottingham: Mental Health Act Commission, 2000)

Twelfth Biennial Report 2005–2007. *Risk, Rights, Recovery*: (London: The Stationery Office, 2008)

Thirteenth Biennial Report 2007–2009, *Coercion and Consent* (London: The Stationery Office, 2009)

Mental Health Commission *Annual Report 2008* (Dublin: Mental Health Commission, 2009)

Meyers, Diana, *Self, Society and Personal Choice* (New York: Columbia University Press, 1989)

Michalowski, Sabine, 'Advance Refusals of Life-Sustaining Medical Treatment: The Relativity of the Absolute Right' (2005) 68 *Modern Law Review* 958

Miles, Steven H and August, Allison, 'Courts, Gender and the Right to Die' (1990) 18 *Law, Medicine and Healthcare* 85

Mill, John Stuart, *On Liberty* (London, 1859) in Grey, John (ed.) *On Liberty and Other Essays* (Oxford University Press, 1991)

Miller, Monica, 'Refusal to Undergo a Caesarean Section: A Woman's Right or a Criminal Act?' (2005) 15 *Health Matrix* 383

Miller, R. D., Bernstein, M. R., Van Rybroek, G. J. and Maier, G. J., 'The Impact of the Right to Refuse Treatment in a Forensic Patient Population: Six Month Review' (1989) 17 *Bulletin of the American Academy of Psychiatry and the Law* 107

Minkowitz, Tina, 'The United Nations Convention on the Rights of Persons With Disabilities and the Right to be Free From Nonconsensual Psychiatric Interventions' (2006–7) 34 *Syracuse Journal of International Law and Commerce* 405

Miola, José, 'Autonomy Rued OK' (2006) 14 *Medical Law Review* 108

Medical Ethics and Medical Law: A Symbiotic Relationship (Oxford: Hart Publishing, 2007)

Monahan, John, Steadman, Henry J., Silver, Eric, Appelbaum, Paul, Clark Robbins, Pamela, Mulvey, Edward P., Roth, Lauren H., Grisso Thomas and Banks, Steven *Rethinking Risk: The MacArthur Study of Mental Disorder and Violence* (New York: Oxford University Press, 2001)

Montgomery, Jonathan, 'Law and the Demoralisation of Medicine' (2006) 26 *Legal Studies* 185

Moorman, S. and Carr, D., 'Spouses' Effectiveness as End-of-Life Health Care Surrogates: Accuracy, Uncertainty and Errors of Overtreatment and Undertreatment' (2008) 48 *Gerontologist* 811

Morris, Anne, 'Once Upon a Time in a Hospital … The Cautionary Tale of *St George's Healthcare NHS Trust* v *S, R* v *Collins and Others ex parte S* [1998] 3 All ER 673' (1999) 7 *Feminist Legal Studies* 75

Morris, Grant, 'Judging Judgment: Assessing the Competence of Mental Patients to Refuse Treatment' (1995) 32 *San Diego Law Review* 343

Mowbray, Alasdair, *The Development of Positive Obligations under the European Convention on Human Rights* (Oxford: Hart Publishing, 2004)

'The Creativity of the European Court of Human Rights' (2005) 5 *Human Rights Law Review* 57

Moye, Jennifer and Marson, Daniel, 'Assessment of Decision-Making Capacity in Older Adults: An Emerging Area of Practice and Research' (2007) 62B *Journal of Gerontology B Psychological Sciences and Social Sciences* 3

Mulhall, Stephen and Swift, Adam, *Liberals and Communitarians* (2nd edn) (Oxford: Blackwell Publishing, 1996)

Murphy, Thérése and Whitty, Noel, 'Is Human Rights Prepared?: Risk, Rights and Public Health Emergencies' (2009) 17 *Medical Law Review* 219

Nagel, Thomas, 'What is it Like to be a Bat?' (1974) 83 *Philosophical Review* 435

National Commission for the Protection of Human Subjects of Biomedical and Behavioural Research, *Ethical Principles and Guidelines for the Protection of Human Subjects of Research* (Washington DC: Department of Health, Education and Welfare, 1979)

Nedelsky, Jennifer, 'Reconceiving Autonomy: Sources, Thoughts and Possibilities' (1989) 1 *Yale Journal of Law and Feminism* 7

Nicholson, T. R. J., Cutter, W. and Hotopf, M., 'Assessing Mental Capacity: The Mental Capacity Act' (2008) 336 *British Medical Journal* 322

Noddings, Nell, *Caring: A Feminine Approach to Ethics and Moral Education* (Berkeley: University of California Press, 1984)

Nozick, Robert, *Anarchy, State and Utopia* (New York: Basic Books, 1974)

Nussbaum, Martha, *Women and Human Development: The Capabilities Approach* (Cambridge University Press, 2000)

Nussbaum, Martha and Sen, Amartya (eds.) *The Quality of Life* (Oxford: Clarendon Press, 1993)

O'Keefe, Shaun, 'A Clinician's Perspective: Issues of Capacity in Care' (2008) 14 *Medico-Legal Journal of Ireland* 41

O'Neill, Onora, *Constructions of Reason: Explorations of Kant's Practical Philosophy* (Cambridge University Press, 1989)

Autonomy and Trust in Bioethics (Cambridge University Press, 2002)

Okai, D., Owen, G., McGuire, H., Singh, S., Churchill, R. and Hotopf M, 'Mental Capacity in Psychiatric Patients: Systematic Review' (2007) 191 *British Journal of Psychiatry* 291, 294

Oshana, Marina, 'Personal Autonomy and Society' (1998) 29 *Journal of Social Philosophy* 81

Owen, G., Richardson, G., David, A., Szmukler, G., Hayward, P. and Hotopf, P., 'Mental Capacity to Make Decisions on Treatment in People admitted to Psychiatric Hospitals: Cross Sectional Study' (2008) 337 *British Medical Journal* 40.

Parfit, Derek, *Reasons and Persons* (Oxford: Clarendon, 1984)

Patrick, Donald, Pearlman, Robert, Starke, Helene, Cain, Kevin, Cole, William and Uhlmann, Richard, 'Validation of Preferences for Life-Sustaining Treatment: Implications for Advance Care Planning' (1997) 127 *Annals of Internal Medicine* 509

Pattinson, S., 'Undue Influence in the Context of Medical Treatment' (2002) 5 *Medical Law International* 305

Peay, Jill, *Tribunals on Trial* (Oxford; Clarendon Press, 1989)

Decisions and Dilemmas: Working With Mental Health Law (Oxford: Hart Publishing, 2003)

Pellegrino, Edmund D. and Thomasma, David C., *For the Patient's Good: The Restoration of Beneficence in Health Care* (New York: Oxford University Press, 1988)

Perlin, Michael, 'Fatal Assumption: A Critical Evaluation of the Role of Counsel in Mental Disability Cases' (1992) 16 *Law and Human Behaviour* 39

'Pretexts and Mental Disability Law: The Case of Competency' (1993) 47 *University of Miami Law Review* 625

'Is it More Than "Dodging Lions and Wastin' Time"? Adequacy of Counsel, Questions of Competence, and the Judicial Process in Individual Right to Refuse Treatment Cases' (1996) 2 *Psychology, Public Policy and Law* 114

'"Where the Winds Hit Heavy on the Borderline": Mental Disability Law, Theory and Practice, "Us" and "Them"' (1998) 31 *Loyola of Los Angeles Law Review* 775

'"Half-Wracked Prejudice Leaped Forth": Sanism, Pretextuality, and Why and How Mental Disability Law Developed as it Did' (1999) 10 *Journal of Contemporary Legal Issues* 3

'A Law of Healing' (2000) 68 *University of Cincinnati Law Review* 407

'Therapeutic Jurisprudence and Outpatient Commitment Law: Kendra's Law as Case Study' (2003) 9 *Psychology, Public Policy & Law* 183

Phillips Griffiths, A. (ed.) *Philosophy, Psychology and Psychiatry* (Cambridge University Press, 1994)

Plath, Sylvia, *The Bell Jar* (London: Faber and Faber, 1966)

Porter, Jill, Ouvry, Carol, Morgan, Maggie and Downs, Caroline, 'Interpreting the Communication of People With Profound and Multiple Learning Difficulties' (2001) 29 *British Journal of Learning Disabilities* 12

Practice Note (Declaratory Proceedings: Medical and Welfare Decisions for Adults Who Lack Capacity) [2002] 1 *Weekly Law Reports* 325

Practice Note (Declaratory Proceedings: Medical and Welfare Decisions for Adults Who Lack Capacity) [2006] 2 *Family Law Reports* 373

President's Commission for the Study of Ethical Problems in Medicine and Biomedical and Behavioural Research, *Making Health Care Decisions: A Report on the Ethical and Legal Implications of Informed Consent in the Patient-Practitioner Relationship* (Washington DC: US Superintendent of Documents, 1982)

Quinlan, Christina and O'Neill, Catherine, *Practitioners' Narrative Submissions* (Unpublished Dublin: Irish Hospice Foundation, 2008)

Quinn, Kevin, 'The Best Interests of Incompetent Patients: The Capacity for Interpersonal Relationships as a Standard for Decisionmaking' (1988) 76 *California Law Review* 897

Ramsey, Sara, 'The Adults With Incapacity (Scotland) Act – Who Knows? Who Cares?' (2005) 45 *Scottish Medical Journal* 20

Rawls, John, *A Theory of Justice* (Cambridge, MA: Harvard University Press, 1971)

  Political Liberalism (New York: Columbia University Press, 1993)

  A Theory of Justice Revised Edition (Cambridge, MA: Harvard University Press, 1999)

  Political Liberalism, Expanded Edition (New York: Columbia University Press, 2005)

Raymont, V., Bingley, W., Buchanan, A., David, A., Hayward, P., Wessely, S. and Hotopf, M, 'Prevalence of Mental Incapacity in Medical Inpatients and Associated Risk Factors: Cross-Sectional Study' (2004) 364 *Lancet* 1421

Raz, Joseph, *The Morality of Freedom* (Oxford: Clarendon Press, 1986)

  Ethics in the Public Domain: Essays in the Morality of Law and Politics (Oxford: Clarendon Press, 1994)

Redelmeier, Don and Shafir, Eldar, 'Medical Decision Making in Situations that Offer Multiple Alternatives' (1995) 273 *Journal of the American Medical Association* 302

Redelmeier, Don, Rozen, Paul and Kahneman, Daniel, 'Understanding Patients' Decisions: Cognitive and Emotional Perspectives' (1993) 279 *Journal of the American Medical Association* 72

Reforming the Mental Health Act: The New Legal Framework (Cm 5015-I, 2000) (London: Department of Health, 2001)

Regnard, Claud, Reynolds, Joanna, Watson, Bill, Matthews, Dorothy, Gibson, Lynn and Clarke, Charlotte, 'Understanding Distress in People With Severe Communication Difficulties: Developing and Assessing the Disability Distress Assessment Tool (DisDAT)' (2006) 51 *Journal of Intellectual Disability Research* 277

Report of the Joint Committee on the Draft Mental Health Bill 2004, (HL Paper 79–1; HC 95–1) (London: The Stationery Office, 2005)

Report of the Review of the Mental Health (Scotland) Act 1984: New Directions (Chair: Rt Hon Bruce Millan) (Edinburgh: Scottish Executive, 2001)

Review of Parts II, V and VI of the Public Health (Control of Disease) Act 1984: A Consultation on Proposals for Changes to Public Health Law in England (Gateway Reference 7742) (London: Department of Health, 2007)

Revised Consensus Statement on High-Dosage Antipsychotic Medication and Polypharmacy (London: Royal College of Psychiatrists, 2006)

Rhoden, Nancy, 'Litigating Life and Death' (1988) 102 *Harvard Law Review* 37

Richardson, Genevra, 'Reforming Mental Health Laws: Principle or Pragmatism?' [2001] *Current Legal Problems* 415

'Autonomy, Guardianship and Mental Disorder: One Problem, Two Solutions' (2002) 65 *Modern Law Review* 702

'The European Convention and Mental Health Law in England and Wales: Moving Beyond Process' (2005) 28 *International Journal of Law and Psychiatry* 127

Richardson, Genevra and Machin, David, 'Judicial Review and Tribunal Decision Making: A Study of the Mental Health Review Tribunal' [2000] *Public Law* 494

Robertson, Gerald, 'Informed Consent Ten Years Later: The Impact of Reibl v Hughes' (1991) 70 *Canadian Bar Review* 423

Robinson, Robert, 'Capacity as the Gateway: An Alternative View' [2000] *Journal of Mental Health Law* 44

Roesch, Ronald, Hart, Steven and Zapf, Patricia, 'Conceptualizing and Assessing Competency to Stand Trial: Implications and Applications of the MacArthur Treatment Competence Model' (1996) 2 *Psychology, Public Policy and Law* 96

Rose, Nikolas, 'Unreasonable Rights: Mental Illness and the Limits of the Law' (1985) 12 *Journal of Law and Society* 199

Roth, Alan, Meisel, Loren and Lidz, Charles W., 'Tests of Competency to Consent to Treatment' (1977) 134 *American Journal of Psychiatry* 279

Roth, L. H., Lidz, C. W., Meisel, A., Soloff, P. H., Kaufman, K., Spiker, D. G. and Forster, F. G., 'Competency to Decide about Treatment or Research' (1982) 5 *International Journal of Law and Psychiatry* 279

Roth, Loren, 'The Right to Refuse Psychiatric Treatment: Law and Medicine at the Interface' (1986) 35 *Emory Law Journal* 139

Rothman, David, *Strangers at the Bedside: A History of how Law and Bioethics Transformed Medical Decision Making* (New York: Basic Books, 1991)

Rudnick, A., 'Depression and Competence to Refuse Psychiatric Treatment' (2002) 28 *Journal of Medical Ethics* 155

Rutledge, E., Kennedy, M., O'Neill, H. and Kennedy, H., 'Functional Mental Capacity is not Independent of the Severity of Psychosis' (2008) 31 *International Journal of Law and Psychiatry* 9

Samantha, Jo, 'Lasting Powers of Attorney for Healthcare Under the Mental Capacity Act 2005: Enhanced Prospective Self-Determination for Future Incapacity or a Simulacrum?' (2009) 17 *Medical Law Review* 377

Sandel, Michael *Liberalism and the Limits of Justice* (Cambridge University Press, 1982); (2nd edn) (Cambridge University Press, 1997)

Sartorius, Norman, Leff, Julian, Lopez-Ibot, Juan José, Maj, Mario and Okasha, Ahmed (eds.) *Families and Mental Disorder: From Burden to Empowerment* (Chichester: John Wiley & Sons, 2005)

Sashidharan, S. P., *Inside Out: Improving Mental Health Services for Black and Minority Ethnic Communities in England* (London: National Institute of Mental Health, 2003)

Scales, A., 'The Emergence of Feminist Jurisprudence: An Essay' (1986) 95 *Yale Law Journal* 1373

Schneider, Carl, *The Practice of Autonomy* (New York: Oxford University Press, 1998)

   'Hard Cases and the Politics of Righteousness' (2005) 35 (3) *Hastings Center Report* 16

Schulman, B. A., 'Active Patient Orientation and Outcomes in Hypertensive Treatment' (1979) 17 *Medical Care* 267

Sclater, Shelley Day, Ebtehaj, Fatemah, Jackson, Emily and Richards, Martin (eds.) *Regulating Autonomy: Sex, Reproduction and Family* (Oxford: Hart Publishing, 2009)

Scott, Rosamund, *Rights, Duties and the Body: Law and Ethics of the Maternal–Fetal Conflict* (Oxford: Hart Publishing, 2002)

Scottish NHS Education for Frontline Staff, accessible at www.nes.scot.nhs.uk.

Secker, Barbara, 'Labelling Patient (In)Competence: A Feminist Analysis of Medico-Legal Discourse' (1999) 30 *Journal of Social Philosophy* 295

'The Appearance of Kant's Deontology in Contemporary Kantianism: Concepts of Patient Autonomy in Bioethics' (1999) 24 *Journal of Medicine and Philosophy* 43

Sedgwick, Peter, *Psycho Politics* (London: Pluto Press, 1982)

Selgelid, Michael, 'Ethics and Infectious Disease' (2005) 19 *Bioethics* 272

Seligman, Martin, *Helplessness: On Depression, Development and Death* (San Francisco: Freeman, 1975)

Seymour, John, '*Parens Patraie* and Wardship Powers: Their Nature and Origins' (1994) 14 *Oxford Journal of Legal Studies* 159

Shaddock, A. J., Dowse, I., Richards, H., Spinks A. T., 'Communicating With People With an Intellectual Disability in Guardianship Board Hearings: An Exploratory Study' (1999) 24 *Journal of Intellectual and Developmental Disability* 279

Shah, Ajit and Mukherjee, Sujoy, 'Ascertaining Capacity to Consent: A Survey of Approaches Used by Psychiatrists' (2003) 43 *Medicine, Science and the Law* 231

Sheldon, Sally and Thompson, Michael (eds.) *Feminist Perspectives on Healthcare Law* (London: Cavendish Publishing, 1998)

Shelford, Leonard, *Practical Treatise on the Law Concerning Lunatics, Idiots, and Persons of Unsound Mind* (Philadelphia: J. S. Littell, 1833)

Sherwin, Susan, *No Longer Patient: Feminist Ethics and Health Care* (Philadelphia: Temple University Press, 1992)

Sherwin, Susan (ed.) *The Politics of Women's Health: Exploring Agency and Autonomy* (Philadelphia: Temple University Press, 1998)

Shore, David (ed.) *The Trust Crisis in Healthcare: Causes, Consequences, and Cures* (New York: Oxford University Press, 2007)

Showalter, Elaine, *The Female Malady: Women, Madness and English Culture: 1830–1985* (New York: Pantheon, 1985)

Sigelman, C., Budd, E., Spanhel, L. and Schoenrock, C, 'When in Doubt, Say Yes: Acquiescence in Interviews With Mentally Retarded Persons' (1981) 19 *Mental Retardation* 53

Silver, Mitchell, 'Reflections on Determining Competency' (2002) 16 *Bioethics* 454

Singer, Peter, *Rethinking Life and Death: The Collapse of Our Traditional Ethics* (New York: Oxford University Press, 1995)

Sklar, Ronald, 'Starson v Swayze: The Supreme Court Speaks Out (Not all that Clearly) on the Question of "Capacity"' (2007) 52 *Canadian Journal of Psychiatry* 390

Slogobin, Christopher, 'Therapeutic Jurisprudence: Five Dilemmas to Ponder' (1995) *Psychology, Public Policy and Law* 1933

Somerville, Margaret, 'Refusal of Medical Treatment in "Captive" Circumstances' (1985) 63 *Canadian Bar Review* 59

Spriggs, Merle, 'Autonomy in the Face of a Devastating Diagnosis' (1998) 24 *Journal of Medical Ethics* 123

Autonomy and Patients' Decisions (Lanham, MD: Lexington Books, 2005)

Stapleton, Jane, 'Occam's Razor Reveals an Orthodox Basis for *Chester* v. *Afshar*' (2006) 122 *Law Quarterly Review* 426

Stefan, Susan, 'Leaving Civil Rights to the "Experts": From Deference to Abdication Under the Professional Judgment Standard' (1992) 102 *Yale Law Journal* 639

   'Silencing the Different Voice: Competence, Feminist Theory and Law' (1993) 47 *University of Miami Law Review* 763

   'Race, Competence Testing, and Disability Law: A Review of the MacArthur Competence Research' (1996) 2 *Psychology, Public Policy and Law* 31

Stern, Kristina, 'Court-ordered Caesarean Sections: In Whose Interests?' (1993) 56 *Modern Law Review* 238

   'Competence to Refuse Life-Sustaining Medical Treatment' (1994) 110 *Law Quarterly Review* 541

Sullivan, Roger J, *An Introduction to Kant's Ethics* (Cambridge University Press, 1994)

Sulmasy, Daniel B., Terry, Peter B., Weisman, Carol S., Miller, Deborah J., Stallings, Rebecca Y., Vetesse, Margaret A. and Haller, Karen B., 'The Accuracy of Substituted Judgments in Patients With Terminal Diagnosis' (1998) 128 *Annals Internal Medicine* 621

Sunstein, Cass and Thaler, Richard, 'Libertarian Paternalism Is Not an Oxymoron' (2003) 70 *University of Chicago Law Review* 1159

Suto, W., Clare I. and Holland A., 'Substitute Financial Decision-making in England and Wales: A Study of the Court of Protection' (2002) 24 *Journal of Social Welfare and Family Law* 37

Suto, W., Clare, Isabel, Holland, Anthony and Watson, Peter, 'Capacity to Make Financial Decisions Among People With Mild Intellectual Disabilities' (2005) 49 *Journal of Intellectual Disability Research* 199

Swanson, J. W., Holzer, C. E., Ganju, V. K., 'Violence and Psychiatric Disorder in the Community: Evidence From the Epidemiologic Catchment Area Surveys' (1990) 41 *Hospital and Community Psychiatry* 761

Szasz, Thomas, *The Myth of Mental Illness: Foundations of a Theory of Personal Conduct* (New York: Paul B. Hoeber, 1961)

Tan, Jacinta, 'The Anorexia Talking' (2003) 362 *Lancet* 1246

Tan, Jacinta and McMillan, J. R., 'The Discrepancy Between the Legal Definition of Capacity and the British Medical Association's Guidelines' (2004) 30 *Journal of Medical Ethics* 427

Tan, Jacinta, Hope, Tony and Stewart, Anne, 'Competence to Refuse Treatment in Anorexia' (2003) 26 *International Journal of Law and Psychiatry* 697

   'Anorexia Nervosa and Personal Identity: The Accounts of Patients and Their Parents' (2003) 26 *International Journal of Law and Psychiatry* 533

Tan, Jacinta, Hope, Tony, Stewart, Anne and Fitzpatrick, Ray, 'Control and Compulsory Treatment in Anorexia Nervosa: The Views of Patient and Parents' (2003) 26 *International Journal of Law and Psychiatry* 627

Tan, Jacinta, Stewart, Anne, Fitzpatrick, Ray and Hope, Tony, 'Competence to Make Treatment Decisions in Anorexia Nervosa: Thinking Processes and Values' (2006) 13 *Philosophy, Psychology and Psychiatry* 267

'Attitudes of Patients With Anorexia Nervosa to Compulsory Treatment and Coercion' (2010) 33 *International Journal of Law and Psychiatry* 13

Taylor, James, 'Autonomy and Informed Consent: A Much Misunderstood Relationship' (2004) 38 *Journal of Value Inquiry* 383

Taylor, Pamela and Gunn, John, 'Homicides by People With Mental Illness: Myth and Reality' (1999) 174 *British Journal of Psychiatry* 9

Teubner, Gunther *Law as an Autopoietic System* (Florence: The European University Institute Press Series, 1993)

Thaler, Richard and Sunstein, Cass, *Nudge: Improving Decisions About Health, Wealth, and Happiness* (New Haven: Yale University Press, 2008)

Theobald, Sir Henry Studdy, *The Law Relating to Lunacy* (London: Stevens and Sons, 1924)

Thornicroft, Graham, *Shunned: Discrimination Against People With Mental Illness* (Oxford University Press, 2007)

Thorpe, Lord Justice, 'The Caesarean Section Debate' [1997] *Family Law* 663

Torrey, E. F. and Zdanowicz, M. T., 'Outpatient Commitment: What, Why and For Whom?' (2001) 52 *Psychiatric Services* 337

Toulmin, Stephen, 'How Medicine Saved the Life of Ethics' (1982) 25 *Perspectives in Biology and Medicine* 736

Tribe, Laurence, *The Invisible Constitution* (New York: Oxford University Press, 2008).

Tversky, Amos and Kahneman, Daniel, 'Availability: a Heuristic for Judging Frequency and Probability' (1973) 5 *Cognitive Psychology* 207

'Judgment under Uncertainty: Heuristics and Biases' (1974) 185 *Science* 1124

'The Framing of Decisions and the Psychology of Choices' (1981) 211 *Science* 453

Tyler, Tom, *The Social Psychology of Procedural Justice* (New York: Plenum, 1988)

Why People Obey the Law (New Haven: Yale University Press, 1990)

Unsworth, Clive, 'Mental Disorder and Tutelary Relationship: From Pre- to Post-carceral Legal Order' (1991) 18 *Journal of Law and Society* 254

The Politics of Mental Health Legislation (Oxford: Clarendon Press, 1987)

Veatch, Robert, *A Theory of Medical Ethics* (New York: Basic Books, 1981)

'Autonomy's Temporary Triumph' (1984) 14 *Hastings Centre Report* 38

Vittoria, Anne, 'The Elderly Guardianship Tribunal Hearing: A Socio-Legal Encounter' (1992) 6 *Journal of Aging Studies* 165

Wadham, John, Mountfield, Helen, Gallagher, Caoilfhionn and Prochaska, Elizabeth *Blackstone's Guide to the Human Rights Act 1998* (5th edn) (Oxford University Press, 2009)

Walker, Nigel (ed.) *Dangerous People* (London: Blackstone Press, 1996)

Wall, S., Buchanan, A., Fahy T, *Systematic Review of Research Relating to the Mental Health Act 1983* (London: Department of Health, 1999)

Walsh, E and Fahy, T, 'Violence in Society' (2002) 325 *British Medical Journal* 507

Ware, Jean, 'Ascertaining the Views of People With Profound and Multiple Learning Disabilities' (2004) 32 *British Journal of Learning Disabilities* 175

Watch Tower Biblical and Tract Society of Pennsylvania, *Family Care and Medical Management for Jehovah's Witnesses* (New York: Watch Tower Biblical and Tract Society, 1995)

Watson, Gary, 'Free Agency' (1975) 72 *Journal of Philosophy* 202

Weller, Penny, 'Supported Decision-Making and the Achievement of Non-Discrimination: The Promise and Paradox of the Disabilities Convention' (2008) 26(2) *Law in Context* 85

Wells, Celia, 'Patients, Consent and Criminal Law' (1994) 16 *Journal of Social Welfare and Family Law* 65

West, R., 'Jurisprudence and Gender' (1988) 55 *University of Chicago Law Review* 1

Wexler, David and Winick, Bruce, *Essays in Therapeutic Jurisprudence* (Durham, NC: Carolina Academic Press, 1991)

Wexler, David and Winick, Bruce (eds.) *Law in a Therapeutic Key: Developments in Therapeutic Jurisprudence* (Durham, NC: Carolina Academic Press, 1996)

Whyte, S., Jacoby, R., Hope, T, 'Testing Doctors' Ability to Assess Patients' Competence' (2004) 27 *International Journal of Law and Psychiatry* 291

Wicclair, Mark, 'Patient Decision-Making Capacity and Risk' (1991) 5 *Bioethics* 91

    Ethics and the Elderly (New York: Oxford University Press, 1993)

    'The Continuing Debate Over Risk-Related Standards of Competence' (1999) 13 *Bioethics* 149

Wilks, Ian, 'The Debate Over Risk-Related Standards of Competence' (1997) 11 *Bioethics* 413

    'Asymmetrical Competence' (1999) 13 *Bioethics* 154

Winick, Bruce, 'The Right to Refuse Mental Health Treatment: A Therapeutic Jurisprudence Analysis' (1994) 17 *International Journal of Law and Psychiatry* 99

    'The Side Effects of Incompetency Labelling and the Implications for Mental Health Law' (1995) 1 *Psychology, Public Policy and Law* 6

    'The MacArthur Treatment Competence Study: Legal and Therapeutic Implications' (1996) 2 *Psychology, Public Policy and Law* 137

    The Right to Refuse Mental Health Treatment (Washington DC: American Psychological Association, 1997)

    Civil Commitment: A Therapeutic Jurisprudence Model (Durham, NC: Carolina Academic Press, 2005)

Wolfson, Jay, 'Erring on the Side of Theresa Schiavo: Reflections of the Special Guardian Ad Litem' (2005) 35 (3) *Hastings Center Report* 16

Wong, J. G., Cheung, E. P. and Chen, E. Y., 'Decision Making Capacity of Inpatients With Schizophrenia in Hong Kong' (2005) 193 *Journal of Nervous and Mental Disease* 316

Woolf, Lord, 'Are the Courts Excessively Deferential to the Medical Profession?' (2001) 9 *Medical Law Review* 1

Young, A. and Chesson, R., 'Obtaining Views on Health Care From People With Learning Disabilities and Severe Mental Health Problems' (2006) 34 *British Journal of Learning Disabilities* 11

Zigmond, Anthony and Holland, A. J., 'Unethical Mental Health Law: History Repeats Itself' (2000) 3 *Journal of Mental Health Law* 49

INDEX

Page numbers with 'n' are notes.

Lightning Source UK Ltd.
Milton Keynes UK
UKOW01f1132260715

255818UK00008B/149/P